Praise for Higher-Order Perl . . .

As a programmer, your bookshelf is probably overflowing with books that did nothing to change the way you program . . . or think about programming.

You're going to need a completely different shelf for this book.

While discussing caching techniques in Chapter 3, Mark Jason Dominus points out how a large enough increase in power can change the fundamental way you think about a technology. And that's precisely what this entire book does for Perl.

It raids the deepest vaults and highest towers of Computer Science, and transforms the many arcane treasures it finds—recursion, iterators, filters, memoization, partitioning, numerical methods, higher-order functions, currying, cutsorting, grammar-based parsing, lazy evaluation, and constraint programming—into powerful and practical tools for real-world programming tasks: file system interactions, HTML processing, database access, web spidering, typesetting, mail processing, home finance, text outlining, and diagram generation.

Along the way it also scatters smaller (but equally invaluable) gems, like the elegant explanation of the difference between "scope" and "duration" in Chapter 3, or the careful exploration of how best to return error flags in Chapter 4. It even has practical tips for Perl evangelists.

Dominus presents even the most complex ideas in simple, comprehensible ways, but never compromises on the precision and attention to detail for which he is so widely and justly admired.

His writing is—as always—lucid, eloquent, witty, and compelling.

Aptly named, this truly /is/ a Perl book of a higher order, and essential reading for every serious Perl programmer.

—Damian Conway, Co-designer of Perl 6

HIGHER-ORDER PERL

HIGHER-ORDER PERL
A GUIDE TO PROGRAM TRANSFORMATION

Mark Jason Dominus

AMSTERDAM • BOSTON • HEIDELBERG • LONDON
NEW YORK • OXFORD • PARIS • SAN DIEGO
SAN FRANCISCO • SINGAPORE • SYDNEY • TOKYO

Morgan Kaufmann Publishers is an imprint of Elsevier

MORGAN KAUFMANN PUBLISHERS

Senior Editor	Tim Cox
Publishing Services Manager	Simon Crump
Assistant Editor	Richard Camp
Cover Design	Yvo Riezebos Design
Cover Illustration	Yvo Riezebos Design
Composition	Cepha Imaging Pvt. Ltd.
Technical Illustration	Dartmouth Publishing, Inc.
Copyeditor	Eileen Kramer
Proofreader	Deborah Prato
Interior Printer	The Maple-Vail Book Manufacturing Group
Cover Printer	Phoenix Color

Morgan Kaufmann Publishers is an imprint of Elsevier.
500 Sansome Street, Suite 400, San Francisco, CA 94111

This book is printed on acid-free paper.

Library of Congress Cataloging-in-Publication Data
Application submitted

ISBN: 1-55860-701-3

For information on all Morgan Kaufmann publications,
visit our Web site at www.mkp.com or www.books.elsevier.com

Printed in the United States of America
05 06 07 08 09   5 4 3 2 1

For Lorrie

CONTENTS

PREFACE

A well-known saying in the programming racket is that a good Fortran programmer can write Fortran programs in any language. The sad truth, though, is that Fortran programmers write Fortran programs in any language whether they mean to or not. Similarly, we, as Perl programmers, have been writing C programs in Perl whether we meant to or not. This is a shame, because Perl is a much more expressive language than C. We could be doing a lot better, using Perl in ways undreamt of by C programmers, but we're not.

How did this happen? Perl was originally designed as a replacement for C on the one hand and Unix scripting languages like Bourne Shell and awk on the other. Perl's first major proponents were Unix system administrators, people familiar with C and with Unix scripting languages; they naturally tended to write Perl programs that resembled C and awk programs. Perl's inventor, Larry Wall, came from this sysadmin community, as did Randal Schwartz, his coauthor on *Programming Perl,* the first and still the most important Perl reference work. Other important early contributors include Tom Christiansen, also a C-and-Unix expert from way back. Even when Perl programmers didn't come from the Unix sysadmin community, they were trained by people who did, or by people who were trained by people who did.

Around 1993 I started reading books about Lisp, and I discovered something important: Perl is much more like Lisp than it is like C. If you pick up a good book about Lisp, there will be a section that describes Lisp's good features. For example, the book *Paradigms of Artificial Intelligence Programming,* by Peter Norvig, includes a section titled *What Makes Lisp Different?* that describes seven features of Lisp. Perl shares six of these features; C shares none of them. These are big, important features, features like first-class functions, dynamic access to the symbol table, and automatic storage management. Lisp programmers have been using these features since 1957. They know a lot about how to use these language features in powerful ways. If Perl programmers can find out the things that Lisp programmers already know, they will learn a lot of things that will make their Perl programming jobs easier.

This is easier said than done. Hardly anyone wants to listen to Lisp programmers. Perl folks have a deep suspicion of Lisp, as demonstrated by Larry Wall's famous remark that Lisp has all the visual appeal of oatmeal with fingernail clippings mixed in. Lisp programmers go around making funny noises like 'cons' and 'cooder,' and they talk about things like the PC loser-ing problem, whatever that is. They believe that Lisp is better than other programming languages, and they say so, which is irritating. But now it is all okay, because now you do not have to listen to the Lisp folks. You can listen to me instead. I will make soothing noises about hashes and stashes and globs, and talk about the familiar and comforting soft reference and variable suicide problems. Instead of telling you how wonderful Lisp is, I will tell you how wonderful Perl is, and at the end you will not have to know any Lisp, but you will know a lot more about Perl.

Then you can stop writing C programs in Perl. I think that you will find it to be a nice change. Perl is much better at being Perl than it is at being a slow version of C. You will be surprised at what you can get done when you write Perl programs instead of C.

WEB SITE

All the code examples in this book are available from my web site at:

```
http://perl.plover.com/hop/
```

When the notation in the margin is labeled with the tag some-example, the code may be downloaded from:

```
http://perl.plover.com/hop/Examples/some-example
```

The web site will also carry the complete text, an errata listing, and other items of interest. Should you wish to send me email about the book, please send your message to mjd-hop@plover.com.

ACKNOWLEDGMENTS

Every acknowledgments section begins with a statement to the effect that "without the untiring support and assistance from my editor, Tim Cox, this book would certainly never have been written". Until you write a book, you will never realize how true this is. Words fail me here; saying that the book would not have been written without Tim's untiring support and assistance doesn't begin to do justice to his contributions, his kindness, and his vast patience. Thank you, Tim.

This book was a long time in coming, and Tim went through three assistants while I was working on it. All these people were helpful and competent, so my thanks to Brenda Modliszewksi, Stacie Pierce, and Richard Camp. "Competent" may sound faint, but I consider it the highest praise.

Many thanks to Troy Lilly and Simon Crump, the production managers, who were not only competent but also fun to work with.

Shortly before the book went into production, I started writing tests for the example code. I realized with horror that hardly any of the programs worked properly. There were numerous small errors (and some not so small), inconsistencies between the code and the output, typos, and so on. Thanks to the heroic eleventh-hour efforts of Robert Spier, I think most of these errors have been caught. Robert was not only unfailingly competent, helpful, and productive, but also unfailingly cheerful, too. If any of the example programs in this book work as they should, you can thank Robert. (If they don't, you should blame me, not Robert.) Robert was also responsible for naming the MOD document preparation system that I used to prepare the manuscript.

The contributions of my wife, Lorrie Kim, are too large and pervasive to note individually. It is to her that this book is dedicated.

A large number of other people contributed to this book, but many of them were not aware of it at the time. I was fortunate to have a series of excellent teachers, whose patience I must sometimes have tried terribly. Thanks to Mark Foster, Patrick X. Gallagher, Joan Livingston, Cal Lobel (who first taught me to program), Harry McLaughlin, David A. J. Meyer, Bruce Piper, Ronnie Rabassa, Michael Tempel, and Johan Tysk. Mark Foster also arrived from nowhere in the nick of time to suggest the title for this book just when I thought all was lost.

This book was directly inspired by two earlier books: *ML for the Working Programmer*, by Lawrence Paulson, and *Structure and Interpretation of Computer Programs*, by Harold Abelson and Gerald Jay Sussman. Other important influences were *Introduction to Functional Programming*, by Richard Bird and Philip Wadler, and *Paradigms of Artificial Intelligence Programming*, by Peter Norvig.

The official technical reviewers had a less rewarding job than they might have on other projects. This book took a long time to write, and although I wanted to have long conversations with the reviewers about every little thing, I was afraid that if I did that, I would never ever finish. So I rarely corresponded with the reviewers, and they probably thought that I was just filing their suggestions in the shredder. But I wasn't; I pored over all their comments with the utmost care, and agonized over most of them. My thanks to the reviewers: Sean Burke, Damian Conway, Kevin Lenzo, Peter Norvig, Dan Schmidt, Kragen Sitaker, Michael Scott, and Adam Turoff.

While I was writing, I ran a mailing list for people who were interested in the book, and sent advance chapters to the mailing list. This was tremendously helpful, and I'd recommend the practice to anyone else. The six hundred and fifty wonderful members of my mailing list are too numerous to list here. All were helpful and supportive, and the book is much better for their input. A few stand out as having contributed a particularly large amount of concrete material: Roland Young, Damien Warman, David "Novalis" Turner, Iain "Spoon" Truskett, Steve Tolkin, Ben Tilly, Rob Svirskas, Roses Longin Odounga, Luc St. Louis, Jeff Mitchell, Steffen Müller, Abhijit Menon-Sen, Walt Mankowski, Wolfgang Laun, Paul Kulchenko, Daniel Koo, Andy Lester, David Landgren, Robin Houston, Torsten Hofmann, Douglas Hunter, Francesc Guasch, Kenneth Graves, Jeff Goff, Michael Fischer, Simon Cozens, David Combs, Stas Bekman, Greg Bacon, Darius Bacon, and Peter Allen. My apologies to the many many helpful contributors whom I have deliberately omitted from this list in the interests of space, and even more so to the several especially helpful contributors whom I have accidentally omitted.

Before I started writing, I received valuable advice about choosing a publisher from Philip Greenspun, Brian Kernighan, and Adam Turoff. Damian Conway and Abigail gave me helpful advice and criticism about my proposal.

Sean Burke recorded my Ivory Tower talk and cut CDs and sent them to me and who supplied RTF-related consulting at the last minute. He also sent me periodic mail to remind me how wonderful my book was, which often arrived at times when I wasn't so sure.

Several specific ideas in Chapter 4 were suggested by other people. Meng Wong suggested the clever and apt "odometer" metaphor. Randal Schwartz helped me with the "append" function. Eric Roode suggested the multiple list iterator.

When I needed to read out-of-print books by Paul Graham, A. E. Sundstrom lent them to me. When I needed a copy of volume 2 of *The Art of Computer Programming*, Hildo Biersma and Morgan Stanley bought it for me. When I needed money, B. B. King lent me some. Thanks to all of you.

The constraint system drawing program of Chapter 9 was a big project, and I was stuck on it for a long time. Without the timely assistance of Wm Leler, I might still be stuck.

Tom Christiansen, Jon Orwant, and Nat Torkington played essential and irreplaceable roles in integrating me into the Perl community.

Finally, the list of things "without which this book could not have been written" cannot be complete without thanking Larry Wall for writing Perl and for founding the Perl community, without which this book could not have been written.

## CHAPTER 1

RECURSION AND CALLBACKS

The first "advanced" technique we'll see is recursion. *Recursion* is a method of solving a problem by reducing it to a simpler problem of the same type.

Unlike most of the techniques in this book, recursion is already well known and widely understood. But it will underlie several of the later techniques, and so we need to have a good understanding of its fine points.

1.1 DECIMAL TO BINARY CONVERSION

Until the release of Perl 5.6.0, there was no good way to generate a binary numeral in Perl. Starting in 5.6.0, you can use `sprintf("%b", $num)`, but before that the question of how to do this was Frequently Asked.

Any whole number has the form $2k + b$, where k is some smaller whole number and b is either 0 or 1. b is the final bit of the binary expansion. It's easy to see whether this final bit is 0 or 1; just look to see whether the input number is even or odd. The rest of the number is $2k$, whose binary expansion is the same as that of k, but shifted left one place. For example, consider the number $37 = 2 \cdot 18 + 1$; here k is 18 and b is 1, so the binary expansion of 37 (100101) is the same as that of 18 (10010), but with an extra 1 on the end.

How did I compute the expansion for 37? It is an odd number, so the final bit must be 1; the rest of the expansion will be the same as the expansion of 18. How can I compute the expansion of 18? 18 is even, so its final bit is 0, and the rest of the expansion is the same as the expansion of 9. What is the binary expansion for 9? 9 is odd, so its final bit is 1, and the rest of its binary expansion is the same as the binary expansion of 4. We can continue in this way, until finally we ask about the binary expansion of 1, which of course is 1.

This procedure will work for any number. To compute the binary expansion of a number n we proceed as follows:

1. If n is 1, its binary expansion is 1, and we may ignore the rest of the procedure. Similarly, if n is 0, the expansion is simply 0. Otherwise:

2. Compute k and b so that $n = 2k + b$ and $b = 0$ or 1. To do this, simply divide n by 2; k is the quotient, and b is the remainder, 0 if n was even, and 1 if n was odd.

3. Compute the binary expansion of k, using this same method. Call the result E.

4. The binary expansion for n is Eb.

Let's build a function called `binary()` that calculates the expansion. Here is the preamble, and step 1:

CODE LIBRARY

binary

```
sub binary {
    my ($n) = @_;
    return $n if $n == 0 || $n == 1;
```

Here is step 2:

```
    my $k = int($n/2);
    my $b = $n % 2;
```

For the third step, we need to compute the binary expansion of k. How can we do that? It's easy, because we have a handy function for computing binary expansions, called `binary()` — or we will once we've finished writing it. We'll call `binary()` with k as its argument:

```
    my $E = binary($k);
```

Now the final step is a string concatenation:

```
    return $E . $b;
}
```

This works. For example, if you invoke `binary(37)`, you get the string 100101.

The essential technique here was to reduce the problem to a simpler case. We were supposed to find the binary expansion of a number n; we discovered that this binary expansion was the concatenation of the binary expansion of a smaller number k and a single bit b. Then to solve the simpler case of the same problem, we used the function `binary()` in its own definition. When we invoke `binary()` with some number as an argument, it needs to compute `binary()` for a different, smaller argument, which in turn computes `binary()` for an even smaller argument. Eventually, the argument becomes 1, and `binary()` computes the trivial binary representation of 1 directly.

This final step, called the *base case* of the recursion, is important. If we don't consider it, our function might never terminate. If, in the definition of `binary()`, we had omitted the line:

```
return $n if $n == 0 || $n == 1;
```

then `binary()` would have computed forever, and would never have produced an answer for any argument.

1.2 FACTORIAL

Suppose you have a list of n different items. For concreteness, we'll suppose that these items are letters of the alphabet. How many different orders are there for such a list? Obviously, the answer depends on n, so it is a function of n. This function is called the *factorial function*. The factorial of n is the number of different orders for a list of n different items. Mathematicians usually write it as a postfix (!) mark, so that the factorial of n is $n!$. They also call the different orders *permutations*.

Let's compute some factorials. Evidently, there's only one way to order a list of one item, so $1! = 1$. There are two permutations of a list of two items: A-B and B-A, so $2! = 2$. A little pencil work will reveal that there are six permutations of three items:

```
C  AB     C  BA
A C B     B C A
AB  C     BA  C
```

How can we be sure we didn't omit anything from the list? It's not hard to come up with a method that constructs every possible ordering, and in Chapter 4 we will see a program to list them all. Here is one way to do it. We can make any list of three items by adding a new item to a list of two items. We have two choices for the two-item list we start with: AB and BA. In each case, we have three choices about where to put the C: at the beginning, in the middle, or at the end. There are $2 \cdot 3 = 6$ ways to make the choices together, and since each choice leads to a different list of three items, there must be six such lists. The preceding left column shows all the lists we got by inserting the C into AB, and the right column shows the lists we got by inserting the C into BA, so the display is complete.

Similarly, if we want to know how many permutations there are of four items, we can figure it out the same way. There are six different lists of three items, and there are four positions where we could insert the fourth item into each of the lists, for a total of $6 \cdot 4 = 24$ total orders:

D ABC	D ACB	D BAC	D BCA	D CAB	D CBA
A D BC	A D CB	B D AC	B D CA	C D AB	C D BA
AB D C	AC D B	BA D C	BC D A	CA D B	CB D A
ABC D	ACB D	BAC D	BCA D	CAB D	CBA D

Now we'll write a function to compute, for any n, how many permutations there are of a list of n elements.

We've just seen that if we know the number of possible permutations of $n - 1$ things, we can compute the number of permutations of n things. To make a list of n things, we take one of the $(n - 1)!$ lists of $n - 1$ things and insert the nth thing into one of the n available positions in the list. Therefore, the total number of permutations of n items is $(n - 1)! \cdot n$:

```perl
sub factorial {
  my ($n) = @_;
  return factorial($n-1) * $n;
}
```

Oops, this function is broken; it never produces a result for any input, because we left out the termination condition. To compute factorial(2), it first tries to compute factorial(1). To compute factorial(1), it first tries to compute factorial(0). To compute factorial(0), it first tries to compute factorial(-1). This process continues forever. We can fix it by telling the function explicitly what 0! is so that when it gets to 0 it doesn't need to make a recursive call:

CODE LIBRARY
factorial

```perl
sub factorial {
  my ($n) = @_;
  return 1 if $n == 0;
  return factorial($n-1) * $n;
}
```

Now the function works properly.

It may not be immediately apparent why the factorial of 0 is 1. Let's return to the definition. factorial($n) is the number of different orders of a given list of $n elements. factorial(2) is 2, because there are two ways to order a list of two elements: ('A', 'B') and ('B', 'A'). factorial(1) is 1, because there is only one way to order a list of one element: ('A'). factorial(0) is 1, because there is only one way to order a list of zero elements: (). Sometimes people are tempted to argue that 0! should be 0, but the example of () shows clearly that it isn't.

Getting the base case right is vitally important in recursive functions, because if you get it wrong, it will throw off all the other results from the function. If we were to erroneously replace return 1 in the preceding function with return 0, it would no longer be a function for computing factorials; instead, it would be a function for computing zero.

1.2.1 Why Private Variables Are Important

Let's spend a little while looking at what happens if we leave out the my. The following version of factorial() is identical to the previous version, except that it is missing the my declaration on $n:

```perl
sub factorial {
  ($n) = @_;
  return 1 if $n == 0;
  return factorial($n-1) * $n;
}
```

Now $n is a global variable, because all Perl variables are global unless they are declared with my. This means that even though several copies of factorial() might be executing simultaneously, they are all using the same global variable $n. What effect does this have on the function's behavior?

Let's consider what happens when we call factorial(1). Initially, $n is set to 1, and the test on the second line fails, so the function makes a recursive call to factorial(0). The invocation of factorial(1) waits around for the new function call to complete. When factorial(0) is entered, $n is set to 0. This time the test on the second line is true, and the function returns immediately, yielding 1.

The invocation of factorial(1) that was waiting for the answer to factorial(0) can now continue; the result from factorial(0) is 1. factorial(1) takes this 1, multiplies it by the value of $n, and returns the result. But $n is now 0, because factorial(0) set it to 0, so the result is $1 \cdot 0 = 0$. This is the final, incorrect return value of factorial(1). It should have been 1, not 0.

Similarly, `factorial(2)` returns 0 instead of 2, `factorial(3)` returns 0 instead of 6, and so on.

In order to work properly, each invocation of `factorial()` needs to have its own private copy of `$n` that the other invocations won't interfere with, and that's exactly what `my` does. Each time `factorial()` is invoked, a new variable is created for that invocation to use as its `$n`.

Other languages that support recursive functions all have variables that work something like Perl's `my` variables, where a new one is created each time the function is invoked. For example, in C, variables declared inside functions have this behavior by default, unless declared otherwise. (In C, such variables are called *auto* variables, because they are automatically allocated and deallocated.) Using global variables or some other kind of storage that isn't allocated for each invocation of a function usually makes it impossible to call that function recursively; such a function is called *non-reentrant*. Non-reentrant functions were once quite common in the days when people used languages like Fortran (which didn't support recursion until 1990) and became less common as languages with private variables, such as C, became popular.

1.3   THE TOWER OF HANOI

Both our examples so far have not actually required recursion; they could both be rewritten as simple loops.

This sort of rewriting is always possible, because after all, the machine language in your computer probably doesn't support recursion, so in some sense it must be inessential. For the factorial function, the rewriting is easy, but this isn't always so. Here's an example. It's a puzzle that was first proposed by Edouard Lucas in 1883, called the Tower of Hanoi.

The puzzle has three pegs, called $\mathcal{A}$, $\mathcal{B}$, and $\mathcal{C}$. On peg $\mathcal{A}$ is a tower of disks of graduated sizes, with the largest on the bottom and the smallest on the top (see Figure 1.1).

The puzzle is to move the entire tower from $\mathcal{A}$ to $\mathcal{C}$, subject to the following restrictions: you may move only one disk at a time, and no disk may ever rest atop a smaller disk. The number of disks varies depending on who is posing the problem, but it is traditionally 64. We will try to solve the problem in the general case, for *n* disks.

Let's consider the largest of the *n* disks, which is the one on the bottom. We'll call this disk "the Big Disk." The Big Disk starts on peg $\mathcal{A}$, and we want it to end on peg $\mathcal{C}$. If any other disks are on peg $\mathcal{A}$, they are on top of the Big Disk, so we will not be able to move it. If any other disks are on peg $\mathcal{C}$, we will not be able to move the Big Disk to $\mathcal{C}$ because then it would be atop a smaller disk. So if

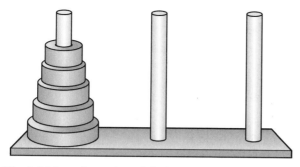

FIGURE I.I The initial configuration of the Tower of Hanoi.

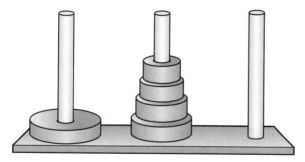

FIGURE I.2 An intermediate stage of the Tower of Hanoi.

we want to move the Big Disk from A to C, all the other disks must be heaped up on peg B, in size order, with the smallest one on top (see Figure 1.2).

This means that to solve this problem, we have a subgoal: we have to move the entire tower of disks, except for the Big Disk, from A to B. Only then we can transfer the Big Disk from A to C. After we've done that, we will be able to move the rest of the tower from B to C; this is another subgoal.

Fortunately, when we move the smaller tower, we can ignore the Big Disk; it will never get in our way no matter where it is. This means that we can apply the same logic to moving the smaller tower. At the bottom of the smaller tower is a large disk; we will move the rest of the tower out of the way, move this bottom disk to the right place, and then move the rest of the smaller tower on top of it. How do we move the rest of the smaller tower? The same way.

The process bottoms out when we have to worry about moving a smaller tower that contains only one disk, which will be the smallest disk in the whole set. In that case our subgoals are trivial, and we just put the little disk wherever we need to. We know that there will never be anything on top of it (because that would be illegal) and we know that we can always move it wherever we like; it's the smallest, so it is impossible to put it atop anything smaller.

Our strategy for moving the original tower looks like this:

To move a tower of *n* disks from the start peg to the end peg,

1. If the "tower" is actually only one disk high, just move it. Otherwise:

2. Move all the disks except for disk *n* (the Big Disk) from the start peg to the extra peg, using this method.

3. Move disk *n* (the Big Disk) from the start peg to the end peg.

4. Move all the other disks from the extra peg to the end peg, using this method.

It's easy to translate this into code:

```perl
# hanoi(N, start, end, extra)
# Solve Tower of Hanoi problem for a tower of N disks,
# of which the largest is disk #N.  Move the entire tower from
# peg 'start' to peg 'end', using peg 'extra' as a work space
sub hanoi {
    my ($n, $start, $end, $extra) = @_;
    if ($n == 1) {
        print "Move disk #1 from $start to $end.\n";     # Step 1
    } else {
        hanoi($n-1, $start, $extra, $end);               # Step 2
        print "Move disk #$n from $start to $end.\n";    # Step 3
        hanoi($n-1, $extra, $end, $start);               # Step 4
    }
}
```

This function prints a series of instructions for how to move the tower. For example, to ask it for instructions for moving a tower of three disks, we call it like this:

```perl
hanoi(3, 'A', 'C', 'B');
```

Its output is:

```
Move disk #1 from A to C.
Move disk #2 from A to B.
Move disk #1 from C to B.
Move disk #3 from A to C.
```

```
Move disk #1 from B to A.
Move disk #2 from B to C.
Move disk #1 from A to C.
```

If we wanted a graphic display of moving disks instead of a simple printout of instructions, we could replace the print statements with something fancier. But we can make the software more flexible almost for free by parametrizing the output behavior. Instead of having a print statement hardwired in, hanoi() will accept an extra argument that is a function that will be called each time hanoi() wants to move a disk. This function will print an instruction, or update a graphical display, or do whatever else we want. The function will be passed the number of the disk, and the source and destination pegs. The code is almost exactly the same:

```perl
sub hanoi {
  my ($n, $start, $end, $extra, $move_disk) = @_;
  if ($n == 1) {
    $move_disk->(1, $start, $end);
  } else {
    hanoi($n-1, $start, $extra, $end, $move_disk);
    $move_disk->($n, $start, $end);
    hanoi($n-1, $extra, $end, $start, $move_disk);
  }
}
```

To get the behavior of the original version, we now invoke hanoi() like this:

```perl
sub print_instruction {
  my ($disk, $start, $end) = @_;
  print "Move disk #$disk from $start to $end.\n";
}

hanoi(3, 'A', 'C', 'B', \&print_instruction);
```

The \&print_instruction expression generates a *code reference*, which is a scalar value that represents the function. You can store the code reference in a scalar variable just like any other scalar, or pass it as an argument just like any other scalar, and you can also use the reference to invoke the function that it represents. To do that, you write:

```perl
$code_reference->(arguments...);
```

This invokes the function with the specified arguments.[1] Code references are often referred to as *coderefs*.

The coderef argument to hanoi() is called a *callback*, because it is a function supplied by the caller of hanoi() that will be "called back" to when hanoi() needs help. We sometimes also say that the $move_disk argument of hanoi() is a *hook*, because it provides a place where additional functionality may easily be hung.

Now that we have a generic version of hanoi(), we can test the algorithm by passing in a $move_disk function that keeps track of where the disks are and checks to make sure we aren't doing anything illegal:

```
@position = ('', ('A') x 3); # Disks are all initially on peg A

sub check_move {
  my $i;
  my ($disk, $start, $end) = @_;
```

The check_move() function maintains an array, @position, that records the current position of every disk. Initially, every disk is on peg A. Here we assume that there are only three disks, so we set $position[1], $position[2], and $position[3] to "A". $position[0] is a dummy element that is never used because there is no disk 0. Each time the main hanoi() function wants to move a disk, it calls check_move().

```
  if ($disk < 1 || $disk > $#position) {
    die "Bad disk number $disk. Should be 1..$#position.\n";
  }
```

This is a trivial check to make sure that hanoi() doesn't try to move a nonexistent disk.

```
  unless ($position[$disk] eq $start) {
    die "Tried to move disk $disk from $start, but it is on peg
                              $position[$disk].\n";
  }
```

---

[1] This notation was introduced in Perl 5.004; users of 5.003 or earlier will have to use a much uglier notation instead: &{$code_reference}(arguments...);. When the $code_reference expression is a simple variable, as in the example, the curly braces may be omitted.

Here the function checks to make sure that hanoi() is not trying to move a disk from a peg where it does not reside. If the start peg does not match check_move()'s notion of the current position of the disk, the function signals an error.

```
    for $i (1 .. $disk-1) {
      if ($position[$i] eq $start) {
        die "Can't move disk $disk from $start because $i is on top of it.\n";
      } elsif ($position[$i] eq $end) {
        die "Can't move disk $disk to $end because $i is already there.\n";
      }
    }
```

This is the really interesting check. The function loops over all the disks that are smaller than the one hanoi() is trying to move, and makes sure that the smaller disks aren't in the way. The first if branch makes sure that each smaller disk is not on top of the one hanoi() wants to move, and the second branch makes sure that hanoi() is not trying to move the current disk onto the smaller disk.

```
    print "Moving disk $disk from $start to $end.\n";
    $position[$disk] = $end;
  }
```

Finally, the function has determined that there is nothing wrong with the move, so it prints out a message as before, and adjusts the @position array to reflect the new position of the disk.

Running:

```
  hanoi(3, 'A', 'C', 'B', \&check_move);
```

yields the same output as before, and no errors — hanoi() is not doing anything illegal.

This example demonstrates a valuable technique we'll see over and over again: by parametrizing some part of a function to call some other function instead of hardwiring the behavior, we can make it more flexible. This added flexibility will pay off when we want the function to do something a little different, such as performing an automatic self-check. Instead of having to clutter up the function with a lot of optional self-testing code, we can separate the testing part from the main algorithm. The algorithm remains as clear and simple as ever, and we can enable or disable the self-checking code at run time if we want to, by passing a different coderef argument.

1.4 HIERARCHICAL DATA

The examples we've seen give the flavor of what a recursive procedure looks like, but they miss an important point. In introducing the Tower of Hanoi problem, I said that recursion is useful when you want to solve a problem that can be reduced to simpler cases of the same problem. But it might not be clear that such problems are common.

Most recursive functions are built to deal with recursive data structures. A recursive data structure is one like a list, tree, or heap that is defined in terms of simpler instances of the same data structure. The most familiar example is probably a file system directory structure. A file is either:

- a plain file, which contains some data, or
- a directory, which contains a list of files

A file might be a directory, which contains a list of files, some of which might be directories, which in turn contain more lists of files, and so on. The most effective way of dealing with such a structure is with a recursive procedure. Conceptually, each call to such a procedure handles a single file. The file might be a plain file, or it might be a directory, in which case the procedure makes recursive calls to itself to handle any subfiles that the directory has. If the subfiles are themselves directories, the procedure will make more recursive calls.

Here's an example of a function that takes the name of a directory as its argument and computes the total size of all the files contained in it, and in its subdirectories, and in their subdirectories, and so on:

CODE LIBRARY
total-size-broken

```
sub total_size {
    my ($top) = @_;
    my $total = -s $top;
```

When we first call the function, it's with an argument $top, which is the name of the file or directory we want to examine. The first thing the function does is use the Perl -s operator to find the size of this file or directory itself. This operator yields the size of the file, in bytes. If the file is a directory, it says how much space the directory itself takes up on the disk, apart from whatever files the directory may contain — the directory is a list of files, remember, and the list takes up some space too. If the top file is actually a directory, the function will add the sizes of its contents to a running total that it will keep in $total.

```
    return $total if -f $top;
    unless (opendir DIR, $top) {
```

```
      warn "Couldn't open directory $top: $!; skipping.\n";
      return $total;
   }
```

The -f operator checks to see if the argument is a plain file; if so, the function can return the total immediately. Otherwise, it assumes that the top file is actually a directory, and tries to open it with opendir(). If the directory can't be opened, the function issues a warning message and returns the total so far, which includes the size of the directory itself, but not its contents.

```
   my $file;
   while ($file = readdir DIR) {
      next if $file eq '.' || $file eq '..';
      $total += total_size("$top/$file");
   }
```

The next block, the while loop, is the heart of the function. It reads filenames from the directory one at a time, calls itself recursively on each one, and adds the result to the running total.

```
      closedir DIR;
      return $total;
   }
```

At the end of the loop, the function closes the directory and returns the total.

In the loop, the function skips over the names . and .., which are aliases for the directory itself and for its parent; if it didn't do this, it would never finish, because it would try to compute the total sizes of a lot of files with names like ././././././fred and dir/../dir/../dir/../dir/fred.

This function has a gigantic bug, and in fact it doesn't work at all. The problem is that directory handles, like DIR, are global, and so our function is not reentrant. The function fails for essentially the same reason that the my-less version of factorial() failed. The first call goes ahead all right, but if total_size() calls itself recursively, the second invocation will open the same dirhandle DIR. Eventually, the second invocation will reach the end of its directory, close DIR, and return. When this happens, the first invocation will try to continue, find that DIR has been closed, and exit the while loop without having read all the filenames from the top directory. The second invocation will have the same problem if it makes any recursive calls itself.

The result is that the function, as written, looks down only the first branch of the directory tree. If the directory hierarchy has a structure like this:

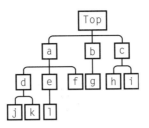

then our function will go down the *top-a-d* path, see files *j* and *k*, and report the total size of $top + a + d + j + k$, without ever noticing *b, c, e, f, g, h, i,* or *l*.

To fix it, we need to make the directory handle DIR a private variable, like $top and $total. Instead of opendir DIR, $top, we'll use opendir $dir, $top, where $dir is a private variable. When the first argument to opendir is an undefined variable, opendir will create a new, anonymous dirhandle and store it into $dir.[2]

Instead of doing this:

```
opendir DIR, $somedir;
print (readdir DIR);
closedir DIR;
```

we can get the same effect by doing this instead:

```
my $dir;
opendir $dir, $somedir;
print (readdir $dir);
closedir $dir;
```

The big difference is that DIR is a global dirhandle, and can be read or closed by any other part of the program; the dirhandle in $dir is private, and can be read

---

[2] This feature was introduced in Perl 5.6.0. Users of earlier Perl versions will have to use the IO::Handle module to explicitly manufacture a dirhandle: my $dir = IO::Handle->new; opendir $dir, $top; .

or closed only by the function that creates it, or by some other function that is explicitly passed the value of $dir.

With this new technique, we can rewrite the total_size() function so that it works properly:

```
sub total_size {
  my ($top) = @_;
  my $total = -s $top;
  my $DIR;

  return $total if -f $top;
  unless (opendir $DIR, $top) {
    warn "Couldn't open directory $top: $!; skipping.\n";
    return $total;
  }

  my $file;
  while ($file = readdir $DIR) {
    next if $file eq '.' || $file eq '..';
    $total += total_size("$top/$file");
  }

  closedir $DIR;
  return $total;
}
```

CODE LIBRARY
total-size

Actually, the closedir here is unnecessary, because dirhandles created with this method close automatically when the variables that contain them go out of scope. When total_size() returns, its private variables are destroyed, including $DIR, which contains the last reference to the dirhandle object we opened. Perl then destroys the dirhandle object, and in the process, closes the dirhandle. We will omit the explicit closedir in the future.

This function still has some problems: it doesn't handle symbolic links correctly, and if a file has two names in the same directory, it gets counted twice. Also, on Unix systems, the space actually taken up by a file on disk is usually different from the length reported by -s, because disk space is allocated in blocks of 1024 bytes at a time. But the function is good enough to be useful, and we might want to apply it to some other tasks as well. If we do decide to fix these problems, we will need to fix them only in this one place, instead of fixing the same problems in fifty slightly different directory-walking functions in fifty different applications.

1.5 APPLICATIONS AND VARIATIONS OF DIRECTORY WALKING

Having a function that walks a directory tree is useful, and we might like to use it for all sorts of things. For example, if we want to write a recursive file lister that works like the Unix `ls -R` command, we'll need to walk the directory tree. We might want our function to behave more like the Unix `du` command, which prints out the total size of every subdirectory, as well as the total for all the files it found. We might want our function to search for dangling symbolic links; that is, links that point to nonexistent files. A frequently asked question in the Perl newsgroups and IRC channels is how to walk a directory tree and rename each file or perform some other operation on each file.

We could write many different functions to do these tasks, each one a little different. But the core part of each one is the recursive directory walker, and we'd like to abstract that out so that we can use it as a tool. If we can separate the walker, we can put it in a library, and then anyone who needs a directory walker can use ours.

An important change of stance occurred in the last paragraph. Starting from here, and for most of the rest of the book, we are going to take a point of view that you may not have seen before: we are no longer interested in developing a complete program that we or someone else might use entirely. Instead, we are going to try to write our code so that it is useful to *another programmer* who might want to re-use it in another program. Instead of writing a program, we are now writing a library or module that will be used by other programs.

One direction that we could go from here would be to show how to write a *user interface* for the `total_size()` function, which might prompt the user for a directory name, or read a directory name from the command line or from a graphical widget, and then would display the result somehow. We are not going to do this. It is not hard to add code to prompt the user for a directory name or to read the command-line arguments. For the rest of this book, we are not going to be concerned with user interfaces; instead, we are going to look at *programmer interfaces*. The rest of the book will talk about "the user," but it's not the usual user. Instead, the user is another programmer who wants to use our code when writing their own programs. Instead of asking how we can make our entire program simple and convenient for an end-user, we will look at ways to make our functions and libraries simple and convenient for other programmers to use in their own programs.

There are two good reasons for doing this. One is that if our functions are well designed for easy re-use, we will be able to re-use them ourselves and save time and trouble. Instead of writing similar code over and over, we'll plug a familiar directory-walking function into every program that needs one. When we improve the directory-walking function in one program, it will be automatically improved in all our other programs as well. Over time, we'll develop a toolkit of useful functions and libraries that will make us more productive, and we'll have more fun programming.

But more importantly, if our functions are well designed for re-use, other programmers will be able to use them, and they will get the same benefits that we do. And being useful to other people is the reason we're here in the first place.[3]

With that change of stance clearly in mind, let's go on. We had written a function, total_size(), which contained useful functionality: it walked a directory tree recursively. If we could cleanly separate the directory-walking part of the code from the total-size-computing part, then we might be able to re-use the directory-walking part in many other projects for many other purposes. How can we separate the two functionalities?

As in the Tower of Hanoi program, the key here is to pass an additional parameter to our function. The parameter will itself be a function that tells total_size() what we want it to do. The code will look like this:

```perl
sub dir_walk {
  my ($top, $code) = @_;
  my $DIR;

  $code->($top);

  if (-d $top) {
    my $file;
    unless (opendir $DIR, $top) {
      warn "Couldn't open directory $top: $!; skipping.\n";
      return;
    }
    while ($file = readdir $DIR) {
      next if $file eq '.' || $file eq '..';
      dir_walk("$top/$file", $code);
    }
  }
}
```

CODE LIBRARY
dir-walk-simple

---

3 Some people find this unpersuasive, so perhaps I should point out that if we make ourselves useful to other people, they will love and admire us, and they might even pay us more.

This function, which I've renamed dir_walk() to honor its new generality, gets two arguments. The first, $top, is the name of the file or directory that we want it to start searching in, as before. The second, $code, is new. It's a coderef that tells dir_walk what we want to do for each file or directory that we discover in the file tree. Each time dir_walk() discovers a new file or directory, it will invoke our code with the filename as the argument.

Now whenever we meet another programmer who asks us, "How do I do *X* for every file in a directory tree?" we can answer, "Use this dir_walk() function, and give it a reference to a function that does *X*." The $code argument is a callback.

For example, to get a program that prints out a list of all the files and directories below the current directory, we can use:

```
sub print_dir {
  print $_[0], "\n";
}

dir_walk('.', \&print_dir );
```

This prints out something like this:

```
.
./a
./a/a1
./a/a2
./b
./b/b1
./c
./c/c1
./c/c2
./c/c3
./c/d
./c/d/d1
./c/d/d2
```

(The current directory contains three subdirectories, named a, b, and c. Subdirectory c contains a sub-subdirectory, named d.)

print_dir is so simple that it's a shame to have to waste time thinking of a name for it. It would be convenient if we could simply write the function without having to write a name for it, analogous to the way we can write:

```
$weekly_pay = 40 * $hourly_pay;
```

without having to name the 40 or store it in a variable. Perl does provide a syntax for this:

```
dir_walk('.', sub { print $_[0], "\n" } );
```

The sub { ... } introduces an *anonymous function*; that is, a function with no name. The value of the sub { ... } construction is a coderef that can be used to call the function. We can store this coderef in a scalar variable or pass it as an argument to a function like any other reference. This one line does the same thing as our more verbose version with the named print_dir function.

If we want the function to print out sizes along with filenames, we need only make a small change to the coderef argument:

```
dir_walk('.', sub { printf "%6d %s\n", -s $_[0], $_[0] } );
```

```
4096 .
4096 ./a
 261 ./a/a1
 171 ./a/a2
4096 ./b
 348 ./b/b1
4096 ./c
 658 ./c/c1
 479 ./c/c2
 889 ./c/c3
4096 ./c/d
 568 ./c/d/d1
 889 ./c/d/d2
```

If we want the function to locate dangling symbolic links, it's just as easy:

```
dir_walk('.', sub { print $_[0], "\n" if -l $_[0] && ! -e $_[0] });
```

-l tests the current file to see if it's a symbolic link, and -e tests to see if the file that the link points at exists.

But my promises fall a little short. There's no simple way to get the new dir_walk() function to aggregate the sizes of all the files it sees. $code is invoked for only one file at a time, so it never gets a chance to aggregate. If the aggregation is sufficiently simple, we can accomplish it with a variable defined outside the callback:

```
my $TOTAL = 0;
```

```
dir_walk('.', sub { $TOTAL += -s $_[0] });
print "Total size is $TOTAL.\n";
```

There are two drawbacks to this approach. One is that the callback function must reside in the scope of the $TOTAL variable, as must any code that plans to use $TOTAL. Often this isn't a problem, as in this case, but if the callback were a complicated function in a library somewhere, it might present difficulties. We'll see a solution to this problem in Section 2.1.

The other drawback is that it works well only when the aggregation is extremely simple, as it is here. Suppose instead of accumulating a single total size, we wanted to build a hash structure of filenames and sizes, like this one:

```
{
  'a' => {
            'a1' => '261',
            'a2' => '171'
         },
  'b' => {
            'b1' => '348'
         },
  'c' => {
            'c1' => '658',
            'c2' => '479',
            'c3' => '889',
            'd' => {
                     'd1' => '568',
                     'd2' => '889'
                   }
         }
}
```

Here the keys are file and directory names. The value for a filename is the size of the file, and the value for a directory name is a hash with keys and values that represent the contents of the directory. It may not be clear how we could adapt the simple $TOTAL-aggregating callback to produce a complex structure like this one.

Our dir_walk function is not general enough. We need it to perform some computation involving the files it examines, such as computing their total size, and to return the result of this computation to its caller. The caller might be the main program, or it might be another invocation of dir_walk(), which can then use the value it receives as part of the computation it is performing for *its* caller.

How can `dir_walk()` know how to perform the computation? In `total_size()`, the addition computation was hardwired into the function. We would like `dir_walk()` to be more generally useful.

What we need is to supply two functions: one for plain files and one for directories. `dir_walk()` will call the plain-file function when it needs to compute its result for a plain file, and it will call the directory function when it needs to compute its result for a directory. `dir_walk()` won't know anything about how to do these computations itself; all it knows is that is should delegate the actual computing to these two functions.

Each of the two functions will get a filename argument, and will compute the value of interest, such as the size, for the file named by its argument. Since a directory is a list of files, the directory function will also receive a list of the values that were computed for each of its members; it may need these values when it computes the value for the entire directory. The directory function will know how to aggregate these values to produce a new value for the entire directory.

With this change, we'll be able to do our `total_size` operation. The plain-file function will simply return the size of the file it's asked to look at. The directory function will get a directory name and a list of the sizes of each file that it contains, add them all up, and return the result. The generic framework function looks like this:

CODE LIBRARY
dir-walk-cb

```perl
sub dir_walk {
  my ($top, $filefunc, $dirfunc) = @_;
  my $DIR;

  if (-d $top) {
    my $file;
    unless (opendir $DIR, $top) {
      warn "Couldn't open directory $code: $!; skipping.\n";
      return;
    }

    my @results;
    while ($file = readdir $DIR) {
      next if $file eq '.' || $file eq '..';
      push @results, dir_walk("$top/$file", $filefunc, $dirfunc);
    }
    return $dirfunc->($top, @results);
  } else {
    return $filefunc->($top);
  }
}
```

To compute the total size of the current directory, we will use this:

```
sub file_size { -s $_[0] }

sub dir_size {
  my $dir = shift;
  my $total = -s $dir;
  my $n;
  for $n (@_) { $total += $n }
  return $total;
}


$total_size = dir_walk('.', \&file_size, \&dir_size);
```

The file_size() function says how to compute the size of a plain file, given its name, and the dir_size() function says how to compute the size of a directory, given the directory name and the sizes of its contents.

If we want the program to print out the size of every subdirectory, the way the du command does, we add one line:

```
sub file_size { -s $_[0] }

sub dir_size {
  my $dir = shift;
  my $total = -s $dir;
  my $n;
  for $n (@_) { $total += $n }
  printf "%6d %s\n", $total, $dir;
  return $total;
}


$total_size = dir_walk('.', \&file_size, \&dir_size);
```

This produces an output like this:

```
 4528 ./a
 4444 ./b
 5553 ./c/d
11675 ./c
24743 .
```

To get the function to produce the hash structure we saw earlier, we can supply
the following pair of callbacks:

CODE LIBRARY
dir-walk-sizehash

```
sub file {
  my $file = shift;
  [short($file), -s $file];
}

sub short {
  my $path = shift;
  $path =~ s{.*/}{};
  $path;
}
```

The file callback returns an array with the abbreviated name of the file (no full
path) and the file size. The aggregation is, as before, performed in the directory
callback:

```
sub dir {
  my ($dir, @subdirs) = @_;
  my %new_hash;
  for (@subdirs) {
    my ($subdir_name, $subdir_structure) = @$_;
    $new_hash{$subdir_name} = $subdir_structure;
  }
  return [short($dir), \%new_hash];
}
```

The directory callback gets the name of the current directory, and a list of name–
value pairs that correspond to the subfiles and subdirectories. It merges these
pairs into a hash, and returns a new pair with the short name of the current
directory and the newly constructed hash for the current directory.

The simpler functions that we wrote before are still easy. Here's the recursive
file lister. We use the same function for files and for directories:

```
sub print_filename { print $_[0], "\n" }
dir_walk('.', \&print_filename, \&print_filename);
```

Here's the dangling symbolic link detector:

```
sub dangles {
  my $file = shift;
```

```
        print "$file\n" if -l $file && ! -e $file;
    }
    dir_walk('.', \&dangles, sub {});
```

We know that a directory can't possibly be a dangling symbolic link, so our directory function is the *null function* that returns immediately without doing anything. If we had wanted, we could have avoided this oddity, and its associated function-call overhead, as follows:

```
sub dir_walk {
  my ($top, $filefunc, $dirfunc) = @_;
  my $DIR;
  if (-d $top) {
    my $file;
    unless (opendir $DIR, $top) {
      warn "Couldn't open directory $code: $!; skipping.\n";
      return;
    }

    my @results;
    while ($file = readdir $DIR) {
      next if $file eq '.' || $file eq '..';
      push @results, dir_walk("$top/$file", $filefunc, $dirfunc);
    }
    return $dirfunc ? $dirfunc->($top, @results) : () ;
  } else {
    return $filefunc ? $filefunc->($top): () ;
  }
}
```

This allows us to write dir_walk('.', \&dangles) instead of dir_walk('.', \&dangles, sub {}).

As a final example, let's use dir_walk() in a slightly different way, to manufacture a list of all the plain files in a file tree, without printing anything:

```
@all_plain_files =
  dir_walk('.', sub { $_[0] }, sub { shift; return @_ });
```

The file function returns the name of the file it's invoked on. The directory function throws away the directory name and returns the list of the files it contains. What if a directory contains no files at all? Then it returns an empty list to `dir_walk()`, and this empty list will be merged into the result list for the other directories at the same level.

1.6 FUNCTIONAL VERSUS OBJECT-ORIENTED PROGRAMMING

Now let's back up a moment and look at what we did. We had a useful function, `total_size()`, which contained code for walking a directory structure that was going to be useful in other applications. So we made `total_size()` more general by pulling out all the parts that related to the computation of sizes, and replacing them with calls to arbitrary user-specified functions. The result was `dir_walk()`. Now, for any program that needs to walk a directory structure and do something, `dir_walk()` handles the walking part, and the argument functions handle the "do something" part. By passing the appropriate pair of functions to `dir_walk()`, we can make it do whatever we want it to. We've gained flexibility and the chance to re-use the `dir_walk()` code by factoring out the useful part and parametrizing it with two functional arguments. This is the heart of the functional style of programming.

Object-oriented (OO) programming style gets a lot more press these days. The goals of the OO style are the same as those of the functional style: we want to increase the re-usability of software components by separating them into generally useful parts.

In an OO system, we could have transformed `total_size()` analogously, but the result would have looked different. We would have made `total_size()` into an abstract base class of directory-walking objects, and these objects would have had a method, `dir_walk()`, which in turn would make calls to two undefined virtual methods called `file` and `directory`. (In C++ jargon, these are called *pure virtual methods*.) Such a class wouldn't have been useful by itself, because the `file` and `directory` methods would be missing. To use the class, you would create a subclass that defined the `file` and `directory` methods, and then create objects in the subclass. These objects would all inherit the same `dir_walk` method.

In this case, I think the functional style leads to a lighter-weight solution that is easier to use, and that keeps the parameter functions close to the places they are used instead of stuck off in a class file. But the important point is that although the styles are different, the decomposition of the original function into useful components has exactly the same structure. Where the functional style uses functional arguments, the object-oriented style uses pure virtual methods. Although the rest of this book is about the functional style of programming, many of the techniques will be directly applicable to object-oriented programming styles also.

1.7 HTML

I promised that recursion was useful for operating on hierarchically defined data structures, and I used the file system as an example. But it's a slightly peculiar example of a data structure, since we normally think of data structures as being in memory, not on the disk.

What gave rise to the tree structure in the file system was the presence of directories, each of which contains a list of other files. Any domain that has items that include lists of other items will contain tree structures. An excellent example is HTML data.

HTML data is a sequence of elements and plain text. Each element has some content, which is a sequence of more elements and more plain text. This is a recursive description, analogous to the description of the file system, and the structure of an HTML document is analogous to the structure of the file system.

Elements are tagged with a *start tag*, which looks like this:

```
<font>
```

and a corresponding *end tag*, like this:

```
</font>
```

The start tag may have a set of *attribute–value pairs*, in which case it might look something like this instead:

```
<font size=3 color="red">
```

The end tag is the same in any case. It never has any attribute–value pairs.

In between the start and end tags can be any sequence of HTML text, including more elements, and also plain text. Here's a simple example of an HTML document:

```
<h1>What Junior Said Next</h1>

<p>But I don't <font size=3 color="red">want</font>
to go to bed now!</p>
```

This document's structure is shown in Figure 1.3.

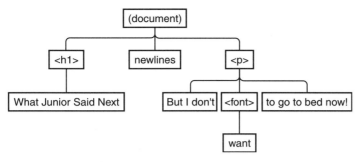

FIGURE 1.3   An HTML document.

The main document has three components: the `<h1>` element, with its contents; the `<p>` element, with its contents; and the blank space in between. The `<p>` element, in turn, has three components: the untagged text before the `<font>` element; the `<font>` element, with its contents; and the untagged text after the `<font>` element. The `<h1>` element has one component, which is the untagged text `What Junior Said Next`.

In Chapter 8, we'll see how to build parsers for languages like HTML. In the meantime, we'll look at a semi-standard module, `HTML::TreeBuilder`, which converts an HTML document into a tree structure.

Let's suppose that the HTML data is already in a variable, say `$html`. The following code uses `HTML::TreeBuilder` to transform the text into an explicit tree structure:

```
use HTML::TreeBuilder;
my $tree = HTML::TreeBuilder->new;
$tree->ignore_ignorable_whitespace(0);
$tree->parse($html);
$tree->eof();
```

The `ignore_ignorable_whitespace()` method tells `HTML::TreeBuilder` that it's not allowed to discard certain whitespace, such as the newlines after the `<h1>` element, that are normally ignorable.

Now `$tree` represents the tree structure. It's a tree of hashes; each hash is a node in the tree and represents one element. Each hash has a `_tag` key whose value is its tag name, and a `_content` key whose value is a list of the element's contents, in order; each item in the `_content` list is either a string, representing tagless text, or another hash, representing another element. If the tag also has attribute–value pairs, they're stored in the hash directly, with attributes as hash keys and the corresponding values as hash values.

So for example, the tree node that corresponds to the <font> element in the example looks like this:

```
{ _tag => "font",
  _content => [ "want" ],
  color => "red",
  size => 3,
}
```

The tree node that corresponds to the <p> element contains the <font> node, and looks like this:

```
{ _tag => "p",
  _content => [ "But I don't ",
               { _tag => "font",
                 _content => [ "want" ],
                 color => "red",
                 size => 3,
               },
               " to go to bed now!",
             ],
}
```

It's not hard to build a function that walks one of these HTML trees and "untags" all the text, stripping out the tags. For each item in a _content list, we can recognize it as an element with the ref() function, which will yield true for elements (which are hash references) and false for plain strings:

```
sub untag_html {
  my ($html) = @_;
  return $html unless ref $html;   # It's a plain string

  my $text = '';
  for my $item (@{$html->{_content}}) {
    $text .= untag_html($item);
  }

  return $text;
}
```

The function checks to see if the HTML item passed in is a plain string, and if so the function returns it immediately. If it's not a plain string, the function assumes that it is a tree node, as described above, and iterates over its content, recursively converting each item to plain text, accumulating the resulting strings, and returning the result. For our example, this is:

```
What Junior Said Next But I don't want to go to bed now!
```

Sean Burke, the author of HTML::TreeBuilder, tells me that accessing the internals of the HTML::TreeBuilder objects this way is naughty, because he might change them in the future. Robust programs should use the accessor methods that the module provides. In these examples, we will continue to access the internals directly.

We can learn from dir_walk() and make this function more useful by separating it into two parts: the part that processes an HTML tree, and the part that deals with the specific task of assembling plain text:

```
sub walk_html {
    my ($html, $textfunc, $elementfunc) = @_;
    return $textfunc->($html) unless ref $html; # It's a plain string


    my @results;
    for my $item (@{$html->{_content}}) {
      push @results, walk_html($item, $textfunc, $elementfunc);
    }
    return $elementfunc->($html, @results);
}
```

CODE LIBRARY
walk-html

This function has exactly the same structure as dir_walk(). It gets two auxiliary functions as arguments: a $textfunc that computes some value of interest for a plain text string, and an $elementfunc that computes the corresponding value for an element, given the element and the values for the items in its content. $textfunc is analogous to the $filefunc from dir_walk(), and $elementfunc is analogous to the $dirfunc.

Now we can write our untagger like this:

```
walk_html($tree, sub { $_[0] },
                 sub { shift; join '', @_ });
```

The $textfunc argument is a function that returns its argument unchanged. The $elementfunc argument is a function that throws away the element itself, then concatenates the texts that were computed for its contents, and returns the concatenation. The output is identical to that of untag_html().

Suppose we want a document summarizer that prints out the text that is inside of <h1> tags and throws away everything else:

```perl
sub print_if_h1tag {
  my $element = shift;
  my $text = join '', @_;
  print $text if $element->{_tag} eq 'h1';
  return $text;
}
walk_html($tree, sub { $_[0] }, \&print_if_h1tag);
```

This is essentially the same as untag_html(), except that when the element function sees that it is processing an <h1> element, it prints out the untagged text.

If we want the function to *return* the header text instead of printing it out, we have to get a little trickier. Consider an example like this:

```
<h1>Junior</h1>

Is a naughty boy.
```

We would like to throw away the text Is a naughty boy, so that it doesn't appear in the result. But to walk_html(), it is just another plain text item, which looks exactly the same as Junior, which we *don't* want to throw away. It might seem that we should simply throw away everything that appears inside a non-header tag, but that doesn't work:

```
<h1>The story of <b>Junior</b></h1>
```

We mustn't throw away Junior here, just because he's inside a <b> tag, because that <b> tag is itself inside an <h1> tag, and we want to keep it.

We could solve this problem by passing information about the current tag context from each invocation of walk_html() to the next, but it turns out to be simpler to pass information back the other way. Each text in the file is either a "keeper," because we know it's inside an <h1> element, or a "maybe," because we don't. Whenever we process an <h1> element, we'll promote all the "maybes" that it contains to "keepers." At the end, we'll print the keepers and throw away the maybes:

```perl
@tagged_texts = walk_html($tree, sub { ['MAYBE', $_[0]] },
                                  \&promote_if_h1tag);

sub promote_if_h1tag {
```

```
    my $element = shift;
    if ($element->{_tag} eq 'h1') {
      return ['KEEPER', join '', map {$_->[1]} @_];
    } else {
      return @_;
    }
  }
```

The return value from walk_html() will be a list of labeled text items. Each text item is an anonymous array whose first element is either MAYBE or KEEPER, and whose second item is a string. The plain text function simply labels its argument as a MAYBE. For the string Junior, it returns the labeled item ['MAYBE', 'Junior']; for the string Is a naughty boy., it returns ['MAYBE', 'Is a naughty boy.'].

The element function is more interesting. It gets an element and a list of labeled text items. If the element represents an <h1> tag, the function extracts all the texts from its other arguments, joins them together, and labels the result as a KEEPER. If the element is some other kind, the function returns its tagged texts unchanged. These texts will be inserted into the list of labeled texts that are passed to the element function call for the element that is one level up; compare this with the final example of dir_walk() in Section 1.5, which returned a list of filenames in a similar way.

Since the final return value from walk_html() is a list of labeled texts, we need to filter them and throw away the ones that are still marked MAYBE. This final pass is unavoidable. Since the function treats an untagged text item differently at the top level than it does when it is embedded inside an <h1> tag, there must be some part of the process that understands when something is at the top level. walk_html() can't do that because it does the same thing at every level. So we must build one final function to handle the top-level processing:

```
sub extract_headers {
  my $tree = shift;
  my @tagged_texts = walk_html($tree, sub { ['MAYBE', $_[0]] },
                                      \&promote_if_h1tag);
  my @keepers = grep { $_->[0] eq 'KEEPER'} @tagged_texts;
  my @keeper_text = map { $_->[1] } @keepers;
  my $header_text = join '', @keeper_text;
  return $header_text;
}
```

Or we could write it more compactly:

```
sub extract_headers {
  my $tree = shift;
```

```
    my @tagged_texts = walk_html($tree, sub { ['MAYBE', $_[0]] },
                                      \&promote_if_h1tag);
    join '', map { $_->[1] } grep { $_->[0] eq 'KEEPER'} @tagged_texts;
}
```

1.7.1   More Flexible Selection

We just saw how to extract all the <h1>-tagged text in an HTML document. The
essential procedure was promote_if_h1tag(). But we might come back next time
and want to extract a more detailed summary, which included all the text from
<h1>, <h2>, <h3>, and any other <h> tags present. To get this, we'd need to make
a small change to promote_if_h1tag() and turn it into a new function:

```
sub promote_if_h1tag {
  my $element = shift;
  if ($element->{_tag} =~ /^h\d+$/) {
    return ['KEEPER', join '', map {$_->[1]} @_];
  } else {
    return @_;
  }
}
```

But if promote_if_h1tag is more generally useful than we first realized, it will be a
good idea to factor out the generally useful part. We can do that by parametrizing
the part that varies:

```
sub promote_if {
  my $is_interesting = shift;
  my $element = shift;
  if ($is_interesting->($element->{_tag})) {
    return ['KEEPER', join '', map {$_->[1]} @_];
  } else {
    return @_;
  }
}
```

Now instead of writing a special function, promote_if_h1tag(), we can express
the same behavior as a special case of promote_if(). Instead of the following:

```
    my @tagged_texts = walk_html($tree, sub { ['maybe', $_[0]] },
                                      \&promote_if_h1tag);
```

we can use this:

```
my @tagged_texts = walk_html($tree,
                            sub { ['maybe', $_[0]] },
                            sub { promote_if(
                                    sub { $_[0] eq 'h1'},
                                    $_[0])
                            });
```

We'll see a tidier way to do this in Chapter 7.

1.8   WHEN RECURSION BLOWS UP

Sometimes a problem appears to be naturally recursive, and then the recursive solution is grossly inefficient. A very simple example arises when you want to compute Fibonacci numbers. This is a rather unrealistic example, but it has the benefit of being very simple. We'll see a more practical example of the same thing in Section 3.7.

1.8.1   Fibonacci Numbers

Fibonacci numbers are named for Leonardo of Pisa, whose nickname was Fibonacci, who discussed them in the 13th century in connection with a mathematical problem about rabbits. Initially, you have one pair of baby rabbits. Baby rabbits grow to adults in one month, and the following month they produce a new pair of baby rabbits, making two pairs:

Month	Pairs of baby rabbits	Pairs of adult rabbits	Total pairs
1	1	0	1
2	0	1	1
3	1	1	2

The following month, the baby rabbits grow up and the adults produce a new pair of babies:

4	1	2	3

The month after that, the babies grow up, and the two pairs of adults each produce a new pair of babies:

5	2	3	5

Assuming no rabbits die, and rabbit production continues, how many pairs of rabbits are there in each month?

Let $A(n)$ be the number of pairs of adults alive in month n and $B(n)$ be the number of pairs of babies alive in month n. The total number of pairs of rabbits alive in month n, which we'll call $T(n)$, is therefore $A(n) + B(n)$:

$$T(n) = A(n) + B(n)$$

It's not hard to see that the number of baby rabbits in one month is equal to the number of adult rabbits the previous month, because each pair of adults gives birth to one pair of babies. In symbols, this is $B(n) = A(n-1)$. Substituting into our formula, we have:

$$T(n) = A(n) + A(n-1)$$

Each month the number of adult rabbits is equal to the total number of rabbits from the previous month, because the babies from the previous month grow up and the adults from the previous month are still alive. In symbols, this is $A(n) = T(n-1)$. Substituting into the previous equation, we get:

$$T(n) = T(n-1) + T(n-2)$$

So the total number of rabbits in month n is the sum of the number of rabbits in months $n-1$ and $n-2$. Armed with this formula, we can write down the function to compute the Fibonacci numbers:

```
# Compute the number of pairs of rabbits alive in month n
sub fib {
    my ($month) = @_;
    if ($month < 2) { 1 }
    else {
        fib($month-1) + fib($month-2);
    }
}
```

This is perfectly straightforward, but it has a problem: except for small arguments, it takes forever.[4] If you ask for fib(25), for example, it needs to make recursive calls to compute fib(24) and fib(23). But the call to fib(24) *also* makes a recursive call to fib(23), as well as another to compute fib(22). Both calls to fib(23) will *also* call fib(22), for a total of three times. It turns out that fib(21) is computed 5 times, fib(20) is computed 8 times, and fib(19) is computed 13 times.

All this computing and recomputing has a heavy price. On my small computer, it takes about four seconds to compute fib(25); it makes 242,785 recursive calls while doing so. It takes about 6.5 seconds to compute fib(26), and makes 392,835 recursive calls, and about 10.5 seconds to make the 635,621 recursive calls for fib(27). It takes as long to compute fib(27) as to compute fib(25) and fib(26) put together, and so the running time of the function increases rapidly, more than doubling every time the argument increases by 2.[5]

The running time blows up really fast, and it's all caused by our repeated computation of things that we already computed. Recursive functions occasionally have this problem, but there's an easy solution for it, which we'll see in Chapter 3.

1.8.2   Partitioning

Fibonacci numbers are rather abstruse, and it's hard to find simple realistic examples of programs that need to compute them.

Here's a somewhat more realistic example. We have some valuable items, which we'll call "treasures," and we want to divide them evenly between two people. We know the value of each item, and we would like to ensure that both people get collections of items whose total value is the same. Or, to recast the problem in a more mundane light: we know the weight of each of the various groceries you bought today, and since you're going to carry them home with one bag in each hand, you want to distribute the weight evenly.

To convince yourself that this can be a tricky problem, try dividing up a set of ten items that have these dollar values:

$9, $12, $14, $17, $23, $32, $34, $40, $42,   and $49

---

4   One of the technical reviewers objected that this was an exaggeration, and it is. But I estimate that calculating fib(100) by this method would take about 2,241,937 billion billion years, which is close enough.

5   In fact, each increase of 2 in the argument increases the running time by a factor of about 2.62.

Since the total value of the items is \$272, each person will have to receive items totalling \$136. Then try:

$9, \quad $12, \quad $14, \quad $17, \quad $23, \quad $32, \quad $34, \quad $40, \quad $38, \quad \text{and} \quad $49

Here I replaced the \$42 item with a \$38 item, so each person will have to receive items totalling \$134.

This problem is called the *partition problem*. We'll generalize the problem a little: instead of trying to divide a list of treasures into two equal parts, we'll try to find some share of the treasures whose total value is a given target amount. Finding an even division of the treasures is the same as finding a share whose value is half of the total value of all the treasures; then the other share is the rest of the treasures, whose total value is the same.

If there is no share of treasures that totals the target amount, our function will return undef:

```
sub find_share {
    my ($target, $treasures) = @_;
    return [] if $target == 0;
    return    if $target < 0 || @$treasures == 0;
```

We take care of some trivial cases first. If the target amount is exactly zero, then it's easy to produce a list of treasures that total the target amount: the empty list is sure to have value zero, so we return that right away.

If the target amount is less than zero, we can't possibly hit it, because treasures are assumed to have positive value. In this case no solution can be found and the function can immediately return failure. If there are no treasures, we know we can't make the target, since we already know the target is larger than zero; we fail immediately.

Otherwise, the target amount is positive, and we will have to do some real work:

```
    my ($first, @rest) = @$treasures;
    my $solution = find_share($target-$first, \@rest);
    return [$first, @$solution] if $solution;
    return         find_share($target      , \@rest);
}
```

Here we copy the list of treasures, and then remove the first treasure from the list. This is because we're going to consider the simpler problem of how to divide up the treasures without the first treasure. There are two possible divisions: either this first treasure is in the share we're computing, or it isn't. If it is, then we have to find a subset of the rest of the treasures whose total value is $target - $first. If it isn't, then we have to find a subset of the rest of the treasures whose total value is $target. The rest of the code makes recursive calls to find_share to investigate these two cases. If the first one works out, the function returns a solution that includes the first treasure; if the second one works out, it returns a solution that omits the first treasure; if neither works out, it returns undef.

Here's a trace of a sample run. We'll call find_share(5, [1, 2, 4, 8]):

Share so far	Total so far	Target	Remaining treasures
	0	5	1 2 4 8

None of the trivial cases apply — the target is neither negative nor zero, and the remaining treasure list is not empty — so the function tries allocating the first item, 1, to the share; it then looks for some set of the remaining items that can be made to add up to 4:

1	1	4	2 4 8

The function will continue investigating this situation until it is forced to give up.

The function then allocates the first remaining item, 2, toward the share of 4, and makes a recursive call to find some set of the last 2 elements that add up to 2:

1 2	3	2	4 8

Let's call this "situation *a*." The function will continue investigating this situation until it concludes that situation *a* is hopeless. It tries allocating the 4 to the share, but that overshoots the target total:

1 2 4	7	−2	8

so it backs up and tries continuing from situation *a without* allocating the 4 to the share:

1 2	3	2	8

The share is still wanting, so the function allocates the next item, 8, to the share, which obviously overshoots:

1 2 8	11	−6	

Here we have $target < 0, so the function fails, and tries omitting 8 instead. This doesn't work either, as it leaves the share short by 2 of the target, with no items left to allocate:

Share so far	Total so far	Target	Remaining treasures
1 2	3	2	

This is the `if (@$treasures == 0) { return undef }` case.

The function has tried every possible way of making situation *a* work; they all failed. It concludes that allocating both 1 and 2 to the share doesn't work, and backs up and tries omitting 2 instead:

Share so far	Total so far	Target	Remaining treasures
1	1	4	4 8

It now tries allocating 4 to the share:

Share so far	Total so far	Target	Remaining treasures
1 4	5	0	8

Now the function has `$target == 0`, so it returns success. The allocated treasures are 1 and 4, which add up to the target 5.

The idea of ignoring the first treasure and looking for a solution among the remaining treasures, thus reducing the problem to a simpler case, is natural. A solution without recursion would probably end up duplicating the underlying machinery of the recursive solution, and simulating the behavior of the function-call stack manually.

Now solving the partition problem is easy; it's a call to `find_share()`, which finds the first share, and then some extra work to compute the elements of the original array that are not included in the first share:

CODE LIBRARY
partition

```
sub partition {
  my $total = 0;
  for my $treasure (@_) {
    $total += $treasure;
  }


  my $share_1 = find_share($total/2, [@_]);
  return unless defined $share_1;
```

First the function computes the total value of all the treasures. Then it asks `find_share()` to compute a subset of the original treasures whose total value is exactly half. If `find_share()` returns an undefined value, there was no equal division, so `partition()` returns failure immediately. Otherwise, it will set about computing the list of treasures that are *not* in `$share_1`, and this will be the second share:

```
my %in_share_1;
for my $treasure (@$share_1) {
  ++$in_share_1{$treasure};
}

for my $treasure (@_) {
  if ($in_share_1{$treasure}) {
    --$in_share_1{$treasure};
  } else {
    push @$share_2, $treasure;
  }
}
```

The function uses a hash to count up the number of occurrences of each value in the first share, and then looks at the original list of treasures one at a time. If it saw that a treasure was in the first share, it checks it off; otherwise, it put the treasure into the list of treasures that make up share 2.

```
    return ($share_1, $share_2);
  }
```

When it's done, it returns the two lists of treasures.

There's a lot of code here, but it mostly has to do with splitting up a list of numbers. The key line is the call to `find_share()`, which actually computes the solution; this is `$share_1`. The rest of the code is all about producing a list of treasures that *aren't* in `$share_1`; this is `$share_2`.

The `find_share` function, however, has a problem: it takes much too long to run, especially if there is no solution. It has essentially the same problem as `fib` did: it repeats the same work over and over. For example, suppose it is trying to find a division of 1 2 3 4 5 6 7 with target sum 14. It might be investigating shares that contain 1 and 3, and then look to see if it can make 5 6 7 hit the target sum of 10. It can't, so it will look for other solutions. Later on, it might investigate shares that contain 4, and again look to see if it can make 5 6 7 hit the target sum of 10. This is a waste of time; `find_share` should remember that 5 6 7 cannot hit a target sum of 10 from the first time it investigated that.

We will see in Chapter 3 how to fix this.

## CHAPTER 2

DISPATCH TABLES

In Chapter 1, we saw how to make functions more flexible by parametrizing their behaviors in terms of other functions. For example, instead of hardwiring the `hanoi()` function to print a certain message every time it wanted to move a disk, we had it call a secondary function that was passed in from outside. By supplying an appropriate secondary function, we could make `hanoi()` print out a list of instructions, or check its own moves, or generate a graphic display, without recoding the basic algorithm. Similarly, we were able to abstract the directory-walking behavior away from the file-size-computing behavior of our `total_size()` function to get a more useful and generally applicable `dir_walk()` function that could be used to do all sorts of different things.

To abstract behavior out of `hanoi()` and `dir_walk()`, we made use of code references. We passed `hanoi()` and `dir_walk()` additional functions as arguments, effectively treating the secondary functions as pieces of data. Code references make this possible.

Now we'll leave recursion for a while and go off in a different direction that shows another use of code references.

2.1 CONFIGURATION FILE HANDLING

Let's suppose that we have an application that reads in a configuration file in the following format:

```
VERBOSITY       8
CHDIR           /usr/local/app
```

```
         LOGFILE         log
         ...             ...
```

We would like to read in this configuration file and take an appropriate action for each directive. For example, for the VERBOSITY directive, we just want to set a global variable. But for the LOGFILE directive, we want to immediately redirect the program's diagnostic messages to the specified file. For CHDIR we might like the program to chdir to the specified directory so that subsequent file operations are relative to the new directory. This means that in the preceding example the LOGFILE is /usr/local/app/log, and not the log file in whatever directory the user happened to be in at the time the program was run.

Many programmers would see this problem and immediately envision a function with a giant if-else switch in it, perhaps something like this:

```perl
sub read_config {
  my ($filename) = @_;
  open my($CF), $filename or return; # Failure
  while (<$CF>) {
    chomp;
    my ($directive, $rest) = split /\s+/, $_, 2;
    if ($directive eq 'CHDIR') {
      chdir($rest) or die "Couldn't chdir to '$rest': $!; aborting";
    } elsif ($directive eq 'LOGFILE') {
      open STDERR, ">>", $rest
        or die "Couldn't open log file '$rest': $!; aborting";
    } elsif ($directive eq 'VERBOSITY') {
      $VERBOSITY = $rest;
    } elsif ($directive eq ...) {
      ...
    } ...
    } else {
      die "Unrecognized directive $directive on line $. of $filename; aborting";
    }
  }
  return 1; # Success
}
```

This function is in two parts. The first part opens the file and reads lines from it one at a time. It separates each line into a $directive part (the first word) and a $rest part (the rest). The $rest part contains the arguments to the directive, such as the name of the log file to open when supplied with the LOGFILE directive. The second part of the function is a big if-else tree that checks the $directive variable to see which directive it is, and aborts the program if the directive is unrecognized.

This sort of function can get very large, because of the many alternatives in the if-else tree. Each time someone wants to add another directive, they change the function by adding another elsif clause. The contents of the branches of the if-else tree don't have much to do with each other, except for the inessential fact that they're all configurable. Such a function violates an important law of programming: Related things should be kept together; unrelated things should be separated.

Following this law suggests a different structure for this function: The part that reads and parses the file should be separate from the actions that are performed when the configuration directives are recognized. Moreover, the code for implementing the various unrelated directives should not be lumped together into a single function.

2.1.1 Table-Driven Configuration

We can do better by separating the code for opening, reading, and parsing the configuration file from the unrelated segments that implement the various directives. Dividing the program into two halves like this will give us better flexibility to modify each of the halves, and to separate the code for the directives.

Here's a replacement for read_config():

```
sub read_config {
  my ($filename, $actions) = @_;
  open my($CF), $filename or return; # Failure
  while (<$CF>) {
    chomp;
    my ($directive, $rest) = split /\s+/, $_, 2;
    if (exists $actions->{$directive}) {
      $actions->{$directive}->($rest);
    } else {
```

CODE LIBRARY
rdconfig-tabular

```
        die "Unrecognized directive $directive on line $. of $filename; aborting";
      }
    }
  return 1; # Success
}
```

We open, read, and parse the configuration file exactly as before. But we dispense with the giant if-else switch. Instead, this version of read_config receives an extra argument, $actions, which is a table of actions; each time read_config() reads a configuration directive, it will perform one of these actions. This table is called a *dispatch table*, because it contains the functions to which read_config() will dispatch control as it reads the file. The $rest variable has the same meaning as before, but now it is passed to the appropriate action function as an argument.

A typical dispatch table might look like this:

```
$dispatch_table =
{ CHDIR       => \&change_dir,
  LOGFILE     => \&open_log_file,
  VERBOSITY   => \&set_verbosity,
  ...         => ...,
};
```

The dispatch table is a hash, whose keys (generically called *tags*) are directive names, and whose values are *actions*, references to subroutines that are invoked when the appropriate directive name is recognized. Action functions expect to receive the $rest variable as an argument; typical actions look like these:

```
sub change_dir {
  my ($dir) = @_;
  chdir($dir)
    or die "Couldn't chdir to '$dir: $!; aborting";
  }

sub open_log_file {
  open STDERR, ">>", $_[0]
    or die "Couldn't open log file '$_[0]': $!; aborting";
}

sub set_verbosity {
  $VERBOSITY = shift
}
```

If the actions are small, we can put them directly into the dispatch table:

```
$dispatch_table =
  { CHDIR       => sub { my ($dir) = @_;
                         chdir($dir) or
                           die "Couldn't chdir to '$dir': $!; aborting";
                       },

    LOGFILE     => sub { open STDERR, ">>", $_[0] or
                           die "Couldn't open log file '$_[0]': $!; aborting";
                       },

    VERBOSITY   => sub { $VERBOSITY = shift },
    ...         => ...,
  };
```

By switching to a dispatch table, we've eliminated the huge if-else tree, but in return we've gotten a table that is only a little smaller. That might not seem like a big win. But the table provides several benefits.

2.1.2   Advantages of Dispatch Tables

The dispatch table is data, instead of code, so it can be modified at run time. You can insert new directives into the table whenever you want to. Suppose the table has:

```
'DEFINE'=> \&define_config_directive,
```

where define_config_directive() is:

```
sub define_config_directive {
  my $rest = shift;
  $rest =~ s/^\s+//;
  my ($new_directive, $def_txt) = split /\s+/, $rest, 2;

  if (exists $CONFIG_DIRECTIVE_TABLE{$new_directive}) {
    warn "$new_directive already defined; skipping.\n";
    return;
  }

  my $def = eval "sub { $def_txt }";
```

CODE LIBRARY
def-conf-dir

```
  if (not defined $def) {
    warn "Could not compile definition for '$new_directive': $@; skipping.\n";
    return;
  }

  $CONFIG_DIRECTIVE_TABLE{$new_directive} = $def;
}
```

The configurator now accepts directives like this:

```
DEFINE HOME          chdir('/usr/local/app');
```

define_config_directive() puts HOME into $new_directive and chdir('/usr/local/app'); into $def_txt. It uses eval to compile the definition text into a subroutine, and installs the new subroutine into a master configuration table, %CONFIG_DIRECTIVE_TABLE, using HOME as the key. If %CONFIG_DIRECTIVE_TABLE were in fact the dispatch table that was passed to read_config() in the first place, then read_config() will see the new definition, and will have an action associated with HOME if it sees the HOME directive on a later line of the input file. Now a config file can say:

```
DEFINE HOME          chdir('/usr/local/app');
CHDIR /some/directory
...
HOME
```

The directives in ... are invoked in the directory /some/directory. When the processor reaches HOME, it returns to its home directory. We can also define a more robust version of the same thing:

```
DEFINE PUSHDIR    use Cwd; push @dirs, cwd(); chdir($_[0])
DEFINE POPDIR     chdir(pop @dirs)
```

PUSHDIR *dir* uses the cwd() function provided by the standard Cwd module to figure out the name of the current directory. It saves the name of the current directory in the variable @dirs, and then changes to *dir*. POPDIR undoes the effect of the last PUSHDIR:

```
PUSHDIR /tmp
A
PUSHDIR /usr/local/app
```

```
B
POPDIR
C
POPDIR
```

The program changes to /tmp, then executes directive A. Then it changes to /usr/local/app and executes directive B. The following POPDIR returns the program to /tmp, where it executes directive C; finally the second POPDIR returns it to wherever it started out.

In order for DEFINE to modify the configuration table, we had to store it in a global variable. It's probably better if we pass the table to define_config_directive explicitly. To do that we need to make a small change to read_config:

CODE LIBRARY
rdconfig-tablearg

```perl
sub read_config {
  my ($filename, $actions) = @_;
  open my($CF), $filename or return; # Failure
  while (<$CF>) {
    chomp;
    my ($directive, $rest) = split /\s+/, $_, 2;
    if (exists $actions->{$directive}) {
      $actions->{$directive}->($rest, $actions);
    } else {
      die "Unrecognized directive $directive on line $. of $filename; aborting";
    }
  }
  return 1; # Success
}
```

Now define_config_directive can look like this:

CODE LIBRARY
def-cdir-tablearg

```perl
sub define_config_directive {
  my ($rest, $dispatch_table) = @_;
  $rest =~ s/^\s+//;
  my ($new_directive, $def_txt) = split /\s+/, $rest, 2;

  if (exists $dispatch_table->{$new_directive}) {
    warn "$new_directive already defined; skipping.\n";
    return;
  }

  my $def = eval "sub { $def_txt }";
```

```
  if (not defined $def) {
    warn "Could not compile definition for '$new_directive': $@; skipping.\n";
    return;
  }

  $dispatch_table->{$new_directive} = $def;
}
```

With this change, we can add a really useful configuration directive:

```
DEFINE INCLUDE    read_config(@_);
```

This installs a new entry into the dispatch table that looks like this:

```
INCLUDE => sub { read_config(@_) }
```

Now, when we write this in the configuration file:

```
INCLUDE extra.conf
```

the main `read_config()` will invoke the action, passing it two arguments. The first argument will be the `$rest` from the configuration file; in this case the filename `extra.conf`. The second argument to the action will be the dispatch table again. These two arguments will be passed directly to a recursive call of `read_config`. `read_config` will read `extra.conf`, and when it's finished it will return control to the main invocation of `read_config`, which will continue with the main configuration file, picking up where it left off.

In order for the recursive call to work properly, `read_config()` must be reentrant. The easiest way to break reentrancy is to use a global variable, for example by using a global filehandle instead of the lexical filehandle we did use. If we had used a global filehandle, the recursive call to `read_config()` would open `extra.conf` with the same filehandle that was being used by the main invocation; this would close the main configuration file. When the recursive call returned, `read_config()` would be unable to read the rest of the main file, because its filehandle would have been closed.

The INCLUDE definition was very simple and very useful. But it was also ingenious, and it might not have occurred to us when we were writing `read_config`. It would have been easy to say "Oh, `read_config` doesn't need to be reentrant." But if we had written `read_config` in a nonreentrant way, the useful INCLUDE definition wouldn't have worked. There's an important lesson to learn here: make functions reentrant by default, because sometimes the usefulness of being able to call a function recursively will be a surprise.

Reentrant functions exhibit a simpler and more predictable behavior than nonreentrant functions. They are more flexible because they can be called recursively. Our INCLUDE example shows that we might not always anticipate all the reasons why someone might want to invoke a function recursively. It's better and safer to make everything reentrant if possible.

Another advantage of the dispatch table over hardwired code in read_config() is that we can use the same read_config function to process two unrelated files that have totally different directives, just by passing a different dispatch table to read_config() each time. We can put the program into "beginner mode" by passing a stripped-down dispatch table to read_config(). Or we can re-use read_config() to process a different file with the same basic syntax by passing it a table with a different set of directives; an example of this appears in Section 2.1.4.

2.1.3 Dispatch Table Strategies

In our implementation of PUSHDIR and POPDIR, the action functions used a global variable, @dirs, to maintain the stack of pushed directories. This is unfortunate. We can get around this, and make the system more flexible, by having read_config() support a *user parameter*. This is an argument, supplied by the caller of read_config(), which is passed verbatim to the actions:

CODE LIBRARY
rdconfig-uparam

```
sub read_config {
  my ($filename, $actions, $user_param) = @_;
  open my($CF), $filename or return; # Failure
  while (<$CF>) {
    my ($directive, $rest) = split /\s+/, $_, 2;
    if (exists $actions->{$directive}) {
      $actions->{$directive}->($rest, $user_param, $actions);
    } else {
      die "Unrecognized directive $directive on line $. of $filename; aborting";
    }
  }
  return 1; # Success
}
```

This eliminates the global variable, because we can now define PUSHDIR and POPDIR like this:

```
DEFINE PUSHDIR  use Cwd; push @{$_[1]}, cwd(); chdir($_[0])
DEFINE POPDIR   chdir(pop @{$_[1]})
```

The $_[1] parameter refers to the user-parameter argument that is passed to read_config(). If read_config() is called with:

```
read_config($filename, $dispatch_table, \@dirs);
```

then PUSHDIR and POPDIR will use the array @dirs as their stack; if it is called with:

```
read_config($filename, $dispatch_table, []);
```

then they will use a fresh, anonymous array as the stack.

It's often useful to pass an action callback the name of the tag on whose behalf it was invoked. To do this, we change read_config() like this:

CODE LIBRARY
rdconfig-tagarg

```
sub read_config {
  my ($filename, $actions, $user_param) = @_;
  open my($CF), $filename or return; # Failure
  while (<$CF>) {
    my ($directive, $rest) = split /\s+/, $_, 2;
    if (exists $actions->{$directive}) {
      $actions->{$directive}->($directive, $rest, $actions, $user_param);
    } else {
      die "Unrecognized directive $directive on line $. of $filename; aborting";
    }
  }
  return 1; # Success
}
```

Why is this useful? Consider the action we defined for the VERBOSITY directive:

```
VERBOSITY => sub { $VERBOSITY = shift },
```

It's easy to imagine that there might be several configuration directives that all follow this general pattern:

```
VERBOSITY => sub { $VERBOSITY = shift },
TABLESIZE => sub { $TABLESIZE = shift },
PERLPATH  => sub { $PERLPATH = shift },
... etc ...
```

We would like to merge the three similar actions into a single function that does the work of all three. To do that, the function needs to know the name of the directive so that it can set the appropriate global variable:

```
VERBOSITY => \&set_var,
TABLESIZE => \&set_var,
PERLPATH  => \&set_var,
... etc ...

sub set_var {
  my ($var, $val) = @_;
  $$var = $val;
}
```

Or, if you don't like a bunch of global variables running around loose, you can store configuration information in a hash, and pass a reference to the hash as the user parameter:

```
sub set_var {
  my ($var, $val, undef, $config_hash) = @_;
  $config_hash->{$var} = $val;
}
```

In this example, not much is saved, because the action is so simple. But there might be several configuration directives that need to share a more complicated function. Here's a slightly more complicated example:

```
sub open_input_file {
  my ($handle, $filename) = @_;
  unless (open $handle, $filename) {
    warn "Couldn't open $handle file '$filename': $!; ignoring.\n";
  }
}
```

This open_input_file() function can be shared by many configuration directives. For example, suppose a program has three sources of input: a history file, a template file, and a pattern file. We would like the locations of all three files to be configurable in the configuration file; this requires three entries in the dispatch table. But the three entries can all share the same open_input_file() function:

```
...
HISTORY  => \&open_input_file,
TEMPLATE => \&open_input_file,
```

```
PATTERN   => \&open_input_file,
...
```

Now suppose the configuration file says:

```
HISTORY             /usr/local/app/history
TEMPLATE            /usr/local/app/templates/main.tmpl
PATTERN             /home/bill/app/patterns/default.pat
```

read_config() will see the first line and dispatch to the open_input_file() function, passing it the argument list ('HISTORY', '/usr/local/app/history'). open_input_file() will take the HISTORY argument as a filehandle name, and open the HISTORY filehandle to come from the /usr/local/app/history file. On the second line, read_config() will dispatch to the open_input_file() again, this time passing it ('TEMPLATE', '/usr/local/app/templates/main.tmpl'). This time, open_input_file() will open the TEMPLATE filehandle instead of the HISTORY filehandle.

2.1.4   Default Actions

Our example read_config() function dies when it encounters an unrecognized directive. This behavior is hardwired in. It would be better if the dispatch table itself carried around the information about what to do for an unrecognized directive. It's easy to add this feature:

CODE LIBRARY
rdconfig-default

```
sub read_config {
  my ($filename, $actions, $userparam) = @_;
  open my($CF), $filename or return; # Failure
  while (<$CF>) {
    chomp;
    my ($directive, $rest) = split /\s+/, $_, 2;
    my $action = $actions->{$directive} || $actions->{_DEFAULT_};
    if ($action) {
      $action->($directive, $rest, $actions, $userparam);
    } else {
      die "Unrecognized directive $directive on line $. of $filename; aborting";
    }
  }
  return 1; # Success
}
```

Here the function looks in the action table for the specified directive; if it isn't there, if looks for a _DEFAULT_ action, and dies only if there is no default specified in the dispatch table. Here's a typical _DEFAULT_ action:

```perl
sub no_such_directive {
  my ($directive) = @_;
  warn "Unrecognized directive $directive at line $.; ignoring.\n";
}
```

Since the directive name is passed as the first argument to the action function, the default action knows what unrecognized directive it was called on behalf of. Since the no_such_directive() function also gets passed the entire dispatch table, it can extract the real directive names and do some pattern matching to figure out what might have been meant. Here no_such_directive() uses a hypothetical score_match() function to decide which table entries are good matches for the unrecognized directive:

```perl
sub no_such_directive {
  my ($bad, $rest, $table) = @_;
  my ($best_match, $best_score);
  for my $good (keys %$table) {
    my $score = score_match($bad, $good);
    if ($score > $best_score) {
      $best_score = $score;
      $best_match = $good;
    }
  }
  warn "Unrecognized directive $bad at line $.;\n";
  warn "\t(perhaps you meant $best_match?)\n";
}
```

The system we have now has only a little code, but it's extremely flexible. Suppose our program is also going to read a list of user IDs and email addresses in the following format:

```
fred          fred@example.com
bill          bvoehno@plover.com
warez         warez-admin@plover.com
...           ...
```

We can re-use `read_config()` and have it read and parse this file, by supplying the appropriate dispatch table:

```
$address_actions =
  { _DEFAULT_ => sub { my ($id, $addr, $act, $aref) = @_;
                       push @$aref, [$id, $addr];
                     },
  };


read_config($ADDRESS_FILE, $address_actions, \@address_array);
```

Here we've given `read_config()` a very small dispatch table; all it has is a `_DEFAULT_` entry. `read_config()` will call this default entry once for each line in the address file, passing it the "directive name" (which is actually the user ID) and the address (which is the `$rest` value). The default action will take this information and add it to `@address_array`, which can be used later by the program.

2.2   CALCULATOR

Let's get away from the configuration file example for a while. Obviously, dispatch tables are going to make sense in many similar situations. For example, a conversational program that must process commands from a user can use a dispatch table to dispatch the user's commands. We'll look at a different example, a very simple calculator.

The input to this calculator is a string that contains an arithmetic expression in *reverse Polish notation* (RPN). Conventional arithmetic notation is ambiguous. If you write $2 + 3 \cdot 4$, it's not immediately clear whether we do the addition or the multiplication first. We have to have special conventions to say that multiplication always happens before addition, or we have to disambiguate the expression by inserting parentheses, for example, $(2 + 3) \cdot 4$.

Reverse Polish notation solves the problem in a different way. Instead of putting the operator symbols in between the arguments that they operate on, RPN puts the operators after their arguments. For example, instead of $2 + 3$ we write 2 3 +. Instead of $(2 + 3) \cdot 4$, we write 2 3 + 4 *. The + follows 2 and 3, so the 2 and 3 are added; the * says to multiply the two preceding expressions, which are 2 3 + and 4. To express $2 + (3 \cdot 4)$ in RPN, we would write 2 3 4 * +. The + applies to the two preceding arguments; the first of these is 2 and the second is 3 4 *. Because the operator always follows its arguments, such expressions are said to be in *postfix form*; this is to contrast them with the usual form, where the operators are in between their arguments, which is called *infix form*.

It's easy to compute the value of an expression in RPN. To do this, we maintain a stack, and read the expression from left to right. When we see a number, we push it on the stack. When we see an operator, we pop the top two elements off the stack, operate on them, and push the result back on the stack. For example, to evaluate 2 3 + 4 *, we first push 2 and then 3, and then when we see the + we pop them off and push back the sum, 5. Then we push 4 on top of the 5, and then the * tells us to pop the 4 and the 5 and push back the final answer, 20. To evaluate 2 3 4 * + we push 2, then 3, then 4. The * tells us to pop back the 3 and the 4 and push the product 12; the + tells us to pop the 12 and the 2 and push the sum, 14, which is the final answer.

Here's a small calculator program that evaluates the RPN expression supplied in its command-line argument:

CODE LIBRARY
rpn-ifelse

```perl
my $result = evaluate($ARGV[0]);
print "Result: $result\n";


sub evaluate {
  my @stack;
  my ($expr) = @_;
  my @tokens = split /\s+/, $expr;
  for my $token (@tokens) {
    if ($token =- /^\d+$/) { # It's a number
      push @stack, $token;
    } elsif ($token eq '+') {
      push @stack, pop(@stack) + pop(@stack);
    } elsif ($token eq '-') {
      my $s = pop(@stack);
      push @stack, pop(@stack) - $s
    } elsif ($token eq '*') {
      push @stack, pop(@stack) * pop(@stack);
    } elsif ($token eq '/') {
      my $s = pop(@stack);
      push @stack, pop(@stack) / $s
    } else {
      die "Unrecognized token '$token'; aborting";
    }
  }
  return pop(@stack);
}
```

The function splits the argument on whitespace into *tokens*, which are the smallest meaningful portions of the input. Then the function loops over the tokens one at a time, from left to right. If a token matches /^\d+$/, then it is a number, so the function pushes it onto the stack. Otherwise, it's an operator, so the function pops two values off the stack, operates on them, and pushes the result back onto the stack. The auxiliary $s variable in the code for subtraction is there because 5 3 - should yield 2, not −2. If we had used:

```
push @stack, pop(@stack) - pop(@stack);
```

then for 5 3 - the first pop would pop the 3, the second would pop the 5, and the result would have been −2. There is similar code in the division branch for the same reason. For multiplication and addition, the order of the operands doesn't matter.

When the function runs out of tokens, it pops the top value off the stack; this is the final result. This code ignores the possibility that the stack might finish with several values; this would mean that the argument contained more than one expression. 10 2 * 3 4 + leaves 20 and 7 on the stack, in that order. It also ignores the possibility that the stack might become empty. For example, 2 * and 2 3 + * are invalid expressions, because in each, the * has only one argument instead of two. In evaluating these, the function finds itself doing an operation when the stack is empty. It should signal an error in that case, but I omitted the error handling to keep the example small.

We can make the example simpler and more flexible by replacing the large if-else switch with a dispatch table:

CODE LIBRARY
rpn-table

```
my @stack;
my $actions = {
  '+'=> sub { push @stack, pop(@stack) + pop(@stack) },
  '*'=> sub { push @stack, pop(@stack) * pop(@stack) },
  '-'=> sub { my $s = pop(@stack); push @stack, pop(@stack) - $s },
  '/'=> sub { my $s = pop(@stack); push @stack, pop(@stack) / $s },
  'NUMBER'=> sub { push @stack, $_[0] },
  '_DEFAULT_'=> sub { die "Unrecognized token '$_[0]'; aborting" }
};


my $result = evaluate($ARGV[0], $actions);
print "Result: $result\n";


sub evaluate {
  my ($expr, $actions) = @_;
  my @tokens = split /\s+/, $expr;
```

```
    for my $token (@tokens) {
      my $type;
      if ($token =~ /^\d+$/) { # It's a number
        $type = 'NUMBER';
      }

      my $action = $actions->{$type}
                || $actions->{$token}
                || $actions->{_DEFAULT_};
      $action->($token, $type, $actions);
    }
    return pop(@stack);
  }
```

The main driver, evaluate(), is now much smaller and more general. It selects an action based on the token's "type," if it has one; otherwise, the action is based on the value of the token itself, and if there is no such action, a default action is used. The evaluate() function does a pattern match on the token to try to determine a token type, and if the token looks like a number, the selected type is NUMBER. We can add a new operator by adding an entry to the %actions dispatch table:

```
    ...
    'sqrt' => sub { push @stack, sqrt(pop(@stack)) },
    ...
```

Again, because of the dispatch table construction, we can get a different behavior from the evaluator by supplying a different dispatch table. Instead of reducing the expression to a number, the evaluator will compile it into an *abstract syntax tree* (AST) if we supply this dispatch table:

```
  my $actions = {
    'NUMBER'   => sub { push @stack,    $_[0] },
    '_DEFAULT_' => sub { my $s = pop(@stack);
                         push @stack,
                            [ $_[0], pop(@stack), $s ]
                       },
  };
```

The result of compiling 2 3 + 4 * is the abstract syntax tree ['*', ['+', 2, 3], 4], which we can also represent as in Figure 2.1.

FIGURE 2.1   The AST for the expression 2 3 + 4 *.

This is the most useful internal form for an expression because all the structure is represented directly. An expression is either a number, or it has an operator and two operands; the two operands are also expressions. An abstract syntax tree is either a number, or a list of an operator and two other ASTs. Once we have an AST, it's easy to write a function to process it. For example, here is a function to convert an AST to a string:

```
sub AST_to_string {
  my ($tree) = @_;
  if (ref $tree) {
    my ($op, $a1, $a2) = @$tree;
    my ($s1, $s2) = (AST_to_string($a1),
                     AST_to_string($a2));
    "($s1 $op $s2)";
  } else {
    $tree;
  }
}
```

Given the tree of Figure 2.1, the AST_to_string() function produces the string "((2 + 3) * 4)". The function first checks to see if the tree is trivial; if it is not a reference, then it must be a number, and the string version is just that number. Otherwise, the string has three parts: an operator symbol, which is stored in $op, and two arguments, which are ASTs. The function calls itself recursively to convert the two argument trees to strings $s1 and $s2, and then produces a new string that has $s1 and $s2 with the appropriate operator symbol in between, surrounded by parentheses to avoid ambiguity. We have just written a system to convert postfix expressions to infix expressions, because we can feed the original postfix expression to evaluate() to generate an AST, and then give the AST to AST_to_string() to generate an infix expression.

The AST_to_string() function is recursive because the definition of an AST is recursive; the definition of an AST is recursive because the structure of an expression is recursive. The structure of AST_to_string() directly reflects the structure of an expression.

2.2.1 HTML Processing Revisited

In Chapter 1 we saw `walk_html()`, a recursive HTML processor. The HTML processor got two functional arguments: `$textfunc`, a function to call for a section of untagged text, and `$elementfunc`, a function to call for an HTML element. But "HTML element" is vague because there are many sorts of elements, and we might want our function to do something different for each kind of element.

We've seen several ways to accomplish this already. The most straightforward is for the user to simply put a giant `if-else` switch into `$elementfunc`. As we've already seen, that has some disadvantages. The user might like to supply a dispatch table to the `$elementfunc` instead. The structure of such a dispatch table is easy to see: the keys of the table will be tag names, and the values will be actions performed for each kind of element. Instead of supplying a single `$elementfunc` that knows how to deal with every possible element, the user will supply a dispatch table that provides one action for each kind of element, and also a generic `$elementfunc` that dispatches the appropriate action.

The `$elementfunc` might get access to the dispatch table in any of several ways. The dispatch table might be hardwired into the element function:

```perl
sub elementfunc {
  my $table = { h1       => sub { shift; my $text = join '', @_;
                                    print $text; return $text ;
                                 }
               _DEFAULT_ => sub { shift; my $text = join '', @_;
                                            return $text ;
              };
  my ($element) = @_;
  my $tag = $element->{_tag};
  my $action = $table->{$tag} || $table{_DEFAULT_};
  return $action->(@_);
}
```

Alternatively, we could build dispatch table support directly into `walk_html()`, so that instead of passing a single `$elementfunc`, the user passes the dispatch table directly to `walk_html()`. In that case, `walk_html()` would look something like this:

CODE LIBRARY
walk-html-disp

```perl
sub walk_html {
  my ($html, $textfunc, $elementfunc_table) = @_;
  return $textfunc->($html) unless ref $html; # It's a plain string
```

```
    my ($item, @results);
    for $item (@{$html->{_content}}) {
      push @results, walk_html($item, $textfunc, $elementfunc_table);
    }
    my $tag = $html->{_tag};
    my $elementfunc = $elementfunc_table->{$tag}
                   || $elementfunc_table->{_DEFAULT_}
                   || die "No function defined for tag '$tag'";
    return $elementfunc->($html, @results);
}
```

Yet another option is to change walk_html() to pass a user parameter to the
$textfunc and $elementfunc. Then the user could have the dispatch table passed
to the $elementfunc via the user parameter mechanism:

CODE LIBRARY
walk-html-uparam

```
sub walk_html {
  my ($html, $textfunc, $elementfunc, $userparam) = @_;
  return $textfunc->($html, $userparam) unless ref $html;
  my ($item, @results);
  for $item (@{$html->{_content}}) {
    push @results, walk_html($item, $textfunc, $elementfunc, $userparam);
  }
  return $elementfunc->($html, $userparam, @results);
}
```

Now it is up to the users to design their $elementfuncs to process the dispatch
table appropriately.

One important and subtle point here: notice that we passed the user parameter to the $textfunc as well as to the $elementfunc. If the user parameter is a
tag dispatch table, it is probably not useful to the $textfunc. Why did we pass
it, then? Because it might not be a tag dispatch table; it might be something else.
For example, the user might have called walk_html() like this:

```
walk_html($html_text,

          # $textfunc
          sub { my ($text, $aref) = @_;
                push @$aref, $text },

          # $elementfunc does nothing
          sub { },
```

```
      # user parameter
      \@text_array
    );
```

Now walk_html() will walk the HTML tree and push all the untagged plain text into the array @text_array. The user parameter is the reference to @text_array; it is passed to the $textfunc, which pushes the text onto the referred-to array. The $elementfunc doesn't use the user parameter at all. Since we, the authors of walk_html(), don't know in advance which sort of user parameter the user will require, we had better pass it to both the $textfunc and the $elementfunc; a function that doesn't need the user parameter is free to ignore it.

## CHAPTER 3

CACHING AND MEMOIZATION

We saw in Section 1.8 that a natural recursive function can sometimes perform extremely badly. An easy and general solution to many of these performance problems, as well as some that arise in nonrecursive contexts, is *caching*.

Let's consider a program that converts images from one format to another. Specifically, let's imagine that the input is in the popular GIF format, and that the output is something we're going to send to the printer. The printer is not the little machine that sits on your desk; it's a big company with giant printing presses that will print one million copies of some magazine by Thursday afternoon.

The printer wants the images in a special CMYK format. CMYK stands for "Cyan-Magenta-Yellow-Black," which are the four colors of the special printer's inks that the printer uses to print the magazines.[1] However, the colors in the GIF image are specified as RGB values, which are the intensities of red, green, and blue light that will be emitted by our computer monitor when it displays the image. We need to convert the RGB values that are suitable for the monitor into CMYK values that are appropriate for printing.

The conversion is just a matter of simple arithmetic:

```
sub RGB_to_CMYK {
  my ($r, $g, $b) = @_;
  my ($c, $m, $y) = (255-$r, 255-$g, 255-$b);
  my $k = $c < $m ? ($c < $y ? $c : $y)
                  : ($m < $y ? $m : $y);   # Minimum
  for ($c, $m, $y) { $_ -= $k }
```

CODE LIBRARY
RGB-CMYK

---

[1] "K" is for "black"; the printers don't use "B" because "B" is for "blue."

```
             [$c, $m, $y, $k];
        }
```

Now we write the rest of the program, which opens the GIF file, reads the pixels one at a time, calls `RGB_to_CMYK()` for each pixel, and writes out the resulting CMYK values in the appropriate format.

There's a minor problem here. Let's suppose that the GIF image is 1024 pixels wide and 768 pixels high, for a total of 786,432 pixels. We will have made 786,432 calls to `RGB_to_CMYK()`. That seems all right, except for one thing: Because of the way the GIF format is defined, no GIF image ever contains more than 256 different colors. That means that at least 786,176 of our 786,432 calls were a waste of time, because we were doing the same computations that we had already done before. If we could figure out how to save the results of our `RGB_to_CMYK()` computations and recover them when appropriate, we might win back some performance.

In Perl, whenever we consider the problem of checking whether we've seen something already, the solution will almost always involve a hash. This is no exception. If we can use the RGB value as a hash key, we can make a hash that records whether we have seen a particular set of RGB values before, and if so, what the corresponding CMYK value was. Then our program logic will go something like this: To convert a set of RGB values to a set of CMYK values, first look up the RGB values in the hash. If they're not there, do the calculation as before, store the result in the hash, and return it as usual. If the values are in the hash, then just get the CMYK values from the hash and return them without doing the calculation a second time.

The code will look something like this:

```
my %cache;

sub RGB_to_CMYK {
  my ($r, $g, $b) = @_;
  my $key = join ',', $r, $g, $b;
  return $cache{$key} if exists $cache{$key};
  my ($c, $m, $y) = (255-$r, 255-$g, 255-$b);
  my $k = $c < $m ? ($c < $y ? $c : $y)
                  : ($m < $y ? $m : $y);   # Minimum
  for ($c, $m, $y) { $_ -= $k }
  return $cache{$key} = [$c, $m, $y, $k];
}
```

Suppose we call `RGB_to_CMYK()` with arguments 128,0,64. The first time we do this, the function will look in the `%cache` hash under the key '128,0,64';

there won't be anything there, so it will continue through the function, performing the calculation as usual, and, on the last line, store the result into $cache{'128,0,64'}, and return the result. The second time we call the function with the same arguments, it computes the same key, and returns the value of $cache{'128,0,64'} without doing any extra calculation. When we find the value we need in the cache without further calculation, that is called a *cache hit*; when we compute the right key but find that no value is yet cached under that key, it is called a *cache miss*.

Of course there's a possibility that the extra program logic and the hash lookups will eat up the gains that we got from avoiding the computation. Whether this is true depends on how time-consuming the original computation was and on the likelihood of cache hits. When the original computation takes a long time, caching is more likely to be a benefit. To be sure, we should run a careful benchmark of both versions of the function. But to help develop an intuition for the kinds of tradeoffs to expect, we will look briefly at the theory.

Suppose the typical call to the real function takes time f. The average time taken by the memoized version will depend on two additional parameters: K, the cache management overhead, and h, the probability of getting a cache hit on any particular call. In the extreme case where we never get a cache hit, h is zero; as the likelihood of cache hits increases, h approaches 1.

For a memoized function, the average time per call will be at least K, since every call must check the cache, plus an additional f if there is a cache miss, for a total of $K + (1 - h)f$. The unmemoized version of the function, of course, always takes time f, so the difference is simply $hf - K$. If $K < hf$, the memoized version of the function will be faster than the unmemoized version. To speed up the memoized version, we can increase the cache hit rate h, or decrease the cache management overhead K. When f is large, it is easier to achieve $K < hf$, so caching is more likely to be effective when the original function takes a long time to run. In the worst case, we never get any cache hits, and $h = 0$, so the "speedup" is actually a slowdown of $-K$.

3.1 CACHING FIXES RECURSION

We saw in Section 1.8 that recursive functions sometimes blow up and take much too long, even on simple inputs, and that the Fibonacci function is an example of this problem:

```
# Compute the number of pairs of rabbits alive in month n
sub fib {
```

```
    my ($month) = @_;
    if ($month < 2) { 1 }
    else {
        fib($month-1) + fib($month-2);
    }
}
```

As we saw in Section 1.8, this function runs slowly for most arguments, because it wastes time recomputing results it has already computed. For example, fib(20) needs to compute fib(19) and fib(18), but fib(19) *also* computes fib(18), as well as fib(17), which is also computed once by each of the calls to fib(18). This is a common problem with recursive functions, and it is fixed by caching. If we add caching to fib, then instead of recomputing fib(18) over again from scratch the second time it is needed, fib will simply retrieve the cached result of the first computation of fib(18). It won't matter that we try to compute fib(17) three times or fib(16) five times because the work will be done only once, and the cached results will be retrieved quickly when they are needed again.

3.2   INLINE CACHING

The most straightforward way to add caching to a function is to give the function a private hash. In this example, we could use an array instead of a hash, since the argument to fib() is always a non-negative integer. But in general, we will need to use a hash, so that's what we'll see here:

CODE LIBRARY
fib-cached

```
# Compute the number of pairs of rabbits alive in month n
{ my %cache;
  sub fib {
    my ($month) = @_;
    unless (exists $cache{$month}) {
      if ($month < 2) { $cache{$month} = 1 }
      else {
        $cache{$month} = fib($month-1) + fib($month-2);
      }
    }
    return $cache{$month};
  }
}
```

Here fib gets the same argument as before. But instead of going into the recursive Fibonacci calculation immediately, it checks the cache first. The cache is a hash, %cache. When the function computes a Fibonacci number fib($month), it will store the value in $cache{$month}. Later calls to fib() will check to see if there is a value in the cache hash. This is the purpose of the exists $cache{$month} test. If the cache element is absent, the function has never been called before for this particular value of $month. The code inside the unless block is just the ordinary Fibonacci computation, including recursive calls if necessary. However, once the function has computed the answer, it doesn't return it immediately; instead, it inserts the value into the cache hash in the appropriate place. For example, $cache{$month} = 1 takes care of populating the cache when $month < 2 is true.

At the end of the function, return $cache{$month} returns the cached value, whether the function just inserted it or it was there to begin with.

With these changes, the fib function is fast. The excessive recursion problem we saw in Chapter 1 simply goes away. The problem was caused by the repeated recomputation of results; adding caching behavior prevents any recomputation from occurring. When the function tries to recompute a result it has computed already, it immediately gets the value from the cache instead.

3.2.1   Static Variables

Why is %cache outside of fib instead of inside, and why is there a bare block around %cache and fib?

If %cache were declared inside of fib, like this:

```
sub fib {
  my %cache;
  ...
}
```

then the cache would not work, because a new, fresh %cache variable would be created on every call to fib, and thrown away when fib returned. By declaring %cache outside of any function, we tell Perl that we want only one instance of %cache, created when the program is first compiled and destroyed only when the program is finished. This allows %cache to accumulate values and retain them in between calls to fib. A variable like %cache that has been declared outside all the functions is called a *static variable* because its value stays the same unless it is explicitly changed, and also because a similar feature of the C language is activated with the keyword static.

%cache has been declared with my, so it is lexically scoped. By default, its scope will continue to the end of the file. If we had defined any functions after fib, they would also be able to see and modify the cache. But this isn't what we want; we want the cache to be completely private to fib. Enclosing both %cache and fib in a separate block accomplishes this. The scope of %cache extends only to the end of the block, which contains only fib and nothing else.

3.3   GOOD IDEAS

There aren't too many ideas that are both good and simple. The few that we have are used everywhere. Caching is one of these. Your web browser caches the documents it retrieves from the network. When you ask for the same document a second time, the browser retrieves the cached copy from local disk or memory, which is fast, instead of downloading it again. Your domain name server caches the responses that it receives from remote servers. When you look up the same name a second time, the local server has the answer ready and doesn't have to carry on another possibly time-consuming network conversation. When your operating system reads data from the disks, it probably caches the data in memory, in case it's read again; when your CPU fetches data from memory, it caches the data in a special cache memory that is faster than the regular main memory.

Caching comes up over and over in real programs. Almost any program will contain functions where caching might yield a performance win. But the best property of caching is that it's *mechanical*. If you have a function, and you would like to speed it up, you might rewrite the function, or introduce a better data structure, or a more sophisticated algorithm. This might require ingenuity, which is always in short supply. But adding caching is a no-brainer; the caching transformation is always pretty much the same. This:

```
sub some_function {
  $result = some computation involving @_;
  return $result;
}
```

turns into this:

```
{ my %cache;
  sub some_function_with_caching {
    my $key = join ',', @_;
    return $cache{$key} if exists $cache{$key};
    $result = the same computation involving @_;
```

```
      return $cache{$key} = $result;
    }
  }
```

The transformation is almost exactly the same for every function. The only part that needs to vary is the join ',', @_ line. This line is intended to turn the function's argument array into a string, suitable for a hash key. Turning arbitrary values into strings like this is called *serialization* or *marshalling*.[2] The preceding join ',', @_ example works only for functions whose arguments are numbers or strings that do not contain commas. We will look at the generation of cache keys in greater detail later on.

3.4   MEMOIZATION

Adding the caching code to functions is not very much trouble. And as we saw, the changes required are the same for almost any function. Why not, then, get the computer to do it for us? We would like to tell Perl that we want caching behavior enabled on a function. Perl should be able to perform the required transformation automatically. Such automatic transformation of a function to add caching behavior is called *memoization* and the function is said to be *memoized*.[3]

The standard Memoize module, which I wrote, does this. If the Memoize module is available, we do not need to rewrite the fib code at all. We simply add two lines at the top of our program:

```
use Memoize;
memoize 'fib';
# Compute the number of pairs of rabbits alive in month n
sub fib {
  my ($month) = @_;
  if ($month < 2) { 1 }
  else {
      fib($month-1) + fib($month-2);
  }
}
```

CODE LIBRARY
fib-automemo

---

2   Data marshalling is so named because it was first studied in 1962 by Edward Waite Marshall, then with the General Electric corporation.

3   The term *memoization* was coined in 1968 by Donald Michie.

fib now exhibits the caching behavior. The code is exactly the same as our original slow version, but the function is no longer slow.

3.5   THE MEMOIZE MODULE

This book isn't about the internals of Perl modules, but some of the techniques used internally by Memoize are directly relevant to things we'll be doing later on, so we'll have a short excursion now.

Memoize gets a function name (or reference) as its argument. It manufactures a new function that maintains a cache and looks up its arguments in the cache. If the new function finds the arguments in the cache, it returns the cached value; if not, it calls the original function, saves the return value in the cache, and returns it to the original caller.

Having manufactured this new function, Memoize then installs it into the Perl symbol table in place of the original function so that when you think you're calling the original function, you actually get the new cache manager function instead.

Rather than looking into the innards of the real Memoize module, which is a 350-line monster, we'll see a tiny, stripped-down memoizer. The most important thing we'll get rid of is the part of the code that deals with the Perl symbol table. (We'll do this manually.) Instead, we'll have a memoize function whose argument is a reference to the subroutine we want to memoize, and which returns a reference to the memoized version — that is, to the cache manager function:

CODE LIBRARY
memoize

```
sub memoize {
  my ($func) = @_;
  my %cache;
  my $stub = sub {
    my $key = join ',', @_;
    $cache{$key} = $func->(@_) unless exists $cache{$key};
    return $cache{$key};
  };
  return $stub;
}
```

To call this, we first use:

```
$fastfib = memoize(\&fib);
```

Now $fastfib is the memoized version of fib(). To install the memoized version of fib() in the symbol table in place of the original, we would write *fib = memoize(\&fib). In this example, the installation is necessary if we want to calculate Fibonacci numbers quickly. Just creating a memoized version of fib() isn't enough, because the recursive calls inside of fib() are calling the function named fib(), and until we do the *fib assignment, this is still the old, slow, unmemoized version.

How does memoize work? We pass it a reference to fib, and memoize sets up a private %cache variable to hold cached data. Then it manufactures a *stub function*, temporarily stored in $stub, which it returns to its caller. This stub function is actually the memoized version of fib; the caller of memoize gets back a reference to it, which we stored in $fastfib in the preceding example.

When we invoke $fastfib, we actually get the stub function that was previously manufactured by memoize. The stub function assembles a hash key by joining the function arguments together with commas; then it looks in the cache to see if the key is a familiar one. If so, the stub returns the cached value immediately.

If the hash key isn't found in the hash, the stub function invokes the original function via $func->(@_), gets the result, stores it in the cache, and returns it (see Figure 3.1).

3.5.1   Scope and Duration

There are some subtleties here. First, suppose we call memoize(\&fib) and get back $fastfib. Then we call $fastfib, which makes use of $func. A common question is why $func didn't go out of scope when memoize returned.

This question betrays a common misconception about scope. A variable has two parts: a name and a value.[4] When you associate a name with a value, you get a variable. Such an association is called a *binding*; we also say that the name is *bound* to its value.

There are two things that might go wrong with our attempt to use $func after memoize returns: The value might have been destroyed, or the binding might have changed, so that the name refers to the wrong value, or to nothing at all.

---

[4] This is not precisely accurate. In imperative languages like Perl, a variable is an association between a name and the part of the computer's memory *in which the value will be stored*. For purposes of our discussion, this distinction is unimportant.

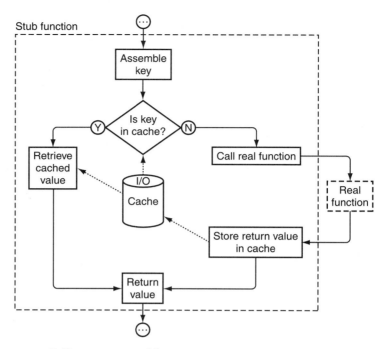

FIGURE 3.1   Calling a memoized function.

SCOPE

scope is the part of the program's source code in which a certain binding is in force. Inside the scope of a binding, the name and value are associated; outside this scope, the binding is *out of scope* and the name and value are no longer associated. The name might mean something else, or nothing at all.

When `memoize` is entered, the `my $func` declaration creates a new, fresh scalar value and binds the name $func to it. The scope of the name declared with `my`, such as $func, begins on the statement following the `my` declaration, and ends at the end of the smallest enclosing block. In this case, the smallest enclosing block is the one labeled `sub memoize`. Inside this block, $func refers to the lexical variable just created; outside, it refers to something else, probably the unrelated global variable $func. Since the stub that uses $func is inside this block, there's no scope problem; $func is in scope inside of the stub, and the name $func retains its binding.

Outside the `sub memoize` block, $func means something different, but the stub is inside the block, not outside. Scope is *lexical*, which means that it's a property of the static program text, not a property of the order in which things execute. The fact that the stub is *called* from outside the `sub memoize` block is irrelevant; its code is "physically within" the scope of the `$func` binding.

The situation is the same for `%cache`.

DURATION

Most people who ask whether `$func` is out of scope are worried about a different problem, which is not a scope issue, but instead concerns something quite different, called *duration*. The duration of a value is the period of time during the program's execution in which the value is valid for use. In Perl, when a value's duration is up, it is destroyed, and the garbage collector makes its memory available for re-use.

The important thing to know about duration is that it is almost completely unrelated to issues of names. In Perl, a value's duration lasts until there are no outstanding references to it. If the value is stored in a named variable, that counts as a reference, but there are other kinds of references. For example:

```
my $x;
{
    $x = 3;
    my $r = \$x;
}
```

Here there is a scalar with the value 3. At the end of the block, there are two references to it:

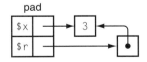

The *pad* is the data structure that Perl uses internally to represent bindings of my variables. (A different structure is used for global variables.) One reference to the 3 is from the pad itself, because the name `$x` is bound to the value 3. The other reference to the 3 is from the reference value that is bound to `$r`.

When control leaves the block, $r goes out of scope, so the binding of $r to its value is dissolved. Internally, Perl deletes the $r binding from the pad:

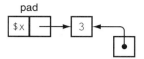

Now there's no reference to the reference value that used to be stored in $r. Since nothing refers to it anymore, its duration is over and Perl destroys it immediately:

This is typical: A variable's name goes out of scope, and its value is destroyed immediately after. Much of the confusion between scope and duration is probably caused by the ubiquity of this simple example. But scope and duration are not always so closely joined, as the next example will show:

```perl
my $r;
{
    my $x = 3;
    $r = \$x;
}
```

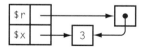

When control leaves the block, the binding of $x is dissolved and $x is deleted from the pad:

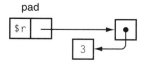

Unlike in the previous example, the unbound value persists indefinitely because it is still referred to by the reference bound to $r. Its duration will not be over until this reference is gone.

This separation of scope and duration is an essential property of Perl variables. For example, a common pattern in Perl object-oriented constructor functions is:

```
sub new {
  ...
  my %self;
  ...
  return \%self;
}
```

This constructor manufactures a hash, which is the object itself; then it returns a reference to the hash. Even though the name %self has gone out of scope, the object persists as long as the caller holds a reference to it. The analogous code in C is erroneous, because in C, the duration of an auto variable ends with its scope:

```
/* This is C */
struct st_object *new(...) {
  struct st_object self;
  ...
  return &self; /* expect a core dump */
}
```

Now let's return to memoize. When memoize returns, $func does indeed go out of scope. But the value is not destroyed, because there is still an outstanding reference from the stub. To really understand what is going on, we need to take a peek into Perl's internals (see Figure 3.2).

The stub is represented by the double box at the top center of the diagram. In Perl jargon, this box is called a *CV*, for "code value"; it is the internal representation of a coderef. (The coderef bound to $func is visible on the right-hand side of the diagram.) A CV is essentially a pair of pointers: one points to the code for the subroutine, and the other points to the pad that was active at the moment that the subroutine was defined. The binding of $func won't be destroyed until the pad it's in is destroyed. The pad won't be destroyed because there is a reference to it from the CV. The CV won't be destroyed because the caller stored it in the caller's pad by assigning it to $fastfib.

Perl knows that the stub might someday be invoked, and if it is, it might examine the value of $func. As long as the stub exists, the value of $func must be

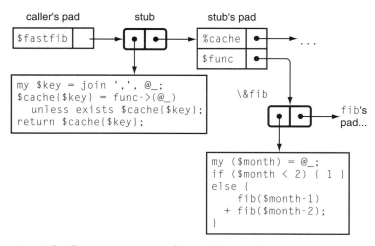

FIGURE 3.2 The data structure manufactured by `memoize`.

preserved intact. There is a reference to the stub stored in `$fastfib`, and as long as the reference is there, the stub must be preserved. Similarly, the cache `%cache` persists as long as the stub does.

3.5.2   Lexical Closure

Now another point might be worrying you. Since the value of `$func` persists as long as the stub does, what happens if we call `memoize` a second time, while the first stub is still extant? Will the assignment to `$func` in the second call clobber the value that the first stub was using?

The answer is no; everything works perfectly. This is because Perl's anonymous functions have a property called *lexical closure*. When an anonymous function is created, Perl packages up its pad, including all the bindings that are in scope, and attaches them to the CV. A function packaged up with an environment in this way is called a *closure*.

When the stub is invoked, the original environment is temporarily reinstated, and the stub function code is run in the environment that was in force at the time the stub was defined. Lexical closure means that an anonymous function carries its native environment wherever it goes, just like some tourists I have met.

The first time we call `memoize`, to memoize `fib()`, a new pad is set up for the bindings of `%cache` and `$func`, new storage is allocated for these new variables, and `$func` is initialized. Then the stub is created; the pad is attached to the CV for the stub, and the CV (let's call it `fastfib()`) is returned back to the caller.

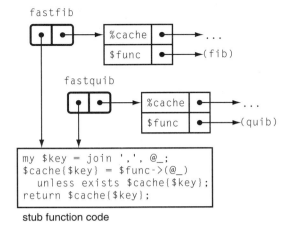

```
my $key = join ',', @_;
$cache{$key} = $func->(@_)
   unless exists $cache{$key};
return $cache{$key};
```

stub function code

FIGURE 3.3   After two calls to memoize.

Now let's call memoize a second time, this time to memoize quib() instead of fib() (see Figure 3.3). Once again, a new pad is created and fresh %cache and $func variables are bound into it. A CV is created (which we'll call fastquib()) that contains a pointer to the new pad. The new pad is completely unrelated to the pad that was attached to fastfib().

When we invoke fastfib, fastfib's pad is temporarily reinstated, and fastfib's code is executed. The code makes use of variables named %cache and $func, and these are looked up in fastfib's pad. Perhaps some data is stored into %cache at this time. Eventually, fastfib returns, and the old pad comes back into force.

Then we invoke fastquib, and almost the same thing happens. fastquib's pad is reinstated, with its own notion of %cache and $func. fastquib's code is run, and it too makes use of variables named %cache and $func. These are looked up in fastquib's pad, which has no connection to fastfib's pad. Data stored into fastfib's %cache is completely inaccessible to fastquib.

Because the code part of the CV is read-only, it is shared between several CVs. This saves memory. When a CV's duration is over, its pad is garbage-collected.

Figure 3.4 shows a simpler example.

CODE LIBRARY
closure-example

```
sub make_counter {
  my $n = shift;
  return sub { print "n is ", $n++ };
}

my $x = make_counter(7);
my $y = make_counter(20);
```

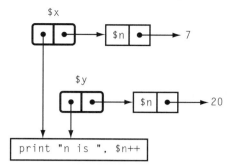

FIGURE 3.4   After two calls to make_counter.

```
$x->(); $x->(); $x->();
$y->(); $y->(); $y->();
$x->();
```

$x now contains a closure whose code is print "n is ", $n++ and whose environment contains a variable $n, set to 7. If we invoke $x a few times:

```
$x->(); $x->(); $x->();
```

the result is

```
n is 7
n is 8
n is 9
```

The new picture is shown in Figure 3.5.

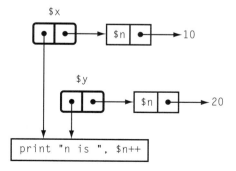

FIGURE 3.5

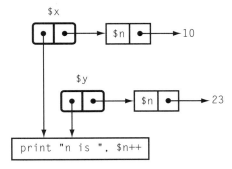

FIGURE 3.6

Now let's run $y a few times:

$y->(); $y->(); $y->();

The same code runs, but this time the name $n is looked up in $y's pad instead of in $x's pad:

```
n is 20
n is 21
n is 22
```

The new picture is shown inFigure 3.6.

Now let's run $x again:

```
n is 10
```

The $n here is the same variable as it was the first three times we invoked $x, and it has retained its value.

3.5.3 Memoization Again

All of the foregoing discussion was by way of explaining just why our memoize function worked. While it's tempting to dismiss this as a triviality — "Of course it worked!" — it's worth noticing that in many languages it won't work and can't be made to work. Several important and complex features had to operate together: delayed garbage collection, bindings, generation of anonymous subroutines, and lexical closure. If you tried to implement a function like memoize in C, for example, you would get stuck, because C doesn't have any of those features. (See Section 3.11.)

3.6 CAVEATS

(That's Latin for "warnings.")

Clearly, memoization is not a suitable solution for all performance problems. It is not even applicable to all functions. There are several kinds of functions that should not be memoized.

3.6.1 Functions Whose Return Values Do Not Depend on Their Arguments

Memoization is most suitable for functions whose return values depend only on their arguments. Imagine the foolishness of memoizing a time-of-day function: The first time you called it, you would get the time of day; subsequent calls would return the *same* time. Similarly, imagine the perversity of a memoized random number generator.

Or imagine a function whose return value indicates a success or failure of some sort. You do not want such a function to be memoized and return the same value every time it is called.

However, memoization is suitable for some such functions. For example, it might be useful to memoize a function whose result depends on the current hour of the day, if the program will run for a long time. (See Section 3.7 for details about how to handle this.)

3.6.2 Functions with Side Effects

Many functions are called not for their return values but for their side effects. Suppose you have written a program that formats a computer uptime report and delivers the report to the printer to be printed. Probably the return value is not interesting, and caching it is silly. Even if the return value is interesting, memoization is still inappropriate. The function might complete much more quickly after the first run, because of the memoization, but your boss would not be impressed, because it would have returned the old cached return value immediately, without bothering to actually print the report.[5]

---

5 I sometimes enjoy the mind-bending exercise of imagining the result of memoizing the Unix `fork()` function.

3.6.3   Functions That Return References

This problem is a little more subtle. Functions that return references to values that may be modified by their callers must not be memoized.

To see the potential problem, consider this example:

```perl
use Memoize;

sub iota {
  my $n = shift;
  return [1 .. $n];
}
memoize 'iota';

$i10 = iota(10);
$j10 = iota(10);
pop @$i10;
print @$j10;
```

The first call to `iota(10)` generates a new, fresh anonymous array of the numbers from 1 to 10, and returns a reference to this array. This reference is automatically placed in the cache, and is also stored into `$i10`. The second call to `iota(10)` fetches the same reference from the cache and stores it into `$j10`. Both `$i10` and `$j10` now refer to the same array — we say that they are *aliases* for the array.

When we change the value of the array via the `$i10` alias, the change affects the value that is stored in `$j10`! This was probably not what the caller was expecting, and it would not have happened if we had not memoized `iota`. Memoization is supposed to be an optimization. This means it is supposed to speed up the program without changing its behavior.

The prohibition on memoizing functions that return references to values that may be modified by the caller probably applies most commonly to object-oriented constructor methods. Consider:

```perl
package Octopus;
sub new {
  my ($class, %args) = @_;
  $args{tentacles} = 8;
  bless \%args => $class;
}

sub name {
```

```
    my $self = shift;
    if (@_) { $self->{name} = shift }
    $self->{name};
}


my $junko = Octopus->new(favorite_food => "crab cakes");
$junko->name("Junko");
my $fenchurch = Octopus->new(favorite_food => "crab cakes");
$fenchurch->name("Fenchurch");


# This prints "Fenchurch" -- oops!
print "The name of the FIRST octopus is ", $junko->name, "\n";
```

Here the programmer is expecting to manufacture two different octopuses, one named "Junko" and the other "Fenchurch." Both octopuses enjoy crab cakes. Unfortunately, someone has foolishly decided to memoize new(), and since the arguments to it are the same on the second call, the memoization stub returns the cached return value from the first call, which is a reference to the "Junko" object. The programmer thinks that there are two octopuses, but really there is only one, masquerading as two.

Functions whose return values depend only on their arguments, and which do not have side effects, and which never return references are called *pure functions*. Caching techniques are most suitable for use with pure functions, although they can sometimes be used even with impure functions.

3.6.4   A Memoized Clock?

A simple and instructive example of a cached impure function is provided by Perl's $^T variable. Perl provides several convenient operators for files, such as -M $filename, which returns the amount of time, in days, since the file named by its argument was last modified. To compute this, Perl asks the operating system for the last-modification time, subtracts this from the current time, and converts to days. Since -M may be performed very frequently, it is important that it be fast: Consider:

```
@result = sort { -M $a <=> -M $b } @files;
```

which sorts a list of files by their last modification time. It's already expensive to look up the last-modified times for many files, and there's no need to make thousands of calls to the time() function on top of that cost. Even worse, the OS may track the time to an accuracy of only one second, and if the system clock happens to advance during the execution of the sort(), the result list might be in the wrong order!

To avoid these problems, Perl does not look up the current time whenever a -M operation is performed. Instead, when the program is first run, Perl caches the current time in the special $^T variable, and uses that as the current time whenever -M is invoked. Most programs are short-lived, and most don't need exact accuracy in the results from -M, so this is usually a good idea. Certain long-running programs need to periodically refresh $^T by doing $^T = time(), to prevent the -M results from getting too far out of date. When caching an impure function, it is usually a good idea to provide an expiration regime, in which old cached values are eventually discarded and refreshed. It is also prudent to allow the programmer a way to flush the entire cache. The Memoize module provides the opportunity to plug in a cache expiry manager.

3.6.5 Very Fast Functions

I once talked to a programmer who complained that when he memoized his function, it got slower instead of faster. It turned out that the function he was trying to speed up was:

```
sub square { $_[0] * $_[0] }
```

Caching, like all techniques, is a tradeoff. The potential benefit is that you make fewer calls to the original function. The cost is that your program must examine the cache on every call. Earlier, we saw the formula $hf - K$, which expresses the amount of time saved by memoization. If $hf < K$, then the memoized version will be slower than the unmemoized version. h is the cache hit rate and is between 0 and 1. f is the original running time of the function, and K is the average time needed to check the cache. If f is smaller than K, $hf < K$ will be inevitable. If the cost of examining the cache is larger than the cost of calling the original function, memoization does not make sense. You can't save time by eliminating "unnecessary" calls because it takes longer to find out that the call is unnecessary than it does to make the call in the first place.

In our square example, the function is doing a single multiplication. Checking a cache requires a hash lookup; this includes computation of a hash value (many multiplications and additions), then indexing into the hash bucket array, and possibly a search of a linked list. There is no way this is going to beat a single multiplication. In fact, almost nothing beats a single multiplication. You can't speed up the square function, by memoization or any other technique, because it is already almost as fast as any function can possibly be.

3.7   KEY GENERATION

The memoizer we saw earlier has at least one serious problem. It needs to turn the function arguments into a hash key, and the way it does that is with join:

```
my $key = join ',', @_;
```

This works for functions with only one argument, and it works for functions whose arguments never contain commas, including all functions whose arguments are numbers. But if the function arguments may contain commas, it might fail, because the same key is computed for these two calls:

```
func("x,", "y");
func("x", ",y");
```

When the first call is made, the return value will be stored in the cache under the key "x,,y". When the second call is made, the true function will not be consulted. Instead the cached value from the first call will be returned. But the function might have wanted to return a different value — the memoization code has confused these two argument lists, resulting in a false cache hit.

Since this can fail only for functions whose arguments may contain commas, it may not be a consideration. Even if the function arguments may contain commas, it's possible that there is some other character that they will never contain. The Perl special variable $; is sometimes used here. It normally contains character #28, which is the control–backslash character. If the key generator uses join $; , @_, it will fail only when the function arguments contain control–backslash; it is often possible to be sure this will never occur. But often we have a function whose argument could contain absolutely anything, and one of these partial hacks won't work reliably.

This can be fixed, because there's always a way to turn any data structure, such as an argument list, into a string in a faithful way, so that different structures become different strings.[6]

---

[6]   To see this, just realize that there must be some difference in the way the two structures are represented in memory, and that the computer's memory is itself nothing more than a very long string.

One strategy would be to use the Storable or FreezeThaw module to turn the argument list into a string. A much more efficient strategy is to use escape sequences:

```
my @args = @_;
s/([\\,])/\\$1/g for @args;
my $key = join ",", @args;
```

Here we insert a backslash character before every comma or backslash in the original arguments, then join the results together with unbackslashed commas. The problem calls we saw earlier are no longer problems, because the two argument lists are transformed to different keys: one to 'x\,,y' and the other to 'x,\,y'. (An exercise: Why is it necessary to put a backslash before every backslash character as well as before every comma?)

However, correctness has been bought at a stiff performance price. The escape character code is much slower than the simple join — about ten times slower even for a simple argument list such as (1,2) — and it must be performed on *every* call to the function. Normally, we laugh at people who are willing to trade correctness for speed, since it doesn't matter how quickly one is able to find the wrong answer. But this is an unusual circumstance. Since the only purpose of memoization is to speed up a function, we want the overhead to be as small as possible.

We'll adopt a compromise. The default behavior of memoize will be fast, but not correct in all cases. We'll give the user of memoize an escape hatch to fix this. If the user doesn't like the default key-generation method, they may supply an alternative, which memoize will use instead.

The change is simple:

```
sub memoize {
  my ($func, $keygen) = @_;
  my %cache;
  my $stub = sub {
    my $key = $keygen ? $keygen->(@_) : join ',', @_;
    $cache{$key} = $func->(@_) unless exists $cache{$key};
    return $cache{$key};
  };
  return $stub;
}
```

The stub returned by memoize looks to see if a $keygen function was supplied when the original function was memoized. If so, it uses the keygen function to construct the hash key; if not, it uses the default method. The extra test is fairly cheap, but we can eliminate it if we want to by performing the test for $keygen once, at the time the function is memoized, instead of once for each call to the memoized function:

```perl
sub memoize {
    my ($func, $keygen) = @_;
    my %cache;
    my $stub = $keygen ?
      sub { my $key = $keygen->(@_);
            $cache{$key} = $func->(@_) unless exists $cache{$key};
            return $cache{$key};
          }
      :
      sub { my $key = join ',', @_;
            $cache{$key} = $func->(@_) unless exists $cache{$key};
            return $cache{$key};
          }
      ;
    return $stub;
}
```

We can pull an even better trick here. In these versions of memoize, $keygen is an anonymous function that has to be invoked on each call to the memoized function. Perl, unfortunately, has a relatively high overhead for function calls, and since the purpose of memoize is to speed things up, we'd like to avoid this if we can.

Perl's eval feature comes to the rescue here. Instead of specifying $keygen as a reference to a key-generation function, we'll pass in a string that contains the code to generate the key, and incorporate this code directly into the stub, rather than as a sub-function that the stub must call.

To use this version of memoize, we will say something like this:

```perl
$memoized = memoize(\&fib, q{my @args = @_;
                             s/([\\,])/\\$1/g for @args;
                             join ',', @args;
                            });
```

memoize will interpolate this bit of code into the appropriate place in a template of the memoized function (this is called *inlining*) and use eval to compile the result into a real function:

```
sub memoize {
  my ($func, $keygen) = @_;
  $keygen ||= q{join ',', @_};

  my %cache;
  my $newcode = q{
    sub { my $key = do { KEYGEN };
          $cache{$key} = $func->(@_) unless exists $cache{$key};
          return $cache{$key};
        }
  };
  $newcode =- s/KEYGEN/$keygen/g;
  return eval $newcode;
}
```

Here we used Perl's q{...} operator, which is identical with '...', except that single-quote characters aren't special inside of q{...}. Instead, the q{...} construction ends at the first matching } character. If we hadn't used q{...} here, the third line would have been rather cryptic:

```
$keygen ||= 'join \',\', @_';
```

We used the s/// operator to inline the value of $keygen, instead of simply interpolating it into a double-quoted string. This is slightly less efficient, but it needs to be done only once per memoized function, so it probably doesn't matter. The benefit is that with the s/// technique, the $newcode variable is easy to read; if we had used string interpolation, it would have been:

```
my $newcode = "
  sub { my \$key = do { $keygen };
        \$cache{\$key} = \$func->(\@_) unless exists \$cache{\$key};
        return \$cache{\$key};
      }
";
```

Here the backslashes clutter up the code. A maintenance programmer reading this might not notice that $keygen is being interpolated even though everything else is backslashed. With the s/// technique, KEYGEN stands out clearly.

For this example, the cache management overhead is about 37% lower with the inlining version of memoize.

It's easy to tweak this version so that it still accepts a function reference the way the previous one did:

```perl
sub memoize {
  my ($func, $keygen) = @_;
  my $keyfunc;
  if ($keygen eq '') {
    $keygen = q{join ',', @_}
  } elsif (UNIVERSAL::isa($keygen, 'CODE')) {
    $keyfunc = $keygen;
    $keygen = q{$keyfunc->(@_)};
  }
  my %cache;
  my $newcode = q{
    sub { my $key = do { KEYGEN };
          $cache{$key} = $func->(@_) unless exists $cache{$key};
          return $cache{$key};
        }
  };
  $newcode =~ s/KEYGEN/$keygen/g;
  return eval $newcode;
}
```

Here, if no key generator is supplied, we inline join ',', @_ as usual. If $keygen is a function reference, we can't simply inline it, because it will turn into something useless like CODE(0x436c1d). Instead, we save the function reference in the $keyfunc variable and inline some code that will call the function via $keyfunc.

The UNIVERSAL::isa($keygen, 'CODE') line requires some explanation. We want to test to see if $keygen is a code reference. The obvious way of doing that is:

```perl
if (ref($keygen) eq 'CODE') { ... }
```

Unfortunately, the Perl ref function is broken, because it confuses two different properties of its argument. If $keygen is a *blessed* code reference, the test above will fail, because ref will return the name of the class into which $keygen has been blessed. It's also possible, although much less likely, that the test could yield true for a non-code reference; this will happen if someone has been silly enough to bless the non-code reference into the class CODE. Using UNIVERSAL::isa avoids all these problems.

3.7.1   More Applications of User-Supplied Key Generators

With any of these key-generation features, users of our `memoize` function have escape hatches if the `join` method doesn't work correctly for the function they are trying to memoize. They can substitute a key generator based on `Storable` or the escape-character method or whatever is appropriate.

User-supplied key generators solve the problems that may occur when two different argument lists hash to the same key. They also solve the converse problem, which occurs when two equivalent argument lists hash to different keys.

Consider a function whose argument is a hash, which might contain any, all, or none of the keys `A`, `B`, and `C`, each with an associated numeric value. Further, suppose that `B`, if omitted, defaults to 17, and `A` defaults to 32:

```
sub example {
  my %args = @_;
  $args{A} = 32 unless defined $args{A};
  $args{B} = 17 unless defined $args{B};
  # ...
}
```

Then the following calls are all equivalent:

```
example(C => 99);
example(C => 99, A => 32);
example(A => 32, C => 99);
example(B => 17, C => 99);
example(C => 99, B => 17);
example(A => 32, C => 99, B => 17);
example(B => 17, A => 32, C => 99);
(etc.)
```

The `join` method of key construction generates a different key for each of these calls (`"C,99"` versus `"A,32,C,99"` versus `"C,99,A,32"` and so forth). The cache manager will therefore miss opportunities to avoid calling the real `example()` function. A call to `example(A => 32, C => 99)` must produce the same result as a call to `example(C => 99, A => 32)`, but the cache manager doesn't know that, because the argument lists are superficially different. If we can arrange that equivalent argument lists are transformed to the same hash key, the cache manager will return the same value for `example(C => 99, A => 32)` that it had previously computed for `example(A => 32, C => 99)`, without the redundant call to example. This will increase the cache hit rate h in the formula $hf - K$ that expresses the speed-up from memoization. The following key generator does the trick:

```
sub {
  my %h = @_;
  $h{A} = 32 unless defined $h{A};
  $h{B} = 17 unless defined $h{B};
  join ",", @h{'A','B','C'};
}
```

Each of the eight equivalent calls (of which example(C => 99, A => 32) was one) receives a key of "32,17,99" from this function. Here we pay an up-front cost: This key generator takes about ten times as long as the simple join generator, so the K in the $hf - K$ formula is larger. Whether this cost is repaid depends on how expensive it is to call the real function, f, and on the size of the increase of cache hits frequency, h. As usual, there is no substitute for benchmarking.

3.7.2   Inlined Cache Manager with Argument Normalizer

Here's an interesting trick we can play with the inlined key-generation code. Consider the following function, a variation on the example we just saw:

```
sub example {
  my ($a, $b, $c) = @_;
  $a = 32 unless defined $a;
  $b = 17 unless defined $b;
  # more calculation here ...
}
```

A suitable key generator might be:

```
my ($a, $b, $c) = @_;
$a = 32 unless defined $a;
$b = 17 unless defined $b;
join ',', $a, $b, $c;
```

It's a little irritating to have to repeat the code that sets the defaults for the arguments, and equally irritating to have to run it twice. If we change the key-generation code as follows, we will be able to remove the argument checking from the example function:

```
$_[0] = 32 unless defined $_[0];
$_[1] = 17 unless defined $_[1];
join ',', @_;
```

When this is inlined into the memoize function, the result is:

```
sub { my $key = do { $_[0] = 32 unless defined $_[0];
                     $_[1] = 17 unless defined $_[1];
                     join ',', @_;
                   };
      $cache{$key} = $func->(@_) unless exists $cache{$key};
      return $cache{$key};
    }
```

Notice what happens here. The key is generated as before, but there is a side effect: @_ is modified. If there is a cache miss, the memoized function calls $func with the modified @_. Since @_ has been modified to include the default values already, we can omit the default-setting code from the original function:

```
sub example {
  my ($a, $b, $c) = @_;
## defaults set by key generation code
##   $a = 32 unless defined $a;
##   $b = 17 unless defined $b;
  # more calculation here ...
}
```

Of course, once we've modified the example function in this way, we can't turn the memoization off, because essential functionality has been moved into the key generator.

Another danger with this technique is that modifying @_ can have peculiar effects back in the *calling* function. Elements of @_ are aliased to the corresponding arguments back in the caller, and assigning to elements of @_ in the memoized function can modify variables outside the memoized function. Here is a simple example:

```
sub set_to_57 {
  $_[0] = 57;
}
```

```
    my $x = 119;
    set_to_57($x);
```

This does set $x to 57, as if we had done $x = 57, even though the assignment is performed outside the scope of $x and shouldn't be able to affect it. Our assignments inside the key-generator code may have similar effects.

Sometimes this feature of Perl is useful, but most often it is more trouble than it is worth, and we normally avoid it. We do this by never operating on @_ directly, but by copying its contents into a series of lexical variables as soon as the function is called:

```
sub safe_function {
  my ($n) = @_;
  $n = 57; # does *not* set $x to 57
}


my $x = 119;
safe_function($x);
```

By combining these techniques, we can get a version of the key-generation code that obviates the need for the default-setting code in the real function, but which is still safe:

```
memoize(\&example, q{
    my ($a, $b, $c) = @_;
    $a = 32 unless defined $a;
    $b = 17 unless defined $b;
    @_ = ($a, $b, $c);              # line 5
    join ',', @_;
});
```

The elements of @_ are aliases for the arguments back in the calling function, but @_ itself isn't. The assignment to @_ on line 5 doesn't overwrite the values back in the caller; it discards the aliases entirely and replaces the contents of @_ with the new values. This trick works only when the key-generation code is inlined into the memoized function; if the key-generation code is called as a subroutine, the change to @_ has no effect after the subroutine returns.

3.7.3 Functions with Reference Arguments

Here's another problem solved by the custom key-generator feature. Consider this function:

```
sub is_in {
  my ($needle, $haystack) = @_;
  for my $item (@$haystack) {
    return 1 if $item == $needle;
  }
  return;
}
```

The function takes $needle, which is a number, and $haystack, which is a list of numbers, and returns true if and only if $haystack contains $needle. A typical call is:

```
if (is_in($my_id, \@employee_ids)) { ... }
```

We might like to try memoizing is_in, but a possible problem is that the $haystack argument is a reference. When it is handled by the join function, it turns into a string like ARRAY(0x436c1d). If we later call is_in() with a $haystack argument that refers to a different array with the same contents, the hash key will be different, which may not be what we want; conversely, if the contents of @employee_ids change, the hash key will still be the same, which certainly isn't what we want. The key generator is generating the key from the identity of the array, but the is_in() function doesn't care about the identity of the array; it cares only about the contents. A more appropriate key-generation function in this case is:

```
sub { join ",", $_[0], @{$_[1]} }
```

Again, whether this actually produces a performance win depends on many circumstances that will be hard to foresee. When performance is important, it is essential to gather real data. Long experience has shown that even experts are likely to guess wrong about what is fast and what is slow.

3.7.4 Partitioning

The find_share function of Chapter 1 provides a convenient example of a function for which memoization fixes slow recursion, as well as requiring a custom key generator:

```
sub find_share {
  my ($target, $treasures) = @_;
  return [] if $target == 0;
  return    if $target < 0 || @$treasures == 0;
  my ($first, @rest) = @$treasures;
  my $solution = find_share($target-$first, \@rest);
  return [$first, @$solution] if $solution;
  return         find_share($target     , \@rest);
}
```

As you'll recall, this function takes an array of treasures and a target value, and tries to select a subset of the treasures that total the target value exactly. If there is such a set, it returns an array with just those treasures; if not, it returns undef.

We saw in Chapter 1 that this function has the same problem as the fib function: It can be slow, because it repeats the same work over and over again. When trying to select treasures from 1 2 3 4 5 6 7 8 9 10 that total 53, find_share comes upon the same situation twice: It finds that $1+2+3+6 = 12$, and invokes find_share([7,8,9,10], 41), which eventually returns undefined. Then later, it finds that $1+2+4+5 = 12$, and invokes find_share([7,8,9,10], 41) a second time. Clearly, this is a good opportunity to try some caching.

For even this simple case, memoization yields a speed-up of about 68%. For larger examples, such as find_share([1..20], 200), the speedup is larger, about 82%. In some cases, memoization can make the difference between a practical and an impractical algorithm. The unmemoized version of find_share([1..20], 210) takes several *thousand* times longer to run than the memoized version. (I used the key generation function sub {join "-", @{$_[0]}, $_[1]}.)

3.7.5 Custom Key Generation for Impure Functions

Custom key generation can also be used to deal with certain kinds of functions that depend on information other than their arguments.

Let's consider a long-running network server program whose job is to sell some product, such as pizzas or weapons-grade plutonium. The cost of a pizza or a canister of plutonium includes the cost of delivery, which in turn depends on the current hour of the day and day of the week. Delivery late at night and on weekends is more expensive because fewer delivery persons are available and nobody likes to work at 3 AM.[7] The server might contain a function something like this:

```perl
sub delivery_charge {
    my ($quantity_ordered) = @_;
    my ($hour, $day_of_week) = (localtime)[2,6];
    # perform complex computatation involving $weight, $gross_cost,
    #       $hour, $day_of_week, and $quantity_ordered
    # ...
    return $delivery_charge;
}
```

Because the function is complicated, we would like to memoize it. The default key generator, join(',', @_), is unsuitable here, because we would lose the time dependence of the delivery charge. But it's easy to solve the problem with a custom key-generation function such as:

```perl
sub delivery_charge_key {
    join ',', @_, (localtime)[2,6];
}
```

delivery_charge is not a pure function, but in this case it may not matter. The only real issue is whether there will be enough cache hits to gain a performance win. We might expect the function to have many cache misses for the first week, until the day of the week rolls over, and then to start seeing more cache hits. In this case the effectiveness of the caching might depend on the longevity of the program. Similarly, we might wonder if the following key-generation function wouldn't be better:

```perl
sub delivery_charge_key {
    my ($hour, $day_of_week) = (localtime)[2,6];
    my $weekend = $day_of_week == 0 || $day_of_week == 6;
    join ',', @_, $hour, $weekend;
}
```

This function takes longer to run, but might get more cache hits because it recognizes that values cached on Monday may be used again on Tuesday and Wednesday. Again, which is best will depend on subtle factors in the program's behavior.

---

7   Most plutonium is ordered late at night in spite of the extra costs.

3.8   CACHING IN OBJECT METHODS

For object methods, it often makes little sense to store the cached values in a separate hash. Consider an `Investor` object in a program written by an investment bank. The object represents one of the bank's customers:

```
package Investor;

# Compute total amount currently invested
sub total {
  my $self = shift;
  # ... complex computation performed here ...
  return $total;
}
```

If the `$total` is not expected to change, we might add caching to it, using the object's identity as a key into the cache hash:

```
# Compute total amount currently invested
{ my %cache;
  sub total {
    my $self = shift;
    return $cache{$self} if exists $cache{$self};
    # ... complex computation performed here ...
    return $cache{$self} = $total;
  }
}
```

However, this technique has a serious problem. When we use an object as a hash key, Perl converts it to a string. The typical hash key will look like `Investor=HASH(0x80ef8dc)`. The hexadecimal numeral is the address at which the object's data is actually stored. It is essential that this key be different for every two objects, or we run the risk of false cache hits, where we retrieve one object's total while thinking that it belongs to a different object. In Perl, these hash keys are indeed distinct for all the live objects in the system at any given time, but no guarantee is made about dead objects. If an object is destroyed and a new object is created, the new object might very well exist at the same memory address formerly occupied by the old object and thus be confused with it:

```
# here 90,000 is returned from the cache
$old_total = $old_object->total();
```

```
undef $old_object;
$new_object = Investor->new();
$new_total = $new_object->total();
```

Here we ask for the total for the new investor. It should be 0, since the investor is new. But instead, the ->total method happens to look in the cache under the same hash key that was used by the $old_object that was recently destroyed; the method sees the 90000 stored there, and returns it erroneously. This problem can be solved with a DESTROY method that deletes an object's data from the cache, or by associating a unique, non-re-usable ID number with every object in the program, and using the ID number as the hash key, but there is a much more straightforward solution.

In an OOP context, the cache hash technique is peculiar, because there is a more natural place to store the cached data: as member data in the object itself. A cached total becomes another property that might or might not be carried by each individual object:

```
# Compute total amount currently invested
sub total {
  my $self = shift;
  return $self->{cached_total} if exists $self->{cached_total};
  # ... complex computation performed here ...
  return $self->{cached_total} = $total;
}
```

Here the logic is exactly the same as before; the only difference is that the method stores the total for each object in the object itself, instead of in an auxiliary hash. This avoids the problem of hash key collision that arose with the auxiliary hash.

Another advantage of this technique is that the space devoted to storage of the cached total is automatically reclaimed when the object is destroyed. With the auxiliary hash, each cached value would persist forever, even after the object to which it belonged was destroyed.

Finally, storing the cached information in each object allows more flexible control over when it is expired. In our example total computes the total amount of money that a certain investor has invested. Caching this total may be appropriate since investors may not invest new money too frequently. But caching it forever is probably not appropriate. In this example, whenever an investor invests more money, we need some way of signalling the total function that the cached total is no longer correct, and must be recomputed from scratch. This is called *expiring* the cached value.

With the auxiliary hash technique, there was no way to do this without adding a special-purpose method in the scope of the cache hash, something like this:

```
# Compute total amount currently invested
{ my %cache;
  sub total {
    my $self = shift;
    return $cache{$self} if exists $cache{$self;
    # ... complex computation performed here ...
    return $cache{$self} = $total;
  }

  sub expire_total {
    my $self = shift;
    delete $cache{$self};
  }
}

sub invest {
  my ($self, $amount, ...) = @_;
  $self->expire_total;
  ...
}
```

With the object-oriented technique, no special method is necessary, because each method can directly expire the cached total if it needs to:

```
# Compute total amount currently invested
sub total {
  my $self = shift;
  return $self->{cached_total} if exists $self->{cached_total};
  # ... complex computation performed here ...
  return $self->{cached_total} = $total;
}

sub invest {
  my ($self, $amount, ...) = @_;
  delete $self->{cached_total};
  ...
}
```

3.8.1   Memoization of Object Methods

As we saw, for object methods, we often like to cache each computed value with the object for which it is relevant, instead of in one separate hash. The `memoize` function we saw earlier doesn't do this, but it's not hard to build one that does:

```
sub memoize_method {
  my ($method, $key) = @_;
  return sub {
    my $self = shift;
    return $self->{$key} if exists $self->{$key};
    return $self->{$key} = $method->($self, @_);
  };
}
```

`$method` is a reference to the true method. `$key` is the name of the slot in each object in which the cached values will be stored. The stub function returned here is suitable for use as a method. When the stub is invoked, it retrieves the object on whose behalf it was called, just like any other method; then it looks in the object for member data named `$key` to see if a value is cached there. If so, the stub returns the cached value; if not, it calls the real method, caches the result in the object, and returns the new cached result.

   To use this, we might write something like this:

```
*Investor::total = memoize_method( \&Investor::total, 'cached_total');
$investor_bob->total;
```

This installs the stub in the symbol table in place of the original method. Alternatively, we might use:

```
$memoized_total = memoize_method(\&Investor::total. 'cached_total');
$investor_bob->$memoized_total;
```

These are not quite the same. In the former case, all calls to `->total` will use the memoized version of the method, including calls from subclasses that inherit the method. In the latter case, we get the memoized version of the method only when we explicitly ask for it by using the `->$memoized(...)` notation.

3.9   PERSISTENT CACHES

Before we leave the topic of automatic memoization, we'll see a few peripheral techniques. We saw how a function could be replaced with a memoized version that stored return values in a cache; the cache was simply a hash variable.

In Perl, one can use the `tie` operator to associate a hash variable with a disk database, so that data stored in the hash is automatically written to the disk, and data fetched back from the hash actually comes from the disk. To add this feature to our `memoize` function is simple:

```perl
use DB_File;

sub memoize {
  my ($func, $keygen, $file) = @_;
  my %cache;
  if (defined $file) {
    tie %cache => 'DB_File', $file, O_RDWR|O_CREAT, 0666
      or die "Couldn't access cache file $file: $!; aborting";
  }
  my $stub = sub {
    my $key = $keygen ? $keygen->(@_) : join ',', @_;
    $cache{$key} = $func->(@_) unless exists $cache{$key};
    return $cache{$key};
  };
  return $stub;
}
```

Here we've added an optional third parameter, which is the name of the disk file that will receive the cached data. If supplied, we use `tie` to tie the hash to the file. Note that if you don't use this feature, you pay hardly any cost at all — a single `defined()` test at the time you call `memoize()`.

When the cache hash is tied to a disk file in this way, the cache becomes persistent. Data stored in the cache on one run of the program remains in the file after the program has exited, and is available to the function the next time the program is run. The program is incrementally replacing the function with a lookup table on the disk. The cost to the programmer is nearly zero, since we did not have to change any of the code in the original function.

If we get tired of waiting for the lookup table to be completely populated, we can force the issue. We can write a tiny program that does nothing but call the memoized function over and over with different arguments each time. We start it up on Friday afternoon and go home for the weekend. When we come back on Monday, the persistent cache will have the values of the function precomputed. When we run our real application, all calls to the memoized function will return almost instantly, since the values have been saved in the database.

Once again, this may not be a win. Remember, the speed-up from memoization is $hf - K$, where K is the overhead of managing the cache. If K is sufficiently large, it will overwhelm the gains from the hf part of the formula, as in the sub { $_[0] * $_[0] } example from Section 3.6. When we store cache data in a disk file, the overhead K can be many times greater than normal, because our program will have to make an operating-system request to look in the disk database.

An alternative and more flexible interface is to allow the user of memoize() to supply their own tied hash:

```
sub memoize {
    my ($func, $keygen, $cache) = @_;
    $cache = {} unless defined $cache;
    my $stub = sub {
        my $key = $keygen ? $keygen->(@_) : join ',', @_;
        $cache->{$key} = $func->(@_) unless exists $cache->{$key};
        return $cache->{$key};
    };
    return $stub;
}
```

This allows the user to supply a cache that is tied to a disk file using their favorite DBM implementation, even one we've never heard of. They could also pass in an ordinary hash; that would allow them to erase the cache or to expire old values from it if they wanted to.

3.10 ALTERNATIVES TO MEMOIZATION

Most pure functions present an opportunity for caching. Although it may appear at first that pure functions are rare, they do appear with some frequency. One place where pure functions are especially common is as the comparator functions used in sorting.

The Perl built-in sort operator is generic, in that it can sort a list of any kind of data into any order desired by the program. By default, it sorts a list of strings into alphabetical order, but the programmer may optionally supply a *comparator function* that tells Perl how to reorder sort's argument list. The comparator function is called repeatedly, each time with two different elements from the list to be sorted, and must return a negative value if the two elements are in the correct order, a positive value if the two elements are in the wrong order, and zero if it doesn't care. Typically, a comparator function's return value depends only on the values of its arguments, the two list items it is comparing, so it is a pure function.

Probably the simplest example of a comparator function is the comparator that compares numbers for sorting into numerical order:

```
@sorted_numbers = sort { $a <=> $b } @numbers;
```

Here `{ $a <=> $b }` is the comparator function. The `sort` operator examines the list of `@numbers`, sets `$a` and `$b` to the numbers it wishes to have compared, and invokes the comparator function. `<=>` is a special Perl operator that returns a negative value if `$a` is less than `$b`, a positive value if `$a` is greater than `$b`, and zero if `$a` and `$b` are equal.[8] `cmp` is an analogous operator for strings; this is the default that Perl uses if you don't specify an explicit comparator.

An alternative syntax uses a named function instead of a bare block:

```
@sorted_numbers = sort numerically @numbers;

sub numerically { $a <=> $b }
```

This is equivalent to the bare-block version.

A more interesting example sorts a list of date strings of the form `"Apr 16, 1945"` into chronological order:

```
@sorted_dates = sort chronologically @dates;

%m2n =
    ( jan =>  1, feb =>  2, mar =>  3,
      apr =>  4, may =>  5, jun =>  6,
      jul =>  7, aug =>  8, sep =>  9,
      oct => 10, nov => 11, dec => 12, );

sub chronologically {
  my ($am, $ad, $ay) =
     ($a =~ /(\w{3}) (\d+), (\d+)/);
```

---

8   Subtraction would work equally well here; `<=>` is used in comparators instead of plain subtraction because of its documentative value.

```
my ($bm, $bd, $by) =
   ($b =~ /(\w{3}) (\d+), (\d+)/);

            $ay  <=>          $by
|| $m2n{lc $am} <=> $m2n{lc $bm}
||          $ad  <=>          $bd;
}
```

The two date strings to be compared are loaded into $a and $b, as before, and then split up into $ay, $by, $am, and so forth. $ay and $by, the years, are compared first. The || operator here is a common idiom in sort comparators for sorting by secondary keys. The || operator returns its left operand, unless that is zero, in which case it returns its right operand. If the years are the same, then $ay <=> $by returns zero, and the || operator passes control to the part of the expression involving the months, which are used to break the tie. But if the years are different, then the result of the first <=> is nonzero, and this is the result of the || expression, instructing sort how to order $a and $b in the result list without ever having looked at the months or the days. If control passes to the $am <=> $bm part, the same thing happens. The months are compared; if the result is conclusive, the function returns immediately, and if the months are the same, control passes to the final tiebreaker of comparing the days.

Internally, Perl's sort operator has been implemented with various algorithms that have $O(n \log n)$ running time. This means that to sort a list that is n times larger than another typically takes somewhat more than n times as long. If the list size doubles, the running time more than doubles. The following table compares the length of the argument list with the number of calls typically made to the comparator function:

Length	# calls	calls / element
5	7	1.40
10	26	2.60
20	60	3.00
40	195	4.87
80	417	5.21
100	569	5.69
1000	9502	9.50
10000	139136	13.91

I got the "# calls" column by generating a list of random numbers of the indicated length and sorting it with a comparator function that incremented a counter each time it was called. The number of calls will vary depending on the list and on the comparator function, but these values are typical.

Now consider a list of 10,000 dates. 139,136 calls are made to the comparator function; each call performs two pattern-match operations, so there are 278,272 pattern matches in all. This means each date is split up into year, month, and day 27.8 times on average. Since the three components for a given date never change, it's clear that 26.8 of these matchings are wasted.

The first thing that might come to mind is to memoize the `chronologically` function, but this doesn't work well in practice. Although `sort` will call `chronologically` repeatedly with the same date, it won't call it twice on the same *pair* of dates. Since the hash keys must incorporate both arguments, the memoized function will never have a cache hit.

Instead, we'll do something slightly different, and memoize just the expensive part of the function. This will require a version of `memoize()` that can handle a function that returns a list.

```
@sorted_dates = sort chronologically @dates;

%m2n =
  ( jan =>  1, feb =>  2, mar =>  3,
    apr =>  4, may =>  5, jun =>  6,
    jul =>  7, aug =>  8, sep =>  9,
    oct => 10, nov => 11, dec => 12, );

sub chronologically {
  my ($am, $ad, $ay) = split_date($a);
  my ($bm, $bd, $by) = split_date($b);

            $ay     <=>          $by
  || $m2n{lc $am} <=> $m2n{lc $bm}
  ||          $ad     <=>          $bd;
}

sub split_date {
  $_[0] =~ /(\w{3}) (\d+), (\d+)/;
}
```

If we set up caching on `split_date`, we'll still make 278,272 calls to it, but 268,272 will result in cache hits, and only the remaining 10,000 will require pattern matching. The only catch is that we'll have to write the caching code by hand, because `split_date` returns a list, and our `memoize` functions deal correctly only with functions that return scalars.

At this point, we could go in three directions. We could enhance our `memoize` function to deal correctly with list-context returns. (Or we could use the CPAN

Memoize module, which does work correctly for functions that return lists.) We could write the caching code manually. But it's more instructive to sidestep the problem by replacing split_date with a function that returns a scalar. If the scalar is constructed correctly, we will be able to dispense with the complicated || logic in chronologically and just use a simple string compare.

Here's the idea: We will split the date, as before, but instead of returning a list of fields, we will pack the fields into a single string. The fields will appear in the string in the order we need to examine them, with the year first, then the month, then the day. The string for "Apr 16, 1945" will be "19450416". When we compare strings with cmp, Perl will stop comparing as soon as possible, so if one string begins with "1998..." and another with "1996..." Perl will know the result as soon as it sees the fourth character, and won't bother to examine the month or day. String comparison is very fast, likely to beat out a sequence of <=>'s and ||s.

Here's the modified code:

```
@sorted_dates = sort chronologically @dates;

%m2n =
   ( jan =>   1, feb =>   2, mar =>   3,
     apr =>   4, may =>   5, jun =>   6,
     jul =>   7, aug =>   8, sep =>   9,
     oct =>  10, nov =>  11, dec =>  12, );

sub chronologically {
   date_to_string($a) cmp date_to_string($b)
}

sub date_to_string {
   my ($m, $d, $y) = ($_[0] =~ /(\w{3}) (\d+), (\d+)/);
   sprintf "%04d%02d%02d", $y, $m2n{lc $m}, $d;
}
```

CODE LIBRARY
chrono-3

Now we can memoize date_to_string. Whether this will win over the previous version depends on whether the sprintf plus cmp is faster than the <=> plus ||. As usual, a benchmark is required; it turns out that the code with the sprintf is about twice as fast.[9]

---

[9] This comes as a surprise to many people, especially C programmers who expect sprintf to be slow. While sprintf is slow, so is Perl, so that dispatching a bunch of extra <=> and || operations

Sorting is often one of those places in the program where we need to squeeze out as much performance as possible. For a list of 10,000 dates, we call sprintf exactly 10,000 times (once date_to_string is memoized) but we still call date_to_string itself 278,272 times. As the list of dates becomes longer, this disparity will increase, and the function calls will eventually come to dominate the running time of the sort.

We can get more speed by simplifying the cache handling and eliminating the 268,272 extra function calls. To do this, we go back to handwritten caching code:

CODE LIBRARY
chrono-orc

```
{ my %cache;
  sub chronologically {
    ($cache{$a} ||= date_to_string($a))
       cmp
    ($cache{$b} ||= date_to_string($b))
  }
}
```

Here we make use of the ||= operator, which seems almost custom-made for caching applications. $x ||= $y yields the value of $x if it is true; if not, it assigns $y to $x and yields the value of $y. $cache{$a} ||= date_to_string($a) checks to see if $cache{$a} has a true value; if so, that is the value used in the comparison with the cmp operator. If nothing is cached yet, then $cache{$a} is false, and chronologically calls date_to_string, stores the result in the cache, and uses the result in the comparison. This inline cache technique is called the *Orcish Maneuver*, because its essential features are the || and the cache.[10]

Memoizing date_to_string yields a two-and-a-half-fold speed-up; replacing the memoization with the Orcish Maneuver yields an *additional* twofold speed-up.

Astute readers will note that the Orcish Maneuver doesn't always work quite right. In this example, it's impossible for date_to_string to ever return a false value. But let's return for a moment to the example where we compute the total amount invested for each investor:

```
{ my %cache;
  sub by_total_invested {
    ($cache{$a} ||= total_invested($a))
```

---

takes a long time compared to sprintf. This is just another example of why the benchmark really is necessary.

10   Joseph Hall, author of *Effective Perl Programming*, is responsible for this name.

```
           <=>
         ($cache{$b} ||= total_invested($b))
     }
  }
```

Suppose Luke the Hermit has invested no money at all. The first time he appears in by_total_invested, we call total_invested for Luke, and we get back 0. We store this 0 in the cache under Luke's key. The next time Luke appears, we check the cache and find that the value stored there is 0. Because this value is false, we call total_invested again, even though we had a cache hit. The problem here is that the ||= operator doesn't distinguish between a cache miss and a cache hit where the cached value happens to be false.

The Lisp people have a name for this phenomenon: They call it the *semipredicate problem*. A *predicate* is a function that returns a boolean value. A *semipredicate* can return a specific false value, indicating failure, or one of many meaningful true values, indicating success. The $cache{$a} is a semipredicate because it might return 0, or any of an infinity of useful true values. We get into trouble when 0 is *also* one of the true values, because we can't distinguish it from the 0 that means false. This is the semipredicate problem.

In our present example, the semipredicate problem won't cause much trouble. The only cost is a few extra calls to total_invested for people who haven't invested any money. If we find that these extra calls are slowing down our sorting significantly (unlikely, but possible) we can replace the comparator function with the following version:

```
{ my %cache;
  sub by_total_invested {
   (exists $cache{$a} ? $cache{$a} : ($cache{$a} = total_invested($a)))
       <=>
   (exists $cache{$b} ? $cache{$b} : ($cache{$b} = total_invested($b)))
  }
}
```

This version uses the reliable exists operator to check to see if the cache is populated. Even if the value stored in the cache is false, exists will still return true. Beware, though, that this costs about 10% more than the simpler version.

There's an alternative that costs hardly anything extra, but does have the disadvantage of being rather bizarre. It's based on the following trick: When the Perl string "0e0" is used as a number, it behaves exactly like 0; the e0 is interpreted by Perl as a scientific notation exponent. But unlike an ordinary 0, the string "0e0" is true rather than false.[11]

If we write by_total_invested like this, we avoid the semipredicate problem with hardly any extra cost:

```
{ my %cache;
  sub by_total_invested {
    ($cache{$a} ||= total_invested($a) || "0e0")
        <=>
    ($cache{$b} ||= total_invested($b) || "0e0")
  }
}
```

If total_invested returns zero, the function caches "0e0" instead. The next time we look up the total invested by the same customer, the function sees "0e0" in the cache, and this value is true, so it doesn't call total_invested a second time. This "0e0" is the value given to the <=> operator for comparison, but in a numeric comparison it behaves exactly like 0, which is just what we want. The speed cost of the additional || operation, invoked only when a false value is returned by total_invested(), is tiny.

3.11 EVANGELISM

If you're trying to explain to a C programmer why Perl is good, automatic memoization makes a wonderful example. Almost all programmers are familiar with caching techniques. Even if they don't use any caching techniques in their own programs, they are certainly familiar with the concept, from caching in web browsers, in the cache memory of their computer, in the DNS server, in their web proxy server, or elsewhere. Caching, like most simple, useful ideas, is ubiquitous.

Adding caching isn't too much trouble, but it takes at least a few minutes to modify the code. With all modifications, there's a chance that you might make a mistake, which has to be factored into the average time. Once you're done, it

---

11   "0e0" is hardly unique; "00" will also work, as will any string that begins with a 0 followed by a non-numeral character, such as "0!!!!". Strings like "0!!!!", however, will generate an "Argument isn't numeric" warning if warnings are enabled. One string commonly used when a zero-but-true value is desired is "0 but true". Perl's warning system has a special case in it that suppresses the usual "isn't numeric" warning for this string.

may turn out that the caching was a bad idea, because the cache management overhead dominates the running time of the function, or because there aren't as many cache hits on a typical run as you expected there to be; then you have to take the caching code out, and again you run the risk of making a mistake. Not to overstate the problems, of course, but it will take at least a few minutes in each direction.

With memoization, adding the caching code no longer takes minutes; it takes seconds. You add one line of code:

```
memoize 'myfunction';
```

and it is impossible to make a serious mistake and break the function. If the memoization turns out to have been a bad idea, you can turn it off again in *one second*. Most programmers can appreciate the convenience of this. If you have five minutes to explain to a C programmer what benefits Perl offers over C, memoization is an excellent example to use.

3.12   THE BENEFITS OF SPEED

It may be tempting at this point to say that memoization is only an incremental improvement over manual caching techniques, because it does the same thing, and the only additional benefit is that you can turn it on and off more quickly. But that isn't really true. When a speed and convenience difference between tools is large enough, it changes the way you think about the tool and the ways you can use it. To automatically memoize a function takes 1/100 as much time as to write caching code for it manually. This is the same as the difference between the speed of an airplane and the speed of an oxcart. To say that the airplane is just a faster oxcart is to miss something essential: The quantitative difference is so large that it becomes a substantive qualitative difference as well.

For example, with automatic memoization, it becomes possible to add caching behavior to functions without having to consider the performance details carefully in advance. Memoization is so easy that it can pay to adopt a strategy of "shoot first and ask questions later." If a function is slow, try slapping some caching onto it and see if it helps matters. If a recursive function might have bad recursion behavior, put in some caching and see if the problem goes away. If not, you can take the caching away again and investigate more thoroughly. When the total cost is ten seconds of programming time, you can try this without having to think much in advance about whether it will be successful. With manual caching, you would have to spend at least a quarter hour, which is too much to invest on a mere fishing expedition.

With automatic memoization, you can enable caching behavior at run time. For example:

```
sub function {
  if (++$CALLS > 100) { memoize 'function'}
  # ...
}
```

Here we don't bother to memoize the function until partway through the program's run. When the function realizes it's being heavily used, it enables caching behavior. To do the same thing without automatic memoization requires a rewrite of the function rather than the addition of a single line.

3.12.1   Profiling and Performance Analysis

Automatic memoization allows caching to be used in profiling and performance analysis in a way that would be impractical otherwise. The typical situation involves a large application that runs too slowly. We would like to speed it up. We will do this by rewriting parts of the program to be faster, perhaps by introducing a better algorithm, and possibly at the expense of a certain amount of clarity or maintainability.

Trying to speed up every part of the program is a bad allocation of resources. This is because of what is known as the "90-10 rule," which says that 90% of the execution time of a program takes place in only 10% of the code, the rest being initialization code that is executed only once, or special-case code such as error handlers that are executed rarely or never. If we work over the entire program and speed up every part by 5%, we have a 5% gain. But if we can identify and rewrite just the crucial 10% to the same degree, we will get a net 4.5% gain in the program's total run time at only 10% of the cost; the cost-benefit ratio is nine times as large. So before we optimize, we would like very much to identify the parts of the program that contribute most to the run time, and concentrate on improving just those parts.

It's sad when a programmer spends a week carefully optimizing a subroutine to run 20% faster, only to discover that the program spent only 2% of its total execution time in that subroutine, and that the week of hard work has yielded only an 0.4% speed-up overall. Historically, programmers have been bad at guessing which parts of the program are heavily used; we need real measurements.

Traditionally, measurements are done using a tool called a *profiler*. The program is run in a special profiling environment that causes it to dump out a record of what it is doing every so often (typically many times per second).

Afterwards, the data is massaged into a report that lists the subroutines in which the program spends the most execution time. There are profiler tools for Perl, but they can be strange and hard to use. Automatic memoization is an alternative.

Run the program once and time how long it takes. Then guess which parts of the program are bottlenecks, and memoize them. Arrange for the memoized data to be stored in a persistent file. (Remember, this requires adding only one line of code to the program.) Run the program a second time; this will populate the cache on the disk. Run the program a third time. All calls to the memoized functions will return almost immediately, because the data is residing in a disk database; the functions do no work at all beyond what is required to get the answers from the database. On the third run, you are simulating how quickly the program would run if it were possible to eliminate the time taken by the target functions. If this run is substantially faster than the unmemoized run time, you have some candidates for optimization; if the times are similar, you know that you should look elsewhere.

You might wonder why not simply leave the memoization in place if the memoized run is substantially shorter, and the answer is that while memoization might cause the target functions to run faster, it might also cause them not to work correctly. Suppose you suspect that the bottleneck function is the one that formats the report. While memoizing this function and having it deliver a precached report may cause it to run faster, it is probably not what the recipient of the report would prefer.

3.12.2 Automatic Profiling

Another profiling technique, one that's even more flexible, uses the techniques we've seen in this chapter, but without any actual caching. The memoize function takes an existing function and puts a cache-managing front-end onto it. There's no reason why this front-end has to do cache management; it could do something else:

```perl
use Time::HiRes 'time';
my (%time, %calls);

sub profile {
  my ($func, $name) = @_;
  my $stub = sub {
    my $start = time;
    my $return = $func->(@_);
    my $end = time;
```

```
    my $elapsed = $end - $start;
    $calls{$name} += 1;
    $time{$name} += $elapsed;
    return $return;
  };
  return $stub;
}
```

The profile function shown here is similar in structure to the memoize function we saw earlier. Like memoize, it takes a function as its argument and constructs and returns a stub, which may be called directly or installed in the symbol table in place of the original.

When the stub is invoked, it records the current time in $start. Normally the Perl time function returns the current time to the nearest second; the Time::HiRes module replaces the time function with one that has finer granularity, if possible. The stub calls the real function and saves its return value. Then it computes the total elapsed time and updates two hashes. One hash records, for each function, how many calls have been made to that function; the stub simply increments that count. The other hash records the total elapsed time spent executing each function; the stub adds the elapsed time for the just-completed call to the total.

At the end of program execution, we can print out a report:

```
END {
  printf STDERR "%-12s %9s %6s\n", "Function", "# calls", "Elapsed";
  for my $name (sort {$time{$b} <=> $time{$a}} (keys %time)) {
    printf "%-12s %9d %6.2f\n", $name, $calls{$name}, $time{$name};
  }
}
```

The output will look something like this:

Function	# calls	Elapsed
printout	1	10.21
searchfor	1	0.34
page	1	0.06
check_file	18	0.01

This is output from the perldoc program that comes standard with Perl. From this output, we can see that most of the execution time is occurring in the printout function; if we want to make perldoc faster, this is the function we should concentrate on.

3.12.3 Hooks

This is clearly a very rudimentary profiling tool. A better version would use the `times()` function to measure CPU time consumed instead of wall-clock time. But the flexibility of the technique should be clear; we can put an arbitrary front-end onto a function, or change the front-end at run time. The front-end can perform caching, or keep track of function call data; it could validate the function arguments if we wanted, enforce pre- and post-conditions, or whatever else we like.

## CHAPTER 4

ITERATORS

4.1 INTRODUCTION

An *iterator* is an object interface to a list.

The object's member data consists of the list and some state information marking a "current position" in the list. The iterator supports one method, which we will call NEXTVAL. The NEXTVAL method returns the list element at the current position and updates the current position so that the next time next is called, the next list element will be returned.

Why would anyone want an object interface to a list? Why not just use a list? There are several reasons. The simplest is that the list might be enormous, so large that you do not want to have it in memory all at once. It is often possible to design iterators to generate list items as they're requested, so that only a small part of the list need ever be in memory at once.

4.1.1 Filehandles Are Iterators

Iterators are familiar to everyone who has ever programmed in Perl, because filehandles are iterators. When you open a file for reading, you get back a filehandle object:

```
open(FILEHANDLE, 'filename');
```

We'll look at filehandles first because they are a familiar example that exhibit all the advantages of iterators. A filehandle does represent a list, namely the list of lines from a file. The next operation is written in Perl as <FILEHANDLE>.

When you do <FILEHANDLE>, Perl returns the line at the current position and updates the current position so that the next time you do <FILEHANDLE> you get the next line.

Imagine an alternate universe in which the Perl open function yielded not a filehandle but instead, a list of lines:

```
@lines = open('filename');    # alternate universe interface
```

Almost any programmer asked to criticize this interface will complain that this would consume too much memory if the file is very large. One of the principal reasons for filehandles is that files can be so large and need to be represented in programs in some way other than as a possibly enormous list of lines.

Another problem with the imaginary iterator-less version is the following common pattern:

```
open(FILEHANDLE, 'filename');
while (<FILEHANDLE>) {
  last if /Plutonium/;
}
close FILEHANDLE;
# do something with $_;
```

This code opens a file and reads through it looking for a record that contains the word "Plutonium". When it finds the record, it exits the loop immediately, closes the file, and then does something with the record it just extracted. On average, it has to search only half of the file, because the plutonium will typically be somewhere near the middle; it might even get lucky and find it right at the beginning. In the worst case, the plutonium is at the end of the file, or is missing entirely, and the program has to read the whole file to discover that.

In the imaginary alternate universe with no filehandles, we get the worst case every time:

```
# alternate universe interface
@lines = open('filename');
for (@lines) {
  last if /Plutonium/;
}
# do something with $_;
```

Even if the plutonium is at the beginning of the file, the alternate universe open() still reads the entire file, a colossal waste of I/O and processor time.

Unix programmers, remembering that Perl's open function can also open a pipe to a command, will object even more strenuously:

```
@lines = open("yes |");        # alternate universe interface
```

Here Perl runs the Unix yes command and reads its output. But there's a terrible problem: the output of yes is infinite. The program will hang in an infinite loop at this line until all memory is exhausted, and then it will drop dead. The filehandle version works just fine.

4.1.2 Iterators Are Objects

The final advantage of an iterator over a plain array is that an iterator is an object, which means it can be shared among functions.

Consider a program that opens and reads a Windows INI file. Here's an example of an INI file:

```
[Display]
model=Samsui

[Capabilities]
supports_3D=y
power_save=n
```

The file is divided into sections, each of which is headed by a title like [Display] or [Capabilities]. Within each section are variable definitions such as model=Samsui. model is the name of a configuration variable and Samsui is its value.

A function to parse a single section of an INI file might look something like this:

```
sub parse_section {
  my $fh = shift;
  my $title = parse_section_title($fh);
  my %variables = parse_variables($fh);
  return [$title, \%variables];
}
```

The function gets a filehandle as its only argument. `parse_section()` passes the filehandle to the `parse_section_title()` function, which reads the first line and extracts and returns the title; then `parse_section()` passes the same filehandle to `parse_variables()`, which reads the rest of the section and returns a hash with the variable definitions. Unlike an array of lines, `$fh` keeps track of the current position in the INI file, so that `parse_section_title()` and `parse_variables()` don't read the same data. Instead, `parse_variables()` picks up wherever `parse_section_title` left off. The corresponding code with an array wouldn't work:

```
sub parse_section {
  my @lines = @_;
  my $title = parse_section_title(@lines);
  my %variables = parse_variables(@lines);
  return [$title, \%variables];
}
```

There would be no way for `parse_section_title()` to remove the section title line from `@lines`. (This is a rather contrived example, but illustrates the possible problem. Packaging up `@lines` as an object, even by doing something as simple as passing `\@lines` instead, solves the problem.)

4.1.3   Other Common Examples of Iterators

Like all good, simple ideas, iterators pop up all over. If you remember only one example, remember filehandles, because filehandles are ubiquitous. But Perl has several other examples of built-in iterators. We'll take a quick tour of the most important ones.

Dirhandles are analogous to filehandles. They are created with the `opendir` function, and encapsulate a list of directory entries that can be read with the `readdir` operator:

```
opendir D, "/tmp";
@entries = readdir D;
```

But `readdir` in scalar context functions as an iterator, reading one entry at a time from D:

```
opendir D, "/tmp";
while (my $entry = readdir D) {
```

```
            # Do something with $entry
        }
```

The built-in `glob` operator is similar, producing one file at a time whose name matches a certain pattern:

```
    while (my $file = glob("/tmp/*.[ch]")) {
        # Do something with $file
    }
```

Perl hashes always have an iterator built in to iterate over the keys or values in the hash. The `keys` and `values` functions produce lists of keys and values, respectively. If the hash is very large, these lists will be large, so Perl also provides a function to operate the iterator directly, namely `each`:

```
    while (my $key = each %hash) {
        # Do something with $key
    }
```

Normally the Perl regex engine just checks to see if a string matches a pattern, and reports true or false. However, it's sometimes of interest what part of the target string matched. In list context, the `m//g` operator produces a list of all matching substrings:

```
    @matches = ("12:34:56" =~ m/(\d+)/g);
```

Here `@matches` contains `("12", "34", "56")`. In scalar context, `m//g` becomes the NEXTVAL operation for an iterator inside the regex, producing a different match each time:

```
    while ("12:34:56" =~ m/(\d+)/g) {
        # do something with $1
    }
```

We will see this useful and little-known feature in more detail in Chapter 8.

Now we'll see how we can build our own iterators.

4.2   HOMEMADE ITERATORS

Our `dir_walk()` function from Chapter 1 took a directory name and a call-back function and searched the directory recursively, calling the callback for each file and directory under the original directory. Now let's see if we can structure dir_walk() as an iterator. If we did, then instead of searching the directory, dir_walk() would return an iterator object. This object would support a NEXTVAL operation, which would return a different file or directory name each time it was called.

First let's make sure that doing this is actually worthwhile. Suppose we had such an iterator. Could we still use it in callback style? Certainly. Suppose make_iterator were a function that constructed an iterator that would return the filenames from a directory tree. Then we would still be able emulate the original dir_walk() like this:

```
sub dir_walk {
  my ($dir, $filefunc, $dirfunc, $user) = @_;
  my $iterator = make_iterator($dir);
  while (my $filename = NEXTVAL($iterator)) {
    if (-f $filename) { $filefunc->($filename, $user) }
    else              {  $dirfunc->($filename, $user) }
  }
}
```

Here I've written NEXTVAL($iterator) to represent the NEXTVAL operation. Since we don't know yet how the iterator is implemented, we don't know what the real syntax of the NEXTVAL operation will be.

This example shows that the iterator version is at least as powerful as the original callback version. However, if we could build it, the iterator version would have several advantages over the callback version. We would be able to stop part way through processing the directory tree, and then pick up later where we left off, and we would have a file-tree-walk object that we could pass around from one function to another.

We'll use a really excellent trick to build our iterator: the iterator will be a function. The NEXTVAL operation on the iterator will simply be to call the function. When we call the iterator function it will do some computing, figure out what the next filename is, and return it. This means that the NEXTVAL($iterator) in our example code is actually doing $iterator->().

The iterator will need to retain some state information inside it, but we've already seen that Perl functions can do that. In Chapter 3, memoized functions were able to retain the cache hash between calls.

Before we get into the details of the dir_walk() iterator, let's try out the idea on a simpler example.

4.2.1   A Trivial Iterator: upto()

Here's a function called upto() that builds iterators, and which is mostly useful as an example. Given two numbers, *m* and *n*, it returns an iterator that will return all the numbers between *m* and *n*, inclusive:

CODE LIBRARY
upto

```perl
sub upto {
  my ($m, $n) = @_;
  return sub {
    return $m <= $n ? $m++ : undef;
  };
}
my $it = upto(3, 5);
```

This constructs an iterator object that will count from 3 up to 5 if we ask it to. The iterator object is just an anonymous subroutine that has captured the values of $m and $n.

The iterator is a subroutine, returned by the final return sub { ... } statement. Because the iterator is a subroutine, its NEXTVAL operation is simply invoking the subroutine. The subroutine runs and returns a value; this is the next value from the iterator. To get the next value ("kick the iterator") we simply do:

```perl
my $nextval = $it->();
```

This stores the number 3 into $nextval. If we do it again, it stores 4. If we do it a third time, it stores 5. Any calls after that will return undef.

To loop over the iterator's values:

```perl
while (defined(my $val = $it->())) {
  # now do something with $val, such as:
  print "$val\n";
}
```

This prints 3, 4, 5, and then quits the loop.

This may have a substantial memory savings over something like:

```perl
for my $val (1 .. 10000000) {
  # now do something with $val
}
```

which, until Perl 5.005, would generate a gigantic list of numbers before starting the iteration.

If you have a sweet tooth, you can put some syntactic sugar on your serial:

```
package Iterator_Utils;
use base Exporter;
@EXPORT_OK = qw(NEXTVAL Iterator
                append imap igrep
                iterate_function filehandle_iterator list_iterator);
%EXPORT_TAGS = ('all'=> \@EXPORT_OK);
sub NEXTVAL { $_[0]->() }
```

Then in place of the preceding examples, we can use this:

```
my $nextval = NEXTVAL($it);
```

and this:

```
while (defined(my $val = NEXTVAL($it))) {
  # now do something with $val
}
```

We'll do this from now on.

The internal operation of the iterator is simple. When the subroutine is called, it returns the value of $m and increments $m for next time. Eventually, $m exceeds $n, and the subroutine returns an undefined value thereafter. When an iterator runs out of data this way, we say it has been *exhausted*. We'll adopt the convention that a call to an exhausted iterator returns an undefined value, and then see some alternatives to this starting in Section 4.5.

SYNTACTIC SUGAR FOR MANUFACTURING ITERATORS

From now on, instead of writing return sub { ... } in a function, we will write return Iterator { ... } to make it clear that an iterator is being constructed:

```
sub upto {
  my ($m, $n) = @_;
```

```
      return Iterator {
        return $m <= $n ? $m++ : undef;
      };
   }
```

This bit of sugar is easy to accomplish:

```
    sub Iterator (&) { return $_[0] }
```

when we write this:

```
    Iterator { ... }
```

Perl behaves as though we had written:

```
    Iterator(sub { ... })
```

instead. Once past the sugar, the Iterator() function itself is trivial. Since the iterator *is* the anonymous function, it returns the argument unchanged.

Using this Iterator() sugar may make the code a little easier to understand. It will also give us an opportunity to hang additional semantics on iterator construction if we want to, by adding features to the Iterator() function. We will see an example of this in Section 4.5.7.

4.2.2 dir_walk()

Now that we've seen a function that builds simple iterators, we can investigate a more useful one, which builds iterators that walk a directory tree and generate filenames one at a time:

```
    # iterator version
    sub dir_walk {
      my @queue = shift;
      return Iterator {
        if (@queue) {
          my $file = shift @queue;
          if (-d $file) {
            opendir my $dh, $file or next;
            my @newfiles = grep {$_ ne "." && $_ ne ".."} readdir $dh;
            push @queue, map "$file/$_", @newfiles;
```

```
      }
      return $file;
    } else {
      return;
    }
  };
}
```

The pattern here is the same as in upto(). dir_walk() is a function that sets up some state variables for the iterator and then returns a closure that captures the state variables. When the closure is executed, it computes and returns the next filename, updating the state variables in the process.

The closure maintains a queue of the files and directories that it hasn't yet examined. Initially, the queue contains only the single top-level directory that the user asked it to search. Each time the iterator is invoked, it removes the item at the front of the queue. If this item is a plain file, the iterator returns it immediately; if the item is a directory, the iterator reads the directory and queues the directory's contents before returning the name of the directory.

After enough calls to the iterator, the queue will become empty. Once this happens, the iterator is exhausted, and further calls to the iterator will return undef. In this case, undef doesn't cause a semipredicate problem, because no valid filename is ever undef.

There is one subtle point to make here. The items in @queue must be full paths like ./src/perl/japh.pl, not basenames like japh.pl, or else the -d operator won't work. A common error when using -d is to get the basenames back from readdir and test them with -d immediately. This doesn't work, because -d, like all file operators, interprets a bare filename as a request to look for that name in the *current* directory. In order to use -d, we have to track the directory names also.

The map function accomplishes this. When we read the filenames out of the directory named $file with readdir, we get only the basenames. The map appends the directory name to each basename before the result is put on the queue. The result is full paths that work properly with -d.

Even if we didn't need the full paths for use with -d, the user of the iterator probably needs them. It's not usually useful to be told that the program has located a file named japh.pl unless you also find out which directory it's in.

4.2.3 On Clever Inspirations

Although this works well, it has one big defect: it appears to have required cleverness. The original dir_walk() from Chapter 1 was reasonably straightforward: process the current file, and if it happens to be a directory, make recursive calls to process its contents. The iterator version is not recursive; in place of recursion, it maintains a queue.

The problem that the queue is solving is that a recursive function maintains a lot of state on Perl's internal call stack. Here's the recursive function dir_walk() again:

```
sub dir_walk {
  my ($top, $code) = @_;
  my $DIR;
  $code->($top);

  if (-d $top) {
    my $file;
    unless (opendir $DIR, $top) {
      warn "Couldn't open directory $top: $!; skipping.\n";
      return;
    }
    while ($file = readdir $DIR) {
      next if $file eq '.'|| $file eq '..'
      dir_walk("$top/$file", $code);
    }
  }
}
```

Each recursive call down in the while loop must save the values of $top, $code, $DIR, and $file on the call stack; when dir_walk() is re-entered, new instances of these variables are created. The values must be saved so that they can be restored when the recursive call returns; at this time, the new instances are destroyed.

When the dir_walk() function finally returns to its original caller, all of the state information that was held in $top, $code, $DIR, and $file has been lost. In order for the iterator to simulate a recursive function, it needs to be able to return to its caller without losing all that state information.

Recursion is essentially an automatic stack-management feature. When our function makes a recursive call, Perl takes care of saving the function's state information on its private, internal stack, and restoring it again as necessary. But here the automatic management isn't what we want; we need manual control over what is saved and restored, so recursion doesn't work. Instead, we replace the call stack with the @queue variable and do all our stack management manually, with push and shift.

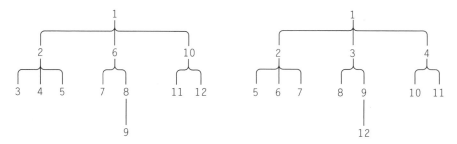

FIGURE 4.1   Depth-first traversal/breadth-first traversal.

The cost of the manual stack management is the trouble we have to go to. But they payoff, as do-it-yourselfers know, is flexibility. A recursive function for directory walking usually traverses the tree in depth-first order, visiting all the contents of each directory before moving on to the next directory. Sometimes we might prefer a breadth-first search, where all the files and directories at one level of the tree are visited before those lower down. Figure 4.1 illustrates both methods.

To get the recursive function to traverse the tree in breadth-first order or in any order other than depth-first is very difficult. But the iterator version accomplishes this easily. The previous iterator code traverses the directory in breadth-first order. If we replace `shift` with `pop`, `@queue` behaves as a stack, rather than a queue, and the iterator generates its output in depth-first order, exactly as the original recursive function did.

Replacing the recursion with the queue seems like a clever inspiration, but clever inspirations are usually in short supply. In Chapter 5, we'll see that any recursive function can be turned into an iterator in a formulaic way, so that we can save our clever inspirations for something else.

4.3   EXAMPLES

Let's see some possibly useful examples of iterators. We'll start with a replacement for `File::Find`, a variation on `dir_walk()`. It searches a directory hierarchy, looking for possibly interesting files:

```
sub interesting_files {
    my $is_interesting = shift;
```

```perl
    my @queue = @_;
  return Iterator {
    while (@queue) {
      my $file = shift @queue;
      if (-d $file) {
        opendir my $dh, $file or next;
        my @newfiles = grep {$_ ne "." && $_ ne ".."} readdir $dh;
        push @queue, map "$file/$_", @newfiles;
      }
      return $file if $is_interesting->($file);
    }
    return;
  };
}
```

Here we've made only a few changes. `interesting_files()` accepts a callback, `$is_interesting`, which will return true if its argument is the name of an "interesting" file. We'll also allow the user to specify more than one initial directory to search. This is trivial: We just take all the given directory names and load them into the initial queue.

The returned iterator is very similar. Instead of returning every file that it finds in the queue, the iterator returns only if the file is interesting, as determined by the callback. Otherwise, the iterator shifts another file off the queue and tries again. If the queue is exhausted before an interesting file is found, control leaves the `while` loop and the iterator returns `undef`. If the user calls the iterator again, the queue is still empty, so the iterator returns `undef` immediately.

To use this, we might write:

```perl
# Files are deemed to be interesting if they mention octopuses
sub contains_octopuses {
  my $file = shift;
  return unless -T $file && open my($fh), "<", $file;
  while (<$fh>) {
    return 1 if /octopus/i;
  }
  return;
}
my $octopus_file =
  interesting_files(\&contains_octopuses, 'uploads', 'downloads');
```

Now that we have the iterator, we can find all the interesting files:

```
while ($file = NEXTVAL($octopus_file)) {
  # do something with the file
}
```

Or perhaps we only want to know if there are any interesting files at all:

```
if (NEXTVAL($next_octopus)) {
  # yes, there is an interesting file
} else {
  # no, there isn't.
}
undef $next_octopus;
```

With a recursive function, we might have had trouble stopping the function when we found the interesting file; with the iterator, it's trivial, since it only searches as far as is necessary to find the first interesting file, and then leaves the rest of the hierarchy unsearched and waiting in the queue. When we undef $next_octopus, this saved state is discarded, and the memory used for storing it is freed.

4.3.1 Permutations

A *permutation* is a rearrangement of the items in a list. A frequently asked question in newsgroups is how to produce all the permutations of a certain list. For example, the permutations of the list ('red', 'yellow', 'blue') are:

```
(   ['red', 'yellow', 'blue'],
    ['red', 'blue', 'yellow'],
    ['yellow', 'red', 'blue'],
    ['yellow', 'blue', 'red'],
    ['blue', 'red', 'yellow'],
    ['blue', 'yellow', 'red'],
)
```

It's not completely clear to me why this is useful. Last time it came up in the newsgroup, I asked the poster, and he explained that he was trying to generate a name for a new product by assembling short phrases or syllables into different orders. Regardless of whether this is a good idea, it does seem to be something people want to do.

A beginner who tries to solve this problem may be completely puzzled. A programmer with more experience will immediately try to write a recursive function to generate the list, and will usually produce something that works. For example, here's the solution from the Perl Frequently Asked Questions List, written by Tom Christiansen and Nathan Torkington:

```
sub permute {
    my @items = @{ $_[0] };
    my @perms = @{ $_[1] };
    unless (@items) {
        print "@perms\n";
    } else {
        my(@newitems,@newperms,$i);
        foreach $i (0 .. $#items) {
            @newitems = @items;
            @newperms = @perms;
            unshift(@newperms, splice(@newitems, $i, 1));
            permute([@newitems], [@newperms]);
        }
    }
}
# sample call:
permute([qw(red yellow blue green)], []);
```

Items are removed from @items and placed onto the end of @perms. When all the items have been so placed, @items is empty and the resulting permutation, which is in @perms, is printed. (We should probably replace the print with a call to a callback.) The important part of this function is the else clause. In this clause, the function removes one of the unused items from the @items array, appends it to the end of the @perms array, and calls itself recursively to distribute the remaining items.

This solution works, but has a glaring problem. If you pass in a list of ten items, it doesn't return until it has printed all 3,628,800 permutations. This is likely to take a lot of time — twenty or thirty minutes on my computer. If we modify the function to generate a list of permutations, it's even worse. It returns a list of 3,628,800 items, each of which is an array of 10 items. This is likely to use up a substantial portion of your computer's real memory; if it does, your OS is likely to start thrashing while trying to compute the result, and it will take an even longer time to finish. The function is inefficient to begin with, because it performs six array copies per call, a total of 24,227,478 copies in our preceding example above. The function is simply too slow to be practical except in trivial cases. And since we probably can't use all of the 3.6 million permutations anyway, most of the work is wasted.

This is the sort of problem that iterators were made to solve. We want to generate a list of permutations, but the list might be enormous. Rather than generating the entire list at once, as the FAQ solution does, we will use an iterator that generates the permutations one at a time.

To make an iterator for permutations requires either an insight, or techniques from later in the chapter. The insight-requiring version is interesting and instructive, so we'll look at it briefly before we move into the more generally useful versions that require less insight.

Regardless of the internals of `permute()`, here's how we'll be using it:

```
my $it = permute('A'..'D');


while (my @p = NEXTVAL($it)) {
  print "@p\n";

}
```

The function `permute()` constructs the iterator itself:

```
sub permute {
  my @items = @_;
  my @pattern = (0) x @items;
  return Iterator {
    return unless @pattern;
    my @result = pattern_to_permutation(\@pattern, \@items);
    @pattern = increment_pattern(@pattern);
    return @result;
  };
}
```

Each permutation is represented by a "pattern" that says in what order to select elements from the original list. Suppose the original list is ('A', 'B', 'C', 'D'). A pattern of 2 0 1 0 selects (and removes) item 2 from the original list, the 'C', leaving ('A', 'B', 'D'); then item 0, 'A', from the remaining items; then item 1, the 'D', then item 0, the 'B'; the result is the permutation ('C', 'A', 'D', 'B'). This selection process is performed by pattern_to_permutation():

```
sub pattern_to_permutation {
  my $pattern = shift;
  my @items = @{shift()};
  my @r;
  for (@$pattern) {
    push @r, splice(@items, $_, 1);
  }
  @r;
}
```

The generation of the patterns is the interesting part. What patterns make sense? If there are four items in the original list, then the first element of the pattern must be a number between 0 and 3, the second element must be a number between 0 and 2, the third must be 0 or 1, and the last element must be 0. Each pattern corresponds to a different permutation; if we can generate all possible patterns, we can generate all possible permutations.

Generating all the patterns is performed by increment_pattern(). For this example, it generates the following patterns in the following order:

0 0 0 0	1 1 0 0	2 2 0 0
0 0 1 0	1 1 1 0	2 2 1 0
0 1 0 0	1 2 0 0	3 0 0 0
0 1 1 0	1 2 1 0	3 0 1 0
0 2 0 0	2 0 0 0	3 1 0 0
0 2 1 0	2 0 1 0	3 1 1 0
1 0 0 0	2 1 0 0	3 2 0 0
1 0 1 0	2 1 1 0	3 2 1 0

What is the pattern here? It turns out that getting from one pattern to the next is rather simple:

1. Scan the numbers in the pattern from right to left.

2. If you can legally increment the current number, do so, and halt.

3. Otherwise, change the current number to 0 and continue.

4. If you fall off the left end, then the sequence was the last one.

This algorithm should sound familiar, because you learned it a long time ago. It's exactly the same as the algorithm you use to *count*:

210397
210398

210399

210400

210401

. . . . . .

To increment a numeral, scan the digits right to left. If you find a digit that you can legally increment (that is, a digit that is less than 9) then increment it, and stop; you are finished. Otherwise, change the digit to 0 and continue leftwards. If you fall off the left end, it's because every digit was 9, so that was the last number. (You can now extend the number by inferring and incrementing an unwritten 0 just past the left end.)

To count in base 2, the algorithm is again the same. Only the definition of "legal digit" changes: instead of "less than 10" it is "less than 2". To generate the permutation patterns, the algorithm is the same, except that this time "legal" means "the digit in the nth column from the right may not exceed n."

The elements of the permutation pattern are like the wheels of an imaginary odometer. But where each wheel on a real odometer is the same size, and carries numbers from 0 to 9 (or 0 to 1 on planets where the odometer reads out in base 2), each wheel in the permutation odometer is a different size. The last one just has a 0 on it; the next has just a 0 and a 1, and so on. But like a real odometer, each wheel turns one notch when the wheel to its right has completed a whole revolution.

The code to manage a regular odometer looks like this:

```
sub increment_odometer {
  my @odometer = @_;
  my $wheel = $#odometer;      # start at rightmost wheel


  until ($odometer[$wheel] < 9 || $wheel < 0) {
    $odometer[$wheel] = 0;
    $wheel--; # next wheel to the left
  }
  if ($wheel < 0) {
    return;    # fell off the left end; no more sequences
  } else {
    $odometer[$wheel]++;  # this wheel now turns one notch
    return @odometer;
  }
}
```

The code to produce the permutation patterns is almost exactly the same:

```
sub increment_pattern {
  my @odometer = @_;
  my $wheel = $#odometer;    # start at rightmost wheel

  until ($odometer[$wheel] < $#odometer-$wheel || $wheel < 0) {
    $odometer[$wheel] = 0;
    $wheel--; # next wheel to the left
  }
  if ($wheel < 0) {
    return;    # fell off the left end; no more sequences
  } else {
    $odometer[$wheel]++; # this wheel now turns one notch
    return @odometer;
  }
}
```

We can simplify the code with a little mathematical trickery. Just as we can predict in advance what positions the wheels of an odometer will hold after we've travelled 19,683 miles, even if it reads out in base 2, we can predict what positions the wheels of our pattern-odometer will hold the 19,683rd time we call it:

```
sub n_to_pat {
  my @odometer;
  my ($n, $length) = @_;
  for my $i (1 .. $length) {
    unshift @odometer, $n % $i;
    $n = int($n/$i);
  }
  return $n ? () : @odometer;
}
```

CODE LIBRARY
permute-n

permute() must change a little to match, since the state information is now a simple counter instead of an entire pattern:

```
sub permute {
  my @items = @_;
  my $n = 0;
  return Iterator {
```

```
        my @pattern = n_to_pat($n, scalar(@items));
        my @result = pattern_to_permutation(\@pattern, \@items);
        $n++;
        return @result;
    };
}
```

This last function is an example of a useful class of iterators that return $f(0), f(1), f(2), \ldots$ for some function f:

```
sub iterate_function {
    my $n = 0;
    my $f = shift;
    return Iterator {
        return $f->($n++);
    };
}
```

This is an iterator that generates values of a function for $n = 0, 1, 2 \ldots$. You might want many values of the function, or few; an iterator may be a more flexible way to get them than a simple loop, because it is a data structure.

The permutation iterators shown here do a lot of splicing. `pattern_to_permutation()` copies the original list of items and then dismantles it; every time an element is removed the other elements must be shifted down in memory to fill up the gap. With enough ingenuity, it's possible to avoid this, abandoning the idea of the patterns. Instead of starting over with a fresh list every time, in the original order, and then using the pattern to select items from it to make the new permutation, we can take the previous permutation and just apply whatever transformation is appropriate to turn it into the new one:

```
sub permute {
    my @items = @_;
    my $n = 0;
    return Iterator {
        $n++, return @items if $n==0;
        my $i;
        my $p = $n;
        for ($i=1; $i<=@items && $p%$i==0; $i++) {
            $p /= $i;
        }
        my $d = $p % $i;
```

```
    my $j = @items - $i;
    return if $j < 0;

    @items[$j+1..$#items] = reverse @items[$j+1..$#items];
    @items[$j,$j+$d] = @items[$j+$d,$j];

    $n++;
    return @items;
  };
}
```

The key piece of code here is the pair of slice assignments of @items. The insight behind this code is that at any given stage, we can ignore the first few items and concentrate only on the last few. Let's say we're rearranging just the last three items. We start with something like ... A B C D and produce the various rearrangements of the last three items, ending with ... A D C B.

At this point, the last three items are in backwards order. We need to put them back in forward order (this is the assignment with the reverse) and then switch the A, the next item over, with one of the three we just finished permuting. (This is the second assignment.) We need to do this three times, first switching A with B, then with C, and finally with D; after each switch, we run again through all possible permutations of the last three items. Of course, there are complications, since permuting the last three items involves applying the same process to the last *two* items, and is itself part of the process of permuting the last four items.

4.3.2 Genomic Sequence Generator

In 1999, I got email from a biologist at the University of Virginia. He was working on the Human Genome Project, dealing with DNA. DNA is organized as a sequence of base pairs, each of which is typically represented by the letter A, C, G, or T. The information carried in the chromosome of any organism can be recorded as a string of these four letters. A bacteriophage will have a few thousand of these symbols, and a human chromosome will have between 30 and 300 million. Much of the Human Genome Project involved data munging on these strings; Perl was invaluable for this munging. (For more details about this, see Lincoln Stein's widely-reprinted article "How Perl Saved the Human Genome Project."[1]

The biologist who wrote to me wanted a function that, given an input pattern like "A(CGT)CGT", would produce the output list ('ACCGT', 'AGCGT',

---

[1] The Perl Journal, Vol 1, #2 (Summer 1996) pp. 5–9.

'ATCGT'). The (CGT) in the input is a wildcard that indicates that the second position may be filled by any one of the symbols C, G, or T. Similarly, an input of "A(CT)G(AC)" should yield the list ('ACGA', 'ATGA', 'ACGC', 'ATGC'). He had written a recursive function to generate the appropriate output list, but was concerned that he would run into memory limitations if he used it on long, ambiguous inputs, where the result would be a list of many thousands of strings.

An iterator is exactly the right solution here:

```perl
sub make_genes {
  my $pat = shift;
  my @tokens = split /[()]/, $pat;
  for (my $i = 1; $i < @tokens; $i += 2) {
    $tokens[$i] = [0, split(//, $tokens[$i])];
  }
  my $FINISHED = 0;
  return Iterator {
    return if $FINISHED;
    my $finished_incrementing = 0;
    my $result = "";
    for my $token (@tokens) {
      if (ref $token eq "") {       # plain string
        $result .= $token;
      } else {                      # wildcard
        my ($n, @c) = @$token;
        $result .= $c[$n];
        unless ($finished_incrementing) {
          if ($n == $#c) { $token->[0] = 0 }
          else { $token->[0]++; $finished_incrementing = 1 }
        }
      }
    }
    $FINISHED = 1 unless $finished_incrementing;
    return $result;
  }
}
```

Here the input pattern "AA(CGT)CG(AT)" is represented by the following data structure, which is stored in @tokens:

```
[ "AA",
  [ 0, "C", "G", "T"],
```

```
        "CG",
        [ 0, "A", "T"],
    ]
```

The code to construct the data structure uses some tricks:

```
    my @tokens = split /[()]/, $pat;
    for (my $i = 1; $i < @tokens; $i += 2) {
        $tokens[$i] = [0,split(//, $tokens[$i])];
    }
```

The peculiar-looking split pattern says that $pat should be split wherever there is an open- or a close- parenthesis character. The return value has the convenient property that the wildcard sections are always in the odd-numbered positions in the resulting list. For example, "AA(CGT)CG(AT)" is split into ("AA", "CGT", "CG", "AT"). Even if the string begins with a delimiter, split will insert an empty string into the initial position of the result: "(A)C" is split into ("", "A", "C").

The following code processes only the wildcard parts of the resulting @tokens list:

```
    for (my $i = 1; $i < @tokens; $i += 2) {
        $tokens[$i] = [0,split(//, $tokens[$i])];
    }
```

The odd-numbered elements of ("AA", "CGT", "CG", "AT") are transformed by this into ("AA", [0, "C", "G", "T"], "CG", [0, "A", "T"]). The iterator then captures this list, which is stored in @tokens. Elements of this list that are plain strings correspond to the non-wildcard parts of the input pattern, and are inserted into the output verbatim. Elements that are arrays correspond to the wildcard parts of the input pattern and indicate choice points.

The internal structure of the iterator is similar to the structure of the permutation generator. When it's run, it scans the token string, one token at a time. During the scan, it does two things: It accumulates an output string, and it adjusts the numeric parts of the wildcard tokens. Tokens are handled differently depending on whether they are plain strings (ref $token eq "") or wildcards. Plain strings are just copied directly to the result.

Wildcard handling is a little more interesting. The wildcard token is first decomposed into its component parts:

```
        my ($n, @c) = @$token;
```

$n says which element of @c should be chosen next:

```
$result .= $c[$n];
```

Then the iterator may need to adjust $n to have a different value so that a different element of @c will be chosen next time. In the permutation-pattern generator, we scanned from right to left, resetting wheels to zero until we found one small enough to be incremented. Here we're scanning from left to right, but the principle is the same. $finished_incrementing is a flag that tells the iterator whether it has been able to increment one of the digits, after which it doesn't need to adjust any of the others:

```
unless ($finished_incrementing) {
  if ($n == $#c) { $token->[0] = 0 }
  else { $token->[0]++; $finished_incrementing = 1 }
}
```

The function can increment the value in a wildcard token if it would still index a valid element of @c afterwards. Otherwise, the value is reset to zero and the iterator keeps looking. This is analogous to the way we used increment_pattern() earlier to cycle through all possible permutation patterns; here we use the same sort of odometer technique to cycle through all possible selections of the wildcards.

When we have cycled through all the possible choices, the numbers in the wildcard tokens all have their maximum possible values; we can recognize this condition because we will have scanned all of them without finding one we could increment, and so $finished_incrementing will still be false after the scan. The iterator sets the $FINISHED flag so that it doesn't start over again from the beginning; thereafter, the iterator returns immediately, without generating a string:

```
$FINISHED = 1 unless $finished_incrementing;
```

There's nothing in this iterator that treats A, C, T, and G specially, so we can use it as a generic string generator:

```
my $it = make_genes('(abc)(de)-(12)');
print "$s\n" while $s = NEXTVAL($it);
```

The output looks like this:

```
ad-1
bd-1
```

```
cd-1
ae-1
be-1
ce-1
ad-2
bd-2
cd-2
ae-2
be-2
ce-2
```

Biologists don't usually use (ACT) to indicate a choice of A, C, or T; they typically use the single letter H. I don't know if the biologist who asked me this question was trying to avoid confusing me with unnecessary detail, or if he really did want to handle patterns like (ACT). But supposing that we want to handle the standard abbreviations, a simple preprocessor will take care of it:

```
%n_expand = qw(N ACGT
               B CGT D AGT H ACT V ACG
               K GT M AC R AG S CG W AT Y CT);
sub make_dna_sequences {
  my $pat = shift;
  for my $abbrev (keys %n_expand) {
    $pat =~ s/$abbrev/($n_expand{$abbrev})/g;
  }
  return make_genes($pat);
}
```

4.3.3 Filehandle Iterators

Now we'll see how to turn an ordinary Perl filehandle into a synthetic closure-based iterator. Why would we want to this? Because in the rest of the chapter we'll develop many tools for composing and manipulating iterators, and these tools apply just as well to Perl filehandles as long as we use the following little wrapper:

```
sub filehandle_iterator {
  my $fh = shift;
  return Iterator { <$fh> };
}
```

We can now use:

```
my $it = filehandle_iterator(*STDIN);
while (defined(my $line = NEXTVAL($it))) {
  # do something with $line
}
```

4.3.4   A Flat-File Database

Now let's do a real application. We'll develop a small flat-file database. A *flat-file database* is one that stores the data in a plain text file, with one record per line.

Our database will have a format something like this:

CODE LIBRARY
db.txt

```
LASTNAME:FIRSTNAME:CITY:STATE:OWES
Adler:David:New York:NY:157.00
Ashton:Elaine:Boston:MA:0.00
Dominus:Mark:Philadelphia:PA:0.00
Orwant:Jon:Cambridge:MA:26.30
Schwern:Michael:New York:NY:149658.23
Wall:Larry:Mountain View:CA:-372.14
```

The first line is a header, sometimes called a *schema*, that defines the names of the fields; the later lines are data records. Each record has the same number of data fields, separated by colons. This sample of the data shows only six records, but the file might contain thousands of records. For large files, the iterator approach is especially important. A flat-file database must be searched entirely for every query, and this is slow. By using an iterator approach, we will allow programs to produce useful results before the entire file has been scanned.

We'll develop the database as an object-oriented class, FlatDB. The FlatDB class will support a new method that takes a data filename and returns a database handle object:

CODE LIBRARY
FlatDB.pm

```
package FlatDB;
my $FIELDSEP = qr/:/;

sub new {
  my $class = shift;
  my $file = shift;
  open my $fh, "<", $file or return;
  chomp(my $schema = <$fh>);
```

```
    my @field = split $FIELDSEP, $schema;
    my %fieldnum = map { uc $field[$_] => $_ } (0..$#field);
    bless { FH => $fh, FIELDS => \@field, FIELDNUM => \%fieldnum,
            FIELDSEP => $FIELDSEP } => $class;
}
```

The database handle object contains a number of items that might be useful, in addition to the open data filehandle itself. For our sample database, the contents of the database handle object look like this:

```
{
  FH => (the handle),
  FIELDS => ['LASTNAME', 'FIRSTNAME', 'CITY', 'STATE', 'OWES'],
  FIELDNUM => { CITY => 2,
                FIRSTNAME => 1,
                LASTNAME => 0,
                OWES => 4,
                STATE => 3,
              },
  FIELDSEP => qr/:/,
}
```

The database handle object will support a query method that takes a field name and a value and returns all the records that have the specified value in the field. But we don't want query to simply read all the records in the data file and return a list of matching records, because that might be very expensive. Instead, query will return an iterator that will return matching records one at a time:

```
# usage: $dbh->query(fieldname, value)
# returns all records for which (fieldname) matches (value)
use Fcntl ':seek';
sub query {
  my $self = shift;
  my ($field, $value) = @_;
  my $fieldnum = $self->{FIELDNUM}{uc $field};
  return unless defined $fieldnum;
  my $fh = $self->{FH};
  seek $fh, 0, SEEK_SET;
  <$fh>;                    # discard schema line

  return Iterator {
    local $_;
    while (<$fh>) {
```

```
        my @fields = split $self->{FIELDSEP};
        my $fieldval = $fields[$fieldnum];
        return $_ if $fieldval eq $value;
      }
      return;
    };
  }
```

query first looks in the FIELDNUM hash to ascertain two things. First, is the requested field name actually a field in the database, and second, if so, what number column is it? The result is stored in $fieldnum; if the field name is invalid, query returns undef to indicate an error. Otherwise, the function seeks the filehandle back to the beginning of the data to begin the search, using the seek function.

seek() has a rather strange interface, inherited from the original design of Unix in the 1970s: seek($fh, $position, $whence) positions the filehandle so that the next read or write will occur at byte position $position. The $whence argument is actually the integer 0, 1, or 2, but mnemonic names for these values are provided by the standard Perl Fcntl module. If $whence is the constant SEEK_SET, $position is interpreted as a number of bytes forward from the beginning of the file. Here we use seek($fh, 0, SEEK_SET), which positions the handle at the beginning of the file, so that the following <$fh> reads and discards the schema line.

The query function then returns the iterator, which captures the values of $self, $fh, $fieldnum, and $value.

The iterator is quite simple. When it's invoked, it starts reading data lines from the database. It splits up each record into fields, and compares the appropriate field value (in $fields[$fieldnum]) with the desired value (in $value). If there's a match, it returns the current record immediately; if not, it tries the next record. When it reaches the end of the file, the while loop exits and the function returns an undefined result to indicate failure.

The iterator is planning to change the value of $_ in the while loop. Since $_ is a global variable, this means that the function calling the iterator might get a nasty surprise:

```
$_ = 'I love you';
NEXTVAL($q);
print $_;
```

We don't want the invocation of $q to change the value of $_. To prevent this, the iterator uses local $_. This saves the old value of $_ on entry to the iterator, and arranges for the old value to be automatically restored when the iterator returns. With this `local` line, it is safe for the iterator to use `$_` any way it wants to. You should probably take this precaution in any function that uses `$_`.

A simple demonstration:

```
use FlatDB;
my $dbh = FlatDB->new('db.txt') or die $!;

my $q = $dbh->query('STATE', 'NY');
while (my $rec = NEXTVAL($q)) {
  print $rec;
}
```

The output is:

```
Adler:David:New York:NY:157.00
Schwern:Michael:New York:NY:149658.23
```

Many obvious variations are possible. We might support different kinds of queries, which return a list of the fields, or a list of just some of the fields. Or instead of passing a field–value pair, we might pass a callback function that will be called with each record and returns true if the record is interesting:

```
use FlatDB;
my $dbh = FlatDB->new('db.txt') or die $!;

my $q = $dbh->callbackquery(sub { my %F=@_; $F{STATE} eq 'NY'});
while (my $rec = NEXTVAL($q)) {
  print $rec;
}

# Output as before
```

With `callbackquery` we can ask for a list of the people who owe more than $10, which was impossible with `->query`:

```
my $q = $dbh->callbackquery(sub { my %F=@_; $F{OWES} > 10 });
```

Similarly, we can now use Perl's full regex capabilities in queries:

```
my $q = $dbh->callbackquery(sub { my %F=@_; $F{FIRSTNAME} =- /^M/ });
```

This callback approach is much more flexible than hardwiring every possible comparison type into the iterator code, and it's easy to support:

```
use Fcntl ':seek';
sub callbackquery {
  my $self = shift;
  my $is_interesting = shift;
  my $fh = $self->{FH};
  seek $fh, 0, SEEK_SET;
  <$fh>;                      # discard header line

  return Iterator {
    local $_;
    while (<$fh>) {
      my %F;
      my @fieldnames = @{$self->{FIELDS}};
      my @fields = split $self->{FIELDSEP};
      for (0 .. $#fieldnames) {
        $F{$fieldnames[$_]} = $fields[$_];
      }
      return $_ if $is_interesting->(%F);
    }
    return;
  }
}
```

The only major change here is in the iterator itself, mostly to set up the %F hash that is passed to the callback. I originally had a hash slice assignment instead of the for loop:

```
@F{@{$self->{fields}}} = split $self->{FIELDSEP};
```

The punctuation made my eyes glaze over, so I used the loop instead.

IMPROVED DATABASE

The database code we've just seen has one terrible drawback: All of the iterators share a single filehandle, and this means that only one iterator can be active at any time. Consider this example:

```
use FlatDB;
my $dbh = FlatDB->new('db.txt') or die $!;
```

```
my $q1 = $dbh->query('STATE', 'MA');
my $q2 = $dbh->query('STATE', 'NY');
for (1..2) {
  print NEXTVAL($q1), NEXTVAL($q2);
}
```

We'd like this to print both NY records and both MA records, but it doesn't; it produces only one of each:

```
Ashton:Elaine:Boston:MA:0.00
Schwern:Michael:New York:NY:149658.23
```

What goes wrong? We would like $q1 to generate records 2 and 4, and $q2 to generate records 1 and 5. The sequence of events is shown in Figure 4.2. $q1 executes the first time, and searches through the database looking for an MA record. In doing so, it skips over record 1 (David Adler) and then locates record 2 (Elaine Ashton), which it returns. The filehandle is now positioned at the beginning of the third record. When we invoke $q2, this is where the search continues. $q2 won't find record 1, because the handle is already positioned past record 1. Instead, the iterator skips the next two records, until it finds record 5 (Michael Schwern), which it returns. The filehandle is now positioned just before record 6 (Larry Wall). When $q1 executes the second time, it skips record 6, reaches the end of the file, and returns undef. All further calls to both iterators produce nothing but undef because the filehandle is stuck at the end of the file. Although some commercial databases (such as Sybase) have this same deficiency, we can do better, and we will.

The obvious solution is to have a separate filehandle for each iterator. But open filehandles are a limited resource, and a program might have many active iterators at any time, so we'll adopt a different solution. Each iterator will remember the position in the file at which its last search left off, and when it is invoked, it will reset the handle to that position and continue. This allows several iterators to share the same filehandle without getting confused.

We need to make only a few changes to query to support this:

```
# usage: $dbh->query(fieldname, value)
# returns all records for which (fieldname) matches (value)
use Fcntl ':seek';
sub query {
  my $self = shift;
  my ($field, $value) = @_;
  my $fieldnum = $self->{FIELDNUM}{uc $field};
```

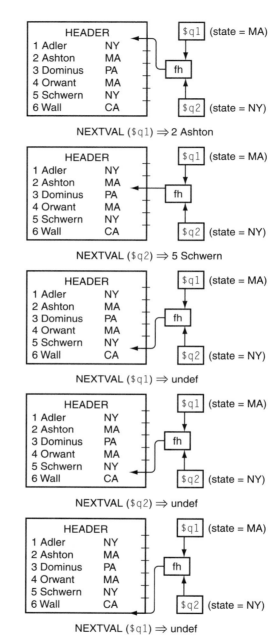

FIGURE 4.2   Interference between two query handles.

```perl
    return unless defined $fieldnum;
  my $fh = $self->{FH};
  seek $fh, 0, SEEK_SET;
  <$fh>;                      # discard header line
  my $position = tell $fh;

  return Iterator {
    local $_;
    seek $fh, $position, SEEK_SET;
    while (<$fh>) {
      $position = tell $fh;
      my @fields = split $self->{FIELDSEP};
      my $fieldval = $fields[$fieldnum];
      return $_ if $fieldval eq $value;
    }
    return;
  };
}


# callbackquery with bug fix
use Fcntl ':seek';
sub callbackquery {
  my $self = shift;
  my $is_interesting = shift;
  my $fh = $self->{FH};
  seek $fh, 0, SEEK_SET;
  <$fh>;                      # discard header line
  my $position = tell $fh;

  return Iterator {
    local $_;
    seek $fh, $position, SEEK_SET;
    while (<$fh>) {
      $position = tell $fh;
      my %F;
      my @fieldnames = @{$self->{FIELDS}};
      my @fields = split $self->{FIELDSEP};
      for (0 .. $#fieldnames) {
        $F{$fieldnames[$_]} = $fields[$_];
      }
      return [$position, $_] if $is_interesting->(%F);
```

```
        }
      return;
    };
  }


  1;
```

The iterators here capture one additional value, $position, which records the current position of the filehandle in the file; initially this position is at the start of the first data record. This position is supplied by the Perl tell operator, which returns the filehandle's current position; if this position is later used with seek $fh, $position, SEEK_SET, the filehandle will be set back to that position. This is precisely what the iterators do whenever they are invoked. Regardless of what other functions have used the filehandle in the meantime, or where they have left it, the first thing the iterators do is to seek the filehandle back to the current position using the seek operator. Each time an iterator reads a record, it updates its notion of the current position, again using tell, so its seek in a future invocation will skip the record that was just read.

With this change, our two-iterators-at-once example works perfectly:

```
Ashton:Elaine:Boston:MA:0.00
Adler:David:New York:NY:157.00
Orwant:Jon:Cambridge:MA:26.30
Schwern:Michael:New York:NY:149658.23
```

4.3.5   Searching Databases Backwards

Perhaps the most common occurrence of a flat-file database is a process log file. Anyone who runs a web server knows that the server can churn out megabytes of log information every day. These logs are essentially flat databases. Each line represents a request for a web page, and includes fields that describe the source of the request, the page requested, the date and time of the request, and the outcome of the request. A sample follows:

```
208.190.220.160 - - [04/Aug/2001:08:14:29 -0400] "GET /- mjd/pictures/new.gif HTTP/1.1"
  200 95 "http://perl.plover.com/" "Mozilla/5.0 (Macintosh; U; PPC; en-US; rv:0.9.2)
  Gecko/20010629"
195.3.19.207 - - [04/Aug/2001:13:39:11 -0400] "GET /pics/small-sigils.gif HTTP/1.1" 200 1586
  "http://perl.plover.com/" "Mozilla/4.0 (compatible; MSIE 5.01; Windows NT 5.0; DigExt)"
```

```
192.94.94.33 - - [07/Aug/2001:12:06:34 -0400] "GET /yak/Identity/slide005.html HTTP/1.0"
  200 821 "http://perl.plover.com/yak/Identity/slide004.html" "Mozilla/4.6 [en]
  (X11; I; SunOS 5.8 sun4u)"
199.93.193.10 - - [13/Aug/2001:13:04:39 -0400] "GET /yak/dirty/miller_glenn_r.jpg HTTP/1.0"
  200 4376 "http://perl.plover.com/yak/dirty/slide009.html" "Mozilla/4.77 [en] (X11; U;
  SunOS 5.6 sun4u)"
216.175.77.248 - - [15/Aug/2001:14:25:20 -0400] "GET /yak/handson/examples/wordsort.pl
  HTTP/1.0" 200 125 "http://perl.plover.com:80/yak/handson/examples/" "Wget/1.5.3"
194.39.218.254 - - [16/Aug/2001:07:44:02 -0400] "GET /pics/medium-sigils.gif HTTP/1.0" 304 -
  "http://perl.plover.com/local.html" "Mozilla/4.0 (compatible; MSIE 5.01; Windows NT 5.0)"
210.239.93.70 - msdw [22/Aug/2001:01:29:28 -0400] "GET /class/msdw-tokyo/ HTTP/1.0" 401 469
  "http://perl.plover.com/class/" "Mozilla/4.0 (compatible; MSIE 5.5; Windows NT 4.0)"
151.204.38.119 - - [25/Aug/2001:13:48:01 -0400] "GET /yak/path/hanoi06.gif HTTP/1.0" 200 239
  "http://perl.plover.com/yak/path/" "Mozilla/4.77 [en] (WinNT; U)"
```

One of the common tasks of system administrators is to search through the log files looking for certain matching records; for example, the last time a certain user visited, or the last time a certain page was fetched. In fact, Perl itself first rose to prominence as a tool for helping system administrators answer exactly these sorts of questions. A typical query will look something like this:

```
perl -ane 'print $F[10] if $F[6] =~ m{/book/$}' access-log
```

The -n option implies a loop; Perl will automatically read the input file access-log line by line and execute the indicated program once for each line. The -a option implies that each line will be automatically split into the special @F array. The -e option introduces the program, which uses the @F array that was set up by -a. In these log files, field #6 is the path of the page that is being requested, and field #10 is the URL of the "referring page," which is the one that contained a link to the page that is being requested. This query will yield the URLs of pages that may contain links to the page that talks about the book you are now reading.

If what you want is all such records, this works very well. But more often, you are more interested in recent activity than in old activity. The preceding perl command example produces the records in chronological order, with the oldest ones first, because that's the order in which they appear in the file. That means that to get to the part of interest, you have to wait until the entire file has been read, analyzed, and printed. If the file is large, this will take a long time.

One solution to this problem is to store the records in reverse order, with the most recent ones first. Unfortunately, under most operating systems, this is impossible. Unix, for example, supports appending records only to the end of a file, not to the beginning.

Instead, we'll build an iterator that can read a file backwards, starting with the most recent records. If we plug this iterator into our existing query system, we'll get a flat-file database query system that produces the most recent records first, with no additional effort.

A QUERY PACKAGE THAT TRANSFORMS ITERATORS

There is one minor technical problem that we have to solve before we can proceed. As written, the FlatDB constructor wants a filename, not another iterator. A few changes are necessary to build a version that accepts an arbitrary iterator:

```
package FlatDB::Iterator;
my $FIELDSEP = qr/\s+/;

sub new {
  my $class = shift;
  my $it = shift;
  my @field = @_;
  my %fieldnum = map { uc $field[$_] => $_ } (0..$#field);
  bless { FH => $it, FIELDS => \@field, FIELDNUM => \%fieldnum,
          FIELDSEP => $FIELDSEP } => $class;
}
```

For the original FlatDB package, we assumed that the data file itself would begin with a schema line. HTTP log files don't have a schema line, so here we've assumed that the field names will be passed to the constructor as arguments. The calling sequence for FlatDB::Iterator::new is:

```
FlatDB::Iterator->new(
  $iterator,
  qw(address rfc931 username datetime tz method page protocol
     status bytes referrer agent)
);
```

The qw(...) list specifies the names of the fields in the data that will be produced by $iterator.

query requires only trivial changes. The code to skip the descriptor records goes away, and the code to fetch the next record changes from:

```
while (<$fh>) {
```

to:

```
while (defined ($_ = NEXTVAL($it))) {
```

A more subtle change is that we must get rid of the seek $fh, 0, SEEK_SET line, because there's no analogous operation for iterators. (We'll see in Chapter 6 how to build iterators that overcome this drawback.) This means that each database object can be used only for one query. After that, we must throw it away, because there's no way to rewind and reread the data:

```
# usage: $dbh->query(fieldname, value)
# returns all records for which (fieldname) matches (value)
sub query {
  my $self = shift;
  my ($field, $value) = @_;
  my $fieldnum = $self->{FIELDNUM}{uc $field};
  return unless defined $fieldnum;
  my $it = $self->{FH};
  # seek $fh, 0, SEEK_SET;
  # <$fh>;                    # discard header line

  return Iterator {
    local $_;
    while (defined ($_ = NEXTVAL($it))) {
      my @fields = split $self->{FIELDSEP};
      my $fieldval = $fields[$fieldnum];
      return $_ if $fieldval eq $value;
    }
    return;
  };
}
```

It's similarly easy to write the amended version of callbackquery. If $it were an iterator that produced the lines from a log file in reverse order, we could use:

```
my $qit =
  FlatDB::Iterator->new($it, @FIELDNAMES)->query($field, $value);
```

And `$qit` would be an iterator that would generate the specified records from the file, one at a time, starting with the most recent.

AN ITERATOR THAT READS FILES BACKWARDS

Building an iterator that reads a file backwards is more an exercise in systems programming than anything else. We'll take the easy way out and use the Unix tac program as our base. The tac program reads a file and emits its lines in reverse order:

```
sub readbackwards {
  my $file = shift;
  open my($fh), "|-", "tac", $file
    or return;
  return Iterator { return scalar(<$fh>) };
}
```

If tac isn't available, we can use the `File::ReadBackwards` module from CPAN instead:

```
use File::ReadBackwards;
sub readbackwards {
  my $file = shift;
  my $rbw = File::ReadBackwards->new($file)
    or return;
  return Iterator { return $rbw->readline };
}
```

PUTTING IT TOGETHER

We can now search a log file backwards:

```
my @fields = qw(address rfc931 username datetime tz method
                page protocol status bytes referrer agent);

my $logfile = readbackwards("/usr/local/apache/logs/access-log")
my $db = FlatDB::Iterator->new($logfile, @fields);
my $q = $db->callbackquery(sub {my %F=@_; $F{PAGE}=~ m{/book/$}});
do {
  for (1..10) {
```

```
        print NEXTVAL($q);
    }
    print "q to quit; CR to continue\n";
    chomp(my $resp = <STDIN>);
    last if $resp =~ /q/i;
}
```

This program starts up fast and immediately produces the most recent few records, without reading through the entire file first. It uses little memory, even when there are many matching records.

We had to do some extra work to read a file backwards in the first place, but once we had done that, we could plug the iterator directly into our existing query system.

4.3.6   Random Number Generation

Perl comes with a built-in random number generator. The random numbers are not truly random; they're what's called *pseudo-random*, which means they're generated by a mechanical process that yields repeatable results. Perl typically uses the `rand`, `random`, or `drand48` function provided by the local C library. A typical random number generator function looks something like this:

```
my $seed = 1;

sub Rand {
  $seed = (27*$seed+11111) & 0x7fff;
  return $seed;
}
```

This example has poor randomness properties. For example, its output alternates between odd and even numbers. Don't use it in any software that needs truly random numbers.

The `Rand()` function takes no arguments and returns a new "random" number. The random number generator has an internal value, called the *seed*. Each time it is invoked, it performs a transformation on the seed, saves the new seed, and returns the new seed. Since the output for `Rand` depends only on the seed, we can think of it as generating a single sequence of numbers:

11138
16925

9334
985
4938
13365
11518
27185
24210
9421

...

We can see that the sequence produced by Rand must eventually repeat. Because the output is always an integer less than 32,768, if we call Rand 32,769 times, two of the calls must have returned the same value, let's say v. This means that the seed was v both times. But since the output of Rand depends only on the value of the seed, the outputs that follow the second appearance of v must be identical to those that followed the first appearance; this shows that the sequence repeats after no more than 32,768 calls. It might, of course, repeat much sooner than that. The length of the repeated portion is called the *period* of the generator. The sample random number generator shown here has a period of only 16384. Changing the 27 to 29 will increase the period to 32768. (The design of random number generators is a topic of some complexity. The interested reader is referred to *The Art of Computer Programming*, Volume II,[2] for more information about this.)

Since the output of the generator depends only on the seed, and the seed is initialized to 1, this random number generator will generate the same sequence of numbers, starting with 1, 11138, 16925, . . . each time the program is run.

Sometimes this is desirable. Suppose the program crashes. You might like to rerun it under the debugger to see what went wrong. But if the program's behavior depended on a sequence of random numbers, it will be important to be able to reproduce the same sequence of numbers, or else the debugging run may not do the same thing and may not reveal the problem.

Nevertheless, when you ask for random numbers, you usually want them to be different every time. For this reason, random number generators come with an auxiliary function for initializing the seed:

```
sub SRand {
  $seed = shift;
}
```

---

2   The Art of Computer Programming, Volume II: Seminumerical Algorithms, Donald E. Knuth, Addison–Wesley.

To get unpredictable random numbers, we call the SRand() function once, at the beginning of the program, with an argument that will vary from run to run, such as the current time or process ID number:

```
SRand($$);
```

The random generator will start at a different place in the sequence each time the program is run. If the program saves the seed in a file, the seed can be re-used later during a debugging run to force the generator to produce the same sequence of random numbers a second time.

This design is very common; C libraries come with paired sets of functions called rand and srand, or random and srandom, or drand48 and srand48, which are analogous to Rand() and SRand(). The Perl built-in rand and srand functions work the same way, and are usually backed by one or another of the C function pairs.

This interface has several problems, however. One is that it's not clear who has responsibility for seeding the random generator. Suppose you have the following program:

```
use CGI::Push;
my $seed = shift || $$ ;
srand($seed);
open LOG, "> $logfile" or die ... ;
print LOG "Random seed: $seed\n";

do_push(...);
```

Normally, the program is run with no command-line argument, and the random number generator is seeded with the process ID as usual. The seed is then saved to the debugging log. If the program fails, it can be rerun, and the same seed can be supplied as a command-line argument.

However, there's a problem. The CGI::Push module also needs to generate random numbers, and it makes its own call to srand when do_push() is called. This will overwrite the seed that the main program wanted to use.

Imagine the problems this could cause. Suppose the main program had saved its seed to a file for use in a later debugging session, and then the program did indeed crash. You start the debugger, and tell the program to re-use the same seed. And it does, up until the call to do_push, which re-seeds the generator, using its own seeding policy, which knows nothing of your debugging strategy. After the call to do_push, all the random numbers produced by rand are unpredictable again. The more separate modules the program uses, the more likely they are to fight over the random number seed like drunken fraternity brothers fighting over the remote control.

A related problem concerns the generator itself. Recall that our example generator generates a sequence of 16,384 numbers before repeating, but with careful choice of the constants, we can improve it to get the maximum possible period of 32,768. Now consider the following program:

```
use Foo;

while (<>) {
  my $random = Rand();
  # do something with $random
  foo();
}
```

Unbeknownst to the author of this program, the foo function, imported from the Foo module, also generates a random number using Rand. This means that the pool of 32,768 random numbers is split between the main program and foo, with the main program getting the first, third, fifth, seventh random numbers, and so on, and the foo function getting the second, fourth, six, eighth, and so on. Since the main program is seeing only half of the pool of numbers, the period of the sequence it sees is only half as big. Whatever is done with $random, it will repeat every 16,384 lines. Even though we were at some pains to make the pool of random numbers as large as possible, our efforts were foiled, because both sources of random data were drawing from the same well of entropy.

The underlying problem here is that the random number generator is a single global resource, and the seed is a global variable. Global variables almost always have this kind of allocation problem. Iterators provide a solution. It's easy to convert the Rand function to an iterator:

CODE LIBRARY
rng-iterator.pl

```
sub make_rand {
  my $seed = shift || (time & 0x7fff);
  return Iterator {
    $seed = (29*$seed+11111) & 0x7fff;
    return $seed;
  }
}
```

Calling make_rand() returns an iterator that generates a different random number each time it is called. The optional argument to make_rand() specifies the seed; if omitted, it is derived from the current time of day. Revisiting the last example:

```
use Foo;
my $rng = make_rand();

while (<>) {
  my $random = NEXTVAL($rng);
  # do something with $random
  foo();
}
```

The main program now has its own private random number generator, represented by $rng. This generator is not available to foo. foo can allocate its own random number generator, which is completely independent of $rng. Each generator is seeded separately, so there is no question about who bears responsibility for the initial seeding. Each part of the program is responsible for seeding its own generators at the time they are created.

If it is desirable for two parts of the program to share a generator for some reason, they can do that simply by sharing the iterator object.

4.4 FILTERS AND TRANSFORMS

Because iterators are objects, we can write functions to operate on them. What might be useful? Since iterators encapsulate lists, we should expect that the same sort of functions that are useful for lists will also be useful for iterators. Two of Perl's most useful list functions are grep and map. grep filters a list, returning a new list of all the elements that possess some property. map transforms a list, applying an operation to each element, and returning a new list. Both of these are useful operations for iterators.

In the diagrams that follow, iterators will be represented as follows:

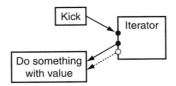

The boxes represent actions, as in a regular flow chart. When an iterator is kicked, it emits a value, which is represented by the dotted line coming out of the left-hand side. Solid arrows represent the flow of control, dotted arrows the flow of data.

4.4.1 imap()

We'll see the iterator version of map first because it's simpler:

```
sub imap {
  my ($transform, $it) = @_;
  return Iterator {
    my $next = NEXTVAL($it);
    return unless defined $next;
    return $transform->($next);
  }
}
```

imap() takes two arguments: a callback function and an iterator. It returns a new iterator whose output is the same as that of the original iterator, but with every element transformed by the callback function:

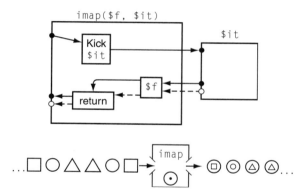

For example, suppose we wanted a random number generator that behaved more like Perl's built-in generator, returning a fraction between 0 and 1 instead of an integer between 0 and 32767. We could rewrite make_rand(), but there's no need if we have imap():

```
my $rng = imap(sub { $_[0] / 37268 }, make_rand());
```

make_rand() constructs an iterator that generates a random integer, as before. We pass the iterator to imap(), which returns a different iterator, which is stored in $rng. When we invoke $rng, it calls the original iterator, which returns an integer; this is stored in $next and passed to $transform, which divides the integer by 32768 and returns the result. The first few outputs from $rng are:

```
0.298915960072985
0.174170870451862
0.0735751851454331
0.673312224965118
0.480626811205324
0.168267682730493
0.781635719652249
0.104996243425995
0.705269936674895
0.528147472362348
...
```

The syntax for imap() is a little cumbersome. Since it's analogous to map, it would be nice if it had the same syntax. Fortunately, Perl allows this. The first step is to add a prototype to imap():

```
sub imap (&$) {
    my ($transform, $it) = @_;
    return Iterator {
        my $next = NEXTVAL($it);
        return unless defined $next;
        return $transform->($next);
    }
}
```

The (&$) tells Perl that imap() will get exactly two arguments, that the first will be a code reference (& symbolizes subroutines) and the second will be a scalar ($ symbolizes scalars). When we announce to Perl that a function's first argument will be a code reference, the announcement triggers a change in the Perl parser to allow the word sub to be omitted from before the first argument and the comma to be omitted after — just as with map and grep. We can now write:

```
my $rng = imap { $_[0] / 37268 } make_rand();
```

The $ in the prototype will ensure that make_rand() will be called in scalar context and will produce a single scalar result; normally, it would be called in list context and might produce many scalars.

The only difference between this syntax and map's is that we had to use $_[0] in the code block instead of $_. If we are willing to commit more trickery, we can use $_ instead of $_[0] in the code reference, just as with map:

```
sub imap (&$) {
   my ($transform, $it) = @_;
   return Iterator {
      local $_ = NEXTVAL($it);
      return unless defined $_;
      return $transform->();
   }
}
```

Instead of storing the output of the underlying iterator into a private $next variable, we store it into $_. Then we needn't pass it explicitly to $transform; $transform can see the value anyway, because $_ is global. As usual, we use local to save the old value of $_ before we overwrite it. We can now write:

```
my $rng = imap { $_ / 37268 } make_rand();
```

which has exactly the same syntax as map.

4.4.2   igrep()

The trickery is the same for igrep(), and only the control flow is different:

```
sub igrep (&$) {
   my ($is_interesting, $it) = @_;
   return Iterator {
      local $_;
      while (defined ($_ = NEXTVAL($it))) {
         return $_ if $is_interesting->();
      }
      return;
   }
}
```

The iterator returned by igrep() kicks the underlying iterator repeatedly until it starts returning undef (at which point igrep() gives up and also returns undef) or it returns an interesting item, as judged by the $is_interesting callback (see Figure 4.3). When it finds an interesting item, it returns it.

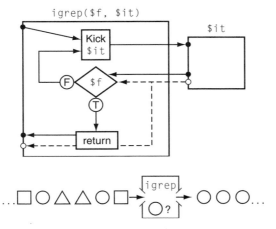

FIGURE 4.3   igrep().

Now that we have igrep(), we no longer need interesting_files(), which searched a directory tree and returned the interesting files. Instead, we can get the same effect by filtering the output of dir_walk():

```
# instead of         my $next_octopus =
#   interesting_files(\&contains_octopuses, 'uploads', 'downloads');

my $next_octopus = igrep { contains_octopuses($_) }
                    dir_walk('uploads', 'downloads');

while ($file = NEXTVAL($next_octopus)) {
  # do something with the file
}
```

4.4.3   list_iterator()

Sometimes it's convenient to have a way to turn a list into an iterator:

```
sub list_iterator {
  my @items = @_;
  return Iterator {
    return shift @items;
  };
}
```

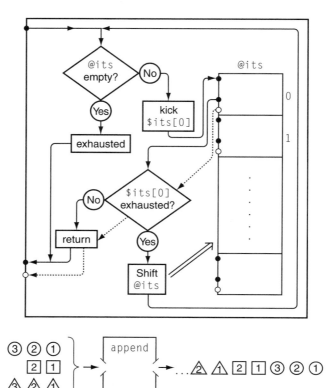

FIGURE 4.4 append().

list_iterator('fish', 'dog', 'carrot') produces an iterator that generates 'fish', then 'dog', then 'carrot', and then an infinite sequence of undefined values.

4.4.4 append()

map and grep aren't the only important operations on lists. Some of the most important operations don't even have names, because they're so common. One of these is the append() operation (see Figure 4.4), which attaches two or more lists together head-to-tail to yield a single list.

```
sub append {
  my @its = @_;
  return Iterator {
    while (@its) {
```

```
      my $val = NEXTVAL($its[0]);
      return $val if defined $val;
      shift @its;  # Discard exhausted iterator
    }
    return;
  };
}
```

We call append() with zero or more iterators as arguments. It returns a new iterator that produces all the items from the first iterator, followed by all the items from the second iterator, and so on. For example, append(upto(1,3), upto(5,8), upto(9,11)) returns an iterator that yields the values 1, 2, 3, 5, 6, 7, 8, 9, 10, 11 in order, and undefined values thereafter.

The while loop invokes the first iterator in the argument list; if it yields an undefined value, the first iterator is exhausted, so it is discarded (by the shift) and the next argument it tried. This continues until a nonempty iterator is found or the argument list is itself exhausted. Then the loop exits and the iterator returns the value from the nonempty iterator, if there was one, or undef if not.

4.5   THE SEMIPREDICATE PROBLEM

So far, our iterators have all indicated exhaustion by returning the undefined value. For the examples we've seen, this is perfectly adequate. An undefined value can never be confused with any number, any file path, any permutation of a list, or any string. But in general, an iterator might generate data that includes the undefined value. For example, consider an iterator whose job is to generate values from certain columns of a SQL database. SQL databases have a special NULL value that is different from every number and every string. It's natural to represent this NULL value in Perl with undef, and in fact the Perl DBI module does this. But if the database field can potentially contain any string value or NULL, then the iterator cannot use undef to indicate end-of-data as well as NULL.

Most of our iterator utility functions, such as imap(), will become confused if the iterator generates undef as a valid data value. If the iterator returns undef to indicate that the database contained NULL, the utility function will erroneously conclude that the iterator has been exhausted.

You may recall from Chapter 3 that this is called the *semipredicate problem*. Our iterators are semipredicates because they return undef to indicate exhaustion, and a data value otherwise. The difficulty occurs when we need undef to sometimes be understood as a data value instead of as a flag indicating exhaustion.

4.5.1   Avoiding the Problem

There are several ways around this. One is simply to declare that no iterator is ever allowed to return an undefined value; if undef is a legal return, the iterator must be restructured to return its data in some other format. Suppose we have an iterator that might return any scalar value, including undef:

```
sub make_iterator {
  ...
  return Iterator {
    my $return_value;
    ...
    if (exhausted) {
      return;
    } else {
      return $return_value;
    }
  }
}
```

This won't work because the caller will not be able to distinguish between an iterator returning undef to indicate exhaustion from one that happens to be returning an undefined value of $return_value. We can restructure this iterator to be unambiguous:

```
# array reference version
sub make_iterator {
  ...
  return Iterator {
    my $return_value;
    ...
    if (exhausted) {
      return;
    } else {
      return [$return_value];
    }
  }
}
```

The iterator now always returns an array reference, except that it returns undef when it is exhausted. When $return_value is undefined, the iterator returns [undef], which is easily distinguished from undef because it *is* defined. In fact, the caller doesn't even need to use defined, because the exhaustion indicator is false, while all other possible returns, including [undef], are true.

Often this simple solution imposes no extra costs. The Perl DBI module uses this strategy in some cases. The $sth->fetchrow_arrayref method returns a row of data from the result of a database query using an undefined return to indicate that there are no more rows available.

Each row may contain undefined values, which represent the database's NULL entries, and if a row contains only one field, it may be a single NULL. But fetchrow_arrayref always returns the row data as an array reference, so a row with a single NULL is easily distinguished from the undef that indicates that no more rows are available:

```
while (my $row = $sth->fetchrow_arrayref) {
  # do something with this $row
}
# no more rows
```

A related solution is to require that the iterator be used only in list context:

```
# list-context-only version
sub make_iterator {
  ...
  return Iterator {
    my $return_value;
    ...
    if (exhausted) {
      return ();
    } else {
      return $return_value;
    }
  }
}
```

Now a successful call to the iterator *always* returns a value, and when the iterator is exhausted it stops returning values. We can use it like this:

```
while (($val) = NEXTVAL($iterator)) {
  # do something with $val
}
# iterator is exhausted
```

The value of a list assignment when used as the condition of a while or if statement is the number of values returned on the right-hand side of the assignment. Even if the iterator returns a list such as (undef) or (0), the condition tested by `while` will be 1, which is true. When the iterator is exhausted, it will return an empty list, the condition will evaluate to 0, and the loop will exit.

4.5.2 Alternative `undef`s

Sometimes we don't want to avoid the semipredicate problem by returning lists or listrefs, or we can't. For DBI, the technique is natural, because the data in a row of a database is naturally represented as an array. But if our iterator returns only single scalars, it may be inconvenient to wrap up every value as an array reference just to unwrap it again in the caller. There are several strategies for dealing with the problem instead of avoiding it this way.

The first strategy is that when we construct the iterator, we could supply a special value that we know will never be returned normally. This value could be captured in the iterator, something like this:

```
sub make_iterator {
  my (..., $final_value, ...) = @_;
  return Iterator {
    ...
    if (exhausted) { return $final_value }
    ...
  }
}
```

However, this would be annoying, since we'd have to inform functions like `imap()` what the special final value was for each iterator they needed to process. It's possible to construct a single value that will work for every iterator in the entire program, so that the iterators and the functions that use them can all assume it.

To construct such a value, we use a trick borrowed from the C language. In C, many functions return pointers; for example, the memory allocator (`malloc`) returns a pointer to a block of unused memory, and the `fopen` function returns a pointer to C's version of a filehandle object. C has a special pointer value, called the *null pointer*, which these functions return when there is an error. The null pointer's only useful property is that it compares unequal to any valid pointer.

Occasionally a C programmer wants to write a function that can return pointers, and indicate two sorts of errors with two different special values. The null pointer will serve for one of these two, but what will be the other one? In C there's an easy solution: use `malloc` to allocate a byte and return a pointer to it; this will serve as the alternative special value. No other valid pointer will ever point to that address, because `malloc` has reserved it.

We can do an analogous thing in Perl. We will invent a new value that can't possibly be confused with any legal data value, including `undef`. We will use this "alternative undef" in place of the real `undef`. How can we do that? It's simple:

```
$EXHAUSTED = [];
```

`$EXHAUSTED` is now guaranteed to be distinct from any other value our program will ever generate. If a value is not an arrayref, we can distinguish it from `$EXHAUSTED`, which is an arrayref. If a value is an arrayref, then it must refer to a different array than `$EXHAUSTED` does, unless it was copied from `$EXHAUSTED` itself. That is,

```
\@a == $EXHAUSTED
```

is guaranteed to be false for all arrays `@a`. Similarly, `[...] == $EXHAUSTED` is guaranteed to be false, because `[...]` generates a new, fresh array, which is different from the one in `$EXHAUSTED`.

We can now write functions, analogous to `undef` and `defined`, to generate and detect special values:

```
{
  my $EXHAUSTED = [];

  # like 'undef()'
  sub special () { return $EXHAUSTED }

  # like 'not defined()'
  sub is_special ($) {
    my $arg = shift;
    ref($arg) && $arg == $EXHAUSTED;
  }
}
```

Having done this, we can build an iterator that uses `$EXHAUSTED` to indicate end-of-data:

```
sub dbi_query_iterator {
  my ($sth, @params) = @_;
```

```
      $sth->execute(@params) or return ;
      return Iterator {
        my $row;
        if ($sth && $row = $sth->fetchrow_arrayref()) {
          return $row->[0];
        } else { # exhausted
          undef $sth;
          return special();
        }
      }
    }
```

$sth is a Perl DBI object that represents a SQL statement. dbi_query_iterator()
takes this object and yields an iterator that will produce the results of the query,
one at a time. It asks the database to execute the query by calling $sth->execute;
if this fails it returns failure. Otherwise, the iterator uses the DBI method
fetchrow_arrayref to fetch the next row of data from the database; it extracts
the first item from the row, if there was one, and returns it. This item might be
undef, which indicates a NULL database value.

When there are no more rows, fetchrow_arrayref returns undef. The iterator discards the private copy of $sth and returns the special value. Since the
special value is distinguishable from any other scalar value, the caller receives an
unambiguous indication that no more data is forthcoming. On future calls, the
iterator continues to return the special value.

The caller can use the iterator this way:

```
    until (is_special(my $value = NEXTVAL($iterator))) {
      # do something with $value
    }
    # no more data
```

It might seem that we could simplify the definition of is_special() by
eliminating the test for ref($arg) eq 'ARRAY':

```
    # MIGHT NOT ALWAYS WORK
    sub is_special {
      my $arg = shift;
      $arg == $EXHAUSTED;
    }
```

But this isn't so. If $arg were an integer, and we were very unlucky, the test
might yield true! Comparing an integer to a reference with == actually compares

the integer to the machine address at which the referenced data is stored, and these two numbers might match. Similarly, using plain eq without the additional ref test wouldn't be enough, because $arg might happen to be the string ARRAY(0x436c1d) and might happen to match the stringized version of the reference exactly. So we need to check $arg for referencehood before using == or eq. This kind of failure is extremely unlikely, but if it *did* happen it could be very difficult to reproduce, and it might take us weeks to track down the problem, so it's better to be on the safe side.

4.5.3   Rewriting Utilities

If we switch from using an undefined value to using a special value, it looks like all the code that uses iterators, including functions like imap(), will have to be rewritten, because we've changed the interface specification. For example, imap() becomes:

```
sub special_imap {
  my ($transform, $it) = @_;
  return Iterator {
    my $next = NEXTVAL($it);
    return special() if is_special($next);
    return $transform->($next);
  }
}
```

It might seem that we need to pick an interface and then stick with it, but we don't necessarily. Suppose we write all our utilities to use the special-value interface; our imap() is actually the special_imap() above.

Now we want to use some iterator, say $uit, that uses the undef convention instead of the special-value convention. Do we have to re-implement imap() and our other utilities to deal with the new undef iterators? No, we don't:

```
sub undef_to_special {
  my $it = shift;
  return Iterator {
    my $val = NEXTVAL($it);
    return defined($val) ? $val : special() ;
  }
}
```

We can't pass $uit directly to imap(), but we can pass undef_to_special($uit) instead, and it will do what we want. undef_to_special() takes an undef-style iterator and turns it into a special-value-style iterator. It is like a mask that an iterator can wear to pretend that its interface is something else. Any undef-style iterator can put on the undef_to_special() mask and pretend to be an special-value-style iterator.

We could also write a similar special_to_undef() mask function to convert the other way. Of course, it wouldn't work correctly on iterators that might return undefined values.

4.5.4   Iterators That Return Multiple Values

The "special value" solution to the semipredicate problem works adequately, but has the disadvantage that the special() and is_special() functions may have to be exported everywhere in the program. (And also the possible disadvantage that it may be peculiar.) Since functions in Perl can return multiple values, and an iterator is just a function, a more straightforward solution may be to have the iterator return two values at a time; the second value will indicate whether the iterator is exhausted:

```perl
sub dbi_query_iterator {
  my ($sth, @params) = @_;
  $sth->execute(@params) or return ;
  return Iterator {
    my $row;
    if ($sth && $row = $sth->fetchrow_arrayref()) {
      return ($row->[0], 1);
    } else { # exhausted
      if ($sth) { $sth->finish; undef $sth; }
      return (undef, 0);
    }
  }
}
```

To use this, the caller writes something like:

```perl
while (my ($val, $continue) = NEXTVAL($iterator)) {
  last unless $continue;
  # do something with $val...
}
# now it is empty
```

4.5.5   Explicit Exhaustion Function

The iterator knows when it is exhausted, and it will tell us if we ask it. But we haven't provided any way to do that; all we can do is ask it for the next value with the NEXTVAL operator. We would like to be able to ask the iterator two types of questions: "Are you empty?" and if not, "Since you're not empty, what is the next item?" There's an obvious hook to hang this expansion on: Since the iterator is simply a function, we will pass it an argument to tell it which question we want answered. To preserve compatibility (and to optimize the common case) we'll leave the iterator's behavior the same when it is called without arguments; calling it with no arguments will continue to ask an iterator to return its next value. But we'll add new semantics: if we pass the iterator the string "exhausted?", it will return a true or false value indicating whether or not it is empty. With this new functionality added, our dbi_query_iterator() becomes:

```perl
sub dbi_query_iterator {
  my ($sth, @params) = @_;
  $sth->execute(@params) or return ;
  my $row = $sth->fetchrow_arrayref();
  return Iterator {
    my $action = shift() || 'nextval';
    if ($action eq 'exhausted?') {
      return ! defined $row;
    } elsif ($action eq 'nextval') {
      my $oldrow = $row;
      $row = $sth->fetchrow_arrayref;
      return $oldrow->[0];
    }
  }
}
```

The iterator now returns undef either when the rows are exhausted or when the value in the row happens to be NULL, and the caller can't tell which. But that doesn't matter, because the caller of this iterator isn't looking for undef to know when to stop reading the iterator. Instead, the caller is doing this:

```perl
until ($iterator->('exhausted?')) {
  my $val = NEXTVAL($iterator);
  ...
}
# now it is empty
```

We can provide syntactic sugar for 'exhausted?' that is analogous to NEXTVAL:

```
sub EXHAUSTED {
  $_[0]->('exhausted?');
}
```

This loop then becomes:

```
until (EXHAUSTED($iterator)) {
  my $val = NEXTVAL($iterator);
  ...
}
# now it is empty
```

Or, if you don't like until, we could define the obvious MORE function, and write:

```
while (MORE($iterator)) {
  my $val = NEXTVAL($iterator);
  ...
}
# now it is empty
```

A mask function allows iterators in the old, undef-returning style to support EXHAUSTED queries:

```
sub undef_to_exhausted {
  my $it = shift;
  my $val = NEXTVAL($it);
  return Iterator {
    my $action = shift || 'nextval';
    if ($action eq 'nextval') {
      my $oldval = $val;
      $val = NEXTVAL($it);
      return $oldval;
    } elsif ($action eq 'exhausted?') {
      return not defined $val;
    }
  }
}
```

If our versions of utilities such as imap() are set up to support the NEXTVAL/EXHAUSTED interface, we can still use the old-style iterators with them, by wrapping them in an undef_to_exhausted() mask. Similarly, the utilities produce iterators with the NEXTVAL/EXHAUSTED interface, so if we want to use one in the old undef style (and we know that's safe) we can build a mask function that goes the other way:

```
sub exhausted_to_undef {
  my $it = shift;
  return Iterator {
    if (EXHAUSTED($it)) { return }
    else                { return NEXTVAL($it) }
  }
}
```

It's better if all our iterators conform to the same interface style, of course, but the mask functions show that they don't have to, and that if we make the wrong choice early on and have to switch to a different system later on, we can do that, or if we want to use the simple style for most iterators and save the more complicated two-operation interface for a few cases, we can do that also.

Interfacing different sorts of iterators is something we've also been doing implicitly through the entire chapter. In Section 4.3 we saw filehandle_iterator(), which is essentially a mask function: it converts one kind of iterator (a filehandle) into another (our synthetic, function-based iterators). If we needed to, we could go in the other direction and write a mask function that would wrap up one of our iterators as a filehandle, using Perl's tied filehandle interface. We will see how to do this in Section 4.6.3.

Similarly, the various versions of dbi_query_iterator() were also mask functions, converting from DBI's statement handles to function-based iterators. We could go in the other direction here if we had to, probably by building an object class that obeyed the DBI statement handle interface, but implementing our own versions of ->fetchrow_arrayref and the like.

4.5.6 Four-Operation Iterators

As long as we're on the topic of iterators that support two kinds of queries (one for exhaustion and one for the next value), we might as well see this idea in its full generality. The C-style for loop has a very general model of iteration:

```
for (initialize; test; update) {
  action;
}
```

Occasionally you may need an equally general iterator:

```
for ($it->('start'); not $it->('exhausted?'); $it->('next')) {
  # do something with $it->('value');
}
```

exhausted? here is as in the previous section. The next operation doesn't return
anything; it just tells the iterator to forget the current value and to get ready to
deliver the next value. value tells the iterator to return the current value; if we
make two calls to $it->('value') without $it->('next') in between, we'll get
the same value both times.

start initializes the iterator. An explicit start call simplifies the code in some
of the iterators we've seen already. For example, dbi_query_iterator() had to
do fetchrow_arrayref() in two places, once to initialize itself, and once after
every NEXTVAL:

```
sub dbi_query_iterator {
  my ($sth, @params) = @_;
  $sth->execute(@params) or return;
  my $row = $sth->fetchrow_arrayref();
  return Iterator {
    my $action = shift() || 'nextval';
    if ($action eq 'exhausted?') {
      return ! defined $row;
    } elsif ($action eq 'nextval') {
      my $oldrow = $row;
      $row = $sth->fetchrow_arrayref;
      return $oldrow;
    }
  }
}
```

Here's the four-operation version of the same function. Although it does more,
the code is almost the same length:

```
sub dbi_query_iterator {
  my ($sth, @params) = @_;
  $sth->execute(@params) or return ;
  my $row;
  return Iterator {
    my $action = shift();
```

```
          if ($action eq 'exhausted?') {
            return ! defined $row;
        } elsif ($action eq 'value') {
            return $row;
        } elsif ($action eq 'next' || $action eq 'start'){
            $row = $sth->fetchrow_arrayref;
        } else {
            die "Unknown iterator operation '$action'";
        }
      }
    }
```

We can still support the old NEXTVAL operation if we want to:

```
    sub dbi_query_iterator {
      my ($sth, @params) = @_;
      $sth->execute(@params) or return ;
      my $row;
      return Iterator {
        my $action = shift() || 'nextval';
        if ($action eq 'exhausted?') {
            return ! defined $row;
        } elsif ($action eq 'value') {
            return $row;
        } elsif ($action eq 'next'|| $action eq 'start'
                || $action eq 'nextval') {
            return $row = $sth->fetchrow_arrayref;
        } else {
            die "Unknown iterator operation '$action'";
        }
      }
    }
```

Here calling start twice has a possibly surprising effect: start and next are identical! Sometimes it's useful to have start mean that the iterator should start over at the beginning, forcing it to go back to the beginning of its notional list. The cost of this is that the iterator has to remember a list of all the values it has ever produced, in case someone tells it to start over. It also complicates the programming. While this is occasionally useful enough to be worth the extra costs, it's usually simpler to declare that calling start twice on the same iterator is erroneous.

4.5.7 Iterator Methods

People can be funny about syntax, and Perl programmers are even more obsessed with syntax than most people. When Larry Wall described the syntax of Perl 6 for the first time, people were up in arms because he was replacing the -> operator with . and the . operator with _. Even though there is only a little difference between:

```
$it->start
```

and:

```
$it->('start')
```

people love the first one and hate the second one. It's easy to make the first syntax available though. The first syntax is an object method call, so we need to make our iterators into Perl objects. We do that with a small change to the Iterator() function:

```
sub Iterator (&) {
  my $it = shift;
  bless $it => 'Iter';
}
```

Now we can add whatever methods we want for iterators:

```
sub Iter::start      { $_[0]->('start')     }
sub Iter::exhausted  { $_[0]->('exhausted?') }
sub Iter::next       { $_[0]->('next')      }
sub Iter::value      { $_[0]->('value'      }
```

The prototypical loop, which looked like this:

```
for ($it->('start'); not $it->('exhausted?'); $it->('next')) {
  # do something with $it->('value');
}
```

can now be written like this:

```
for ($it->start; not $it->exhausted; $it->next) {
  # do something with $it->value;
}
```

4.6 ALTERNATIVE INTERFACES TO ITERATORS

We've already seen that there are two ways to get the next value from any of these iterators. We can use:

```
$next_value = NEXTVAL($iterator);
```

or, equivalently, we can write:

```
$next_value = $iterator->();
```

which is just what NEXTVAL is doing behind the scenes.

So much for syntax; semantics is more interesting. Since an iterator is just a function, we aren't limited to iterators that return scalar values.

4.6.1 Using foreach to Loop Over More Than One Array

An occasional question is how to loop over two arrays simultaneously. Perl provides for, which is convenient when you want to loop over a single array:

```
for $element (@a) {
  # do something with $element
}
```

But suppose you want to write a function that compares two arrays element by element and reports whether they are the same? (The obvious notation, @x == @y, returns true whenever the two arrays have the same length.) You'd like to loop over pairs of corresponding elements, but there's no way to do that. The only obvious way out is to loop over the array indices instead:

```
sub equal_arrays (\@\@) {
  my ($x, $y) = @_;
  return unless @$x == @$y;      # arrays are the same length?
  for my $i (0 .. $#$x) {
    return unless $x->[$i] eq $y->[$i];   # mismatched elements
  }
  return 1;                      # arrays are equal
}
```

To call this function, we write:

```
if (equal_arrays(@x, @y)) { ... }
```

The (\@\@) prototype tells Perl that the two argument arrays should be passed by reference, instead of being flattened into a single list of array elements. Inside the function, the two references are stored into $x and $y. The @$x == @$y test makes sure that the two arrays have equal lengths before examining the elements.

An alternative approach is to build an iterator that can be used whenever this sort of loop is required:

```
sub equal_arrays (\@\@) {
  my ($x, $y) = @_
  return unless @$x == @$y;
  my $xy = each_array(@_);
  while (my ($xe, $ye) = NEXTVAL($xy)) {
    return unless $xe eq $ye;
  }
  return 1;
}
```

The following iterator, invented by Eric Roode, does the trick:

```
sub each_array {
  my @arrays = @_;
  my $cur_elt = 0;
  my $max_size = 0;

  # Get the length of the longest input array
  for (@arrays) {
    $max_size = @$_ if @$_ > $max_size;
  }

  return Iterator {
    $cur_elt = 0, return () if $cur_elt >= $max_size;
    my $i = $cur_elt++;
    return map $_->[$i], @arrays;
  };
}
```

The caller of this function passes in references to one or more arrays, which are stored into @arrays. The iterator captures this variable, as well as $cur_elt, which records its current position. Each time the iterator is invoked, it gathers one element from each array and returns the list of elements; it also increments $cur_elt for next time. When $cur_elt is larger than the last index of the

largest array, the iterator is exhausted and returns the empty list instead, resetting
$cur_elt so that the iterator can be used again.

Another place where this function might be useful is in generating HTML
forms. Suppose @labels contains a list of user-visible labels for radio buttons,
say ('Alaska', 'Alabama', ... 'Yukon Territory'), and @values contains the
internal tags that will be sent back by the browser when the user selects each
button, say ('AK', 'AL', ..., 'YT').

Probably these arrays should have been structured as an array of arrays,
(['Alaska', 'AK'], ['Alabama', 'AL'], ...), but that's not always convenient or even possible. (It's tempting to say that the structure should have been
a hash, but that's a mistake for several reasons: the hash loses the order of the
data; also, neither labels nor values are required to be distinct.)

With the multiple-list iterator, we can write things like:

```
my $buttons = each_array(\@labels, \@values);

...


while (my ($label, $value) = NEXTVAL($buttons)) {
  print HTML qq{<input type=radio value="$value"> $label<br>\n};
}
```

The version Eric Roode uses has a clever twist:

```
sub each_array (\@;\@\@\@\@\@\@\@\@\@\@\@\@\@\@\@\@\@\@\@\@\@\@\@\@\@\@) {
  my @arrays    = @_;
  ...
}
```

The prototype here says that the arguments will be arrays, and will be passed
implicitly by reference, and that there will be at least one. The ; character separates the required arguments from the optional ones. Because of the prototype,
Eric can leave off the backslashes in calls to each_array(), and write:

```
$ea = each_array(@a, @b, @c, @d);
```

While this is slightly more convenient for his common case, it forecloses the
possibility of passing literal array references or array references contained in scalar
variables, so that:

```
$aref = \@a;
$ea = each_array($aref, [1,2,3]);
```

becomes illegal; it must be written in this somewhat bizarre form:

```
$ea = each_array(@$aref, @{[1,2,3]});
```

Besides, a more interesting use for the argument space is coming up.

It's not clear what the best behavior is when the function is passed arrays of different lengths, say (1,2,3) and ('A','B','C','D'). The preceding version returns four pairs: (1, 'A'), (2, 'B'), (3, 'C'), and (undef, 'D'). It might be preferable in some circumstances to have the iterator become exhausted at the end of the shortest input array, instead of the longest. To get this behavior, just replace the maximum computation with a minimum. We can also provide a version of each_array that has either behavior, depending on an optional argument:

```
sub each_array {
  my @arrays    = @_;
  my $stop_type = ref $arrays[0] ? 'maximum': shift @arrays;
  my $stop_size = @{$arrays[0]};
  my $cur_elt   = 0;

  # Get the length of the longest (or shortest) input array
  if ($stop_type eq 'maximum') {
    for (@arrays) {
      $stop_size = @$_ if @$_ > $stop_size;
    }
  } elsif ($stop_type eq 'minimum') {
    for (@arrays) {
      $stop_size = @$_ if @$_ < $stop_size;
    }
  } else {
    croak "each_array: unknown stopping behavior '$stop_type'";
  }

  return Iterator {
    return ()  if $cur_elt >= $stop_size;
    my $i = $cur_elt++;
    return map $_->[$i], @arrays;
  };
}
```

If the first argument is not an array ref, we shift it off into $stop_type, which otherwise defaults to "maximum". Only "maximum" and "minimum" are supported

here. As usual, we can gain flexibility and eliminate the repeated code by allowing
a callback argument to specify the method for selecting the stopping point:

```
sub each_array {
  my @arrays    = @_;
  my $stop_func = UNIVERSAL::isa($arrays[0], 'ARRAY') ? 'maximum': shift @arrays;
  my $stop_size = @{$arrays[0]};
  my %stop_funcs = ('maximum'=>
                       sub { $_[0] > $_[1] ? $_[0] : $_[1] },
                     'minimum'=>
                       sub { $_[0] < $_[1] ? $_[0] : $_[1] },
                   );

  unless (ref $stop_func eq 'CODE') {
    $stop_func = $stop_funcs{$stop_func}
      or croak "each_array: unknown stopping behavior '$stop_func'";
  }

  # Get the length of the longest (or shortest) input array
  for (@arrays) {
    $stop_size = &$stop_func($stop_size, scalar @$_);
  }

  my $cur_elt   = 0;
  return Iterator {
    return ()  if $cur_elt >= $stop_size;
    my $i = $cur_elt++;
    return map $_->[$i], @arrays;
  };
}
```

each_array now has several calling conventions. The basic one we've seen already:

```
my $each = each_array(\@x, \@y, ...);
```

This builds an iterator that produces one list for each element in the longest
input array. The first argument to each_array may also be a callback function
that is used to generate the array limit:

```
sub max { $_[0] > $_[1] ? $_[0] : $_[1] };
my $each = each_array(\&max, \@x, \@y, ...);
```

The callback function is given two arguments: the current stopping size and the size of one of the arrays. It returns a new choice of stopping size. In the preceding example, it returns the maximum. The third way of calling each_array is to pass a string key that symbolizes a commonly chosen function:

```
my $each = each_array('maximum', \@x, \@y, ...);
```

This selects a canned maximum function from the table %stop_funcs.

We can get a different behavior by supplying a more interesting function:

```
my $all_equal = sub {
    if ($_[0] == $_[1]) { return $_[0] }
    croak "each_array: Not every array has length $_[0]";
};

my $each = each_array($all_equal, \@x, \@y, ...);
```

Here each_array croaks unless every input array has the same length. If this behavior turns out to be frequently needed, we can add the $all_equal function to the %stop_funcs table and support:

```
my $each = each_array('all_equal', \@x, \@y, ...);
```

without breaking backward compatibility.

4.6.2 An Iterator with an each-Like Interface

Every Perl hash contains an iterator component, which is accessed by each(). Each call to each() produces another key from the hash, and, in list context, the corresponding value.

Following this model, we can make a transformation function, analogous to imap(), that may produce a more useful result:

```
sub eachlike (&$) {
  my ($transform, $it) = @_;
  return Iterator {
    local $_ = NEXTVAL($it);
    return unless defined $_;
    my $value = $transform->();
    return wantarray ? ($_, $value) : $value;
  }
}
```

eachlike() transforms an iterator by applying a function to every element of the iterator. In scalar context, the iterators produced by eachlike() behave exactly the same as those produced by imap(). But in list context, an eachlike() iterator returns two values: the original, unmodified value, and the transformed value. For example:

```
my $n = eachlike { $_ * 2 } upto(3,5);
```

This loop will print the values 6, 8, 10, just as if we had used imap():

```
while (defined(my $q = NEXTVAL($n))) {
  print "$q\n";
}
```

This loop will print 3 6, 4 8, 5 10:

```
while (my @q = NEXTVAL($n)) {
  print "@q\n";
}
```

Our implementation of dir_walk() took a callback argument; the callback function was applied to each filename in the directory tree, and the iterator returned the resulting values. This complicated the implementation of dir_walk(). eachlike() renders this complication entirely unnecessary. It's quite enough for dir_walk() to return plain filenames, because in place of:

```
my $it = dir_walk($DIR, sub { ... } );
```

We can now use:

```
my $it = eachlike { ... } dir_walk($DIR);
```

In scalar context, $it will behave as if it had been generated by the former, more complicated version of dir_walk(). But in addition, it can also be used like this:

```
while (my ($filename, $value) = NEXTVAL($it)) {
  # do something with the filename or the value or both
}
```

For example, print out all the dangling symbolic links in a directory:

```
my $it = eachlike { -l && ! -e } dir_walk($DIR);
while (my ($filename, $badlink) = NEXTVAL($it)) {
  print "$filename is a dangling link" if $badlink;
}
```

4.6.3 Tied Variable Interfaces

The ordinary interface to an iterator may be unfamiliar. By using Perl's `tie` feature, which allows us to associate any semantics we want with a perl variable, we can make an iterator look like an ordinary scalar. Or rather, it will look like one of Perl's magical scalars, such as `$!` or `$.`, which might contain different values depending on when it's examined.

SUMMARY OF `tie`

In Perl, scalar variables may be *tied*. This means that access to the variable is mediated by a Perl object. The `tie` function associates the variable with a particular object, which we say is *tied to* the variable.

Suppose the scalar `$s` is tied to the object `$o`.

When you write this: Perl actually does this instead:

```
print $s;              print $o->FETCH();
$r = $s;               $r = $o->FETCH();

$s = $value;           $o->STORE($value);
```

If anyone tries to read from or write to `$s`, then instead of doing whatever it would usually do, Perl makes a method call on `$o` instead. An attempt to read `$s` turns into `$o->FETCH()`. The return value of the FETCH method is reported as being the value stored in `$s`.

Similarly, an attempt to do `$s = $value` turns into `$o->STORE($value)`. It is the responsibility of the STORE method to store the value somewhere so that it can be retrieved by a later call to FETCH.

To tie a scalar variable in Perl, we use the built-in `tie` operator:

```
tie $scalar, 'Package', ARGUMENTS...
```

This makes a method call to `Package->TIESCALAR(ARGUMENTS...)`. TIESCALAR must be an object constructor. The object that it returns is the one that will be associated with `$scalar` and which will receive subsequent FETCH and STORE messages.

Here's a (silly) example:

```
package CIA;
sub TIESCALAR {
  my $package = shift;
```

```
    my $self = {};
    bless $self => $package;
  }
  sub STORE { }
  sub FETCH { "<<Access forbidden>>" }
```

This is an implementation of an extra-secret tied scalar. If we tie a scalar into the CIA package, all data stored into it becomes inaccessible:

```
    tie $secret, 'CIA';
```

This creates the association between $secret and the object constructed by CIA::TIESCALAR. Accesses to $secret will turn into FETCH and STORE methods on the object:

```
    $secret = 'atomic ray';
```

Instead of storing 'atomic ray' in the usual way, STORE is invoked. It's passed the object and new value as arguments, but it just throws them away, without storing the data anywhere. That's OK, because if you later ask the hash what's stored under that key:

```
    print "The secret weapon is '$secret'.\n"
```

The output is:

```
    The secret weapon is '<<Access forbidden>>'.
```

which is pleasantly mysterious, and has the side benefit of defending national security.

TIED SCALARS

We can use this feature to associate a tied scalar variable with an iterator. When the value of the scalar variable is examined, Perl gets control behind the scenes, kicks the iterator, and reports the next iterator value as the current value of the variable.

```
    package Iterator2Scalar;

    sub TIESCALAR {
      my ($package, $it) = @_;
```

```
      my $self = { It => $it };
      bless $self => $package;
    }

    sub FETCH {
      my ($self) = @_;
      NEXTVAL($self->{It});
    }

    sub STORE {
      require Carp;
      Carp::croak("Iterator is read-only");
    }
```

Now we can use:

```
tie $nextfile, 'Iterator2Scalar', dir_walk($DIR);

while ($filename = $nextfile) {
  # do something with $filename
}
```

TIED FILEHANDLES

A tied scalar interface to an iterator produces a magical variable that encapsulates the iterator. This may be an intuitive interface in some cases, but it may also be peculiar. The user may be surprised to find that the variable's value changes spontaneously, or that the variable can't be assigned to.

Since Perl 5.004, filehandles have also been tie-able. A filehandle is often the most natural interface for a synthetic iterator. Since filehandles *are* examples of iterators, nobody will get any surprises when our filehandle behaves like an iterator or displays iterator-like limitations. People won't be surprised if a filehandle returns a different value each time it's read. They won't be surprised that they can't assign a value to it. They won't be surprised when a filehandle refuses to be rewound back to the beginning, since even ordinary filehandles don't always support that. They might be surprised by the handle's failure to support the getc operator, but more likely they won't even notice that it's missing.

The interface to tied filehandles is similar to that for tied scalars. Since filehandles aren't first-class variables in Perl, the caller passes an entire glob, and the tie operator ties the filehandle part of the glob:

```
tie *IT, 'Iterator2Handle', $iterator;
```

This calls the `Iterator2Handle::TIEHANDLE` constructor method, which is analogous to `TIESCALAR`:

```
package Iterator2Handle;

sub TIEHANDLE {
   my ($package, $iterator) = @_;
   my $self = { IT => $iterator };
   bless $self => $package;
}
```

When the user tries to read from the handle using the usual <IT> notation, Perl will call the `READLINE` method on the tied object:

```
sub READLINE {
   my $self = shift;
   return NEXTVAL($self->{IT});
}
```

To use the iterator, the user now does:

```
$some_value = <IT>;

# ... or ...

while ($nextval = <IT>) {
   # do something with $nextval
}
```

They can even use Perl's shortcut for reading a filehandle in a `while` loop:

```
while (<IT>) {
   # do something with $_
}
```

4.7 AN EXTENDED EXAMPLE: WEB SPIDERS

We'll now use the tools provided to build a replacement for Ave Wrigley's `WWW::SimpleRobot` module, which traverses a web site, invoking a callback for each page. SimpleRobot provides two callback hooks, one of which is called for documents that can't be retrieved, the other for documents that can. It also supports options to specify whether the traversal will be breadth- or depth-first, and a regex that the URLs of the retrieved documents must match.

Our robot, which we'll call Grasshopper, will be at once simpler and more flexible. The robot will be embedded in an iterator, and the iterator will simply return URLs. If the user wants a callback invoked for each URL, they can add one with imap.

Our basic tools will be the LWP::Simple and HTML::LinkExtor modules. LWP::Simple provides a simple interface for building web clients. HTML::LinkExtor parses an HTML page and returns a list of all the links found on the page. Here is the first cut:

```
use HTML::LinkExtor;
use LWP::Simple;

sub traverse {
  my @queue = @_;
  my %seen;

  return Iterator {
    while (@queue) {
      my $url = shift @queue;
      $url =~ s/#.*$//;
      next if $seen{$url}++;

      my ($content_type) = head($url);
      if ($content_type eq 'text/html') {
        my $html = get($url);
        push @queue, get_links($url, $html);
      }
      return $url;
    }
    return;      # exhausted
  }
}
```

The pattern here should be familiar; it's the same as the pattern we followed for walk_tree. The iterator maintains a queue of unvisited URLs, initialized with the list of URLs the user requests that it visit. Whenever the iterator is invoked, it gets the first item in the queue, reads it for more URLs, adds these URLs to the end of the queue, and returns the URL. When the queue is empty, the iterator is exhausted.

Use of the iterator structure was essential. A simple recursive formulation just doesn't work. Recursive searches always do DFS, so a recursive robot will follow the first link on the first page to arrive at the second page, then follow the first link on the second page, then the first link on the third page, and so on, never returning to any page to process the other links there until it hits a dead end. Dead ends on the web are unusual, so the recursive robot goes wandering off into cyberspace and never comes back. Breadth-first search is almost always preferable for this application, but with a simple recursive function there's no way to get BFS.

There are a few web-specific features in the code. Some URLs may contain an anchor component, indicated by a # sign followed by the anchor name; this doesn't identify a document, so we discard it. (The specification for URLs guarantees that any other # sign in the URL will be represented as %23, so this substitution should be safe.) The iterator maintains a hash, %seen, which records whether or not it has visited a URL already; if it has, then the URL is skipped. It uses the head function, supplied by LWP::Simple, to find out whether the URL represents an HTML document, and if not it doesn't bother searching that document for links. In theory, head is supposed to indicate to the server that we do not want the entire document content; we want only meta-information, such as its content-type and length. In practice, the world is full of defective servers (and working servers running defective CGI programs) that send the entire document anyway. We've done the best we can here; if the server is going to send the document even though we asked it not to, there's nothing we can do about that.

If the document does turn out to be HTML, we use the get function, also supplied by LWP::Simple, to retrieve the content, which we then pass into get_links. get_links will parse the HTML and return a list of all the link URLs found in the document. Here it is:

```
sub get_links {
  my ($base, $html) = @_;
  my @links;
  my $more_links = sub {
    my ($tag, %attrs) = @_;
    push @links, values %attrs;
  };

  HTML::LinkExtor->new($more_links, $base)->parse($html);
  return @links;
}
```

The structure of get_links is a little peculiar, because HTML::LinkExtor uses an unfortunate interface. The new call constructs an HTML::LinkExtor object. We give the constructor a callback function, $more_links, and a base URL, $base. The callback function is invoked whenever the object locates an HTML element that contains a link. The link URLs themselves will be transformed into absolute URLs, interpreted relative to $base.

Parsing the document is triggered by the ->parse method. We pass the HTML document as the argument. The object parses the document, invoking the callback each time it finds an HTML element that contains links. When we're done parsing the document, the object is no longer needed, so we never store it anywhere; we create it just long enough to call a single method on it.

The callback we supply to the HTML::LinkExtor object is called once for each link-bearing HTML element. The arguments are the tag of the element, and a sequence of attribute–value pairs for its link-bearing attributes. For example, if the element is:

```
<img border=0 src="pics/medium-sigils.gif" height=71 width=151
     align=right lowsrc="pics/small-sigils.gif" alt="$@%">
```

The arguments to the callback will be:

```
('IMG', 'SRC'=> 'pics/medium-sigils.gif',
        'LOWSRC'=> 'pics/small-sigils.gif',)
```

Our callback discards the tag, extracts the URLs, and pushes them into the @links array. When the parse is complete, we return @links.

4.7.1 Pursuing Only Interesting Links

The first cut of Grasshopper is almost useful. The one thing it's missing is a way to tell the robot not to pursue links to other web sites. We'll do that by inserting a callback filter function into get_links(). After get_links() extracts a list of links, it will invoke the user-supplied callback on this list. The callback will filter out the links that it doesn't want the robot to pursue, and return a list of the interesting links. The call to traverse will now look like this:

```
traverse($is_interesting_link, $url1, ...);
```

We need to make some minor changes to traverse():

```
# Version with 'interesting links' callback
sub traverse {
  my $interesting_links = sub { @_ };
  $interesting_links = shift if ref $_[0] eq 'CODE';

    ...

        push @queue, $interesting_links->(get_links($url, $html));
    ...
}
```

Now we can ask it to traverse a single web site:

```
my $top = 'http://perl.plover.com/';
my $interesting = sub { grep /^\Q$top/o, @_ };

my $urls = traverse($interesting, $top);
```

This is already reasonably useful. Here's a program that copies every reachable file on a site:

```
use File::Basename;
while (my $url = NEXTVAL($urls)) {
  my $file = $url;
  $file =~ s/^\Q$top//o;
  my $dir = dirname($file);
  system('mkdir', '-p', $dir) == 0 or next;
  open F, ">", $file or next;
  print F, get($url);
}
```

Here's a program to check whether any internal links on the site are bad:

```
while (my $url = NEXTVAL($urls)) {
  print "Bad link to: $url" unless head($url);
}
```

This last example exposes two obvious weaknesses in the current design. We can find out that $url is bad, but the iterator never tells us what page that bad URL appeared on, so we can't do anything about it. And the way we find out that $url is bad is rather silly. The iterator itself has just finished doing a head operation on this very URL, so we're repeating work that was just done a moment ago. The second of these is easier to repair. Since the information is available anyway, we'll just have the iterator return it. In scalar context, it will return a URL; in list context, it will return a URL, a hash of header information, and the content, if available:

```
sub traverse {
    ...
    my (%head, $html);
    @head{qw(TYPE LENGTH LAST_MODIFIED EXPIRES SERVER)} = head($url);
    if ($head{TYPE} eq 'text/html') {
      $html = get($url);
      push @queue, $interesting_links->(get_links($url,$html));
    }
    return wantarray ? ($url, \%head, $html) : $url;
    ...
}
```

The bad link detector now becomes:

```
while (my ($url, $head) = NEXTVAL($urls)) {
  print "Bad link to: $url\n" unless $head->{TYPE};
}
```

The site copier is:

```
use File::Basename;
while (my ($url, $head, $content) = NEXTVAL($urls)) {
  next unless $head->{TYPE};
  my $file = $url;
  $file =~ s/^\Q$top//o;
  my $dir = dirname($file);
  system('mkdir', '-p', $dir) == 0 or next;
  open F, ">", $file or next;
  $content = get($url) unless defined $content;
  print F, $content;
}
```

4.7.2 Referring URLs

Including the referring URL is a little trickier, because by the time a URL shows up at the front of the queue, we've long since forgotten where we saw it. The solution is to record the referring URLs in the queue also. Queue members will now be pairs of URLs. We will make the queue into an array of references to two-element arrays:

```
[ URL to investigate,
  URL of the page where we saw it (the 'referrer') ]
```

The traverse function is now:

```
sub traverse {
  my $interesting_links = sub { shift; @_ };
  $interesting_links = shift if ref $_[0] eq 'CODE';
  my @queue = map [$_, 'supplied by user'], @_;
  my %seen;

  return Iterator {
    while (@queue) {
      my ($url, $referrer) = @{shift @queue};
      $url =~ s/#.*$//;
      next if $seen{$url}++;

      my (%head, $html);
      @head{qw(TYPE LENGTH LAST_MODIFIED EXPIRES SERVER)} = head($url);
      if ($head{TYPE} eq 'text/html') {
        my $html = get($url);
        push @queue,
          map [$_, $url],
            $interesting_links->($url, get_links($url, $html));
      }
      return wantarray ? ($url, \%head, $referrer, $html) : $url;
    }
    return;      #exhausted
  }
}
```

Instead of just copying the original URL list into the queue, we now annotate each one with a fake referrer. When we shift an item off the queue, we dismantle it into a URL and a referrer. The URL is treated as before. The referrer is passed to the $interesting_links callback, and each interesting link in the resulting list is annotated with its own referrer, the current URL, before being put into the queue. In list context, we return the referrer of each URL along with the other information about the document.

Our bad link detector is now :

```
my $top = 'http://perl.plover.com/'
my $interesting = sub { shift; grep s/^\Q$top/o, @_ };

my $urls = traverse($interesting, $top);

while (my ($url, $head, $referrer) = NEXTVAL($urls)) {
  next if $head->{TYPE};
  print "Page '$referrer' has a bad link to '$url'\n";
}
```

Or, using igrep in the natural way:

```
my $top = 'http://perl.plover.com/';
my $interesting = sub { shift; grep /^\Q$top/o, @_ };

my $urls = igrep_l { not $_[1]{TYPE} } traverse($interesting, $top);

while (my ($url, $head, $referrer) = NEXTVAL($urls)) {
  print "Page '$referrer' has a bad link to '$url'\n";
}
```

The igrep_l here is a variation on igrep that filters a sequence of list values instead of a sequence of scalar values:

```
sub igrep_l (&$) {
  my ($is_interesting, $it) = @_;
  return Iterator {
    while (my @vals = NEXTVAL($it)) {
      return @vals if $is_interesting->(@vals);
    }
    return;
  }
}
```

Returning to the web spider, we might write:

```
while (my ($url, $head, $referrer) = NEXTVAL($urls)) {
  print "Page '$referrer' has a bad link to '$url'\n";
  print "Edit now? ";
```

```
    my $resp = <>;
    if ($resp =- /^y/i) {
      system $ENV{EDITOR}, url_to_filename($referrer);
    } elsif ($resp =-/^q/i) {
      last;
    }
  }
```

Note that if the user enters quit to exit the loop and go on with the rest of the program, this *doesn't* foreclose the possibility that sometime later, they might continue from where they left off.

We now have a library good enough to check for bad offsite links as well as bad intrasite links:

```
my $top = 'http://perl.plover.com/';
my $interesting = sub { my $ref = shift;
                        $ref =- /^\Q$top/o ? @_ : () };

my $urls = igrep_l { not $_[1]{TYPE} } traverse($interesting, $top);

while (my ($url, $head, $referrer) = NEXTVAL($urls)) {
  ...
}
```

The only thing that has changed is the $interesting callback that determines which links are worth pursuing. Formerly, links were worth pursuing if they *pointed to* a http://perl.plover.com/ page. Now they're worth pursuing as long as they're *referred to* by some http://perl.plover.com/ page. The checker will investigate pages at other sites, but it won't investigate the links on the pages at those sites.

This works well, but there's a more interesting solution available. If we think about how we're using the queue, we can see that the queue itself could be an iterator! We kick it periodically to produce another item for consideration by traverse()'s iterator, and then apply various transformations (s/#.*$//) and filters (next if $seen{$url}++) to the result. This is only going to get more complicated, so we'll probably get a win if we can leverage the tools we've developed for dealing with such structures:

```
sub traverse {
  my $interesting_link;
  $interesting_link = shift if ref $_[0] eq 'CODE';
```

```
  my @queue = map [$_, 'supplied by user'], @_;
  my %seen;
  my $q_it = igrep { ! $seen{$_->[0]}++ }
                 imap { $_->[0] =~ s/#.*$//; $_}
                   Iterator { return shift(@queue) };

  if ($interesting_link) {
    $q_it = igrep {$interesting_link->(@$_)} $q_it;
  }

  return imap {
      my ($url, $referrer) = @$_;
      my (%head, $html);

      @head{qw(TYPE LENGTH LAST_MODIFIED EXPIRES SERVER)} = head($url);
      if ($head{TYPE} eq 'text/html') {
        my $html = get($url);
        push @queue,
          map [$_, $url],
            get_links($url, $html);
      }
      return wantarray ? ($url, \%head, $referrer, $html) : $url;
  } $q_it;
}
```

The innermost iterator, the one that actually accesses the queue, shifts the first item off, as before, and returns it. Applications of imap and igrep trim fragment anchors off the URL and filter out URLs that have been seen already. Inside of the callbacks, `$_->[0]` is the URL and `$_->[1]` is the referrer. `$q_it` is the main queue iterator. NEXTVAL($q_it) will return the next URL/referrer pair that traverse should process.

If the user has supplied an $interesting_link function, we insert it into the queue iterator $q_it, where it will discard uninteresting links. If not, we ignore it completely, rather than inserting the identity function as a placeholder. Another change here is that because $interesting_link is filtering the output of the queue iterator, it processes only one URL at a time, rather than an entire list.

The $interesting_link function will receive the same implicit $_ that the other segments of $q_it do, but for convenience we also pass the URL and referrer via the usual @_ mechanism. Our earlier examples:

```
# Do not pursue links to other sites
my $interesting = sub { shift; grep /^\Q$top/o, @_ };
```

```
# Do not pursue links found on other sites
my $interesting = sub { my $ref = shift;
                        $ref =~ /^\Q$top/o ? @_ : () };
```

now become:

```
# Do not pursue links to other sites
my $interesting = sub { $_[0] =~ /^\Q$top/o };

# Do not pursue links found on other sites
my $interesting = sub { $_[1] =~ /^\Q$top/o };
```

The main `while(@queue) { ... shift @queue .. }` control is replaced with a call to `imap`, which maps the `head`, `get`, and queue updating behavior over `$q_it`.

Note that although we've added some code to support the new style, we've also deleted corresponding old code, so that both versions of the function are about the same length. This is to be expected, since the two functions are doing the same thing.

4.7.3 `robots.txt`

Let's add one more feature, one not supported by `WWW::SimpleRobot`. Some sites don't want to be walked by robots, or want to warn robots away from certain portions of their web space. For example, `/finance/admin/reports/` might actually be a CGI program, and asking for the document at `/finance/admin/reports/2000/12/24/08.html` would actually execute the program, which would compile the appropriate report and return it. Rather than storing 87,000 reports on the disk, on the off-chance that someone might want one, they are generated on demand. This is a good strategy when normal usage patterns are to request only a few reports per day.

A web robot that blunders into this part of the HTML space can waste a lot of network bandwidth and processing time on both ends of the connection, requesting thousands of reports. In the worst case, the report space might be infinite, and the robot will never get out.

To prevent this sort of accident, many sites advertise lists of the parts of their web space that robots should stay away from. Each site stores its robot policy in a file named/`robots.txt`. Good robots respect the policy laid out in this file.[3]

---

3   There are, unfortunately, very few good robots.

Here is a segment of `http://www.pathfinder.com/robots.txt`:

```
# Welcome to Pathfinder's robots.txt
#
...
#
# ------------------------

User-agent: *
Disallow: /cgi-bin/
Disallow: /event.ng/
Disallow: /money/money101/
Disallow: /offers/cp/
Disallow: /FoodWine/images/
# Disallow: /FoodWine/trecipes/
Disallow: /FoodWine/aspen/
...


User-agent: Mozilla
Disallow: /cgi-bin/Money/netc/story.cgi


User-agent: MSIECrawler
Disallow: /
```

Blank lines and lines beginning with # signs are comments and are ignored. User-agent: * marks the beginning of a section that applies to all robots. The Disallow lines are requests that robots not retrieve any documents whose URLs have any of the indicated prefixes. The sections at the bottom labelled Mozilla and MSIECrawler apply only to those browsers; other browsers can ignore them.

The Perl module WWW::RobotRules parses these files and returns an object that can be queried about the status of any URL:

```
my $rules = WWW::RobotRules->('Grasshopper/1.0');
```

Grasshopper/1.0 is the name of our robot. This instructs the WWW::RobotRules object to pay attention to directives addressed to Grasshopper/1.0, and to ignore those addressed to Mozilla, MSIECrawler, and other browsers.

We add a set of rules to the object with the ->parse method. It has two arguments: the contents of the robots.txt file, and the URL at which we found it. We can call ->parse multiple times to add rules files for different sites.

To query the object about a URL, we use $rules->allowed($url). This returns true if the rules allow us to visit the URL, false otherwise.

We will use igrep() to add a filter to the queue iterator $q_it. The filter will check each URL against the currently known set of robot rules and will discard it unless the rules allow it. Additionally, if the URL appears to refer to a site that hasn't been visited yet, the filter will attempt to load the robots.txt file from that site and add it to the current set of rules.

The filter callback will be manufactured by the following function:

```
use WWW::RobotRules;
use URI::URL;

sub make_robot_filter {
  my $agent = shift;
  my %seen_site;
  my $rules = WWW::RobotRules->new($agent);
  return sub {
    my $url = url(shift());
    return 1 unless $url->scheme eq 'http';
    unless ($seen_site{$url->netloc}++) {
      my $robots = $url->clone;
      $robots->path('/robots.txt');
      $robots->frag(undef);
      $rules->parse($robots, get($robots));
    }
    $rules->allowed($url)
  };
}
```

We can't simply use a single, named function, because the robot filter function needs to be able to capture private versions of the variables $rules and %seen_site, and named functions don't capture properly. We could have embedded the robot filter closure as a private function inside of traverse(), but I felt that traverse() was getting a little too long.

We're using the URI::URL module here, which provides convenience methods for parsing and constructing URLs. In the URL http://perl. plover.com/perl.html#search, http is the *scheme*, perl.plover.com is the *netloc*, /perl.html is the *path*, and #search is the *fragment*. scheme, netloc, path, and frag methods retrieve or set these sections of a URL. The clone method copies a URL object and returns a new object.

URLs for schemes other than http are always allowed by the filter, because other schemes don't have any mechanisms analogous to robots.txt. You could make an argument that we should filter out `mailto` URLs and the like, but that would be more appropriately done by a different filter; this one is only about enforcing `robots.txt` rules.

If the URL is from a new site, as recorded in the private `%seen_site` hash, the filter constructs the URL for the `robots.txt` file and attempts to retrieve and parse it. It then consults the rules to decide whether the original URL will be discarded.

```perl
my $ROBOT_NAME = 'Grasshopper/1.0';

sub traverse {
    my $interesting_link;
    $interesting_link = shift if ref $_[0] eq 'CODE';
    my @queue = map [$_, 'supplied by user'], @_;
    my %seen;
    my $robot_filter = make_robot_filter($ROBOT_NAME);
    my $q_it = igrep { ! $seen{$_->[0]}++ && $robot_filter->($_->[0]) }
                 imap { $_->[0] =~ s/#.*$//; $_ }
                   Iterator { return shift(@queue) };

    ...
}
```

4.7.4 Summary

The are only two major features of `WWW::SimpleRobot` that we've omitted. One is depth-first instead of breadth-first searching, which we've already seen is trivial to support; we just change `shift` to `pop` to turn the queue into a stack. With our iterator-structured queue, this is as simple as replacing:

```perl
Iterator { return shift(@queue) };
```

with:

```perl
$depth_first ? Iterator { return   pop(@queue) }
             : Iterator { return shift(@queue) };
```

The other feature is the `depth` feature, which allows the user to tell `WWW::SimpleRobot` how far to pursue chains of links. If `depth` is 5, then the robot will visit all the pages that are reachable by a path of five or fewer links, but no pages that can be reached only by paths of six or more links.

With a sufficiently ingenious $interesting_links callback, we can emulate this feature in the current system. But we might want to add it to the traverse() function for convenience. This is also only a small change: add the link depth of each URL to the queue items. It will then be passed automatically to the $interesting_links callback, which can cut off deep searches by saying:

```
return unless $_->[2] < $max_depth;
```

These are the missing features. On the other hand, Grasshopper supports robots.txt, a major benefit. It also has the feature that it can be incorporated into a larger program as an auxiliary component. WWW::SimpleRobot will tend to take over the behavior of any program it's part of, because once you call the WWW::SimpleRobot::traverse function, you won't get control back until it has traversed the entire site, which could be a very long time. Grasshopper never takes control for longer than it takes to retrieve one page (plus possibly the robots.txt file for a new site), and if the program wants to do something else afterwards, it can pick up where it left off.

I don't want to make too much of the operational differences between these two modules. They both have serious defects stemming from the design of LWP::Simple. But I think there's one other difference that's worth pointing out: Grasshopper requires less than half as much code; one-third if you don't count the code required to support robots.txt handling, which WWW::SimpleRobot doesn't do.

Where did this benefit come from? The queue structure itself didn't gain us much, because WWW::SimpleRobot is using the same queue technique that we are. The object-oriented style of WWW::SimpleRobot imposes some overhead; with the functional approach there are no classes to declare. Some of the extra code in WWW::SimpleRobot is to support diagnostics, which shouldn't count, because I omitted diagnostics from the iterator module. (On the other hand, a 49-line module probably doesn't need many diagnostics.)

Probably the greatest contributor to overhead is option checking. With the functional approach, the module hardly supports any options directly. WWW:SimpleRobot has all its options on the inside. To support a new option, we have to attach it inside the module. Grasshopper is a module that has been turned inside out, all of its useful hooks are exposed to the caller, who can apply whatever options they want afterwards via functions like igrep.

## CHAPTER 5

FROM RECURSION TO ITERATORS

We've already seen that iterators are useful when a source of data is prepared to deliver more data than we want, or when it takes a long time to come up with each data item and we don't want to waste time by computing more of them than we need to.

Both conditions occur frequently in conjunction with recursive functions. Recursive functions are often used for searching large, hierarchical spaces for solutions to some specification. If solutions are common, the space will contain more of them than we want to use; if solutions are rare, they will take a long time to find. In either case, we don't want our program to have to populate an array with all the possible solutions before it can continue, and it is natural to use an iterator.

We saw another reason to get rid of recursion in the web robot example in Chapter 4: Recursive functions naturally perform depth-first searches. When this is inappropriate, as for a web robot, recursion offers no escape. With an iterator solution, we can order the queue any way we like or even reorder it dynamically when new information arrives.

But recursive functions are often easy to write, whereas iterators seemed to require ingenuity. In this chapter, we'll look at techniques for transforming general recursive functions into iterators.

5.1   THE PARTITION PROBLEM REVISITED

As our prototypical example of such a problem, we're going to look at the *partition problem*, which we saw in Chapters 1 and 3. This is a simple but common problem that arises in many contexts, most commonly in optimization and operations research problems.

Recall that in the partition problem, we are given a list of treasures, each with a known value, and a target value, which represents the share of the treasures that we are trying to allocate to someone whom we will call the wizard. The question is whether there is any collection of treasures that will add up to the wizard's share exactly, and if so, which treasures?

One runs into this problem and closely related problems everywhere. For example, I once was talking to Jonathan Hoefler, owner of the Hoefler Type Foundry. Hoefler needed to produce type samples for his catalog. For each font, he needed to find an English word or phrase that would fit in a column *exactly* 3.25 inches wide. He had a dictionary, and could compute a table of the length of each word. For large font sizes, this was enough, because a single word such as "Hieroglyph" or "Cherrypickers" at 48- or 42-point size (respectively) would exactly fill the column; solving the problem for large sizes is a simple matter of scanning the table for the single word closest in size to 3.25 inches. But the same column must accommodate fonts of all sizes, from large to small, and there is no word that is 3.25 inches wide when set in 20-point type. Several words have to be put together to add up to the required length. For 20-point type, the example is "The Defenestration of Prague."[1] (See Figure 5.1.)

In regular text, the typesetter will expand the spaces between words slightly to take up extra space when needed, or will press the words more closely together. In ordinary typesetting, this is acceptable. But in a font specimen catalog, the font designer wants everything to look perfect, and the spacing has to be just so. The designer wants to pick text, which, when spaced in the most natural way, happens to fill the column as exactly as possible.

The problem of finding words to fit as perfectly as possible into the space in a font specimen catalog is very similar to the partition problem we saw in Chapter 3. The differences are that some allowance has to be made in the programming to handle appropriate inter-word space that follows every word but the last, that

---

1   Stay away from the windows if you're ever in Prague; the city is famous for its defenestrations. Probably the most important was on 23 March, 1618, when Bohemian nobles flung two imperial governors out the window into a ditch, touching off the Thirty Years' War. Other notable defenestrations have occurred in 1419 and 1948.

SEL *Avez*

UNE *Remy*

DANS *Pierrot*

ALSACE *Maitresse*

ARIADNE *Hieroglyph*

COLLEGIAN *Cherrypickers*

CONGRESSMEN *Baroque Musicians*

RELINQUISHMENTS *Wilson's Fourteen Points*

AQUEDUCT DESIGNED *The Defenestration of Prague*

HMS BRITANNIA SETS SAIL FOR *Works of the Impressionists 1885–1912*

THE REIGNS OF THE GREAT KINGS *The few remaining examples of Pompeian*

EDWARD VIII, FIRST ROYAL SOVEREIGN *Ceramics from the site date to late in this century*

THE WORKS OF SAMUEL TAYLOR COLERIDGE *An excavation at Herculaneum revealed an odd example*

WILHELM FRIEDMANN BACH WAS FOREMOST AMONG *The copy from type specimen books is not traditionally entertaining*

120 pt
96 pt
84 pt
64 pt
48 pt
42 pt
32 pt
24 pt
20 pt
16 pt
14 pt
12 pt
10 pt
9 pt

MUSE N° I   HTF DIDOT LIGHT ITALIC · XVII

FIGURE 5.1   A page from Hoefler's type specimen catalog.

words may be re-used, and that it is permissible to miss the target value by a small amount.

Another related problem is how to back up your files from your hard disk onto floppy diskettes, using as few diskettes as possible. It is not permitted to split any file across two or more diskettes. This problem was intensely interesting to me in 1986, because the file backup program for my Macintosh did have just these restrictions, and as a penurious college student, I couldn't afford to buy lots of diskettes.

We've seen the code for a recursive version of this problem already. It looks like this:

```perl
sub find_share {
    my ($target, $treasures) = @_;
    return [] if $target == 0;
    return    if $target < 0 || @$treasures == 0;
    my ($first, @rest) = @$treasures;
    my $solution = find_share($target-$first, \@rest);
    return [$first, @$solution] if $solution;
    return         find_share($target      , \@rest);
}
```

This function returns an array of treasures that add up to the target sum, if there is such a solution, and undef if there is no solution.

5.1.1   Finding All Possible Partitions

We could easily modify it to return *all* possible solutions, instead of only one:

CODE LIBRARY
partition-all

```perl
sub partition {
    my ($target, $treasures) = @_;
    return [] if $target == 0;
    return () if $target < 0 || @$treasures == 0;

    my ($first, @rest) = @$treasures;
    my @solutions = partition($target-$first, \@rest);
    return ((map {[$first, @$_]} @solutions),
            partition($target, \@rest));
}
```

Why might we want to do such a thing? Suppose we're trying to allocate shares to several people, say a wizard, a barbarian, and a plumber, out of the same pool of treasure. First we allocate the wizard's share. There might be several ways to do this, so we choose one. Next we want to allocate the barbarian's share, but we find that there's no way to do this. It might be that if we had allocated the wizard's share differently, we wouldn't have gotten into trouble over the barbarian's share later. When we find out that we can't allocate the barbarian's share correctly, we want to *backtrack* and try the wizard's share in a different way.

Here's a particularly simple example: Suppose that there are four treasures worth 1, 2, 3, and 4. The wizard is owed treasures worth 5 gold pieces, and the barbarian is owed 3. If we give treasures 2 and 3 to the wizard, we foreclose the only possible solutions for the barbarian. We need to backtrack and try a different distribution of treasures; in this case we should give treasures 1 and 4 to the wizard, and treasure 3 to the barbarian. (The plumber works for union scale and is paid by the hour.)

The preceding partition function delivers all possible shares for the wizard; so if we try [2,3] and discover that this causes problems later for the barbarian, we can backtrack and try the other solution, [1,4], instead.

But this function has a serious problem that we might have foreseen: Even simple instances of the partition problem often have many different solutions. For example, the call partition(105, [1..20]) generates 15,272 solutions. Since we probably won't need to find all these solutions, we would like to convert this function to an iterator.

In Chapter 4, we saw a technique for doing this. It involved replacing the implicit recursion stack with an explicit queue, and appeared to require ingenuity. But it turns out that this technique always works, and doesn't require much ingenuity at all.

This tactic for turning a recursive function into an iterator is to have the iterator retain an agenda[2] or to-do list of partially-complete partition attempts that it has not yet investigated. Each time we invoke the iterator, it will remove an item from the to-do list and investigate it. If the item represents a solution to the problem, the iterator will return it immediately. If the item requires further investigation, the iterator will investigate it a little further, possibly producing some new partially-investigated items, which it will put onto the to-do list be investigated later, and will continue to look through the agenda for solutions. If the agenda is exhausted before a solution is found, the iterator will report failure. Since the agenda is part of the iterator's state, the iterator can return a solution to its caller, and the agenda state will remain intact until the next time the iterator is called.

We saw several examples of this approach, including the web spider, in Chapter 4.

---

2   *Agenda* is the Latin word for "to-do list."

For this problem, each item in the queue must contain the following information:

- A current target sum

- The *pool* of treasures still available for use

- The *share* containing the treasures already allocated toward the target

In general, with this technique, each agenda item must contain all the information that would have been passed as arguments to the recursive version of the function.

```
sub make_partitioner {
    my ($n, $treasures) = @_;
    my @todo = [$n, $treasures, []];
```

Initially, the queue contains only one item that the iterator must investigate: The target sum is $n, the number originally supplied by the user; the pool contains all the treasures; the share is empty. The iterator will move treasures from the pool to the share, deducting their values from the target, until the target is zero.

```
sub {
  while (@todo) {
    my $cur = pop @todo;
    my ($target, $pool, $share) = @$cur;
```

Here the iterator extracts the tail item from the agenda. This is the "current" item that it must investigate. The iterator extracts the target sum, the available pool of treasures, and the list of treasures already allocated to the share. The presence of this item in the to-do list indicates that if some subset of the treasures in $pool can be made to add up to $target, then those treasures, plus the ones in $share, constitute a solution to the original problem.

The iterator can return under two circumstances. If it finds that the current item represents a solution, it will return the solution immediately. But if the agenda is exhausted before this occurs, then there is nothing left to investigate, there are no more solutions, and the iterator will immediately return failure.

```
if ($target == 0) { return $share }
```

If the target sum is zero, the current share is already a winner. The iterator returns it immediately. Any items that are still uninvestigated remain on the to-do list, awaiting the next call to the iterator.

```
next if $target < 0 || @$pool == 0;
```

On the other hand, if the target is negative, the current item is hopeless, and the iterator should immediately discard it and investigate another item; similarly if the pool of treasures in the current item has been exhausted. The next restarts the while loop from the top, which begins by extracting a new current item from the agenda.

With these simple cases out of the way, the bulk of the code follows:

```
        my ($first, @rest) = @$pool;
        push @todo, [$target-$first, \@rest, [@$share, $first]],
                   [$target       , \@rest,  $share          ];
    }
```

In the typical case, the current item has two sub-items that must be investigated separately: Either the first treasure in the pool is included in the share, and the target is smaller, or it isn't included, and the target is the same. For example, to satisfy (28, [10,18,27], [1]) we can either investigate (18, [18,27], [1,10]) or we can investigate (28, [18,27], [1]).

The iterator appends the two new items to the end of the queue and returns to the top of the while loop to investigate another item.

```
        return undef;
    } # end of anonymous iterator function
} # end of make_partitioner
```

If the to-do list is exhausted, the while loop exits, and the iterator returns undef to indicate failure.

5.1.2 Optimizations

There are a few obvious ways to improve the preceding code. Suppose the current item is [12, [12, ...], [...]]. The function then constructs two new items, [0, [...], [..., 12]] and [12, [...], [...]], and pushes them onto the end of the to-do list. But the first item is obviously a solution (because its target sum is 0), so there's no point in putting it on the end of the queue and working through every other item on the queue looking for a different solution; clearly we should return it right away.

Similarly, if the function constructs an item that is obviously useless, it could throw it away immediately rather than putting it on the queue to be thrown away later:

```
sub make_partitioner {
  my ($n, $treasures) = @_;
  my @todo = [$n, $treasures, []];
  sub {
    while (@todo) {
      my $cur = pop @todo;
      my ($target, $pool, $share) = @$cur;
      if ($target == 0) { return $share }
      next if $target < 0 || @$pool == 0;

      my ($first, @rest) = @$pool;

      push @todo, [$target, \@rest, $share ] if @rest;
      if ($target == $first) {
         return [@$share, $first];
      } elsif ($target > $first && @rest) {
         push @todo, [$target-$first, \@rest, [@$share, $first]],
      }
    }
    return undef;
  } # end of anonymous iterator function
} # end of make_partitioner
```

The first new line here appends to the queue what was previously the second new item. But here it's conditionalized: The item is placed on the queue only if its treasure pool will still contain an unused item. If its pool is empty, then it can't possibly result in a solution, so the function discards it immediately.

The following if-elsif block handles what was previously the first new item. The function is about to put the first treasure into the share and to subtract its size from the target sum. But unlike the previous version of the code, here it puts the new item on the queue only if the size of the first treasure is smaller than the target sum. If the first treasure is equal to the target sum, then the item it is about to put on the queue is actually a solution to the problem, so the iterator returns it immediately instead of queuing it. Conversely, if the first treasure is larger than the target sum, then the item the iterator was about to queue would have had a negative target sum, and would have been discarded the next time it was encountered; instead, the iterator never puts it in the queue at all. The && @rest condition makes sure the iterator doesn't queue an item with a positive target sum and an empty pool, which is guaranteed to fail.

It's tempting to remove the:

```
if ($target == 0) { return $share }
next if $target < 0 || @$pool == 0;
```

lines now. They're much less useful, since the cases they check for are all detected at the bottom of the loop, and items that have $target <= 0 or @$pool == 0 aren't put into the queue to begin with. The only cases they do catch are when such items are placed directly into the queue by the caller of make_partitioner.

There are at least three ways we can deal with this. We can leave the checks in place. We can remove the checks and document the resulting deficiency in the function: If the initial value of $n is 0, the iterator fails to report the empty solution. (Even with the extra checks, the function has a few boundary condition errors of this type. For example, it reports only three of the eight possible solutions to make_partitioner(0, [0,0,0]).) Or we can remove the checks and add preprocessing code that works around the bug. For example:

```
sub make_partitioner {
  my ($n, $treasures) = @_;
  my @todo = $n ? [$n, $treasures, []] : [$n, [], []];
  sub {
    ...
  }
}
```

If make_partitioner sees that we're about to exercise the bug, which occurs only for $n = 0$ and a nonempty treasure pool, it silently adjusts the pool behind the scenes to a case that *will* produce the correct answer.

These three tactics are presented in increasing order of "cleverness." Such cleverness should be used only when necessary, since it requires a corresponding application of cleverness on the part of the maintenance programmer eight weeks later, and such cleverness may not be available.

5.1.3   Variations

The space searched by this function is organized like a tree:

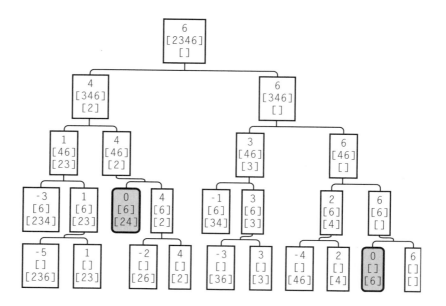

Each node of this tree represents one of the items that the partitioner investigates, showing the target sum, the pool, and the share so far. For example, the root node represents an item with a target sum of 6, a pool containing 2, 3, 4, and 6, and an empty share. The root node is the item that the user of make_partitioner first inserted into the to-do list. Each node has two child nodes, which are the two derived items: one moves the first treasure from pool to share and subtracts it from the target sum, and the other removes the first treasure from the pool and discards it without changing the share or the target sum. The leaf nodes are those from which no further searching is done, because the pool is empty (bottom row) or the target sum is too small.

The partitioner always searches a node before searching its children, so it searches the tree in a generally top-to-bottom order. In fact, the version we saw first searches the nodes in depth-first order, visiting the root node, then the nodes down the leftmost branch, then the three nodes just to the right of the leftmost branch, and so on.

The second version of the partitioner saves time by refusing to investigate items that it sees will be leaves, effectively searching the smaller tree of Figure 5.2 instead.

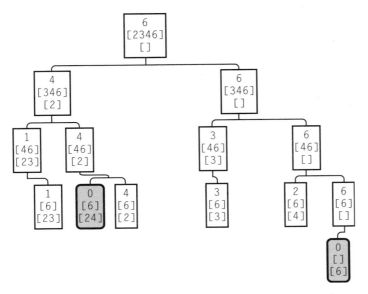

FIGURE 5.2   The search space of `partition(6, [2,3,4,6])`, pruned.

Whether to choose breadth- or depth-first search depends on the nature of the problem. Each has major contraindications. *Depth-first search (DFS)* tends to yield shorter to-do lists. In any depth-first search of a tree, if each node in the tree has no more than n children, and the depth of the tree is d nodes, then the to-do list will contain at most $(n - 1)(d - 1) + 1$ items at any time. For the partition problem, n is 2, and d is no more than the number of items in the original pool. So in depth-first search, the to-do list will never exceed the size of the original pool.

In contrast, *breadth-first search (BFS)* can sometimes lead to enormous to-do lists. The tree is searched top-down, and if all the solutions are in the leaves, each interior tree node must be put on the to-do list and taken off again before the search reaches the leaves where the solutions are. In the unpruned partition search example, shown on page 212, breadth-first search starts with the root node on the agenda, then removes it and replaces it with the two second-level nodes, then removes these and replaces them with the four third-level nodes, then replaces these with the eight fourth-level nodes. These are eventually replaced with the ten fifth-level nodes; if the problem had been bigger, there would have been sixteen fifth-level nodes instead of only ten. Breadth-first search may be contraindicated when the tree branches rapidly or when the solutions are all to be found among the leaves. Depth-first search, which dives straight down to where the solutions are, may be a better choice.

For some applications, however, depth-first search is a loser. Web spidering is one of these. I was once teaching a class in which one of the students decided to write a web spider. The central control of his program was a recursive function, something like this:

```
sub handle_page {
  my $url = shift;
  get the document from the network;
  if (the document is HTML) {
    parse it;
    extract the links;
    for (links) {
      handle_page($_);
    }
  }
}
```

Because the function was recursive, it naturally did a depth-first search on the web space. The result was completely useless. The spider started by reading the initial page and making a list of all the links from that first page. Then it followed the first link on the first page and made a list of all the links on the second page. Then it followed the first link on the second to a third page and made a list of all the links on that page, and so on. The spider went dashing off toward the horizon, never to return, except perhaps by accident. Clearly this wasn't particularly useful. This is the major contraindication for depth-first search: a very large, or infinite search space.

To see a particularly simple example of this, consider a search for strings of the letters A, B, and C that read the same forwards as backwards (see Figure 5.3). We might imagine a search of the space of all strings.

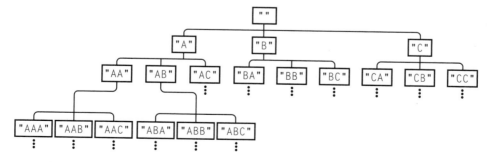

FIGURE 5.3   Searching for palindromes in the space of all strings.

Breadth-first search eventually finds all the desired strings, in order by length: "", "A", "B", "C", "AA", "BB", "CC", "AAA", "ABA", "ACA", "BAB", ...

Depth-first search, however, goes diving down the leftmost branch, finding "", "A", "AA", "AAA", "AAAA"... and never even looking at any branches that contain Bs or Cs.

5.2 HOW TO CONVERT A RECURSIVE FUNCTION TO AN ITERATOR

We've seen several such techniques, including the odometer method and the agenda method. It appears that these took some ingenuity to find. What if they don't happen to work for a particular function, and you don't have enough ingenuity that day to find something that does work?

It turns out that that won't happen, because the agenda method *always* works. This is because we can consider every recursive function to be doing a tree search!

Ordinary function call semantics create a notional tree of function calls. Imagine that we have a node for each time a function is called, and node A is the parent node of B when the function invocation represented by A is responsible for invoking the function represented by B. The root node is the main program, which is started by some agency outside of the program itself. A simple program like this:

```perl
# !/usr/bin/perl

$data = read_the_input();
$result = process_the_data($data);
print_the_output($result);
```

evolves the simple tree depicted below. Such a tree is called a *call tree*:

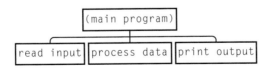

It's important to realize that the call tree has one tree node not for each subroutine, but for each *invocation* of each subroutine (see Figure 5.4).

```perl
sub read_input {
  for (1..8){
```

read_input
read_block(1)
read_block(2)
read_block(3)
...
read_block(8)
read_addendum
read_addendum

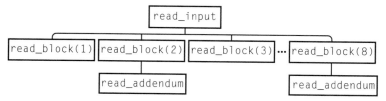

FIGURE 5.4 A more complicated call tree.

```
    read_block($_);
  }
  ...
}

sub read_block {
  my $n = shift;
  if ($n %  2 == 0) { read_addendum() }
  ...
}

sub read_addendum { ... }
```

In the call tree for a recursive function, the node for a subroutine may have children that represent calls to the same subroutine. For a recursive directory tree walker like `walk_tree`, the call tree is exactly the same as the directory tree itself. Figure 5.5 shows a more arbitrary example.

```
sub rec {
  my ($n, $k) = @_;
  print $k x $n, "\n";
  for (1 .. $n-1) {
    rec($n-$_, $_);
  }
}
```

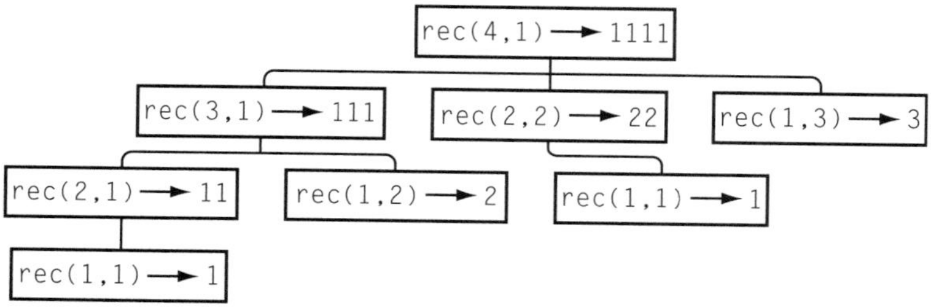

rec(4,1) → 1111
rec(3,1) → 111
rec(2,2) → 22
rec(1,3) → 3
rec(2,1) → 11
rec(1,2) → 2
rec(1,1) → 1
rec(1,1) → 1

FIGURE 5.5 A call tree for a recursive function.

When a recursive function runs, we can imagine that it is performing a depth-first tree search on its own call tree. It starts at the root, which represents the initial invocation of the function. Each time the function calls itself, it is moving down the tree to a child node; when the call returns, it moves back up the parent. When run, the preceding code example does indeed produce the data from the tree nodes of Figure 5.7 in depth-first order:

```
1111
111
11
1
2
22
1
3
```

As a result, every recursive function is really doing a depth-first tree search. Whenever we want to convert a recursive function to an iterator, we can use the agenda method. Each agenda item will represent one call to the recursive function and will contain all the state information that the recursive function needed to do its work: in general, all its private variables, but often, just the arguments. When the iterator removes an item from the agenda, it starts pretending that it's the recursive function, with the arguments described by the item it removed. If the recursive function would have called itself recursively, the iterator puts an item onto the agenda to represent the new arguments.

Let's look at a new example to see how this works. Some time ago, a friend, Jeff Goff, was working on a game and asked how to write a function that would take a positive integer n and produce a list of all the different ways it could be split into smaller integers. For example, if $n = 6$, the desired list is:

```
6
5 1
4 2
4 1 1
3 3
3 2 1
3 1 1 1
2 2 2
2 2 1 1
2 1 1 1 1
1 1 1 1 1 1
```

Rather confusingly, this is called the *partitions of an integer problem*, and each of the rows in the table is a *partition* of the number 6.

First we have to suppose we have a recursive function that solves this problem. The function will take a number and split a chunk off it. For example, it might split 5 into 4 + 1 or 6 into 3 + 3. It will do this in every possible way. Then it will recurse, and split another chunk off the remainder, and so on:

```perl
sub partition {
    print "@_\n";
    my ($n, @parts) = @_;
    for (1 .. $n-1) {
        partition($n-$_, $_, @parts);
    }
}
```

This isn't quite what we want, because it generates some of the partitions more than once. For example, if we start with 6, and split off 2 and then 3, we get 1 + 3 + 2; if we split off 3 first and then 2, we get 1 + 2 + 3, which is the same. The preceding function generates 32 partitions of 6, including 3 + 1 + 1 + 1, 1 + 3 + 1 + 1, 1 + 1 + 3 + 1, and 1 + 1 + 1 + 3, but there are only 11 different partitions.

The trick for eliminating extra items in a listing like this is to adopt a *canonical form* for the output. Where there are several items that are essentially the same, a canonical form is just a convention about which item you'll choose to represent all of them.

This idea should be familiar. Suppose we wanted to read a list of words, and report on the ones that appeared more than once. Easy; just use a hash:

```perl
for (@words) { $seen{$_}++ }
@repeats = grep $seen{$_} > 1, keys %seen;
```

But what if the words are in mixed-case, and the case doesn't matter, so that we want to consider "perl", "Perl", and "PERL" as being the same? There's only one easy way to do it: Use a hash, and store the all-lowercase version of the codes:

```perl
for (@words) { $seen{lc $_}++ }
@repeats = grep $seen{$_} > 1, keys %seen;
```

The all-lowercase version is the canonical form for the words. Words are divided into groups of equivalent words, sometimes called *equivalence classes*, and a representative is chosen from each group. For the group of equivalent words containing:

perl	Perl	pErl	peRl
perL	PErl	PeRl	PerL
pERl	pErL	peRL	PERl
PErL	PeRL	pERL	PERL

we choose "perl" as the canonical representative. Choosing the all-uppercase member of each group would work as well, of course, as would any other method that chooses exactly one representative from every equivalence class. Another familiar example is numerals: We might consider the numerals "0032.50," "32.5," and "325e-01" to be equivalent; when Perl converts these strings to an internal floating-point format, it is converting them to a canonical representation so that equivalent numerals have the same representation.

Returning to our problem of duplicate partitions, it appears that one solution will be to find a canonical form for partitions, and then discard any partitions that aren't already in canonical form. Sometimes it can be difficult to find an appropriate canonical form. But not in the case of the partition problem. The partitions are lists of numbers, and since every list has one and only one sorted version, we'll just say that the sorted version of the list is its canonical form.

We will produce partitions whose elements are in decreasing order, and no others. (We'll say "decreasing" when what we really mean is "nonincreasing," so we say that 5, 5, 4, 3, 3 is a "decreasing" sequence of numbers. This is more convenient than using the clumsy word "nonincreasing" everywhere.[3])

We could refit our subroutine to suppress the printing for the elements that aren't in decreasing order:

```perl
sub partition {
  print "@_\n" if decreasing_order(@_);
  my ($n, @parts) = @_;
  for (1 .. $n-1) {
    partition($n-$_, $_, @parts);
  }
}
```

However, it's more efficient to avoid generating noncanonical partitions in the first place. To generate only those partitions whose members are in decreasing

---

3   If anyone complains about this abuse of terminology, I will just point out that Edsger Dijkstra, a computer scientist famous for precision, did the same thing. See page 3 of *An Introductory Example*, http://www.cs.utexas.edu/users/EWD/ewd10xx/EWD1063.PDF.

order, we just have to take care not to split off any parts that are smaller than a part we have already split off:

```
sub partition {
  print "@_\n";
  my ($largest, @rest) = @_;
  my $min = $rest[0] || 1;
  my $max  = int($largest/2);
  for ($min .. $max) {
    partition($largest-$_, $_, @rest);
  }
}
```

Here instead of splitting off parts with any size at all between 1 and $n-1, we put conditions on the size of the parts we can split off. We know that the arguments to the function are in decreasing order, so that the first argument is the largest part, the next is the next largest (if it exists), and the rest (if there are any) are no bigger than these two. We don't want to split off a part that is smaller than one we split off before, so it is sufficient to make sure the split-off part is at least as large as $rest[0], if it exists; if not, we haven't split anything off yet, so it's okay to split off any amount down to and including 1.

The split-off value must not be larger than half the largest element, or else the part left over after it is subtracted will be smaller than the part that was split off: we would go from partition(5,2) to partition(2,3,2), and then the arguments wouldn't be in decreasing order.

Figure 5.6 shows the call tree for the invocation partition(7).

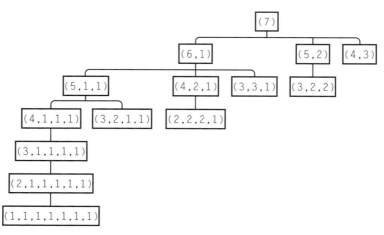

FIGURE 5.6   Partitions of the integer 7, organized as a search space.

The large left branch contains all the partitions that include a part of size 1. The much smaller second branch contains just the partitions whose parts are all at least 2. The third branch contains the single partition, (4, 3), whose parts are all at least 3.

Incidentally, it's quite easy to change the function to solve the slightly different problem of producing the partitions where the parts are all different: Just change $rest[0] to $rest[0]+1 and $largest to ($largest-1).

The function works just fine, producing each partition exactly once, and every partition in decreasing order, so now we'll try to turn it into an iterator.

To do this, we need to identify the state that the function tracks during each invocation. We'll then package up each state into an agenda item. In general, the state might include all of the function's lexical variables, and it has four: @rest, $largest, $min, and $max:

CODE LIBRARY
partition-
iterator-2

```
sub make_partition {
  my $n = shift;
  my @agenda = (([$n,                  # $largest
                 [],                   # \@rest
                 1,                    # $min
                 int($n/2),            # $max
                ]);
  return Iterator {
    while (@agenda) {
      my $item = pop @agenda;
      my ($largest, $rest, $min, $max) = @$item;
      for ($min .. $max) {
        push @agenda, [$largest - $_,           # $largest
                       [$_, @$rest],            # \@rest
                       $_,                      # $min
                       int(($largest - $_)/2),  # $max
                      ];
      }
      return [$largest, @$rest];
    }
    return;
  };
}
```

The code here has a strong resemblance to the original recursive function. We can see the int($largest/2) and the for ($min .. $max) loop lurking inside. But it's rather clumsy. The iterator we've just constructed is more closely analogous to a different version of the recursive function, one that passes all four quantities as arguments:

```
sub partition {
  my ($largest, $rest, $min, $max) = @_;
  for ($min .. $max) {
    partition($largest-$_, [$_, @$rest], $_, int(($largest - $_)/2));
  }
  return [$largest, @$rest];
}
```

This does work, but it's not how we did it originally. Instead, we derived $min and $max from $largest and $rest, and these in turn were derived from @_, which is the true state of the recursive function. Realizing this leads us to a simpler iterator:

CODE LIBRARY
make-partition-1

```
sub make_partition {
  my $n = shift;
  my @agenda = [$n];
  return Iterator {
    while (@agenda) {
      my $item = pop @agenda;
      my ($largest, @rest) = @$item;
      my $min = $rest[0] || 1;
      my $max  = int($largest/2);
      for ($min .. $max) {
        push @agenda, [$largest-$_, $_, @rest];
      }
      return $item;
    }
    return;
  };
}
```

The code here is quite similar to that of the original function.

Now that we have an iterator, we can play around with it. There's no point to the while loop, because it executes at most once, and a while loop that executes at most once is just an if in disguise:

CODE LIBRARY
make-partition-2

```
sub make_partition {
  my $n = shift;
  my @agenda = [$n];
  return Iterator {
    return unless @agenda;
```

```
    my $item = pop @agenda;
    my ($largest, @rest) = @$item;
    my $min = $rest[0] || 1;
    my $max  = int($largest/2);
    for ($min .. $max) {
      push @agenda, [$largest-$_, $_, @rest];
    }
    return $item;
  };
}
```

Because we return each partition immediately, after putting its children onto the agenda, old nodes are never preempted by new ones, regardless of whether we use pop or shift. Consequently this iterator always produces partitions in breadth-first order. The output lists the partitions in increasing order of number of elements:

```
6
5 1
4 2
3 3
4 1 1
3 2 1
2 2 2
3 1 1 1
2 2 1 1
2 1 1 1 1
1 1 1 1 1 1
```

We might prefer it to return the partitions in a different order, say one listing all the partitions with large parts before those with small parts:

```
6
5 1
4 2
4 1 1
3 3
3 2 1
3 1 1 1
2 2 2
2 2 1 1
2 1 1 1 1
1 1 1 1 1 1
```

This is equivalent to sorting the partitions. And we can get this order by sorting the agenda before we process it. To do that, we'll need a comparison function for partitions:

```
# Compare two partitions for preferred order
sub partitions {
  for my $i (0 .. $#$a) {
    my $cmp = $b->[$i] <=> $a->[$i];
    return $cmp if $cmp;
  }
}
```

To compare two partitions, we just scan through them both one element at a time until we find a difference; when we do, that's the answer. Since two partitions must have a difference somewhere before the end of either, we don't have to worry what happens if we fall off the end.[4] Now we make a small change to the iterator:

```
sub make_partition {
  my $n = shift;
  my @agenda = [$n];
  return Iterator {
    return unless @agenda;
    my $item = pop @agenda;
    my ($largest, @rest) = @$item;
    my $min = $rest[0] || 1;
    my $max  = int($largest/2);
    for ($min .. $max) {
      push @agenda, [$largest-$_, $_, @rest];
    }
    @agenda = sort partitions @agenda;
    return $item;
  };
}
```

We sort the agenda into the order we want before extracting items from it. Rather than sorting the entire array so that the item we want is at the end, a computationally cheaper approach is to scan the agenda looking for the maximal element and

---

4   With ordinary lexical sorting, we have to worry about cases where one value is a prefix of another, such as "fan" and "fandango". In such a case, we *do* fall off the end. But that can't happen with partitions, because two such sequences of positive numbers can't possibly add up to the same thing.

then to `splice` it out once we find it. If we plan to do a lot of heuristically-guided searches, we should invest in building a priority-queue structure for the agenda. A priority queue contains a collection of items, each with an associated priority; it efficiently supports the operations of adding a new item to the collection, and of extracting and removing the item with the largest priority.

5.3 A GENERIC SEARCH ITERATOR

You've probably noticed by now that all these agenda-type iterators look more or less the same. We can abstract out the sameness and make a generic tree-search iterator. To do that, we need to describe the tree. The constructor function will receive two arguments: the root node, and a callback function, which, given a node, generates its children in the tree. It will then carry out a tree search, returning the tree nodes one at a time:

CODE LIBRARY
make-dfs-simple

```perl
use Iterator_Utils 'Iterator';

sub make_dfs_search {
  my ($root, $children) = @_;
  my @agenda = $root;
  return Iterator {
    return unless @agenda;
    my $node = pop @agenda;
    push @agenda, $children->($node);
    return $node;
  };
}
```

With this formulation, `make_partition` becomes:

CODE LIBRARY
make-part-dfs-1

```perl
sub make_partition {
  my $n = shift;
  my $root = [$n];
  my $children = sub {
    my ($largest, @rest) = @{shift()};
    my $min = $rest[0] || 1;
    my $max  = int($largest/2);
    map [$largest-$_, $_, @rest], ($min .. $max);
  };
  make_dfs_search($root, $children);
}
```

Factoring make_partition into two parts in this way allows us to re-use the make_dfs_search part.

We might outfit make_dfs_search with a filter that rejects uninteresting items, since this is sure to be a common usage:

```
use Iterator_Utils 'Iterator';

sub make_dfs_search {
  my ($root, $children, $is_interesting) = @_;
  my @agenda = $root;
  return Iterator {
    while (@agenda) {
      my $node = pop @agenda;
      push @agenda, $children->($node);
      return $node if !$is_interesting || $is_interesting->($node);
    }
    return;
  };
}

1;
```

We don't need this for make_partition, since every node represents a correct partition. But we might have needed it if we had used a slightly clumsier implementation of the search:

```
require 'make-dfs-search';

sub make_partition {
  my $n = shift;
  my $root = [$n, 1, []];
```

Here the nodes will have three parts: $n, the part of the original number that we haven't yet split off to any of the parts of the partition; a minimum part size, initially 1; and a list of the parts we've split off so far, initially empty:

```
my $children = sub {
  my ($n, $min, $parts) = @{shift()};
  map [$n-$_, $_, [@$parts, $_]], ($min .. $n);
};
```

For each possible part size $_, from the minimum $min up to the maximum $n, we split off a new part of size $_. To do this, we subtract the size from $n, indicating that we now have to apportion a smaller value among the remaining parts; we adjust the minimum value up to the new part size, so that any future parts are at least that big and therefore the parts will be generated in order of increasing size; and we append the new part to the list of parts.

Note that if $n < $min, there's no possible solution. An example of such a node will occur when we try to partition the number 6 and we first split off parts of sizes 2 and then 3. Then we're stuck: Only 1 remains, but 2, 3, 1 is forbidden because the parts aren't in increasing order.

```
my $is_complete = sub {
  my ($n) = @{shift()};
  $n == 0;
};
```

The partition is complete once we've reduced $n to exactly 0.

By default, make_dfs_search() returns interesting nodes from the agenda. Here the nodes have extraneous information in them in addition to the partitions themselves. So we'll wrap make_dfs_search() in a call to imap() that strips out the extra data, returning only the partition itself:

```
    imap { $_->[2] }
      make_dfs_search($root, $children, $is_complete);
  }
```

We could similarly outfit make_dfs_search() with a callback to evaluate nodes and allow the most valuable ones to be processed first. If we did, we would want to rename it, because it would no longer be doing DFS. To do this properly requires a good priority-queue implementation, which is outside the scope of this chapter. Here's an inefficient implementation:

```
sub make_dfs_value_search {
  my ($root, $children, $is_interesting, $evaluate) = @_;
  $evaluate = memoize($evaluate);
  my @agenda = $root;
  return Iterator {
    while (@agenda) {
      my $best_node_so_far = 0;
      my $best_node_value = $evaluate->($agenda[0]);
      for (0 .. $#agenda) {
        my $val = $evaluate->($agenda[$_]);
        next unless $val > $best_node_value;
        $best_node_value = $val;
        $best_node_so_far = $_;
```

```
        }
        my $node = splice @agenda, $best_node_so_far, 1;
        push @agenda, $children->($node);
        return $node if !$is_interesting || $is_interesting->($node);
      }
      return;
    };
  }
```

The inefficient part is the scan over the entire agenda and the splice. There are a number of ways to speed this up, but if it matters, the priority queue is probably the best approach.

If we did do this, it would include DFS and BFS as easy special cases, since we could use the following two valuations:

```
    {
      my ($d, $b) = (0, 0);
      sub dfs_value { return $d++ }
      sub bfs_value { return $b-- }
    }
```

bfs_value, like a cantankerous grandfather, always reports the value of an old node as being greater than that of the newer nodes; dfs_value, like the staff at *Wired* magazine, does just the opposite.

One possible trap to be aware of when using make_dfs_search() is that "depth first" doesn't necessarily define the search order uniquely. Consider the tree shown here.

DFS says that once we visit a node, we must visit its children before its siblings. But it doesn't say what order the siblings must be visited in. Both of the orders shown in Figure 5.7 are depth-first for this tree.

Since the nodes generated by the call to $children are pushed onto the end of the agenda and then popped off from the end, the items will be processed in the reverse of the order that $children returned them, with the last item in

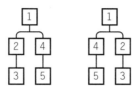

FIGURE 5.7 Two different DFS orders for the same tree.

$children's return list processed immediately. To prevent surprises, we'll make one final change to make_dfs_search:

```
sub make_dfs_search {
  my ($root, $children, $is_interesting) = @_;
  my @agenda = $root;
  return Iterator {
    while (@agenda) {
      my $node = pop @agenda;
      push @agenda, reverse $children->($node);
      return $node if !$is_interesting || $is_interesting->($node);
    }
    return;
  };
}
```

CODE LIBRARY
make-dfs-final

Now branches will be traversed in the order they were generated.

5.4 OTHER GENERAL TECHNIQUES FOR ELIMINATING RECURSION

5.4.1 Tail-Call Elimination

In addition to the agenda technique we looked at in detail in the previous section, there are a few other techniques that are generally useful for turning recursive functions into iterative ones. One of the most useful is *tail-call elimination*.

First, let's consider the implementation of function calls generally. Usually there is a stack. When function B wants to call C, it pushes C's arguments onto this stack and transfers control to C. C then removes the arguments from the stack, does its computations (possibly including other function calls), pushes its intended return value onto the stack, and transfers control back to B. B then pops the return value off the stack and continues. If there are three functions, as follows:

```
sub A { A1; $B = B(...); A2; }
sub B { B1; $C = C(...); B2; return $Bval; }
sub C { C1; return $Cval; }
```

then the sequence of events is:

A: A1;
        Push B's arguments
B: Pop B's arguments
        B1;
        Push C's arguments
C: Pop C's arguments
        C1;
        Push C's return value
B: Pop C's return value
        B2;
        Push B's return value
A: Pop B's return value
        A2;

Now let's suppose that function B is a little simpler, and doesn't do anything except return after it calls C:

```
sub A { A1; $B = B(...); A2; }
sub B { B1; return C(...); }
sub C { C1; return $Cval; }
```

The sequence of events is as before, up to B2, which was eliminated; and then goes like this:

        ...
C: Push C's return value
B: Pop C's return value
        (There is no B2 any more)
        Push B's return value (the same as C's)
A: Pop B's return value
        A2;

All of B's work here is useless. Because B's return value is the same as C's, all B is doing is removing C's return value from the stack and then putting it back again immediately. A common optimization in programming-language implementations is to eliminate the return to B entirely. The final call to C is known as a *tail call*, and the optimization is called *tail-call elimination*. When function B is compiled, the compiler will notice that the call from B to C is a tail call, and will arrange for it to be done in a special way. Normally, B would record its own address so that C would know where to transfer control back to when it was finished. Instead, B erases its own frame from the stack and lets C borrow the return information that B originally got from A. When C returns, it will return directly to A, bypassing B entirely:

```
       . . .
C:     Push C's return value
A:     Pop C's return value (thinking it is B's)
       A2;
```

This is the *tail-call optimization*. Perl could in principle perform this optimization, but as of 5.8.6, it doesn't.

Now let's consider the *greatest common divisor function* or *GCD* function. This function takes two numbers, *m* and *n*, and yields the greatest number *g* such that *g* divides evenly into both *m* and *n*. There is always such a number, since 1 divides evenly into both *m* and *n*, although the GCD is often larger than 1. For example, the GCD of 42 and 360 is 6, and the GCD of 48 and 20 is 4. Probably the most well-known application of the GCD is in putting fractions into lowest terms. Given a fraction, say 42/360, one finds the GCD of the numerator and denominator, in this case 6, and then cancels that factor from the top and bottom of the fraction, giving $42/360 = 7 \cdot 6 / 60 \cdot 6 = 7/60$. Similarly $48/20 = 12 \cdot 4 / 5 \cdot 4 = 12/5$.

There is a simple algorithm for calculating the GCD of two numbers, called *Euclid's algorithm*, which is in fact the oldest surviving nontrivial numeric algorithm. Here it is translated into Perl:

CODE LIBRARY
gcd

```perl
sub gcd {
  my ($m, $n) = @_;
  if ($n == 0) {
    return $m;
  }
  return gcd($n, $m % $n);
}
```

The execution of gcd(48, 20) goes like this:

```
call gcd(48, 20)          # Call A
  call gcd(20, 8)         # Call B
    call gcd(8, 4)        # Call C
      call gcd(4, 0)      # Call D
```

```
            return 4
         return 4
      return 4
   return 4
```

The stack manipulations are as follows:

original
caller: push 48, 20 onto stack
            transfer control to gcd
A: pop 48, 80 from stack

...

C: push 4, 0 onto stack
            transfer control to gcd
D: pop 4, 0 from stack
            push 4 onto stack
            transfer control to gcd
C: pop 4 from stack
            push 4 onto stack
            transfer control to gcd
B: pop 4 from stack
            push 4 onto stack
            transfer control to gcd
A: pop 4 from stack
            push 4 onto stack
            transfer control back to original caller

The tail-call optimization allows call D to return the 4 directly back to the original caller, skipping all the steps at the end.

Since Perl doesn't perform the tail-call optimization automatically, we can help it out. The tail-call optimization would normally replace the current call frame with the one for the function being called. Perl won't do that internally, but since the call frame has nothing in it except a bunch of variable bindings, we can accomplish the same thing by just rebinding the variables to the appropriate variables. "Transfer control to gcd," which normally means "create a new call frame and activate it" just becomes "transfer control back the top of the current function" — in other words, a local goto. Since goto itself is considered naughty, we'll use a loop, which is the same thing:

```
sub gcd {
    my ($m, $n) = @_;
    until ($n == 0) {
```

```
        ($m, $n) = ($n, $m % $n);
    }
    return $m;
}
```

The condition for performing the until loop is the same as the one guarding the recursive call in the old code. The original function made a recursive call unless $n was zero; here it performs the loop body. The body of the loop transforms the arguments $m and $n in the same way that the recursive code in the original function did, replacing $m with $n and $n with $m % $n. Thus the until loop sets up the new values of $m and $n that would have been seen by the recursively-called instance of gcd, and then effectively restarts the function. In the case $n == 0, there is no recursively-called instance, so the function skips that step and returns immediately.

Here's another example: printing the elements of a sorted binary tree in order. The recursive code looks like this:

```perl
sub print_tree {
    my $t = shift;
    return unless $t;   # Null tree
    print_tree($t->left);
    print $t->root, "\n";
    print_tree($t->right);
}
```

Replacing the tail call with a loop yields this version:

```perl
sub print_tree {
    my $t = shift;
    while ($t) {
        print_tree($t->left);
        print $t->root, "\n";
        $t = $t->right;
    }
}
```

Here we've replaced the tail call, print_tree($t->right), with code that modifies $t appropriately, replacing it with $t->right, and then jumps back up to the top of the function. Since print_tree($t->left) isn't a tail call, we can't eliminate it in this way. We'll eliminate it in a different way later on.

A variation of print_tree() handles the empty-tree case before the recursive calls, instead of afterwards, potentially optimizing away many such calls:

```perl
sub print_tree {
  my $t = shift;
  print_tree($t->left) if $t->left;
  print $t->root, "\n";
  print_tree($t->right) if $t->right;
}
```

Eliminating the tail call yields:

```perl
sub print_tree {
  my $t = shift;
  do {
    print_tree($t->left) if $t->left;
    print $t->root, "\n";
    $t = $t->right;
  } while $t;
}
```

SOMEONE ELSE'S PROBLEM

Here's a particularly interesting example, taken from *Mastering Algorithms with Perl*[5]. Given a set of key–value pairs (represented as a hash, of course), it returns the *power set* of that set. This is the set of all hashes that can be obtained from the original hash by deleting zero or more of the pairs.

For example, the power set of {apple => 'red', banana => 'yellow', grape => 'purple'} is:

```
{apple => 'red', banana => 'yellow', grape => 'purple'}
{apple => 'red', banana => 'yellow'}
{apple => 'red',                     grape => 'purple'}
{apple => 'red'}
                {banana => 'yellow', grape => 'purple'}
                {banana => 'yellow'}
                                     {grape => 'purple'}
{}
```

---

5   This example is taken from Orwant, Hietaniemi, and Macdonald, *Mastering Algorithms with Perl*, pp. 237–238. O'Reilly and associates, 1999.

The power set is returned as a hash of hashes. The keys of the return value are unimportant, and the values are the elements of the power set. Here's the code that Hietaniemi presents:

CODE LIBRARY
powerset-0

```
sub powerset_recurse ($;@) {
    my ( $set, $powerset, $keys, $values, $n, $i ) = @_;

    if ( @_ == 1 ) { # Initialize.
        my $null    = { };
        $powerset = { $null, $null };
        $keys     = [ keys   %{ $set } ];
        $values   = [ values %{ $set } ];
        $nmembers = keys %{ $set };   # This many rounds.
        $i        = 0;                # The current round.
    }

    # Ready?
    return $powerset if $i == $nmembers;

    # Remap.

    my @powerkeys   = keys   %{ $powerset };
    my @powervalues = values %{ $powerset };
    my $powern      = @powerkeys;
    my $j;

    for ( $j = 0; $j < $powern; $j++ ) {
        my %subset = ( );

        # Copy the old set to the subset.
        @subset{keys   %{ $powerset->{ $powerkeys [ $j ] } }} =
                values %{ $powerset->{ $powervalues[ $j ] } };

        # Add the new member to the subset.
        $subset{$keys->[ $i ]} = $values->[ $i ];

        # Add the new subset to the powerset.
        $powerset->{ \%subset } = \%subset;
    }

    # Recurse.
```

```
        powerset_recurse( $set, $powerset, $keys, $values, $nmembers, $i+1 );
    }
```

Clearly, the recursive call here is a tail call. Applying the usual tail-call optimization, we can replace the recursive call with a loop. The special case initialization for the last five parameters no longer needs to be a special case; we just take care of the initialization before we enter the loop. The peculiar ($;@) prototype goes away entirely, or maybe becomes ($):

CODE LIBRARY
powerset-1

```
sub powerset_recurse ($) {
  my ( $set ) = @_;
  my $null = { };
  my $powerset  = { $null, $null };
  my $keys      = [ keys   %{ $set } ];
  my $values    = [ values %{ $set } ];
  my $nmembers  = keys %{ $set };    # This many rounds.
  my $i         = 0;                 # The current round.

  until ($i == $nmembers) {

    # Remap.
    my @powerkeys   = keys   %{ $powerset };
    my @powervalues = values %{ $powerset };
    my $powern      = @powerkeys;
    my $j;

    for ( $j = 0; $j < $powern; $j++ ) {
      my %subset = ( );

      # Copy the old set to the subset.
      @subset{keys   %{ $powerset->{ $powerkeys [ $j ] } }} =
            values %{ $powerset->{ $powervalues[ $j ] } };

      # Add the new member to the subset.
      $subset{$keys->[ $i ]} = $values->[ $i ];

      # Add the new subset to the powerset.
      $powerset->{ \%subset } = \%subset;
    }

    $i++;
```

```
      }


      return $powerset;
  }
```

Now we can see that $i, the loop counter variable, just runs from 0 up to
$nmembers-1, so we can rewrite the while loop as a for loop:

```
sub powerset_recurse ($) {
    my ( $set ) = @_;
    my $null = { };
    my $powerset  = { $null, $null };
    my $keys      = [ keys   %{ $set } ];
    my $values    = [ values %{ $set } ];
    my $nmembers = keys %{ $set };      # This many rounds.

    for my $i (0 .. $nmembers-1) {

      #  Remap.
      my @powerkeys   = keys   %{ $powerset };
      my @powervalues = values %{ $powerset };
      my $powern      = @powerkeys;
      my $j;

      for ( $j = 0; $j < $powern; $j++ ) {
          my %subset = ( );

          # Copy the old set to the subset.
          @subset{keys   %{ $powerset->{ $powerkeys  [ $j ] } }} =
                  values %{ $powerset->{ $powervalues[ $j ] } };

          # Add the new member to the subset.
          $subset{$keys->[ $i ]} = $values->[ $i ];

          # Add the new subset to the powerset.
          $powerset->{ \%subset } = \%subset;
      }
    }

    return $powerset;
}
```

CODE LIBRARY
powerset-2

Now that we've done this, it appears that the only purpose of $i is to index @$keys and @$values. Since these are precisely the keys and values of %$set, we can eliminate all three variables in favor of a simple while (each %$set) loop:

```perl
sub powerset_recurse ($) {
    my ( $set ) = @_;
    my $null = { };
    my $powerset = { $null, $null };

    while (my ($key, $value) = each %$set) {

        # Remap.

        my @powerkeys   = keys   %{ $powerset };
        my @powervalues = values %{ $powerset };
        my $powern      = @powerkeys;
        my $j;

        for ( $j = 0; $j < $powern; $j++ ) {
            my %subset = ( );

            # Copy the old set to the subset.
            @subset{keys   %{ $powerset->{ $powerkeys [ $j ] } }} =
                    values %{ $powerset->{ $powervalues[ $j ] } };

            # Add the new member to the subset.
            $subset{$key} = $value;

            # Add the new subset to the powerset.
            $powerset->{ \%subset } = \%subset;
        }
    }

    return $powerset;
}
```

If we're feeling sharp, we might notice the same thing about $j:

```perl
sub powerset_recurse ($) {
    my ( $set ) = @_;
    my $null = { };
```

```
    my $powerset  = { $null, $null };

    while (my ($key, $value) = each %$set) {

        my @newitems;

        while (my ($powerkey, $powervalue) = each %$powerset) {
            my %subset = ( );

            # Copy the old set to the subset.
            @subset{keys   %{ $powerset->{$powerkey} } } =
                    values %{ $powerset->{$powervalue} };

            # Add the new member to the subset.
            $subset{$key} = $value;

            # Prepare to add the new subset to the powerset.
            push @newitems, \%subset;
        }

        $powerset->{ $_ } = $_ for @newitems;

    }

    return $powerset;
}
```

Getting rid of the unnecessary recursion made the state changes of the variables clearer and kicked off a series of simplifications that left the function with about one-third less code.

5.4.2 Creating Tail Calls

Often, a function that doesn't have a tail call can be easily converted into one that does. For example, consider the decimal-to-binary conversion function of Chapter 1:

```
sub binary {
  my ($n) = @_;
  return $n if $n == 0 || $n == 1;
```

```
        my $k = int($n/2);
        my $b = $n % 2;
        my $E = binary($k);
        return $E . $b;
    }
```

Here the recursive call isn't in the tail position. The return value from the recursive call isn't returned directly, but rather is concatenated to $b.

The general technique for converting such a function to one that does a tail call is to add an auxiliary parameter that records the return value so far. When the other parameters indicate that the recursion is complete, the function returns the return-value parameter. Instead of making a recursive call, waiting for the return value, modifying it, and returning the result, the modified version takes the return value parameter, modifies it appropriately, and passes it along. When we apply this idea to the binary() function, we get this:

CODE LIBRARY

binary-1

```
sub binary {
    my ($n, $RETVAL) = @_;
    $RETVAL = "" unless defined $RETVAL;
    my $k = int($n/2);
    my $b = $n % 2;
    $RETVAL = "$b$RETVAL";
    return $RETVAL if $n == 0 || $n == 1;
    binary($k, $RETVAL);
}
```

$RETVAL records the bit sequence computed so far; if unspecified, it defaults to the empty string. On each call, the function appends a new bit to this bit string. If $n is 0 or 1, that's the base case, and the function just returns the bit string; otherwise, it makes a recursive call with the new value of $n and the new bit string.

Applying the tail-call optimization to this version of binary() yields:

CODE LIBRARY

binary-2

```
sub binary {
    my ($n, $RETVAL) = @_;
    $RETVAL = "";
    while (1) {
        my $k = int($n/2);
        my $b = $n % 2;
        $RETVAL = "$b$RETVAL";
        return $RETVAL if $n == 0 || $n == 1;
```

```
      $n = $k;
    }
  }
}
```

and then optimizing away the unnecessary $k:

```
sub binary {
  my ($n, $RETVAL) = @_;
  $RETVAL = "";
  while (1) {
    my $b = $n % 2;
    $RETVAL = "$b$RETVAL";
    return $RETVAL if $n == 0 || $n == 1;
    $n = int($n/2);
  }
}
```

CODE LIBRARY
binary-3

Adding an extra parameter to the factorial() function of Chapter 1 transforms this:

```
sub factorial {
  my ($n) = @_;
  return 1 if $n == 0;
  return factorial($n-1) * $n;
}
```

CODE LIBRARY
factorial-0

into this:

```
sub factorial {
  my ($n, $product) = @_;
  $product = 1 unless defined $product;
  return $product if $n == 0;
  return factorial($n-1, $n * $product);
}
```

CODE LIBRARY
factorial-1

Then we can eliminate the tail call:

```
sub factorial {
  my ($n) = @_;
  my $product = 1;
  until ($n == 0) {
    $product *= $n;
    $n--;
```

CODE LIBRARY
factorial-2

```
      }
      return $product;
  }
```

5.4.3 Explicit Stacks

When we last saw the `print_tree()` example, it looked like this:

```
sub print_tree {
  my $t = shift;
  do {
    print_tree($t->left) if $t->left;
    print $t->root, "\n";
    $t = $t->right;
  } while $t;
}
```

The original function had two recursive calls, one of which was a tail call, and was eliminated in this version. The other call remains.

To get rid of a recursive call embedded in the middle of a function may require heavy machinery. The heaviest machinery is to explicitly simulate the same stack operations that Perl normally performs implicitly on function call and return. Making a recursive call records the function's current state on the stack, and returning from a call pops the stack. The function's current state, as we saw earlier, may in general include all of its local variables and parameters.

The state of `print_tree()` comprises nothing more than $t, the tree argument itself. So our state-saving operation will be simple. We replace the recursive call `print_tree($t->left)` with a stack push:

```
sub print_tree {
  my $t = shift;
  my @STACK;
  do {
    push(@STACK, $t), $t = $t->left if $t->left;
```

and then, in place of the function return, we add a stack pop and a jump back to the line right after the recursive call:

```
RETURN:
    print $t->root, "\n";
```

```
      $t = $t->right;
    } while $t;
    return unless @STACK;
    $t = pop @STACK;
    goto RETURN;
  }
```

(Or, if the stack is empty, then the function returns for real instead of popping.)

One objection to this is likely to be that it uses goto, which people think is naughty. We can get rid of the goto by transforming the code to this:

```
sub print_tree {
  my $t = shift;
  my @STACK;
RIGHT: {
    push(@STACK, $t), $t = $t->left while $t->left;
    do {
      print $t->root, "\n";
      $t = $t->right;
      redo RIGHT if $t;
      return unless @STACK;
      $t = pop @STACK;
    } while 1;
  }
}
```

This is really the same thing, except we have cosmetically disguised the goto as a do-while loop, and turned the old do-while loop into a redo. Loop control statements such as next, last, and redo are no more than gotos in disguise, of course, and in fact so are loops.

ELIMINATING RECURSION FROM fib()

Let's apply the same process to the Fibonacci function:

CODE LIBRARY
fib-0

```
sub fib {
  my $n = shift;
  if ($n < 2) { return $n }
  fib($n-2) + fib($n-1);
}
```

There are no tail calls here. The fib($n-1) looks like it might be, but it isn't, because it's not the very last thing the function does before it returns; the addition is. So we can't use tail-call elimination. Instead, we'll roll out the heavy guns and manage the stack explicitly.

The state tracked by fib() is more complicated than in the print_tree() example. The parameter $n is clearly part of the state, but there is some additional state that isn't so obvious. Since there are two recursive calls to fib, after we return from a recursive call, we have to remember how to pick up where we left off: Were we about to make the second call, or were we about to perform the addition? Moreover, during the second recursive call, the function's state must include the result from the first recursive call.

In difficult cases, the first step in eliminating recursive calls is to make this state explicit. We rewrite fib() as follows:

CODE LIBRARY
fib-1

```
sub fib {
  my $n = shift;
  if ($n < 2) {
    return $n;
  } else {
    my $s1 = fib($n-2);
    my $s2 = fib($n-1);
    return $s1 + $s2;
  }
}
```

The second step is to introduce a loop to separate the initialization of the function from the body:

CODE LIBRARY
fib-2

```
sub fib {
  my $n = shift;
  while (1) {
    if ($n < 2) {
      return $n;
    } else {
      my $s1 = fib($n-2);
      my $s2 = fib($n-1);
      return $s1 + $s2;
    }
  }
}
```

Eventually, we'll have a stack that simulates Perl's call stack; the loop we just introduced is simulating Perl itself.

The third step is to break the body into chunks, each of which contains the code from the end of one recursive call to the beginning of the next. Breaks may occur in the middle of a statement. For example, in my $s1 = fib($n-1), the $n-1 is computed before the call, but the assignment is done after the call, in a separate chunk. Put each chunk in a separate branch of an if-else tree:

CODE LIBRARY
fib-3

```perl
sub fib {
  my $n = shift;
  my ($s1, $s2, $return);
  while (1) {
    if ($n < 2) {
      return $n;
    } else {
      if ($BRANCH == 0) {
        $return = fib($n-2);
      } elsif ($BRANCH == 1) {
        $s1 = $return;
        $return = fib($n-1);
      } elsif ($BRANCH == 2) {
        $s2 = $return;
        $return = $s1 + $s2;
      }
    }
  }
}
```

Because a statement like $s1 = fib($n-2) was split across chunks, I've introduced a temporary value, $return, to hold the return value from fib($n-2) until it can be assigned to $s1. I've also moved the declaration of $s1 and $s2 up to the top of the function. Our new fib() function is effectively simulating the behavior of the old one, and $s1 and $s2 represent information about the function's internal state that are normally traced internally by Perl. They are therefore global to the function itself.

Similarly, $BRANCH will record where in the function we left off to make a recursive call. This is another thing Perl normally tracks internally. Initially, it's 0, indicating that we want to start at the top of the body. When we simulate a return from a recursive call, it will be 1 or 2, telling us to pick up later on in the body where we left off:

CODE LIBRARY
fib-4

```perl
sub fib {
  my $n = shift;
```

```
      my ($s1, $s2, $return);
      my $BRANCH = 0;
      while (1) {
        if ($n < 2) {
          return $n;
        } else {
          if ($BRANCH == 0) {
            $return = fib($n-2);
          } elsif ($BRANCH == 1) {
            $s1 = $return;
            $return = fib($n-1);
          } elsif ($BRANCH == 2) {
            $s2 = $return;
            $return = $s1 + $s2;
          }
        }
      }
    }
```

Returning directly from the middle of the while loop is inappropriate, because
the simulated stack might not be empty. So for step 4, we'll convert any remaining
returns into assignments to $return. Later on in the function, we'll return the
contents of $return if the simulated stack is empty:

```
sub fib {
  my $n = shift;
  my ($s1, $s2, $return);
  my $BRANCH = 0;
  while (1) {
    if ($n < 2) {
      $return = $n;
    } else {
      if ($BRANCH == 0) {
        $return = fib($n-2);
      } elsif ($BRANCH == 1) {
        $s1 = $return;
        $return = fib($n-1);
      } elsif ($BRANCH == 2) {
        $return = $s1 + $s2;
      }
    }
  }
}
```

Step 5 is the important one: Replace all the recursive calls with code that pushes the function state onto the synthetic stack and then transfers control back to the top of the function:

```perl
sub fib {
  my $n = shift;
  my ($s1, $s2, $return);
  my $BRANCH = 0;
  my @STACK;
  while (1) {
    if ($n < 2) {
      $return = $n;
    } else {
      if ($BRANCH == 0) {
        push @STACK, [ $BRANCH, $s1, $s2, $n ];
        $n -= 2;
        $BRANCH = 0;
        next;
      } elsif ($BRANCH == 1) {
        $s1 = $return;
        push @STACK, [ $BRANCH, $s1, $s2, $n ];
        $n -= 1;
        $BRANCH = 0;
        next;
      } elsif ($BRANCH == 2) {
        $s2 = $return;
        $return = $s1 + $s2;
      }
    }
  }
}
```

Since this is important, let's look at one of the calls in detail. When fib() calls fib($n-2), it saves all its state and then transfers control back to the top of fib(), which starts up just as before, but with argument $n-2 instead of $n. The code we put in is doing exactly that. It saves the current state on the stack:

```perl
push @STACK, [ $BRANCH, $s1, $s2, $n ];
```

Then it adjusts the value of the argument from $n to $n-2:

```perl
$n -= 2;
```

Then it adjusts the value of $BRANCH to say that control should continue from the top of the function, not the middle:

```
$BRANCH = 0;
```

This was unnecessary in this case, since $BRANCH was already 0, but I left it in for symmetry with the second branch, where it is needed.

Finally, we transfer control back up to the top:

```
next;
```

We're almost done. We've simulated the recursive calls, and the last thing we need to do is simulate the returns. The function's desired return value is in $return. To simulate a function return, check to see if the synthetic stack is empty. If so, then the function is really returning to its caller, and should just return $return. Otherwise, we pop the saved state off the stack and resume execution where we left off:

```
sub fib {
  my $n = shift;
  my ($s1, $s2, $return);
  my $BRANCH = 0;
  my @STACK;
  while (1) {
    if ($n < 2) {
      $return = $n;
    } else {
      if ($BRANCH == 0) {
        push @STACK, [ $BRANCH, $s1, $s2, $n ];
        $n -= 2;
        $BRANCH = 0;
        next;
      } elsif ($BRANCH == 1) {
        $s1 = $return;
        push @STACK, [ $BRANCH, $s1, $s2, $n ];
        $n -= 1;
        $BRANCH = 0;
        next;
      } elsif ($BRANCH == 2) {
        $s2 = $return;
        $return = $s1 + $s2;
```

```
      }
    }

    return $return unless @STACK;
    ($BRANCH, $s1, $s2, $n) = @{pop @STACK};
    $BRANCH++;
  }
}
```

We increment $BRANCH so that execution will resume with the chunk *following* the one we were in when we made the call.

And amazingly, we're now done. This function does indeed compute Fibonacci numbers.

Because I was showing a general transformation of a recursive into a nonrecursive function, the result has some unnecessary code. For example, I included an unnecessary $BRANCH = 0 line for symmetry. In branch 1, we assign $s1 from $return and then immediately push its value onto the stack; we may as well push $return directly onto the stack without the intervening assignment. In branch 0, we push $s1 into the stack, but its value is always undefined at this point, so we may as well just push 0 directly:

CODE LIBRARY
fib-8

```
sub fib {
  my $n = shift;
  my ($s1, $s2, $return);
  my $BRANCH = 0;
  my @STACK;
  while (1) {
    if ($n < 2) {
      $return = $n;
    } else {
      if ($BRANCH == 0) {
        push @STACK, [ $BRANCH, 0, $s2, $n ];
        $n -= 2;
        next;
      } elsif ($BRANCH == 1) {
        push @STACK, [ $BRANCH, $return, $s2, $n ];
        $n -= 1;
        $BRANCH = 0;
        next;
      } elsif ($BRANCH == 2) {
        $s2 = $return;
```

```
                             $return = $s1 + $s2;
                           }
                        }

             return $return unless @STACK;
             ($BRANCH, $s1, $s2, $n) = @{pop @STACK};
             $BRANCH++;
           }
        }
```

Performing the same sort of eliminations for $s2 as we did for $s1, we discover that $s2 is *entirely unnecessary*. The only place it's used is in branch 2, and it's used immediately after it's assigned:

```
sub fib {
  my $n = shift;
  my ($s1, $return);
  my $BRANCH = 0;
  my @STACK;
  while (1) {
    if ($n < 2) {
      $return = $n;
    } else {
      if ($BRANCH == 0) {
        push @STACK, [ $BRANCH, 0, $n ];
        $n -= 2;
        next;
      } elsif ($BRANCH == 1) {
        push @STACK, [ $BRANCH, $return, $n ];
        $n -= 1;
        $BRANCH = 0;
        next;
      } elsif ($BRANCH == 2) {
        $return += $s1;
      }
    }

    return $return unless @STACK;
    ($BRANCH, $s1, $n) = @{pop @STACK};
    $BRANCH++;
  }
}
```

We might also optimize branch 0 a little. In branch 0, we push the stack, decrement $n by 2, and pass control back to the top of the function. Typically, we then come back immediately and do it again, forming a loop. We can tighten up the loop:

```
sub fib {
  my $n = shift;
  my ($s1, $return);
  my $BRANCH = 0;
  my @STACK;
  while (1) {
    if ($n < 2) {
      $return = $n;
    } else {
      if ($BRANCH == 0) {
        push (@STACK, [ $BRANCH, 0, $n ]), $n -= 2 while $n >= 2;
        $return = $n;
      } elsif ($BRANCH == 1) {
        push @STACK, [ $BRANCH, $return, $n ];
        $n -= 1;
        $BRANCH = 0;
        next;
      } elsif ($BRANCH == 2) {
        $return += $s1;
      }
    }

    return $return unless @STACK;
    ($BRANCH, $s1, $n) = @{pop @STACK};
    $BRANCH++;
  }
}
```

Since that tight loop is more efficient than the large main loop, we'd like to do it as often as possible. As it is, though, we do it only about *n*/2 times. Since it doesn't matter whether fib() makes the fib($n-2) or the fib($n-1) call first, we can exchange the first and second chunks, giving us:

```
sub fib {
  my $n = shift;
  my ($s1, $return);
```

```
        my $BRANCH = 0;
        my @STACK;
        while (1) {
          if ($n < 2) {
            $return = $n;
          } else {
            if ($BRANCH == 0) {
              push (@STACK, [ $BRANCH, 0, $n ]), $n -= 1 while $n >= 2;
              $return = $n;
            } elsif ($BRANCH == 1) {
              push @STACK, [ $BRANCH, $return, $n ];
              $n -= 2;
              $BRANCH = 0;
              next;
            } elsif ($BRANCH == 2) {
              $return += $s1;
            }
          }

          return $return unless @STACK;
          ($BRANCH, $s1, $n) = @{pop @STACK};
          $BRANCH++;
        }
      }
```

This is a little faster than the previous version.

We can also clean up one more line of code by eliminating $BRANCH++ at the bottom. Instead of pushing the old value of $BRANCH onto the stack and then incrementing it after we pop it again, we'll just push the value of $BRANCH that we want to have when we return:

CODE LIBRARY
fib-12

```
sub fib {
  my $n = shift;
  my ($s1, $return);
  my $BRANCH = 0;
  my @STACK;
  while (1) {
    if ($n < 2) {
      $return = $n;
    } else {
      if ($BRANCH == 0) {
```

```
        push (@STACK, [ 1, 0, $n ]), $n -= 1 while $n >= 2;
        $return = $n;
      } elsif ($BRANCH == 1) {
        push @STACK, [ 2, $return, $n ];
        $n -= 2;
        $BRANCH = 0;
        next;
      } elsif ($BRANCH == 2) {
        $return += $s1;
      }
    }


    return $return unless @STACK;
    ($BRANCH, $s1, $n) = @{pop @STACK};
  }
}
```

There are several things we can learn from all of this. Most important, it affords us a detailed look into what is really required to implement recursive calls. Many of the small tweaks and optimizations we applied at the end of the conversion process are directly analogous to optimizations that compilers and interpreters can perform internally.

Recursion elimination may also be useful in reducing the memory footprint of a function. With Perl's built-in recursion, you don't get a choice about what state is saved on the stack: Absolutely everything is saved. Once we have the stack represented explicitly in the program, it may become clear that not everything needs to be saved on every call, and we may be able to reduce stack usage, as we did by eliminating $s2.

Finally, in some cases it will turn out that the iterative version of the code is faster or simpler than the recursive version. In these cases, such as the power set function example, the simplifications suggested by recursion elimination may lead to a cascade of further simplifications.

6

INFINITE STREAMS

There's a special interface that we can put on iterators that makes them easier to deal with in many cases. One drawback of the iterators we've seen so far is that they were difficult or impossible to rewind; once data came out of them, there was no easy way to put it back again. Later on, in Chapter 8, we will want to scan forward in an input stream, looking for a certain pattern; if we don't see it, we might want to rescan the same input, looking for a different pattern. This is inconvenient to do with the iterators of Chapter 4, but the variation in this chapter is just the thing, and we will use it extensively in Chapter 8.

What we need is a data structure more like an array or a list. We can make the iterators look like linked lists, and having done so we get another benefit: We can leverage the enormous amount of knowledge and technique that already exists for dealing with linked lists.

A linked list is a data structure common in most languages, but seldom used in Perl, because Perl's arrays usually serve as a good enough replacement. We'll take a moment to review linked lists.

6.1 LINKED LISTS

A *linked list* is made up of *nodes*; each node has two parts: a *head*, which contains some data, and a *tail*, which contains (a pointer to) another linked list node, or possibly an undefined value, indicating that the current node is the last one in the list:

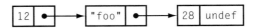

Here's typical Perl code that uses arrays to represent nodes:

```
sub node {
  my ($h, $t) = @_;
  [$h, $t];
}

sub head {
  my ($ls) = @_;
  $ls->[0];
}

sub tail {
  my ($ls) = @_;
  $ls->[1];
}

sub set_head {
  my ($ls, $new_head) = @_;
  $ls->[0] = $new_head;
}

sub set_tail {
  my ($ls, $new_tail) = @_;
  $ls->[1] = $new_tail;
}
```

Linked lists are one of the data structures that's ubiquitous in all low-level programming. They hold a sequence of data, the way an array does, but unlike an array they needn't be allocated all at once. To add a new data item to the front of a linked list, all that's needed is to allocate a new node, store the new data item in the head of the node, and store the address of the old first node into the tail of the new node; none of the data needs to be moved. This is what node() does:

```
$my_list = node($new_data, $my_list);
```

In contrast, inserting a new item at the start of an array requires all the array elements to be moved over one space to make room.

Similarly, it's easy to splice a data item into the middle of a linked list by tweaking the tail of the node immediately before it:

```
sub insert_after {
  my ($node, $new_data) = @_;
  my $new_node = node($new_data, tail($node));
  set_tail($node, $new_node);
}
```

To splice data into the middle of an array requires that all of the following elements in the array be copied to make room, and the entire array may need to be moved if there isn't any extra space at the end for the last item to move into.

Scanning a linked list takes about twice as long as scanning the corresponding array, since you spend as much time following the pointers as you do looking at the data; with the array, there are no pointers. The big advantage of the array over the list is that the array supports fast indexed access. You can get or set array element $a[$n] instantly, regardless of what $n is, but accessing the nth element of a list requires scanning the entire list starting from the head, taking time proportional to n.

6.2 LAZY LINKED LISTS

As you'll recall from Chapter 4, one of the primary reasons for using iterators is to represent lists that might be enormous, or even infinite. Using a linked list as an implementation of an iterator won't work if all the list nodes must be in memory at the same time.

The lazy computation version of the linked list has a series of nodes, just like a regular linked list. And it might end with an undefined value in the tail of the last node, just like a regular linked list. But the tail might instead be an object called a *promise*. The promise is just that: a promise to compute the rest of the list, if necessary. We can represent it as an anonymous function, which, if called, will return the rest of the list nodes. We'll add code to the tail() function so that if it sees it's about to return a promise, it will collect on the promise and return the head node of the resulting list instead. Nobody accessing the list with the head() or tail() functions will be able to tell that anything strange is going on:

```perl
package Stream;
use base Exporter;
@EXPORT_OK = qw(node head tail drop upto upfrom show promise
                filter transform merge list_to_stream cutsort
                iterate_function cut_loops);

%EXPORT_TAGS = ('all' => \@EXPORT_OK);

sub node {
  my ($h, $t) = @_;
  [$h, $t];
}

sub head {
  my ($s) = @_;
  $s->[0];
}

sub tail {
  my ($s) = @_;
  if (is_promise($s->[1])) {
    return $s->[1]->();
  }
  $s->[1];
}

sub is_promise {
  UNIVERSAL::isa($_[0], 'CODE');
}
```

The modified version of the tail() function checks to see if the tail is actually a promise; if so, it invokes the promise function to manufacture the real tail, and returns that. This is sometimes called *forcing* the promise.

If nobody ever tries to look at the promise, then so much the better. The code will never be invoked, and we'll never have to go to the trouble of computing the tail.

We'll call these trick lists *streams*.

As is often the case, the most convenient representation of an empty stream is an undefined value. If we do this, we won't need a special test to see if a stream is empty; a stream value will be true if and only if it's nonempty. This also means that we can create the last node in a stream by calling node($value); the result is a stream node whose head contains $value and whose tail is undefined.

Finally, we'll introduce some syntactic sugar for making promises, as we did for making iterators:

```
sub promise (&) { $_[0] }
```

6.2.1   A Trivial Stream: upto()

To see how this all works, let's look at a trivial stream. Recall the upto() function from Section 4.2.1: Given two numbers, *m* and *n*, it returned an iterator that would return all the numbers between *m* and *n*, inclusive. Here's the linked list version:

```
sub upto_list {
  my ($m, $n) = @_;
  return if $m > $n;
  node($m, upto_list($m+1, $n));
}
```

This might consume a large amount of memory if $n is much larger than $m. Here's the lazy-stream version:

```
sub upto {
  my ($m, $n) = @_;
  return if $m > $n;
  node($m, promise { upto($m+1, $n) } );
}
```

It's almost exactly the same. The only difference is that instead of immediately making a recursive call to construct the tail of the list, it defers the recursive call and manufactures a promise instead. The node it returns has the right value ($m) in the head, but the tail is an IOU. If someone looks at the tail, the tail() function sees the promise and invokes the anonymous promise function, which in turn invokes upto($m+1, $n), which returns another stream node. The new node's head is $m+1 (which is what was wanted) and its tail is another IOU.

If we keep examining the successive tails of the list, we see node after node, as if they had all been constructed in advance. Eventually we get to the end of the list, and $m is larger than $n; in this case when the tail() function invokes the promise, the call to upto() returns an empty stream instead of another node.

If we want an *infinite* sequence of integers, it's even easier: Get rid of the code that terminates the stream:

```
sub upfrom {
  my ($m) = @_;
  node($m, promise { upfrom($m+1) } );
}
```

Let's return to upto(). Notice that although the upto() function was obtained by a trivial transformation from the recursive upto_list() function, it is not itself recursive; it returns immediately. A later call to tail() may call it again, but the new call will again return immediately. Streams are therefore another way of transforming recursive list functions into nonrecursive, iterative functions.

We could perform the transformation in reverse on upfrom() and come up with a recursive list version:

```
sub upfrom_list {
  my ($m) = @_;
  node($m, upfrom_list($m+1) );
}
```

This function does indeed compute an infinite list of integers, taking an infinite amount of time and memory to do so.

6.2.2 Utilities for Streams

The first function you need when you invent a new data structure is a diagnostic function that dumps out the contents of the data structure. Here's a stripped-down version:

```
sub show {
  my $s = shift;
  while ($s) {
```

```
        print head($s), $";
        $s = tail($s);
    }
    print $/;
}
```

If the stream $s is empty, the function exits, printing $/, normally a newline. If not, it prints the head value of $s followed by $" (normally a space), and then sets $s to its tail to repeat the process for the next node.

Since this prints every element of a stream, it's clearly not useful for infinite streams; the while loop will never end. So the version of show() we'll actually use will accept an optional parameter *n*, which limits the number of elements printed. If *n* is specified, show() will print only the first *n* elements:

```
sub show {
  my ($s, $n) = @_;
  while ($s && (! defined $n || $n-- > 0)) {
    print head($s), $";
    $s = tail($s);
  }
  print $/;
}
```

For example:

```
use Stream 'upfrom', 'show';

show(upfrom(7), 10);
```

CODE LIBRARY
show-example-1

This prints:

```
7 8 9 10 11 12 13 14 15 16
```

We can omit the second argument of show(), in which case it will print all the elements of the stream. For an infinite stream like upfrom(7), this takes a long time. For finite streams, there's no problem:

```
use Stream 'upto', 'show';

show(upto(3,6));
```

CODE LIBRARY
show-example-2

The output:

```
3 4 5 6
```

The line $s = tail($s) in show() is a fairly common operation, so we'll introduce an abbreviation:

```
sub drop {
  my $h = head($_[0]);
  $_[0] = tail($_[0]);
  return $h;
}
```

Now we can call drop($s), which is analogous to pop for arrays: It removes the first element from a stream, modifying the stream in place, and returns that element. show() becomes:

```
sub show {
  my ($s, $n) = @_;
  while ($s && (! defined $n || $n-- > 0)) {
    print drop($s), $";
  }
  print $/;
}
```

As with the iterators of Chapter 4, we'll want a few basic utilities such as versions of map and grep for streams. Once again, the analogue of map is simpler:

```
sub transform (&$) {
  my $f = shift;
  my $s = shift;
  return unless $s;
  node($f->(head($s)),
        promise { transform($f, tail($s)) });
}
```

This example is prototypical of functions that operate on streams, so you should examine it closely. It's called in a way that's similar to map():

```
transform {...} $s;
```

For example,

```
my $evens = transform { $_[0] * 2 } upfrom(1);
```

generates an infinite stream of all positive even integers. Or rather, it generates the first node of such a stream, and a promise to generate more, should we try to examine the later elements.

The analog of grep() is only a little more complicated:

```
sub filter (&$) {
  my $f = shift;
  my $s = shift;
  until (! $s || $f->(head($s))) {
    drop($s);
  }
  return if ! $s;
  node(head($s),
       promise { filter($f, tail($s)) });
}
```

filter() scans the elements of $s until either it runs out of nodes (! $s) or the predicate function $f returns true ($f->(head($s))). In the former case, there are no matching elements, so it returns an empty stream; in the latter case, it returns a new stream whose head is the matching element it found and whose tail is a promise to filter the rest of the stream in the same way. It would probably be instructive to compare this with the igrep() function of Section 4.4.2.

Another utility that will be useful is one to iterate a function repeatedly. Given an initial value x and a function f, it produces the (infinite) stream containing x, $f(x), f(f(x)), \ldots$. We could write it this way:

```
sub iterate_function {
  my ($f, $x) = @_;
  node($x, promise { iterate_function($f, $f->($x)) });
}
```

But there's a more interesting and even simpler way to do it that we'll see in Section 6.6.1.

6.3   RECURSIVE STREAMS

The real power of streams arises from the fact that it's possible to define a stream in terms of itself. Let's consider the simplest possible example, a stream that contains an infinite sequence of carrots. Following the upfrom() example of the previous section, we begin like this:

```
sub carrots {
  node('carrot', promise { carrots() });
}
my $carrots = carrots();
```

It's silly to define a function that we're going to call from only one place; we might as well do this:

```
my $carrots = node('carrot', promise { carrots() });
```

except that we now must eliminate the call to carrots() from inside the promise. But that's easy too, because the carrots() and $carrots will have the same value:

```
my $carrots = node('carrot', promise { $carrots });
```

This looks good, but it doesn't quite work, because of an oddity in the Perl semantics. The scope of the my variable $carrots doesn't begin until the *next* statement, and that means that the two mentions of $carrots refer to different variables. The declaration creates a new lexical variable, which is assigned to, but the $carrots on the right-hand side of the assignment is the *global* variable $carrots, not the same as the one we're creating. The line needs a tweak:

```
my $carrots;
$carrots = node('carrot', promise { $carrots });
```

We've now defined $carrots as a stream whose head contains 'carrot' and whose tail is a promise to produce the rest of the stream — which is identical to the entire stream. And it does work:

```
show($carrots, 10);
```

The output:

```
carrot carrot carrot carrot carrot carrot carrot carrot carrot carrot
```

6.3.1 Memoizing Streams

Let's look at an example that's a little less trivial than the one with the carrots: We'll construct a stream of all powers of 2. We could follow the upfrom() pattern:

```
sub pow2_from {
  my $n = shift;
  node($n, promise {pow2_from($n*2)})
}
my $powers_of_2 = pow2_from(1);
```

but again, we can get rid of the special-purpose pow2_from() function in the same way that we did for the carrot stream:

```
my $powers_of_2;
$powers_of_2 =
  node(1, promise { transform {$_[0]*2} $powers_of_2 });
```

This says that the stream of powers of 2 begins with the element 1, and then follows with a copy of itself with every element doubled. The stream itself contains 1, 2, 4, 8, 16, 32, . . . ; the doubled version contains 2, 4, 8, 16, 32, 64, . . . ; and if you append a 1 to the beginning of the doubled stream, you get the original stream back. Unfortunately, a serious and subtle problem arises with this definition. It does produce the correct output:

```
show($powers_of_2, 10);
1 2 4 8 16 32 64 128 256 512
```

But if we instrument the definition, we can see that the transformation subroutine is being called too many times:

```
$powers_of_2 =
  node(1, promise {
          transform {
            warn "Doubling $_[0]\n";
            $_[0]*2
          } $powers_of_2
    });
```

The output is now:

```
1 Doubling 1
2 Doubling 1
Doubling 2
4 Doubling 1
Doubling 2
Doubling 4
8 Doubling 1
Doubling 2
Doubling 4
Doubling 8
16 Doubling 1

...
```

The show() method starts by printing the head of the stream, which is 1. Then it goes to get the tail, using the tail() method:

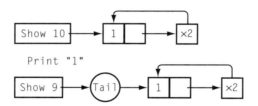

```perl
sub tail {
  my ($s) = @_;
  if (is_promise($s->[1])) {
    return $s->[1]->();
  }
  $s->[1];
}
```

Since the tail is a promise, this forces the promise, which calls transform {...} $powers_of_2. transform() gets the head of $powers_of_2, which is 1, and doubles it, yielding a stream whose head is 2 and whose tail is a promise to double the rest of the elements of $powers_of_2. This stream is the tail of $powers_of_2, and show() prints its head, which is 2.

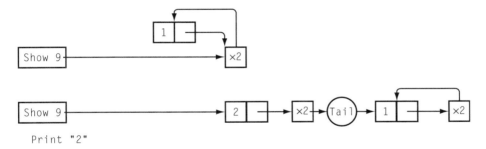

Print "2"

show() now wants to get the tail of the tail. It applies the tail() method to the tail stream. But the tail of the tail is a promise to double the tail of $powers_of_2. This promise is invoked, and the first thing it needs to do is compute the tail of $powers_of_2. This is the key problem, because computing the tail of $powers_of_2 is something we've already done. Nevertheless, the promise is forced a second time, causing another invocation of transform and producing a stream whose head is 2 and whose tail is a promise to double the rest of the elements of $powers_of_2:

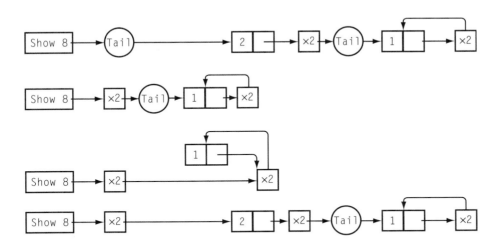

transform doubles the 2 and returns a new stream whose head is 4 and whose tail is (deep breath now) a promise to double the elements of the tail of a stream that was created by doubling the elements of the tail of $powers_of_2, which was itself created by doubling its own tail. show() prints the 4, but when it tries to get the tail of the new stream, it sets off a cascade of called promises, to get the tail of the doubled stream, which itself needs to get the tail of another stream, which is the doubled version of the tail of the main stream:

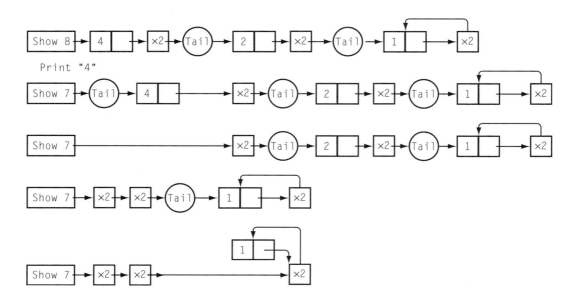

Each element of the stream depends on calculating the tail of the original stream, and every time we look at a new element, we calculate the tail of $powers_of_2, including the act of doubling the first element. We're essentially computing each element from scratch by building it up from 1, and what we should be doing is building each element on the previous element. Our basic problem is that we're forcing the same promises over and over. But by now we have a convenient solution to problems that involve repeating the same work over and over: *memoization*. We should remember the result whenever we force a promise, and then if we need the same result again, instead of calling the promise function, we'll get it from the cache.

There's a really obvious, natural place to cache the result of a promise, too. Since we don't need the promise itself anymore, we can store the result in the tail of the stream — which was where it would have been if we hadn't deferred its computation in the first place.

The change to the code is simple:

```
sub tail {
  my ($s) = @_;
  if (is_promise($s->[1])) {
    $s->[1] = $s->[1]->();
```

```
        }
        $s->[1];
    }
```

If the tail is a promise, we force the promise, and throw away the promise and replace it with the result, which is the real tail. Then we return the real tail. If we try to look at the tail again, the promise will be gone, and we'll see just the correct tail.

With this change, the $powers_of_2 stream is both correct *and* efficient. The instrumented version produces output that looks like this:

```
1 Doubling 1
2 Doubling 2
4 Doubling 4
8 Doubling 8
16 Doubling 16
32 Doubling 32
...
```

6.4 THE HAMMING PROBLEM

As an example of a problem that's easy to solve with streams, we'll turn to an old chestnut of computer science, Hamming's Problem.[1] Hamming's problem asks for a list of the numbers of the form $2^i 3^j 5^k$. The list begins as follows:

```
1 2 3 4 5 6 8 9 10 12 15 16 18 20 24 25 27 30 32 36 40 ...
```

It omits all multiples of 7, 11, 13, 17, and any other primes larger than 5.

The obvious method for generating this list is to try every number starting with 1. Suppose we want to learn whether the number n is on this list. If n is a multiple of 2, 3, or 5, then divide it by 2, 3, or 5 (respectively) until the result is no longer a multiple of 2, 3, or 5. If the final result is 1, then the original number n was a Hamming number. The code might look like this:

```
sub is_hamming {
    my $n = shift;
    $n/=2 while $n%2 == 0;
```

---

[1] Named for Richard W. Hamming, who also invented Hamming codes.

```
    $n/=3 while $n%3 == 0;
    $n/=5 while $n%5 == 0;
    return $n == 1;
}


# Return the first $N hamming numbers
sub hamming {
  my $N = shift;
  my @hamming;
  my $t = 1;
  until (@hamming == $N) {
    push @hamming, $t if is_hamming($t);
    $t++;
  }
  @hamming;
}
```

Unfortunately, this is completely impractical. It starts off well enough. But the example Hamming numbers above are misleading — they're too close together. As you go further out in the list, the Hamming numbers get farther and farther apart. The 2999th Hamming number is 278,628,139,008. Nobody has time to test 278,628,139,008 numbers; even if they did, they would have to test 314,613,072 more before they found the 3000th Hamming number.

But there's a better way to solve the problem. There are four kinds of Hamming numbers: multiples of 2, multiples of 3, multiples of 5, and 1. And moreover, every Hamming number except 1 is either 2, 3, or 5 times some other Hamming number. Suppose we took the Hamming sequence and doubled it, tripled it, and quintupled it:

Hamming:	1	2	3	4	5	6	8	9	10	12	15	16	18	20	...

Doubled:	2	4	6	8	10	12	16	18	20	24	30	32	36	40	...
Tripled:	3	6	9	12	15	18	24	27	30	36	45	48	54	60	...
Quintupled:	5	10	15	20	25	30	40	45	50	60	75	80	90	100	...

and then merged the doubled, tripled, and quintupled sequences in order:

Merged: 2 3 4 5 6 8 9 10 12 15 16 18 20 24 25 27 30 32 36 40 ...

The result would be exactly the Hamming sequence, except for the 1 at the beginning. Except for the merging, this is similar to the way we constructed the sequence of powers of 2 earlier. To do it, we'll need a merging function:

```
sub merge {
   my ($S, $T) = @_;
   return $T unless $S;
   return $S unless $T;
   my ($s, $t) = (head($S), head($T));
   if ($s > $t) {
      node($t, promise {merge(     $S,  tail($T))});
   } elsif ($s < $t) {
      node($s, promise {merge(tail($S),      $T)});
   } else {
      node($s, promise {merge(tail($S), tail($T))});
   }
}
```

This function takes two streams of numbers, $S and $T, which are assumed to be in sorted order, and merges them into a single stream of numbers whose elements are also in sorted order. If either $S or $T is empty, the result of the merge is simply the other stream. (If both are empty, the result is therefore an empty stream.) If neither is empty, the function examines the head elements of $S and $T to decide which one should come out of the merged stream first. It then constructs a stream node whose head is the lesser of the two head elements, and whose tail is a promise to merge the rest of $S and $T in the same way. If the heads of $S and $T are the same number, the duplicate is eliminated in the output.

To avoid cluttering up our code with many calls to transform(), we'll build a utility that multiplies every element of a stream by a constant:

```
use Stream qw(transform promise merge node show);
```

CODE LIBRARY
hamming.pl

```
sub scale {
   my ($s, $c) = @_;
   transform { $_[0]*$c } $s;
}
```

Now we can define a Hamming stream as a stream that begins with 1 and is otherwise identical to the merge of the doubled, tripled, and quintupled versions of itself:

```
my $hamming;
$hamming = node(1,
               promise {
                   merge(scale($hamming, 2),
                   merge(scale($hamming, 3),
                         scale($hamming, 5),
                   ))
               }
           );


show($hamming, 3000);
```

This stream generates 3000 Hamming numbers (up to 278, 942, 752, 080 =
24 · 320 · 5) in about 14 seconds. Its structure looks like this:

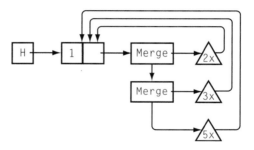

6.5   REGEX STRING GENERATION

Here's a question that comes up fairly often on IRC and in Perl-related newsgroups: Given a regex, how can one generate a list of all the strings matched by
the regex? The problem can be rather difficult to solve. But the solution with
streams is straightforward and compact.

There are a few complications that we should note first. In the presence of
assertions and other oddities, there may not be any string that matches a given
regex. For example, nothing matches the regex /a\bz/, because it requires the
letters a and z to be adjacent, with a zero-length word boundary in between,
and by definition, a word boundary does not occur between two adjacent letters.
Similarly, /a^b/ can't match any string, because the b must occur *at* the beginning
of the string, but the a must occur *before* the beginning of the string.

Also, if our function is going to take a real regex as input, we have to worry about parsing regexes. We'll ignore this part of the problem until Chapter 8, where we'll build a parsing system that plugs into the string generator we'll develop here.

Most of the basic regex features can be reduced to combinations of a few primitive operators. These operators are concatenation, union, and *.[2] We'll review; if *A* and *B* are regexes, then:

- *AB*, the concatenation of *A* and *B*, is a regex that matches any string of the form *ab*, where *a* is a string that matches *A* and *b* is a string that matches *B*.

- *A* | *B*, the union of *A* and *B*, is a regex that matches any string *s* that matches *A* or *B*.

- *A** matches the empty string, or the concatenation of one or more strings that each individually match *A*.

With these operators, and the trivial regexes that match literal strings, we can build most of Perl's other regex operations. For example, /A+/ is the same as /AA*/, and /A?/ is the same as /|A/. Character classes are equivalent to unions; for example, /[abc]/ and /a|b|c/ are equivalent. Similarly /./ is a union of 255 different characters (everything but the newline.)

^ and $ are easier to remove than to add, so we'll include them by default, so that all regexes are implicitly anchored at both ends. Our system will be able to generate the strings that match a regex only if the regex begins with ^ and ends with $. This is really no restriction at all, however. If we want to generate the strings that match /A$/, we can generate the strings that match /^.*A$/ instead; these are exactly the same strings. Similarly the strings that match /^A/ are the same as those that match /^A.*$/ and the strings that match /A/ are the same as those that match /^.*A.*$/. Every regex is therefore equivalent to one that begins with ^ and ends with $.

We'll represent a regex as a (possibly infinite) stream of the strings that it matches. The Regex class will import from Stream:

```
package Regex;
use Stream ':all';
use base 'Exporter';
@EXPORT_OK = qw(literal union concat star plus charclass show
                matches);
```

---

2   The * operator is officially called the *closure operator*, and the set of strings that match /A*/ is the *closure* of the set of those that match /A/. This has nothing to do with anonymous function closures.

```
┌─────┬───────┐
│ foo │ undef │
└─────┴───────┘
```

FIGURE 6.1   The stream generated by `literal()`.

Literal regexes are trivial. The corresponding stream has only one element, as shown in Figure 6.1:

```
sub literal {
  my $string = shift;
  node($string, undef);
}
show(literal("foo"));
foo
```

Union is almost as easy. We have some streams, and we want to merge all their elements into a single stream. We can't append the streams beginning-to-end as we would with ordinary lists, because the streams might not have ends. Instead, we'll interleave the elements. Here's a demonstration function that mingles two streams this way:

```
sub mingle2 {
  my ($s, $t) = @_;
  return $t unless $s;
  return $s unless $t;
  node(head($s),
      node(head($t),
              promise { mingle2(tail($s),
                                    tail($t))
                      }
      ));
}
```

Later on it will be more convenient if we have a more general version that can mingle any number of streams:

```
sub union {
  my ($h, @s) = grep $_, @_;
  return unless $h;
  return $h unless @s;
  node(head($h),
      promise {
```

```
        union(@s, tail($h));
    });
}
```

The function starts by throwing out any empty streams from the argument list. Empty streams won't contribute anything to the output, so we can discard them. If all the input streams are empty, union() returns an empty stream. If there is only one nonempty input stream, union() returns it unchanged. Otherwise, the function does the mingle: The first element of the first stream is at the head of the result, and the rest of the result is obtained by mingling the rest of the streams with the rest of the first stream. The key point here is that the function puts tail($h) at the *end* of the argument list in the recursive call, so that a different stream gets assigned to $h next time around. This will ensure that all the streams get cycled through the $h position in turn. The behavior is depicted in Figure 6.2. Here's a simple example:

```
# generate infinite stream ($k:1, $k:2, $k:3, ...)
sub constant {
  my $k = shift;
  my $i = shift || 1;
  my $s = node("$k:$i", promise { constant($k, $i+1) });
}

my $fish = constant('fish');
show($fish, 3);
fish:1 fish:2 fish:3

my $soup = union($fish, constant('dog'), constant('carrot'));

show($soup, 10);
fish:1 dog:1 carrot:1 fish:2 dog:2 carrot:2 fish:3 dog:3 carrot:3 fish:4
```

Now we'll do concatenation. If either of regexes S or T never matches anything, then ST also can't match anything. Otherwise, S is matched by some list of strings, and this list has a head s and a tail s_{tail}; similarly T is matched by some other list of strings with head t and tail t_{tail}. What strings are matched by ST? We can choose one string that matches S and one that matches T, and their concatenation is one of the strings that matches ST. Since we split each of the two lists into two parts, we have four choices for how to construct a string that matches ST:

1. st matches ST

2. s followed by any string from t_{tail} matches ST

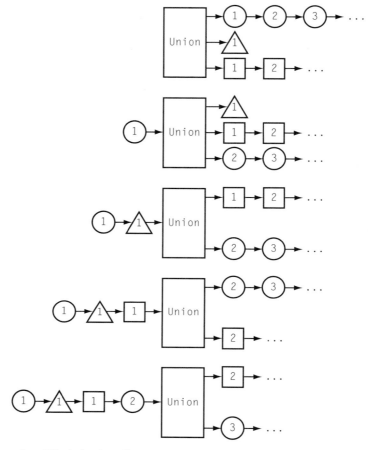

FIGURE 6.2   The behavior of union().

3.   Any string from s_{tail} followed by t matches ST

4.   Any string from s_{tail} followed by any string from t_{tail} matches ST

Notationally, we write:

$$(s \mid s_{\text{tail}}).(t \mid t_{\text{tail}}) = s.t \mid s.t_{\text{tail}} \mid s_{\text{tail}}.t \mid s_{\text{tail}}.t_{\text{tail}}$$

The first of these contains only one string. The middle two are simple transformations of the tails of S and T. The last one is a recursive call to the concat() function itself. So the code is simple:

```
sub concat {
  my ($S, $T) = @_;
```

```
    return unless $S && $T;

  my ($s, $t) = (head($S), head($T));

  node("$s$t", promise {
    union(postcat(tail($S), $t),
          precat(tail($T), $s),
          concat(tail($S), tail($T)),
      )
  });
}
```

precat() and postcat() are simple utility functions that concatenate a string to the beginning or end of every element of a stream:

```
sub precat {
  my ($s, $c) = @_;
  transform {"$c$_[0]"} $s;
}

sub postcat {
  my ($s, $c) = @_;
  transform {"$_[0]$c"} $s;
}
```

An example:

```
# I'm /^(a|b)(c|d)$/
my $z = concat(union(literal("a"), literal("b")),
               union(literal("c"), literal("d")),
              );
show($z);
ac bc ad bd
```

The behavior of concat() is illustrated in Figure 6.3.

Now that we have concat(), the * operator is trivial, because of this simple identity:

```
s* = "" | ss*
```

That is, *s** is either the empty string or else something that matches *s* followed by something else that matches *s**. We want to generate *s**; let's call this result *r*.

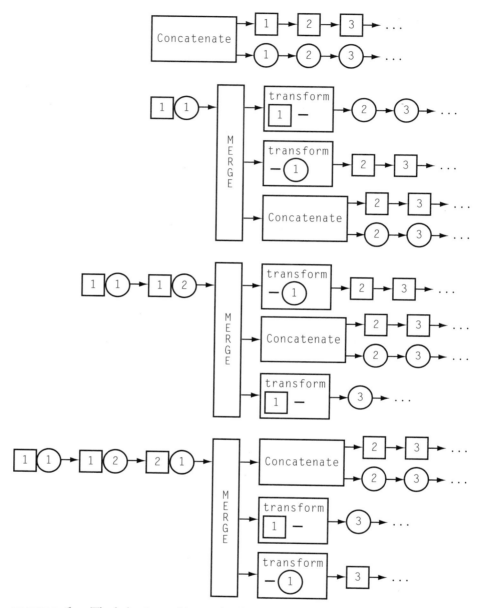

FIGURE 6.3 The behavior and internals of concat().

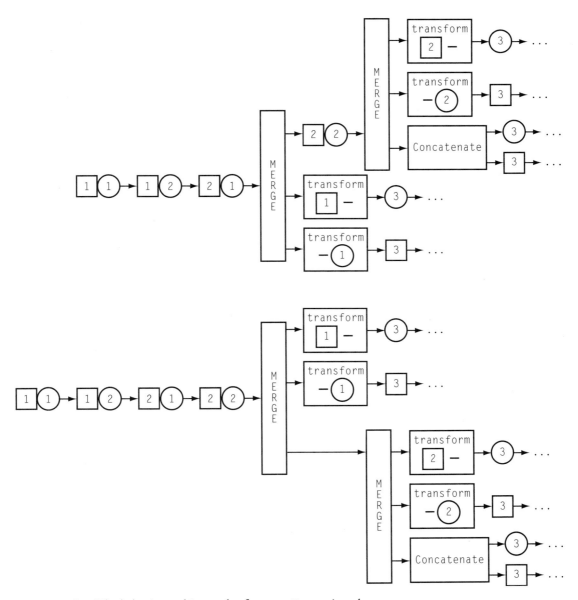

FIGURE 6.3 The behavior and internals of concat(), continued.

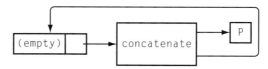

FIGURE 6.4   The behavior and internals of star().

Then:

```
r = "" | sr
```

Now we can use the wonderful recursive definition capability of streams:

```
sub star {
  my $s = shift;
  my $r;
  $r = node("", promise { concat($s, $r) });
}
```

$r, the result, will be equal to the * of $s. It begins with the empty string, and the rest of $r is formed by concatenating something in $s with $r itself: Figure 6.4 shows how it works; here's an example:

```
# I'm /^(HONK)*$/
show(star(literal('HONK')), 6)
 HONK  HONKHONK  HONKHONKHONK  HONKHONKHONKHONK  HONKHONKHONKHONKHONK
```

The empty string is hiding at the beginning of that output line. Let's use a modified version of show() to make it visible:

```
sub show {
  my ($s, $n) = @_;
  while ($s && (! defined $n || $n-- > 0)) {
    print qq{"}, drop($s), qq{"\n};
  }
  print "\n";
}
```

Now the output is:

```
""

"HONK"
```

```
"HONKHONK"
"HONKHONKHONK"
"HONKHONKHONKHONK"
"HONKHONKHONKHONKHONK"
```

We can throw in a couple of extra utilities if we like:

```
# charclass('abc') = /^[abc]$/
sub charclass {
  my ($s, $class) = @_;
  union(map literal($_), split(//, $class));
}


# plus($s) = /^s+$/
sub plus {
  my $s = shift;
  concat($s, star($s));
}
```

And now a demonstration:

```
use Regex qw(concat star literal show);
# I represent /^ab*$/
my $regex1 = concat(     literal("a"),
                    star(literal("b"))
                  );
show($regex1, 10);
```

The output is:

```
"a"
"ab"
"abb"
"abbb"
"abbbb"
"abbbbb"
"abbbbbb"
"abbbbbbb"
"abbbbbbbb"
"abbbbbbbbb"
```

Let's try something a little more interesting:

```
# I represent /^(aa|b)*$/
my $regex2 = star(union(literal("aa"),
                        literal("b"),
                       ));
show($regex2, 16);
```

The output is:

```
""
"aa"
"b"
"aaaa"
"baa"
"aab"
"bb"
"aaaaaa"
"baaaa"
"aabaa"
"bbaa"
"aaaab"
"baab"
"aabb"
"bbb"
"aaaaaaaa"
...
```

One last example:

```
# I represent /^(ab+|c)*$/
my $regex3 = star(union(concat(    literal("a"),
                               plus(literal("b")))),
                        literal("c")
                       ));
show($regex3, 20);
```

The output is:

```
""
"ab"
```

```
"c"
"abab"
"cab"
"abb"
"abc"
"abbab"
"abbb"
"ababab"
"cc"
"abbbb"
"abcab"
"abbc"
"abbbbb"
"ababb"
"abbbab"
"abbbbbb"
"ababc"
"cabab"
...
```

6.5.1 Generating Strings in Order

It's hard to be sure, from looking at this last output, that it really is generating all the strings that will match /^(ab+|c)*/. Will cccc really show up? Where's cabb? We might prefer the strings to come out in some order, say in order by length. It happens that this is also rather easy to do. Let's say that a stream of strings is "ordered" if no string comes out after a longer string has come out, and see what will be necessary to generate ordered streams.

The streams produced by literal() contain only one string, so those streams are already ordered, because one item can't be disordered.[3] concat(), it turns out, is already generating its elements in order as best it can. The business end is:

```
my ($s, $t) = (head($S), head($T));

node("$s$t", promise {
    union( precat(tail($T), $s),
```

---

3 Perhaps I should have included a longer explanation of this point, since I seem to be the only person in the world who is bothered by the phrase "Your call will be answered in the order it was received." It always seems to me that my call could not have an order.

```
                    postcat(tail($S), $t),
                    concat(tail($S), tail($T)),
                  )
        });
```

Let's suppose that the inputs, $S and $T, are already ordered. In that case, $s is one of the shortest elements of $S, and $t is one of the shortest elements of $T. st therefore can't be any longer than any other concatenation of elements from $S and $T, so it's all right that it will come out first. As long as the output of the union() call is ordered, the output of concat() will be too.

union() does need some rewriting. It currently cycles through its input streams in sequence. We need to modify it to find the input stream whose head element is shortest and to process that stream first:

```
sub union {
  my (@s) = grep $_, @_;
  return unless @s;
  return $s[0] if @s == 1;
  my $si = index_of_shortest(@s);
  node(head($s[$si]),
            promise {
              union(map $_ == $si ? tail($s[$_]) : $s[$_],
                        0 .. $#s);
            });
}
```

The first two returns correspond to the early returns in the original version of union(), handling the special cases of zero or one argument stream. If there's more than one argument stream, the function calls index_of_shortest(), which will examine the heads of the streams to find the shortest string. index_of_shortest() returns $si, the index number of the stream with the shortest head string. union() pulls off this string and puts it first in the output, then calls itself recursively to process the remaining data. index_of_shortest() is quite ordinary:

```
sub index_of_shortest {
  my @s = @_;
  my $minlen = length(head($s[0]));
  my $si = 0;
  for (1 .. $#s) {
    my $h = head($s[$_]);
    if (length($h) < $minlen) {
```

```
      $minlen = length($h);
      $si = $_;
    }
  }
  $si;
}
```

The last function to take care of is star(). But star(), it turns out, has taken care of itself:

```
sub star {
  my $s = shift;
  my $r;
  $r = node("", promise { concat($s, $r) });
}
```

The empty string, which comes out first, is certainly no longer than any other element in $r's output. And since we already know that concat produces an ordered stream, we're finished.

That last example again:

```
# I represent /^(ab+|c)*$/
my $regex3 = star(union(concat(      literal("a"),
                                plus(literal("b")))),
                      literal("c")
                  ));
$regex3->show(30);
```

And the now-sorted output:

```
""
"c"
"ab"
"cc"
"abb"
"cab"
"ccc"
"abc"
"abbb"
"cabb"
"ccab"
```

```
"cccc"
"cabc"
"abbc"
"abab"
"abcc"
"abbbb"
"cabbb"
"ccabb"
"cccab"
"ccccc"
"ccabc"
"cabbc"
"cabab"
"cabcc"
"abbbc"
"ababb"
"abcab"
"abccc"
"ababc"
...
```

Aha, cccc and cabb *were* produced, after all.

6.5.2 Regex Matching

At this point we've built a system that can serve as a regex engine: Given a regex and a target string, it can decide whether the string matches the regex. A regex is a representation of a set of strings that supports operations like concatenation, union, and closure. Our regex-string-streams fit the bill. Here's a regex-matching engine:

```
sub matches {
  my ($string, $regex) = @_;
  while ($regex) {
    my $s = drop($regex);
    return 1 if $s eq $string;
    return 0 if length($s) > length($string);
  }
  return 0;
}
```

The $regex argument here is one of our regex streams. (After we attach the parser from Chapter 8, we'll be able to pass in a regex in standard Perl notation instead.) The function looks at the shortest string matched by the regex; if it's the target string, then we have a match. If it's longer than the target string, then the match fails, because every other string in the regex is also too long. Otherwise, the function throws away the head and repeats with the next string. If the regex runs out of strings, the match fails.

This is just an example; it should be emphasized that, in general, streams are *not* a good way to do regex matching. To determine whether a string matches /^[ab]*$/, this method generates all possible strings of a's and b's and checks each one to see if it is the target string. This is obviously a silly way to do it. The amount of time it takes is exponential in the length of the target string; an obviously better algorithm is to scan the target string left to right, checking each character to make sure it is an a or a b, which requires only linear time.

Nevertheless, in some ways this implementation of regex matching is actually *more* powerful than Perl's built-in matcher. For example, there's no convenient way to ask Perl if a string contains a balanced arrangement of parentheses. (Starting in 5.005, you can use the (?{...}) operator, but it's nasty.[4]) But our "regexes" are just lists of strings, and the lists can contain whatever we want. If we want a regex that represents balanced arrangements of parentheses, all we need to do is construct a stream that contains the strings we want.

Let's say that we would like to match strings of a, (, and) in which the parentheses are balanced. That is, we'd like to match the following strings:

```
""
"a"
"aa"
"()"
"aaa"
"a()"
"()a"
"(a)"
"aaaa"
"aa()"
"a()a"
"()aa"
"a(a)"
"(a)a"
```

---

4   /^(?{local$d=0})(?:\((?{$d++})|\)(?{$d--})(?(?{$d<0})(?!))|(?>[^()]*))*(?(?{$d!=0})(?!))$/.

```
"(aa)"
"()()"
"(())"
"aaaaa"
...
```

Suppose *s* is a regex that matches the expressions that are legal between parentheses. Then a sequence of these expressions with properly balanced parentheses is one of the following:

- the empty string, or

- something that matches *s*, or

- (*b*), where *b* is some balanced string, or

- a balanced string followed by one of the above

Then we can almost read off the definition:

```
sub bal {
  my $contents = shift;
  my $bal;
  $bal = node("", promise {
    concat($bal,
           union($contents,
                 transform {"($_[0])"} $bal,
                 )
          )
       });
}
```

And now the question "Does $s contain a balanced sequence of parentheses, a's, and b's" is answered by:

```
if (match($s, bal(charclass('ab')))) {
  ...
}
```

6.5.3 Cutsorting

The regex-string generator suggests another problem that sometimes comes up. It presently generates strings in order by length, but strings of the same length

come out in no particular order, as in the following column on the left. Suppose
we want the strings of the same length to come out in sorted order, as in the
column on the right:

""	""
"c"	"c"
"ab"	"ab"
"cc"	"cc"
"abb"	"abb"
"cab"	"abc"
"ccc"	"cab"
"abc"	"ccc"
"abbb"	"abab"
"cabb"	"abbb"
"ccab"	"abbc"
"cccc"	"abcc"
"cabc"	"cabb"
"abbc"	"cabc"
"abab"	"ccab"
"abcc"	"cccc"
"abbbb"	"ababb"
"cabbb"	"ababc"
"ccabb"	"abbab"
"cccab"	"abbbb"
"ccccc"	"abbbc"
"ccabc"	"abbcc"
"cabbc"	"abcab"
"cabab"	"abccc"
"cabcc"	"cabab"
"abbbc"	"cabbb"
"ababb"	"cabbc"
"abcab"	"cabcc"
"abccc"	"ccabb"
"ababc"	"ccabc"
"abbab"	"cccab"
"abbcc"	"ccccc"
. . .	. . .

We should note first that although it's reasonable to ask for the strings sorted into
groups by length and then lexicographically within each group, it's *not* reasonable
to ask for *all* the strings to be sorted lexicographically. This is for two reasons.

First, even if we could do it, the result wouldn't be useful:

```
""
"ab"
"abab"
"ababab"
"abababab"
"ababababab"
"abababababab"
. . .
```

None of the strings that contains c would ever appear, because there would always be some other string that was lexicographically earlier that we had not yet emitted. But the second reason is that in general it's not possible to sort an infinite stream at all. In this example, the first string to be emitted is clearly the empty string. The second string out should be "ab". But the sorting process can't know that. It can't emit the "ab" unless it's sure that no other string would come between "" and "ab". It doesn't know that the one-billionth string in the input won't be "a". So it can never emit the "ab", because no matter how long it waits to do so, there's always a possibility that "a" will be right around the corner.

But if we know in advance that the input stream will be sorted by string length, and that there will be only a finite number of strings of each length, then we certainly can sort each group of strings of the same length.

In general, the problem with sorting is that, given some string we want to emit, we don't know whether it's safe to emit it without examining the entire rest of the stream, which might be infinite. But suppose we could supply a function that would say whether or not it was safe. If the input stream is already sorted by length, then at the moment we see the first length–3 string in the input, we know it's safe to emit all the length–2 strings that we've seen already; the function could tell us this. The function effectively "cuts" the stream off, saying that enough of the input has been examined to determine the next part of the output, and that the cut-off part of the input doesn't matter yet.

This idea is the basis of *cutsorting*. The cutting function will get two arguments: the element we would like to emit, which should be the smallest one we have seen so far, and the current element of the input stream. The cutting function will return true if we have seen enough of the input stream to be sure that it's safe to emit the element we want to, and false if the rest of the input stream might contain an element that precedes the one we want the function to emit.

For sorting by length, the cutting function is trivial:

```
sub cut_bylen {
  my ($a, $b) = @_;
```

```
      # It's OK to emit item $a if the next item in the stream is $b
      length($a) < length($b);
    }
```

Since the cutsorter may need to emit several items at a time, we'll build a utility function for doing that:

```
    sub list_to_stream {
      my $node = pop;
      while (@_) {
        $node = node(pop, $node);
      }
      $node;
    }
```

list_to_stream(h1, h2, ... t) returns a stream that starts with h1, h2, ... and whose final tail is t. t may be another (possibly empty) stream or a promise. list_to_stream(h, t) is equivalent to node(h, t).

The cutsorting function gets four arguments: $s, the stream to sort; $cmp, the sorting comparator (analogous to the comparator function of sort()); and $cut, the cutting test. It also gets an auxiliary argument @pending that we'll see in a moment:

```
    sub insert (\@$$);

    sub cutsort {
      my ($s, $cmp, $cut, @pending) = @_;
      my @emit;

      while ($s) {
        while (@pending && $cut->($pending[0], head($s))) {
          push @emit, shift @pending;
        }

        if (@emit) {
          return list_to_stream(@emit,
                                promise { cutsort($s, $cmp, $cut, @pending) });
        } else {
          insert(@pending, head($s), $cmp);
          $s = tail($s);
        }
      }
```

```
        return list_to_stream(@pending, undef);
    }
```

The idea of the cutsorter is to scan through the input stream, maintaining a buffer of items that have been seen so far but not yet emitted; this is @pending. @pending is kept in sorted order, so that if any element is ready to come out, it will be $pending[0]. The while (@pending...) loop checks to see if any elements can be emitted; if so, the emittable elements are transferred to @emit. If there are any such elements, they are emitted immediately: cutsort() returns a stream that begins with these elements and that ends with a promise to cutsort the remaining elements of $s. Any unemitted elements of @pending are passed along in the promise to be emitted later.

If no elements are ready for emission, the function discards the head element of the stream after inserting it into @pending. insert() takes care of inserting head($s) into the appropriate place in @pending so that @pending is always properly sorted.

If $s is exhausted, all items in @pending immediately become emittable, so the function calls list_to_stream() to build a finite stream that contains them and that ends with an empty tail.

Now if we'd like to generate strings in sorted order, we call cutsort() like this:

```
my $sorted =
  cutsort($regex3,
          sub { $_[0] cmp $_[1] },  # comparator
          \&cut_bylen              # cutting function
          );
```

The one piece of this that we haven't seen is insert(), which inserts an element into the appropriate place in a sorted array:

```
sub insert (\@$$) {
  my ($a, $e, $cmp) = @_;
  my ($lo, $hi) = (0, scalar(@$a));
  while ($lo < $hi) {
    my $med = int(($lo + $hi) / 2);
    my $d = $cmp->($a->[$med], $e);
    if ($d <= 0) {
      $lo = $med+1;
    } else {
      $hi = $med;
```

```
          }
        }
        splice(@$a, $lo, 0, $e);
      }
```

This is straightforward, except possibly for the prototype. The prototype (\@$$) says that insert() will be called with three arguments: an array and two scalars, and that it will be passed a reference to the array argument instead of a list of its elements. It then performs a binary search on the array @$a, looking for the appropriate place to splice in the new element $e. A linear scan is simpler to write and to understand than the binary search, but it's not efficient enough for heavy-duty use.

At all times, $lo and $hi record the indices of elements of @$a that are known to satisfy $a->[$lo] ≤ $e < $a->[$hi], where ≤ here represents the comparison defined by the $cmp function. Each time through the while loop, the function compares $e to the element of the array at the position halfway between $lo and $hi. Depending on the outcome of the comparison, it now know, a new element $a->[$med] with $a->[$med] ≤ $e or with $e < $a->[$med]. We can then replace either $hi or $lo with $med while still preserving the condition $a->[$lo] ≤ $e < $a->[$hi]. When $lo and $hi are the same, the function has located the correct position for $e in the array, and uses splice() to insert $e in the appropriate place. For further discussion of binary search, see *Mastering Algorithms with Perl*, pp. 162–165.

LOG FILES

For a more practical example of the usefulness of cutsorting, consider a program to process a mail log file. The popular qmail mail system generates a log in the following format:

```
@400000003e382910351ebf4c new msg 706430
@400000003e3829103573e42c info msg 706430: bytes 2737 from <boehm5@email.com> qp 31064 uid 1001
@400000003e38291035d359ac starting delivery 190552: msg 706430 to local guitar-tpj-regex@plover.com
@400000003e38291035d3cedc status: local 1/5 remote 2/10
@400000003e3829113084e7f4 delivery 190552: success: did_0+1+0/qp_31067/
@400000003e38291130aa3aa4 status: local 1/5 remote 2/10
@400000003e3829120762c51c end msg 706430
```

The first field in each line is a time stamp in *tai64n* format. The rest of the line describes what the mail system is doing. new msg indicates that a new message has been added to one of the delivery queues and includes the ID number of the new message. `info msg` records the sender of the new message. (A message always has exactly one sender, but may have any number of recipients.) `starting delivery` indicates that a delivery attempt is being started, the address of the intended recipient, and a unique delivery ID number. `delivery` indicates the outcome of the delivery attempt, which may be a successful delivery, or a temporary or permanent failure, and includes the delivery ID number. `end msg` indicates that delivery attempts to all the recipients of a message have ended in success or permanent failure, and that the message is being removed from the delivery queue. `status` lines indicate the total number of deliveries currently in progress.

This log format is complete and not too difficult to process, but it is difficult for humans to read quickly. We might like to generate summary reports in different formats; for example, we might like to reduce the life of the previous message to a single line:

```
706430 29/Jan/2003:14:18:30 29/Jan/2003:14:18:32 <boehm5@email.com> 1 1 0 0
```

This records the message ID number, the times at which the message was inserted into and removed from the queue, the sender, the total number of delivery attempts, and the number of attempts that were respectively successful, permanent failures, and temporary failures.

`qmail` writes its logs to a file called `current`; when `current` gets sufficiently large, it is renamed and a new `current` file is started. We'll build a stream that follows the `current` file, notices when a new `current` is started, and switches files when necessary. First we need a way to detect when a file's identity has changed. On Unix systems, a file's identity is captured by two numbers: the device number of the device on which it resides, and an *i-number* which is a per-device identification number. Both numbers can be obtained with the Perl `stat()` function:

CODE LIBRARY
logfile-process

```
sub _devino {
  my $f = shift;
  my ($dev, $ino) = stat($f);
  return unless defined $dev;
  "$dev;$ino";
}
```

The next function takes a filename, an open filehandle, and a device and i-number pair and returns the next record from the filehandle. If the handle is at the end of its file, the function checks to see if the filename now refers to a different file.

If so, the function opens the handle to the new file and continues; otherwise it waits and tries again:

```
sub _next_record {
  while (1) {
    my ($fh, $filename, $devino, $wait) = @_;
    $wait = 1 unless defined $wait;
    my $rec = <$fh>;
    return $rec if defined $rec;
    if (_devino($filename) eq $devino) {
      # File has not moved
      sleep $wait;
    } else {
      # $filename refers to a different file
      open $_[0], "<", $filename or return;
      $_[2] = _devino($_[0]);
    }
  }
}
```

Note that if $fh and $devino are initially unspecified, _next_record will initialize them when it is first called.

The next function takes a filename and returns a stream of records from the file, using _next_record to follow the file if it is replaced:

```
sub follow_file {
  my $filename = shift;
  my ($devino, $fh);
  tail(iterate_function(sub { _next_record($fh, $filename, $devino) }));
}

my $raw_mail_log = follow_file('/service/qmail/log/main/current');
```

Now we can write functions to transform this stream. For example, a quick-and-dirty function to convert tai64n format timestamps to Unix epoch format is:

```
sub tai64n_to_unix_time {
  my $rec = shift;
  return [undef, $rec] unless s/^\@([a-f0-9]{24})\s+//;
  [hex(substr($1, 8, 8)) + 10, $rec];
}
my $mail_log = &transform(\&tai64n_to_unix_time, $raw_mail_log);
```

Next is the function to analyze the log. Its input is a stream of log records from which the timestamps have been preprocessed by tai64n_to_unix_time(), and its output is a stream of hashes, each of which represents a single email message. The function gets two auxiliary arguments, $msg and $del, which are hashes that represent the current state of the delivery queue. The keys of $del are delivery ID numbers; each value is the ID number of the message with which the delivery is associated. The keys of $msg are message ID numbers; the values are structures that record information about the corresponding message, including the time it was placed in the queue, the sender, the total number of delivery attempts, and other information. A complete message structure looks like this:

```
{
    'id' => 706430,            # Message id number
    'bytes' => 2737,           # Message length
    'from' => '<boehm5@email.com>',  # Sender
    'deliveries' => [190552], # List of associated delivery ids

    'start' => 1043867776,  # Start time
    'end' => 1043867778,    # End time

    'success' => 1,            # Number of successful delivery attempts
    'failure' => 0,            # Number of permanently failed delivery attempts
    'deferral' => 0,           # Number of temporarily failed delivery attempts
    'total_deliveries' => 1,# Total number of delivery attempts
}
```

The stream produced by digest_maillog() is a sequence of these structures. To produce a structure, digest_maillog() scans the input records, adjusting $msg and $del as necessary, until it sees an end msg line; at that point it knows that it has complete information about a message, and it emits a single data item representing that message. If the input stream is exhausted, digest_maillog() terminates the output:

```
sub digest_maillog {
    my ($s, $msg, $del) = @_;
    for ($msg, $del) { $_ = {} unless $_ }
    while ($s) {
        my ($date, $rec) = @{drop($s)};
        next unless defined $date;
        if ($rec =~/^new msg (\d+)/) {
            $msg->{$1} = {start => $date, id => $1,
```

```
                             success => 0, failure => 0, deferral => 0};

     } elsif ($rec =~/^info msg (\d+): bytes (\d+) from (<[^\>]*>)/) {
       next unless exists $msg->{$1};
       $msg->{$1}{bytes} = $2;
       $msg->{$1}{from} = $3;

     } elsif ($rec =~/^starting delivery (\d+): msg (\d+)/) {
       next unless exists $msg->{$2};
       $del->{$1} = $2;
       push @{$msg->{$2}{deliveries}}, $1;

     } elsif ($rec =~/^delivery (\d+): (success|failure|deferral)/) {
       next unless exists $del->{$1} && exists $msg->{$del->{$1}};
       $msg->{$del->{$1}}{$2}++;

     } elsif ($rec =~/^end msg (\d+)/) {
       next unless exists $msg->{$1};
       my $m = delete $msg->{$1};
       $m->{total_deliveries} = @{$m->{deliveries}};
       for (@{$m->{deliveries}}) { delete $del->{$_} };
       $m->{end} = $date;
       return node($m, promise { digest_maillog($s, $msg, $del) });
     }
   }
   return;
}
```

Now we can generate reports by transforming the stream of message structures into a stream of log records:

```
use POSIX 'strftime';

sub format_digest {
  my $h = shift;
  join " ",
    $h->{id},
    strftime("%d/%b/%Y:%T", localtime($h->{start})),
    strftime("%d/%b/%Y:%T", localtime($h->{end})),
    $h->{from},
    $h->{total_deliveries},
```

```
                              $h->{success},
                              $h->{failure},
                              $h->{deferral},
                                ;
                      }


              show(&transform(\&format_digest, digest_maillog($mail_log)));
```

Typical output looks like this:

```
...
707045 28/Jan/2003:12:10:03 28/Jan/2003:12:10:03 <Paulmc@371.net> 1 1 0 0
707292 28/Jan/2003:12:10:03 28/Jan/2003:12:10:06 <Paulmc@371.net> 1 1 0 0
707046 28/Jan/2003:12:10:06 28/Jan/2003:12:10:07 <Paulmc@371.net> 4 3 1 0
707293 28/Jan/2003:12:10:07 28/Jan/2003:12:10:07 <guido@odiug.zope.com> 1 1 0 0
707670 28/Jan/2003:12:10:06 28/Jan/2003:12:10:08 <spam-return-133409-@plover.com-@[]> 2 2 0 0
707045 28/Jan/2003:12:10:07 28/Jan/2003:12:10:11 <guido@odiug.zope.com> 1 1 0 0
707294 28/Jan/2003:12:10:11 28/Jan/2003:12:10:11 <guido@odiug.zope.com> 1 1 0 0
707047 28/Jan/2003:12:10:22 28/Jan/2003:12:10:23
        <ezmlm-return-10817-mjd-ezmlm=plover.com@list.cr.yp.to> 1 1 0 0
707048 28/Jan/2003:12:11:02 28/Jan/2003:12:11:02
        <perl5-porters-return-71265-mjd-p5p2=plover.com@perl.org> 1 1 0 0
707503 24/Jan/2003:11:29:49 28/Jan/2003:12:11:35
        <perl-qotw-discuss-return-1200-@plover.com-@[]> 388 322 2 64
707049 28/Jan/2003:12:11:35 28/Jan/2003:12:11:45 <> 1 1 0 0
707295 28/Jan/2003:12:11:41 28/Jan/2003:12:11:46
        <perl6-internals-return-14784-mjd-perl6-internals=plover.com@perl.org> 1 1 0 0
...
```

That was all a lot of work, and at this point it's probably not clear why the stream method has any advantage over the more usual method of reading the file one record at a time, tracking the same data structures, and printing output records as we go, something like this:

```
while (<LOG>) {
  # analyze current record
  # update $msg and $del
  if (/^end msg/) {
    print ...;
  }
}
```

One advantage was that we could encapsulate the follow-the-changing-file behavior inside its own stream. In a more conventionally structured program, the logic to track the moving file would probably have been threaded throughout the rest of the program. But we could also have accomplished this encapsulation by using a tied filehandle.

A bigger advantage of the stream approach comes if we want to reorder the output records. As written, the output stream contains message records in the order in which the messages were removed from the queue; that is, the output is sorted by the third field. Suppose we want to see the messages sorted by the second field, the time at which each message was first sent. In the preceding example output, notice the line for message 707503. Although the time at which it was removed from the queue (12:11:35 on 28 January) is in line with the surrounding messages, the time it was sent (11:29:49 on 24 January) is quite different. Most messages are delivered almost immediately, but this one took more than four days to complete. It represents a message that was sent to a mailing list with 324 subscribers. Two of the subscribers had full mailboxes, causing their mail systems to temporararily refuse new message for these subscribers. After four days, the mail system finally gave up and removed the message from the queue. Similarly, message 707670 arrived a second earlier but was delivered (to India) a second later than message 707293, which was delivered (locally) immediately after it arrived.

The ordinary procedural loop provides no good way to emit the log entries sorted in order by the date the messages were sent rather than by the date that delivery was completed. We can't simply use Perl's sort() function, since it works only on arrays, and we can't put the records into an array, because they extend into the indefinite future.

But in the stream-based solution, we can order the records with the cutsorting method, using the prefabricated cutsorting function we have already. There's an upper bound on how long messages can remain in the delivery queue; after four days any temporary delivery failures are demoted to permanent failures, and the message bounces. Suppose we have in hand the record for a message that was first queued on January 1 and that has been completely delivered. We can't emit it immediately, since the next item out of the stream might be the record for a message that was first queued on December 28 whose delivery didn't complete until January 2; this record should come out before the January 1 record because we're trying to sort the output by the start date rather than the end date. But we can tell the cutsorter that it's safe to emit the January 1 record once we see a January 5 record in the stream, because by January 5 any messages queued before January 1 will have been delivered one way or another:

```perl
my $QUEUE_LIFETIME = 4;       # Days
my $by_entry_date =
```

```
cutsort($mail_log,
        sub { $_[0]{start} <=> $_[1]{start} },
        sub { $_[1]{end} - $_[0]{end} >= $QUEUE_LIFETIME*86400 },
       );
```

The first anonymous function argument to cutsort() says how to order the elements of the output; we want them ordered by {start}, the date each message was placed into the queue. The second anonymous function argument is the cutting function; this function says that it's safe to emit a record *R* with a certain start date if the next record in the stream was for a message that was completed at least $QUEUE_LIFETIME days after *R*; any record that was queued before *R* would have to be removed less than $QUEUE_LIFETIME days later, and therefore there are no such records remaining in the stream. The output from $by_entry_date includes the records in the preceding sample, but in a different order:

```
...

707503 24/Jan/2003:11:29:49 28/Jan/2003:12:11:35 <perl-qotw-discuss-return-1200-@plover.com-@[]>
       388 322 2 64


... (many records omitted) ...

707045 28/Jan/2003:12:10:03 28/Jan/2003:12:10:03 <Paulmc@371.net> 1 1 0 0
707292 28/Jan/2003:12:10:03 28/Jan/2003:12:10:06 <Paulmc@371.net> 1 1 0 0
707046 28/Jan/2003:12:10:06 28/Jan/2003:12:10:07 <Paulmc@371.net> 4 3 1 0
707670 28/Jan/2003:12:10:06 28/Jan/2003:12:10:08 <spam-return-133409-@plover.com-@[]> 2 2 0 0
707293 28/Jan/2003:12:10:07 28/Jan/2003:12:10:07 <guido@odiug.zope.com> 1 1 0 0
707045 28/Jan/2003:12:10:07 28/Jan/2003:12:10:11 <guido@odiug.zope.com> 1 1 0 0
...
```

Even on a finite segment of the log file, cutsorting offers advantages over a regular sort. To use regular sort, the program must first read the entire log file into memory. With cutsorting, the program can begin producing output after only $QUEUE_LIFETIME days worth of records have been read in.

6.6   THE NEWTON-RAPHSON METHOD

How does Perl's sqrt() function work? It probably uses some variation of the *Newton-Raphson method*. You may have spent a lot of time toiling in high school to solve equations; if so, rejoice, because the Newton-Raphson method is a general technique for solving any equation whatsoever.[5]

Suppose we're trying to calculate sqrt(2). This is a number, which, when multiplied by itself, will give 2. That is, it's a number x such that $x^2 = 2$, or, equivalently, such that $x^2 - 2 = 0$.

If you plot the graph of $y = x^2 - 2$ you get a parabola illustrated in Figure 6.5. Every point on the parabola has $x^2 - 2 = y$. Points on the x-axis have $y = 0$. Where the parabola crosses the x-axis, we have $x^2 - 2 = 0$, and so the x-coordinate of the crossing point is equal to $\sqrt{2}$. This value is the solution, or *root*, of the equation.

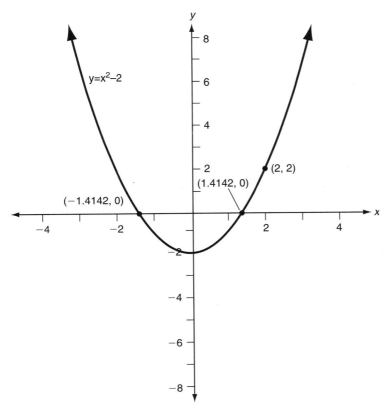

FIGURE 6.5   The parabola $y = x^2 - 2$.

5   Isaac Newton discovered and wrote about the method first, but his write-up wasn't published until 1736. Joseph Raphson discovered the technique independently and published it in 1671.

The Newton-Raphson method takes an approximation to the root and produces a closer approximation. We get the method started by guessing a root. Techniques for making a good first guess are an entire field of study themselves, but for the parabola in Figure 6.5, any guess except 0 will work. To show that the initial guess doesn't have to be particularly good, we'll guess that $\sqrt{2} = 2$. The method works by observing that a smooth curve, such as the parabola, can be approximated by a straight line, and constructs the tangent line to the curve at the current guess, which is $x = 2$. This is the straight line that touches the curve at that point, and that proceeds in the same direction that the curve was going. The curve will veer away from the straight line (because it's a curve) and eventually intersect the x-axis in a different place than the straight line does. But if the curve is reasonably well-behaved, it won't veer away too much, so the line's intersection point will be close to the curve's intersection point, and closer than the original guess.

The tangent line in this case happens to be the line $y = 4x - 6$. This line intersects the x-axis at $x = 1.5$, as shown in Figure 6.6. This value, 1.5, is our new guess for the value of $\sqrt{2}$. It is indeed more accurate than the original guess.

To get a better approximation, we repeat the process. The tangent line to the parabola at the point (1.5, 0.25) has the equation $y = 3x - 4.25$. This line intersects the x-axis at 1.41667, which is correct to two decimal places.

Now we'll see how these calculations were done. Let's suppose our initial guess is g, so we want to construct the tangent at $(g, g^2 - 2)$. If a line has slope m and passes through the point (p, q), its equation is $y - q = m(x - p)$. We'll see later how to figure out the slope of the tangent line without calculus, but in the meantime calculus tells us that the slope of the tangent line to the parabola at the point $(g, g^2 - 2)$ is $2g$, and therefore that the tangent line itself has the equation $(y - (g^2 - 2)) = 2g(x - g)$. We want to find the value of x for which this line intersects the x-axis; that is, we want to find the value of x for which y is 0. This gives us the equation $(0 - (g^2 - 2)) = 2g(x - g)$. Solving for x yields $x = g - (g^2 - 2)/2g = (g^2 + 2)/2g$. That is, if our initial guess is g, a better guess will be $(g^2 + 2)/2g$. A function that computes $\sqrt{2}$ is therefore:

CODE LIBRARY
Newton.pm

```
sub sqrt2 {
    my $g = 2; # Initial guess
    until (close_enough($g*$g, 2)) {
        $g = ($g*$g + 2) / (2*$g);
    }
    $g;
}
```

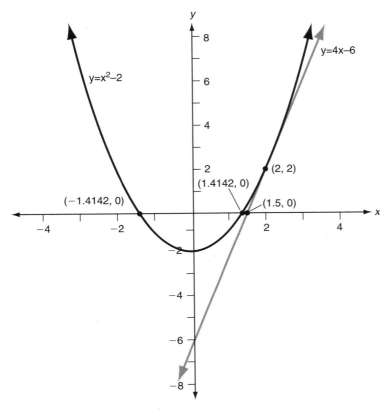

FIGURE 6.6 The parabola $y = x^2 - 2$.

```
sub close_enough {
  my ($a, $b) = @_;
  return abs($a - $b) < 1e-12;
}
```

This code rapidly produces a good approximation to $\sqrt{2}$, returning 1.414213562373095 after only five iterations. (This is correct to 15 decimal places.) To calculate the square root of a different number, we do the mathematics the same way, this time replacing the 2 with a variable n; the result is:

```
sub sqrtn {
  my $n = shift;
  my $g = $n;   # Initial guess
  until (close_enough($g*$g, $n)) {
    $g = ($g*$g + $n) / (2*$g);
```

```
        }
      $g;
    }
```

6.6.1 Approximation Streams

But what does all this have to do with streams? One of the most useful and interesting uses for streams is to represent the results of an approximate calculation.
Consider the following stream definition, which delivers the same sequence of
approximations that the sqrtn() function would compute:

```
use Stream 'iterate_function';

sub sqrt_stream {
  my $n = shift;
  iterate_function (sub { my $g = shift;
                          ($g*$g + $n) / (2*$g);
                        },
                    $n);
}


1;
```

We saw iterate_function() back in Section 6.2.2. At the time, I promised a
simpler and more interesting version. Here it is:

```
sub iterate_function {
  my ($f, $x) = @_;
  my $s;
  $s = node($x, promise { &transform($f, $s) });
}
```

Recall that iterate_function($f, $x) produces the stream $x, $f->($x),
$f->($f->($x)),.... The preceding recursive version relies on the observation
that the stream begins with $x, and the rest of the stream can be gotten by apply-
ing the function $f to each element in turn. The & on the call to transform()
disables transform()'s prototype-derived special synatax. Without it, we'd have
to write:

```
transform { $f->($_[0]) } $s
```

which would introduce an unnecessary additional function call.

6.6.2 Derivatives

The problem with the Newton-Raphson method as I described it in the previous section is that it requires someone to calculate the slope of the tangent line to the curve at any point. When we needed the slope at any point of the parabola $g^2 - 2$, I magically pulled out the formula $2g$. The function $2g$ that describes the slope at the tangent line at any point of the parabola $g^2 - 2$ is called the *derivative function* of the parabola; in general, for any function, the related function that describes the slope is called the *derivative*. Algebraic computation of derivative functions is the subject of the branch of mathematics called *differential calculus*.

Fortunately, though, you don't need to know differential calculus to apply the Newton-Raphson method. There's an easy way to compute the slope of a curve at any point. What we really want is the slope of the tangent line at a certain point. But if we pick two points that are close to the point we want, and compute the slope of the line between them, it won't be too different from the slope of the actual tangent line.

For example, suppose we want to find the slope of the parabola $y = x^2 - 2$ at the point (2, 2). We'll pick two points close to that and find the slope of the line that passes through them. Say we choose (2.001, 2.004001) and (1.999, 1.996001). The slope of the line through two points is the y difference divided by the x difference; in this case, $0.008/0.002 = 4$. And this does match the answer from calculus exactly. It won't always be an exact match, but it will always be close, because differential calculus uses exactly the same strategy, augmented with algebraic techniques to analyze what happens to the slope as the two points get closer and closer together.

It's not hard to write code that, given a function, calculates the slope at any point:

```
sub slope {
  my ($f, $x) = @_;
  my $e = 0.00000095367431640625;
  ($f->($x+$e) - $f->($x-$e)) / (2*$e);
}
```

The value of $e that I chose is exactly 2^{-20}; I picked it because it was the power of 2 closest to one one-millionth. Powers of 2 work better than powers of 10 because they can be represented exactly; with a power of 10 you're introducing round-off error before you even begin. Smaller values of $e will give us more accurate answers, up to a point. The computer's floating-point numbers have only a fixed amount of accuracy, and as the numbers we deal with get smaller, the round-off error will tend to dominate the answer. For the function $f = sub { $_[0] * $_[0] - 2 }$ and $x = 2$ our slope() function produces the correct answer (4) for values of e down to 2^{-52}; at that point the round-off error takes over, and when e is 2^{-54}, the calculated slope is 0 instead of 4. It's not hard to see what has happened: e has become so small that when it's added to or subtracted from x, and the result is rounded off to the computer's precision, the e disappears entirely and we're left with exactly 2. So the calculated values of $f->($x+$e)$ and $f->($x-$e)$ are both exactly the same, and the slope() function returns 0.

Once we have this slope() function, it's easy to write a generic equation solver using the Newton-Raphson method:

```
# Return a stream of numbers $x that make $f->($x) close to 0
sub solve {
  my $f = shift;
  my $guess = shift || 1;
  iterate_function(sub { my $g = shift;
                         $g - $f->($g)/slope($f, $g);
                    },
                  $guess);
}
```

Now if we want to find $\sqrt{2}$, we do:

```
my $sqrt2 = solve(sub { $_[0] * $_[0] - 2 });

{ local $" = "\n";
  show($sqrt2, 10);
}
```

This produces the following output:

```
1
1.5
1.41666666666667
1.41421568627464
1.41421356237469
1.4142135623731
1.41421356237309
1.4142135623731
1.41421356237309
1.4142135623731
```

At this point the round-off error in the calculations has caused the values to alternate between 1.41421356237309 and 1.4142135623731.[6] The correct value is 1.41421356237309504880, so our little bit of code has produced an answer that is accurate to better than four parts per quadrillion.

If we want more accurate answers, we can use the standard Perl multi-precision floating-point library, `Math::BigFloat`. Doing so requires only a small change to the code:

```
use Math::BigFloat;

my $sqrt2 = solve(sub { $_[0] * $_[0] - 2 },
                  Math::BigFloat->new(2));
```

Using `Math::BigFloat` produces extremely accurate answers, but after only a few iterations, the numbers start coming out more and more slowly.

Because `Math::BigFloat` *never* rounds off, every multiplication of two numbers produces a number twice as long. The results increase in size exponentially, and so do the calculation times. The third iteration produces 1.41666666666666666666666666666666666666667, which is an extremely precise but rather inaccurate answer. There's no point in retaining or calculating with all the 6's at the end, because we know they're wrong, but `Math::BigFloat` does it anyway, and the fourth iteration produces a result that has five accurate digits followed by 80 inaccurate digits.

One solution to this is to do more mathematics to produce an estimate of how many digits are accurate, and to round off the approximations to leave only the correct digits for later calculations. But this requires sophisticated technique. A simple solution is to improve the initial guess. Since Perl has a built-in square root function that is fast, we'll use it to generate our initial guess, which will already be accurate to about thirteen decimal places. Any work done by `Math::BigFloat` afterwards will only improve this:

```
my $sqrt2 = solve(sub { $_[0] * $_[0] - 2 },
                  Math::BigFloat->new(sqrt(2)));
```

The approximations still double in size at every step, and each one still takes twice as long as the previous one, but many more of the digits are correct, so the extra time spent isn't being wasted as it was before.

---

6   Actually they're alternating between 1.414213562373094923430016933708 and 1.414213562373095145474621858739, but who's counting?

You may wait twice as long to get the answer, but you get an answer that has twice as many correct digits. The second element of the stream is 1.**41421356237309504880168872421**83652153338124600441037, of which the first 28 digits after the decimal point are correct. The next element has 58 correct digits. In general, the Newton-Raphson method will double the number of correct digits at every step, so if you start with a reasonably good guess, you can get extremely accurate results very quickly.

6.6.3   The Tortoise and the Hare

The `$sqrt2` stream we built in the previous section is infinite, but after a certain point the approximations it produces won't get any more accurate because they'll be absorbed by the inherent error in the computer's floating-point numbers. The output of `$sqrt2` was:

```
1
1.5
1.41666666666667
1.41421568627464
1.41421356237469
1.4142135623731
1.41421356237309
1.4142135623731
1.41421356237309
...
```

`$sqrt2` is stuck in a loop. A process that was trying to use `$sqrt2` might decide that it needs more than 13 places of precision, and might search further and further down the stream, hoping for a better approximation that never arrives. It would be better if we could detect the loop in `$sqrt2` and cut off its tail.

The obvious way to detect a loop is to record every number that comes out of the stream and compare it to the items that came out before; if there is a repeat, then cut off the tail:

```
sub cut_loops {
  my $s = shift;
  return unless $s;
  my @previous_values = @_;
  for (@previous_values) {
    if (head($s) == $_) {
      return;
```

```
        }
      }
      node(head($s),
            promise { cut_loops(tail($s), head($s), @previous_values) });
    }
```

`cut_loops($s)` constructs a stream that is the same as `$s`, but that stops at the point where the first loop begins. Unfortunately, it does this with a large time and memory cost. If the argument stream doesn't loop, the `@previous_values` array will get bigger and bigger and take longer and longer to search. There is a better method, sometimes called the *tortoise and hare algorithm*.

Imagine that each value in the stream is connected to the next value by an arrow. If the values form a loop, the arrows will too. Now imagine that a tortoise and a hare both start at the first value and proceed along the arrows. The tortoise crawls from one value to the next, following the arrows, but the hare travels twice as fast, leaping over every other value. If there is a loop, the hare will speed around the loop and catch up to the tortoise from behind. When this happens, you know that the hare has gone all the way around the loop once.[7] If there is no loop, the hare will vanish into the distance and will never meet the tortoise again:

```
        sub cut_loops {
          my ($tortoise, $hare) = @_;
          return unless $tortoise;

          # The hare and tortoise start at the same place
          $hare = $tortoise unless defined $hare;

          # The hare moves two steps every time the tortoise moves one
          $hare = tail(tail($hare));

          # If the hare and the tortoise are in the same place, cut the loop
          return if head($tortoise) == head($hare);

          return node(head($tortoise),
                      promise { cut_loops(tail($tortoise), $hare) });
        }
```

---

[7] It may not be obvious that the hare will necessarily catch the tortoise, but it is true. For details, see Donald Knuth, *The Art of Computer Programming: Volume 2, Seminumerical Algorithms*, exercise 3.1.6.

show(cut_loops($sqrt2)) now generates:

```
1
1.5
1.41666666666667
1.41421568627464
1.41421356237469
1.4142135623731
```

and nothing else.

Notice that the entire loop didn't appear in the output. The loop consists of:

```
1.4142135623731
1.41421356237309
```

but we saw only the first of these. The tortoise and hare algorithm guarantees to cut the stream somewhere in the loop, *before* the values start to repeat; it might therefore place the cut sometime before all of the values in the loop have appeared. Sometimes this is acceptable behavior. If not, send the hare around the loop an extra time:

```
sub cut_loops2 {
  my ($tortoise, $hare, $n) = @_;
  return unless $tortoise;
  $hare = $tortoise unless defined $hare;

  $hare = tail(tail($hare));
  return if head($tortoise) == head($hare)
          && $n++;
  return node(head($tortoise),
          promise { cut_loops(tail($tortoise), $hare, $n) });
}
```

6.6.4   Finance

The square root of two is beloved by the mathematics geeks, but normal humans are motivated by other things, such as money. Let's suppose I am paying off a loan, say a mortgage. Initially I owe P dollars. (P is for "principal", which is the finance geeks' jargon word for it.) Each month, I pay *pmt* dollars, of which some goes to pay the interest and some goes to reduce the principal. When the principal reaches zero, I own the house.

For concreteness, let's say that the principal is $100,000, the interest rate is 6% per year, or 0.5% per month, and the monthly payment is $1,000. At the end of the first month, I've racked up $500 in interest, so my $1,000 payment reduces the principal to $99,500. At the end of the second month, the interest is a little lower, only $99,500 \times 0.5\% = $495.50, so my payment reduces the principal by $504.50, to $98,995.50. Each month, my progress is a little faster. How long will it take me to pay off the mortgage at this rate?

First let's figure out how to calculate the amount owed at the end of any month. The first two months are easy:

Month Amount owed

0   P

In the first month, we pay interest on the principal in the amount of $P \times .005$, bringing the total to $P \times 1.005$. But we also make a payment of *pmt* dollars, so that at the end of month 1, the amount owed is:

1      $P \cdot 1.005 - pmt$

The next month, we pay interest on the amount still owed. That amount is $P \times 1.005 - pmt$, so the interest is $(P \times 1.005 - pmt) \times .005$, and the total is $(P \times 1.005 - pmt) + (P \times 1.005 - pmt) \times 0.005)$, or $(P \times 1.005^2 - pmt \times 1.005)$. Then we make another payment, bringing the total down to:

2      $P \cdot (1.005)^2 - pmt \cdot (1 + 1.005)$

The pattern continues in the third month:

3      $P \cdot (1.005)^3 - pmt \cdot (1 + 1.005 + (1.005)^2)$

4      $P \cdot (1.005)^4 - pmt \cdot (1 + 1.005 + (1.005)^2 + (1.005)^3)$

This pattern is simple enough that we can program it without much trouble:

```
sub owed {
    my ($P, $N, $pmt, $i) = @_;
    my $payment_factor = 0;
    for (0 .. $N-1) {
        $payment_factor += (1+$i) ** $_;
    }
    return $P * (1+$i)**$N - $pmt * $payment_factor;
}
```

It requires a little high school algebra to abbreviate the formula.[8] $1 + 1.005 + (1.005)^2 + \cdots + 1.005^{N-1}$ is equal to $(1.005^N - 1)/.005$, which is quicker to calculate:

4          $P \cdot (1.005)^4 - pmt \cdot ((1.005)^4 - 1)/0.005$

5          $P \cdot (1.005)^5 - pmt \cdot ((1.005)^5 - 1)/0.005$

6          $P \cdot (1.005)^6 - pmt \cdot ((1.005)^6 - 1)/0.005$

so the code gets simpler:

CODE LIBRARY
owed

```
sub owed {
    my ($P, $N, $pmt, $i) = @_;
    return $P * (1+$i)**$N - $pmt * ((1+$i)**$N - 1) / $i;
}
```

Now, the question that everyone with a mortgage wants answered: How long before my house is paid off?

We could try solving the equation $P \cdot (1 + i)^N - pmt \cdot \frac{(1+i)^N - 1}{i}$ for N, but doing that requires a lot of mathematical sophistication, much more than coming up with the formula in the first place.[9] It's much easier to hand the owed() function to solve() and let it find the answer:

```
sub owed_after_n_months {
    my $N = shift;
    owed(100_000, $N, 1_000, 0.005);
}

my $stream = cut_loops(solve(\&owed_after_n_months));
my $n;
$n = drop($stream) while $stream;
print "You will be paid off in only $n months!\n";
```

According to this, we'll be paid off in 138.9757 months, or eleven and a half years. This is plausible, since if there were no interest we would clearly have

---

8   It also requires a bit of a trick. Say $S = 1 + k + k^2 + \cdots + k^{n-1}$. Multiplying both sides by k gives $Sk = k + k^2 + \cdots + k^{n-1} + k^n$. These two equations are almost the same, and if we subtract one from the other almost everything cancels out, leaving only $Sk - S = k^n - 1$ and so $S = (k^n - 1)/(k - 1)$.

9   I'm afraid I am out of tricks.

the loan paid off in exactly 100 months. Indeed, after the 138th payment, the principal remains at $970.93, and a partial payment the following month finishes off the mortgage.

But we can ask more interesting questions. I want a thirty-year mortgage, and I can afford to pay $1,300 per month, or $15,600 per year. The bank is offering a 6.75% annual interest rate. How large a mortgage can I afford?

```
sub affordable_mortgage {
  my $mortgage = shift;
  owed($mortgage, 30, 15_600, 0.0675);
}


my $stream = cut_loops(solve(\&affordable_mortgage));
my $n;
$n = drop($stream) while $stream;
print "You can afford a \$$n mortgage.\n";
```

Apparently with a $1,300 payment I can pay off any mortgage up to $198,543.62 in 30 years.

6.7 POWER SERIES

We've seen that the Newton-Raphson method can be used to evaluate the sqrt() function. What about other built-in functions, such as sin() and cos()?

The Newton-Raphson method won't work here. To evaluate something like sqrt(2), we needed to find a number x with $x^2 = 2$. Then we used the Newton-Raphson method, which required only simple arithmetic to approximate a solution. To evaluate something like sin(2), we would need to find a number x with $\sin^{-1}(x) = 2$. This is at least as difficult as the original problem. x^2 is easy to compute; $\sin^{-1}(x)$ isn't.

To compute values of the so-called "transcendental functions" like sin() and cos(), the computer uses another strategy called *power series expansion*.[10]

A *power series* is an expression of the form:

$$a_0 + a_1x + a_2x^2 + a_3x^3 + \cdots$$

---

10   These series are often called *Taylor series* or *Maclaurin series* after English mathematicians Brook Taylor and Colin Maclaurin who popularized them. The general technique for constructing these series was discovered much earlier by several people, including James Gregory and Johann Bernoulli.

for some numbers a_0, a_1, a_2, ... Many common functions can be expressed as power series, and in particular, it turns out that for all x, $\sin(x) = x - x^3/3! + x^5/5! - x^7/7! + \cdots$. (Here $a_0 = 0$, $a_1 = 1$, $a_2 = 0$, $a_3 = -1/3!$, etc.) The formula is most accurate for x close to 0, but if you carry it out to enough terms, it works for any x at all. The terms themselves get small rather quickly in this case, because the factorial function in the denominator increases more rapidly than the power of x in the numerator, particularly for small x. For example, $0.1 - (0.1)^3/3! + (0.1)^5/5! - (0.1)^7/7!$ is **.09983341664682**539683; the value of $\sin(0.1)$ is **.09983341664682**815230. When the computer wants to calculate the sine of some number, it plugs the number into the power series and calculates an approximation. The code to do this is simple:

CODE LIBRARY
sine

```
# Approximate sin(x) using the first n terms of the power series
sub approx_sin {
    my $n = shift;
    my $x = shift;
    my ($denom, $c, $num, $total) = (1, 1, $x, 0);
    while ($n--) {
        $total += $num / $denom;
        $num *= $x*$x * -1;
        $denom *= ($c+1) * ($c+2);
        $c += 2;
    }
    $total;
}
1;
```

At each step, $num holds the numerator of the current term and $denom holds the denominator. This is so simple that it's even easy in assembly language.

Similarly, $\cos(x) = 1 - x^2/2! + x^4/4! - x^6/6! + \cdots$.

Streams seem almost tailor-made for power series computations, because the power series itself is infinite, and with a stream representation we can look at as many terms as are necessary to get the accuracy we want. Once the terms become sufficiently small, we know that the rest of the stream won't make a significant contribution to the result.[11]

---

11   This shouldn't be obvious, since there are an infinite number of terms in the rest of the stream, and in general the infinite tail of a stream may make a significant contribution to the total. However, in a power series, the additional terms *do* get small so quickly that they can be disregarded, at least for sufficiently small values of x. For details, consult a textbook on numerical analysis or basic calculus.

We could build a sin function that, given a numeric argument, used the power series expansion to produce approximations to sin(x). But we can do better. We can use a stream to represent the entire power series itself, and then manipulate it as a single unit.

We will represent the power series $a_0 + a_1 x + a_2 x^2 + \cdots$ with a stream that contains $(a_0, a_1, a_2, \ldots)$. With this interpretation, we can build a function that evaluates a power series for a particular argument by substituting the argument into the series in place of x.

Since the nth terms of these power series depend in simple ways on n itself, we'll make a small utility function to generate such a series:

```
package PowSeries;
use base 'Exporter';
@EXPORT_OK = qw(add2 mul2 partial_sums powers_of term_values
                evaluate derivative multiply recip divide
                $sin $cos $exp $log_ $tan);
use Stream ':all';

sub tabulate {
  my $f = shift;
  &transform($f, upfrom(0));
}
```

Given a function f, this produces the infinite stream $f(0), f(1), f(2), \ldots$. Now we can define sin() and cos():

```
my @fact = (1);
sub factorial {
  my $n = shift;
  return $fact[$n] if defined $fact[$n];
  $fact[$n] = $n * factorial($n-1);
}


$sin = tabulate(sub { my $N = shift;
                      return 0 if $N % 2 == 0;
                      my $sign = int($N/2) % 2 ? -1 : 1;
                      $sign/factorial($N)
                    });


$cos = tabulate(sub { my $N = shift;
                      return 0 if $N % 2 != 0;
```

```
                  my $sign = int($N/2) % 2 ? -1 : 1;
                  $sign/factorial($N)
            });
```

$sin is now a stream that begins (0, 1, 0, −0.16667, 0, 0.00833, 0, ...); $cos begins (1, 0, −0.5, 0, 0.041667, ...).

Before we evaluate these functions, we'll build a few utilities for performing arithmetic on power series. First is add2(), which adds together the elements of two streams, element-by-element:

```
sub add2 {
  my ($s, $t) = @_;
  return unless $s && $t;
  node(head($s) + head($t),
      promise { add2(tail($s), tail($t)) });
}
```

add2($s, $t) corresponds to the addition of two power series. (Multiplication of power series is more complicated, as we will see later.) Similarly, scale($s, $c), which we've seen before, corresponds to the multiplication of the power series $s by the constant $c.

mul2(), which multiplies streams element-by-element, is similar to add2():

```
sub mul2 {
  my ($s, $t) = @_;
  return unless $s && $t;
  node(head($s) * head($t),
      promise { mul2(tail($s), tail($t)) });
}
```

We will also need a utility function for summing up a series. Given a stream (a_0, a_1, a_2, ...), it should produce the stream (a_0, $a_0 + a_1$, $a_0 + a_1 + a_2$, ...) of successive partial sums of elements of the first stream. This function is similar to several others we've already defined:

```
sub partial_sums {
  my $s = shift;
  my $r;
  $r = node(head($s), promise { add2($r, tail($s)) });
}
```

One of the eventual goals of all this machinery is to compute sines and cosines. To do that, we will need to evaluate the partial sums of a power series for a particular value of x. This function takes a number x and produces the stream $(1, x, x^2, x^3, \ldots)$:

```
sub powers_of {
    my $x = shift;
    iterate_function(sub {$_[0] * $x}, 1);
}
```

When we multiply this stream element-wise by the stream of coefficients that represents a power series, the result is a stream of the terms of the power series evaluated at a point x:

```
sub term_values {
    my ($s, $x) = @_;
    mul2($s, powers_of($x));
}
```

Given a power series stream $\$s = (a_0, a_1, a_2, \ldots)$, and a value $x, \texttt{term\_values()}$ produces the stream $(a_0, a_1 x, a_2 x^2, \ldots)$.

Finally, `evaluate()` takes a function, as represented by a power series, and evaluates it at a particular value of x:

```
sub evaluate {
    my ($s, $x) = @_;
    partial_sums(term_values($s, $x));
}
```

And lo and behold, all our work pays off:

```
my $pi = 3.1415926535897932;
show(evaluate($cos, $pi/6), 20);
```

producing the following approximations to $\cos(\pi/6)$:

```
1
1
0.862922161095981
0.862922161095981
0.866053883415747
```

0.866053883415747
0.866025264100571
0.866025264100571
0.866025404210352
0.866025404210352
0.866025403783554
0.866025403783554
0.866025403784440
0.866025403784440
0.866025403784439
0.866025403784439
0.866025403784439
0.866025403784439
0.866025403784439
0.866025403784439

This is correct. (The answer happens to be exactly $\sqrt{3}/2$.)

We can even work it in reverse to calculate π:

```
# Get the n'th term from a stream
sub nth {
  my $s = shift;
  my $n = shift;
  return $n == 0 ? head($s) : nth(tail($s), $n-1);
}


# Calculate the approximate cosine of x
sub cosine {
  my $x = shift;
  nth(evaluate($cos, $x), 20);
}
```

If we know that $\cos(\pi/6) = \sqrt{3}/2$, then to find π we need only solve the equation $\cos(x/6) = \sqrt{3}/2$, or equivalently, $\cos^2(x/6) = 3/4$:

```
sub is_zero_when_x_is_pi {
  my $x = shift;
  my $c = cosine($x/6);
  $c * $c - 3/4;
}


show(solve(\&is_zero_when_x_is_pi), 20);
```

And the output from this is:

```
1
5.07974473179368
3.19922525384188
3.14190177620487
3.14159266278343
3.14159265358979
3.14159265358979

...
```

which is correct. The initial guess of 1, you will recall, is the default for solve().
Had we explicitly specified a better guess, such as 3, the process would have
converged more quickly; had we specified a much larger guess, like 10, the
results would have converged to a different solution, such as 11π.

6.7.1 Derivatives

We used slope() to calculate the slope of the curve $\cos^2(x/6) - 3/4$ at various
points; recall that slope() calculates an approximation of the slope by picking
two points close together on the curve and calculating the slope of the line
between them. If we had known the derivative function of $\cos^2(x/6) - 3/4$, we
could have plugged it in directly. But calculating a derivative function requires
differential calculus.

However, if you know a power series for a function, calculating its derivative
is trivial. If the power series for the function is $a_0 + a_1x + a_2x^2 + \cdots$, the power
series for the derivative is $a_1 + 2a_2x + 3a_3x^2 + \cdots$. That is, it's simply:

```
sub derivative {
  my $s = shift;
  mul2(upfrom(1), tail($s));
}
```

If we do:

```
show(derivative($sin), 20);
```

we get exactly the same output as for:

```
show($cos, 20);
```

demonstrating that the cosine function is the derivative of the sine function.

6.7.2   Other Functions

Many other common functions can be calculated with the power series method. For example, Perl's built-in exp() function is:

```
$exp = tabulate(sub { my $N = shift; 1/factorial($N) });
```

The hyperbolic functions sinh() and cosh() are like sin() and cos() except without the extra $sign factor in the terms. Perl's built-in log() function is almost:

```
$log_ = tabulate(sub { my $N = shift;
                       $N==0 ? 0 : (-1)**$N/-$N });
```

This actually calculates $\log(x + 1)$; to get $\log(x)$, subtract 1 from x before plugging it in. (Unlike the others, it works only for x between -1 and 1.) The power series method we've been using won't work for an unmodified log() function, because it approximates every function's behavior close to 0, and $\log(0)$ is undefined.

The tangent function is more complicated. One way to compute $\tan(x)$ is by computing $\sin(x)/\cos(x)$. We'll see another way in the next section.

6.7.3   Symbolic Computation

As one final variation on power series computations, we'll forget about the numbers themselves and deal with the series as single units that can be manipulated algebraically. We've already seen hints of this earlier. If $f and $g are streams that represent the power series for functions $f(x)$ and $g(x)$, then add2($f,$g) is the power series for the function $f(x) + g(x)$, scale($f,$c) is the power series for the function $c \cdot f(x)$, and derivative($f) is the power series for the function $f'(x)$, the derivative of f.

Multiplying and dividing power series is more complex. In fact, it's not immediately clear how to divide one infinite power series by another. Or even, for that matter, how to multiply them. mul2() is *not* what we want here, because algebra tells us that $(a_0 + a_1x + \cdots) \times (b_0 + b_1x + \cdots) = a_0b_0 + (a_0b_1 + a_1b_0)x + \cdots$, and mul2() would give us $a_0b_0 + a_1b_1x + \cdots$ instead.

Our regex-string generator comes to the rescue: Power series multiplication is formally almost identical to regex concatenation. First note that if $S represents some power series, say $a_0 + a_1x + a_2x^2 + \cdots$ then tail($S) represents

$a_1 + a_2x + a_3x^2 + \cdots$. Then:

$$\begin{aligned}
S &= a_0 && + a_1x + a_2x^2 + a_3x^3 + \cdots \\
&= a_0 && + x \cdot (a_1 + a_2x + a_3x^2 + \cdots) \\
&= \text{head}(S) + x \cdot \text{tail}(S)
\end{aligned}$$

Now we want to multiply two series, $S and $T:

$$\begin{aligned}
S &= \text{head}(S) && + x\,\text{tail}(S) \\
T &= \text{head}(T) && + x\,\text{tail}(T)
\end{aligned}$$

$$\begin{aligned}
S \cdot T &= \text{head}(S)\text{head}(T) + x\,\text{head}(S)\text{tail}(T) \\
&\qquad + x\,\text{head}(T)\text{tail}(S) + x^2\text{tail}(T)\text{tail}(S) \\
&= \text{head}(S)\text{head}(T) + x\,(\text{head}(S)\text{tail}(T) + \text{head}(T)\text{tail}(S) \\
&\qquad + x\,(\text{tail}(T)\text{tail}(S)))
\end{aligned}$$

The first term of the result, head(S) * head(T), is simply the product of two numbers. The rest of the terms can be found by summing three series. The first is head(S) * tail(T), which is the tail of T scaled by head(S), or scale(tail(T), head(S)). The second is head(T) * tail(S), which is similar. The last term, x * tail(S) * tail(T), is the product of two power series and can be computed with a recursive call; the extra multiplication by x just inserts a 0 at the front of the stream, since $x \cdot (a_0 + a_1x + a_2x^2 + \cdots) = 0 + a_0x + a_1x^2 + a_2x^3 + \cdots$.
    Here is the code:

```
sub multiply {
  my ($S, $T) = @_;
  my ($s, $t) = (head($S), head($T));
  node($s*$t,
       promise { add2(scale(tail($T), $s),
                   add2(scale(tail($S), $t),
                       node(0,
                         promise {multiply(tail($S), tail($T))}),
                     ))
             }
         );
}
```

For power series, we can get a more efficient implementation by optimizing scale() slightly:

```
sub scale {
  my ($s, $c) = @_;
  return    if $c == 0;
  return $s if $c == 1;
  transform { $_[0]*$c } $s;
}
```

To test this, we can try out the identity $\sin^2(x) + \cos^2(x) = 1$:

```
my $one = add2(multiply($cos, $cos), multiply($sin, $sin));
show($one, 20);
```

```
1 0 0 0 0 0 0 4.33680868994202e-19 0 0 0 0 0 0 0 0 6.46234853557053e-27 0
```

Exactly 1, as predicted, except for two insignificant round-off errors.

We might like to make multiply() a little cleaner and faster by replacing the two calls to add2() with a single call to a function that can add together any number of series:

```
sub sum {
  my @s = grep $_, @_;
  my $total = 0;
  $total += head($_) for @s;
  node($total,
      promise { sum(map tail($_), @s) }
    );
}
```

sum() first discards any empty streams from its arguments, since they won't contribute to the sum anyway. It then adds up the heads to get the head of the result and returns a new stream with the sum at its head; the tail promises to add up the tails similarly. With this new function, multiply() becomes:

```
sub multiply {
  my ($S, $T) = @_;
  my ($s, $t) = (head($S), head($T));
  node($s*$t,
```

```
promise { sum(scale(tail($T), $s),
                scale(tail($S), $t),
              node(0,
                promise {multiply(tail($S), tail($T))}),
            )
      }
   );
}
```

The next step is to calculate the reciprocal of a power series. If $s is the power series for a function $f(x)$, then the reciprocal series $r is the series for the function $1/f(x)$. To get this requires a little bit of algebraic ingenuity. Let's suppose that the first term of $s is 1. (If it's not, we can scale $s appropriately, and then scale the result back when we're done.)

$$
\begin{aligned}
r &= 1/f(x) \\
r &= 1/s \\
r &= 1/(1 + \text{tail}(s)) \\
r \cdot (1 + \text{tail}(s)) &= 1 \\
r + r \cdot \text{tail}(s) &= 1 \\
r &= 1 - r \cdot \text{tail}(s)
\end{aligned}
$$

And now, amazingly, we're done. We now know that the first term of $r must be 1, and we can compute the rest of the terms recursively by using our trick of defining the $r stream in terms of itself:

```
# Works only if head($s) = 1
sub recip {
  my ($s) = shift;
  my $r;
  $r = node(1,
           promise { scale(multiply($r, tail($s)), -1) });
}
```

The heavy lifting is done; dividing power series is now a one-liner:

```
# Works only if head($t) = 1
sub divide {
  my ($s, $t) = @_;
```

```
    multiply($s, recip($t));
}


$tan = divide($sin, $cos);
show($tan, 10);
```

0 1
0 0.333333333333333
0 0.133333333333333
0 0.053968253968254
0 0.0218694885361552

My *Engineering Mathematics Handbook*[12] says that the coefficients are 0, 1, 0, 1/3, 0, 2/15, 0, 17/315, 0, 62/2835,..., so it looks as though the program is working properly. If we would like the program to generate the fractions instead of decimal approximations, we should download the Math::BigRat module from CPAN and use it to initialize the factorial() function that is the basis of $sin and $cos.

Math::BigRat values are infectious: if you combine one with an ordinary number, the result is another Math::BigRat object. Since the @fact table is initialized with a Math::BigRat, its other elements will be constructed as Math::BigRats also; since the return values of fact() are Math::BigRats, the elements of $sin and $cos will be too; and since these are used in the computation of $tan, the end result will be Math::BigRat objects. Changing one line in the source code causes a ripple effect that propagates all the way to the final result:

```
my @fact = (Math::BigRat->new(1));

sub factorial {
  my $n = shift;
  return $fact[$n] if defined $fact[$n];
  $fact[$n] = $n * factorial($n-1);
}
```

The output is now:

```
0 1 0 1/3 0 2/15 0 17/315 0 62/2835
```

---

12   Jan J. Tuma, McGraw-Hill, 1970.

7

HIGHER-ORDER FUNCTIONS AND CURRYING

Our `memoize()` function of Chapter 3 was a "function factory," building stub functions that served as replacements for other functions. The technique of using functions to build other functions is extremely powerful. In this chapter, we'll look at a technique called *currying*, which transforms an ordinary function into a function factory for manufacturing more functions, and at other techniques for transforming one function into another.

A higher-order function is a function that operates on other functions instead of on data values. Some of these take data arguments and manufacture functions to order; others, like the `imap()` function of Chapter 4, transform one function into another one.

7.1 CURRYING

We have seen several times how to use callbacks to parametrize the behavior of a function so that it can serve many purposes. For example, in Section 1.5 we saw how a generic directory-walking function could be used to print a list of dangling symbolic links, to return a list of interesting files, or to copy an entire directory.

Callbacks are a way to make functions more general by supplying other functions to them as arguments. We saw how to write functions that used closures to generate other functions as return values. The *currying* technique we'll see combines closures and callbacks, turning an ordinary function into a factory that manufactures functions on demand.

Recall our walk_html() function from Chapter 1. Its arguments were an HTML tree and a pair of callbacks, one to handle plain text and one to handle tagged text. We found a way to use this to extract all the text that was enclosed in <h1> tags:

```
@tagged_texts = walk_html($tree, sub { ['MAYBE', $_[0]] },
                                 \&promote_if_h1tag);


sub promote_if_h1tag {
  my $element = shift;
  if ($element->{_tag} eq 'h1') {
    return ['KEEPER', join '', map {$_->[1]} @_];
  } else {
    return @_;
  }
}
sub extract_headers {
  my $tree = shift;
  my @tagged_texts = walk_html($tree, sub { ['MAYBE', $_[0]] },
                                      \&promote_if_h1tag);
  my @keepers = grep { $_->[0] eq 'KEEPER' } @tagged_texts;
  my @keeper_text = map { $_->[1] } @keepers;
  my $header_text = join '', @keeper_text;
  return $header_text;
}
```

We then observed that it would make sense to abstract the <h1> out of promote_if_h1tag(), to make it more general:

```
sub promote_if {
  my $is_interesting = shift;
  my $element = shift;
  if ($is_interesting->($element->{_tag})) {
    return ['keeper', join '', map {$_->[1]} @_];
  } else {
```

```
        return @_;
      }
    }


  my @tagged_texts = walk_html($tree,
                        sub { ['maybe', $_[0]] },
                        sub { promote_if(
                                sub { $_[0] eq 'h1' },
                                $_[0])
                        });
```

The second callback in walk_html() is rather peculiar. It's an anonymous function that we manufactured solely to call promote_if() with the right arguments. The previous version of the code was tidier. What we need is a way to get promote_if() to *manufacture* the promote_if_h1tag() function we need. This seems like it should be possible, because promote_if() already knows how to perform the task that we want promote_if_h1tag() to perform. All that we need to do is to have promote_if() wrap up that behavior into a new function:

```
  sub promote_if {
    my $is_interesting = shift;
    return sub {
      my $element = shift;
      if ($is_interesting->($element->{_tag}) {
        return ['keeper', join '', map {$_->[1]} @_];
      } else {
        return @_;
      }
    }
  }
```

Instead of accepting both arguments right away, promote_if() now gets the $is_interesting callback only, and manufactures a new function that, given an HTML element, promotes it if it's considered interesting. Making this change to promote_if(), to turn it from a function of two arguments into a function of one argument that returns a function of one argument, is called *currying* it, and the version of promote_if() immediately above is the *curried* version of promote_if().[1]

---

[1]   Currying is so-named because it was popularized by Haskell B. Curry in 1930, although it had been discovered by Gottlob Frege in 1893 and rediscovered by Moses Schönfinkel in 1924.

The happy outcome is that the call to walk_html() is now much simpler:

```
my @tagged_texts = walk_html($tree,
                             sub { ['maybe', $_[0]] },
                             promote_if('h1'),
                             });
```

Once you get used to the idea of currying, you start to see opportunities to do it all over. Recall our functions from Chapter 6 for adding and multiplying two streams together element-by-element: add2() and mul2():

```
sub add2 {
  my ($s, $t) = @_;
  return unless $s && $t;
  node(head($s) + head($t),
       promise { add2(tail($s), tail($t)) });
}
sub mul2 {
  my ($s, $t) = @_;
  return unless $s && $t;
  node(head($s) * head($t),
       promise { mul2(tail($s), tail($t)) });
}
```

These functions are almost identical. We saw in Chapter 1 that two functions with similar code can often be combined into a single function that accepts a callback parameter. In this case, the callback, $op, specifies the operation to use to combine head($s) and head($t):

```
sub combine2 {
  my ($s, $t, $op) = @_;
  return unless $s && $t;
  node($op->(head($s), head($t)),
       promise { combine2(tail($s), tail($t), $op) });

}
```

Now we can build add2() and mul2() from combine2():

```
sub add2 { combine2(@_, sub { $_[0] + $_[1] }) }
sub mul2 { combine2(@_, sub { $_[0] * $_[1] }) }
```

Since a major use of combine2() is to manufacture such functions, it would be more convenient for combine2() to do what we wanted in the first place. We can turn combine2() into a factory that manufactures stream-combining functions by currying it:

```
sub combine2 {
    my $op = shift;
    return sub {
      my ($s, $t) = @_;
      return unless $s && $t;
      node($op->(head($s), head($t)),
           promise { combine2($op)->(tail($s), tail($t))}});
    };
}
```

Now we have simply:

```
$add2 = combine2(sub { $_[0] + $_[1] });
$mul2 = combine2(sub { $_[0] * $_[1] });
```

This may also be fractionally more efficient, since we won't have to do an extra function call every time we call add2() or mul2(). add2() is the function to add the two streams, rather than a function that re-invokes combine2() in a way that adds two streams.

If we want these functions to stick around, we can give them names, as we just did; alternatively, we can use them anonymously:

```
my $catstrs = combine2(sub { "$_[0]$_[1]" })->($s, $t);
```

Instead of the scale() function we saw earlier, we might prefer this curried version:

```
sub scale {
    my $s = shift;
    return sub {
      my $c = shift;
      return if $c == 0;
      transform { $_[0] * $c } $s;
    }
}
```

scale() is now a function factory. Instead of taking a stream and a number and returning a new stream, it takes a stream and manufactures a function that produces new streams. $scale_s = scale($s) returns a function for scaling $s; given a numeric argument, say $n, $scale_s produces a stream that has the elements of $s scaled by $n. For example, $scale_s->(2) returns a stream whose every element is twice $s's, and $scale_s->(3) returns a stream whose every element is three times $s's. If we're planning to scale the same stream by several different factors, it might make sense to have a single scale function to generate all the outputs.

Depending on how we're using it, we might have preferred to curry the function arguments in the other order:

CODE LIBRARY

scale

```
sub scale {
    my $c = shift;
    return sub {
        my $s = shift;
        transform { $_[0] * $c } $s;
    }
}
```

Now scale() is a factory for manufacturing scaling functions. scale(2) returns a function that takes any stream and doubles it; scale(3) returns a function that takes any stream and triples it. We could write $double = scale(2) and then use $double->($s) to double $s, or scale(2)->($s) to double $s.

If you don't like the extra arrows in $double->($s) you can get rid of them by using Perl's glob feature, as we did in Chapter 3:

```
*double = scale(2);
$s2 = double($s);
```

Similarly, in Chapter 6, we defined a slope() function that returned the slope of some other function at a particular point:

```
sub slope {
    my ($f, $x) = @_;
    my $e = 0.00000095367431640625;
    ($f->($x+$e) - $f->($x-$e)) / (2*$e);
}
```

We could make this more flexible by currying the $x argument:

CODE LIBRARY
slope0

```
sub slope {
  my $f = shift;
  my $e = 0.00000095367431640625;
  return sub {
    my $x = shift;
    ($f->($x+$e) - $f->($x-$e)) / (2*$e);
  };
}
```

slope() now takes a function and returns its derivative function! By evaluating the derivative function at a particular point, we compute the slope at that point.

If we like, we can use Perl's polymorphism to put both behaviors into the same function:

CODE LIBRARY
slope

```
sub slope {
  my $f = shift;
  my $e = 0.00000095367431640625;
  my $d = sub {
    my ($x) = shift;
    ($f->($x+$e) - $f->($x-$e)) / (2*$e);
  };
  return @_ ? $d->(shift) : $d;
}
```

Now we can call slope($f, $x) as before, to compute the slope of $f at the point $x, or we can call slope($f) and get back the derivative function of $f.

Currying can be a good habit to get into. Earlier, we wrote:

```
sub iterate_function {
  my ($f, $x) = @_;
  my $s;
  $s = node($x, promise { &transform($f, $s) });
}
```

But it's almost as easy to write it this way instead:

CODE LIBRARY
iterate_function

```
sub iterate_function {
  my $f = shift;
```

```
    return sub {
      my $x = shift;
      my $s;
      $s = node($x, promise { &transform($f, $s) });
    };
  }
```

It requires hardly any extra thought to do it this way, and the payoff is substantially increased functionality. We now have a function that manufactures stream-building functions to order. We could construct upfrom() as a special case of iterate_function(); for example:

```
    *upfrom = iterate_function(sub { $_[0] + 1 });
```

Or similarly, our earlier example of pow2_from():

```
    *pow2_from = iterate_function(sub { $_[0] * 2 });
```

One final lexical point about currying: When currying a recursive function, it's often possible to get a small time and memory performance improvement by tightening up the recursion. For example, consider combine2() again:

```
    sub combine2 {
      my $op = shift;
      return sub {
        my ($s, $t) = @_;
        return unless $s && $t;
        node($op->(head($s), head($t)),
            promise { combine2($op)->(tail($s), tail($t)) });
      };
    }
```

combine2($op) will return the same result function every time. So we should be able to get a speed-up by caching its value and using the cached value in the promise instead of repeatedly calling combine2($op). Moreover, combine2($op) is precisely the value that combine2() is about to return anyway. So we can change this to:

```
    sub combine2 {
      my $op = shift;
```

```
    my $r;
    $r = sub {
      my ($s, $t) = @_;
      return unless $s && $t;
      node($op->(head($s), head($t)),
          promise { $r->(tail($s), tail($t)) });
    };
  }
```

Now the promise no longer needs to call combine2(); we've cached the value that combine2() is about to return by storing it in $r, and the promise can call $r directly. The code is also easier to understand this way: Now the promise says explicitly that the function will be calling itself on the tails of the two streams.

These curried functions are examples of *higher-order functions*. Ordinary functions operate on values: You put some values in, and you get some other values out. Higher-order functions are functions that operate on other functions: You put some functions in, and you get some other functions out. For example, in combine2() we put in a function to operate on two scalars and we got out an analogous function to operate on two streams.

7.2 COMMON HIGHER-ORDER FUNCTIONS

Probably the two most fundamental higher-order functions for any list or other kind of sequence are analogs of map() and grep(). map() and grep() are higher-order functions because each of them takes an argument that is itself another function. We've already seen versions of map() and grep() for iterators and streams. Perl's standard map() and grep() each take a function and a list and return a new list; for example:

```
map { $_ * 2 } (1..5);          # returns 2, 4, 6, 8, 10
grep { $_ % 2 == 0 } (1..10);   # returns 2, 4, 6, 8, 10
```

Often it's more convenient to have curried versions of these functions:

```
sub cmap (&) {
  my $f = shift;
  my $r = sub {
```

```
      my @result;
      for (@_) {
        push @result, $f->($_);
      }
      @result;
    };
    return $r;
  }
```

```
sub cgrep (&) {
  my $f = shift;
  my $r = sub {
    my @result;
    for (@_) {
      push @result, $_ if $f->($_);
    }
    @result;
  };
  return $r;
}
```

These functions should be called like this:

```
$double = cmap { $_ * 2 };
$find_slashdot = cgrep { $_->{referer} =~ /slashdot/i };
```

After which `$double->(1..5)` returns (2, 4, 6, 8, 10) and `$find_slashdot`
`->(weblog())` returns the web log records that represent referrals from Slashdot.

It may be tempting to try to make cmap() and cgrep() polymorphic, as we
did with slope() (I was tempted, anyway.):

```
sub cmap (&;@) {
  my $f = shift;
  my $r = sub {
    my @result;
    for (@_) {
      push @result, $f->($_);
    }
    @result;
  };
```

```
      return @_ ? $r->(@_) : $r;
  }
```

Then we would also be able to use cmap() and cgrep() like regular map() and grep():

```
@doubles = cmap { $_ * 2 } (1..5);
@evens = cgrep { $_ % 2 == 0 } (1..10);
```

Unfortunately, this apparently happy notation hides an evil surprise:

```
@doubles = cmap { $_ * 2 } @some_array;
```

If @some_array is empty, @doubles is assigned a reference to a doubling function.

7.2.1 Automatic Currying

We've written the same code several times to implement curried functions:

```
sub some_curried_function {
  my $first_arg = shift;
  my $r = sub {
     ...
  };
  return @_ ? $r->(@_) : $r;
}
```

(Possibly with the polymorphism trick omitted from the final line.)

As usual, once we recognize this pattern, we should see if it makes sense to abstract it into a function:

```
package Curry;
use base 'Exporter';
@EXPORT = ('curry');
@EXPORT_OK = qw(curry_listfunc curry_n);

sub curry {
  my $f = shift;
  return sub {
    my $first_arg = shift;
    my $r = sub { $f->($first_arg, @_) };
```

```
           return @_ ? $r->(@_) : $r;
        };
    }

    sub curry_listfunc {
      my $f = shift;
      return sub {
        my $first_arg = shift;
        return sub { $f->($first_arg, @_) };
      };
    }

    1;
```

curry() takes any function and returns a curried version of that function. For example, consider the imap() function from Chapter 4:

```
    sub imap (&$) {
      my ($transform, $it) = @_;
      return sub {
        my $next = NEXTVAL($it);
        return unless defined $next;
        return $transform->($next);
      }
    }
```

imap() is analogous to map(), but operates on iterators rather than on lists. We might use it like this:

```
    my $doubles_iterator = imap { $_[0] * 2 } $it;
```

If we end up doubling a lot of iterators, we have to repeat the {$_[0] * 2} part:

```
    my $doubles_a = imap { $_[0] * 2 } $it_a;
    my $doubles_b = imap { $_[0] * 2 } $it_b;
    my $doubles_c = imap { $_[0] * 2 } $it_c;
```

We might wish we had a single, special-purpose function for doubling every element of an iterator, so that we could write instead:

```
    my $doubles_a = double $it_a;
    my $doubles_b = double $it_b;
    my $doubles_c = double $it_c;
```

or even:

```
my ($doubles_a, $doubles_b, $doubles_c)
  = map double($_), $it_a, $it_b, $it_c;
```

If we had written imap() in a curried style, we could have done:

```
*double = imap { $_[0] * 2 };
```

but we didn't, so we can't. But that's no problem, because curry() will manufacture a curried version of imap() on the fly:

```
*double = curry(\&imap)->(sub { $_[0] * 2 });
```

Since the curried imap() function came in handy once, perhaps we should keep it around in case we need it again:

```
*c_imap = curry(\&imap);
```

Then to manufacture double() we do:

```
*double = c_imap(sub { $_[0] * 2 });
```

7.2.2 Prototypes

The only drawback of this approach is that we lose imap()'s pretty calling syntax, which is enabled by the (&@) prototype at compile time. We can get it back, although the results are somewhat peculiar. First, we modify curry() so that the function it manufactures has the appropriate prototype:

```
sub curry {
   my $f = shift;
   return sub (&;@) {
     my $first_arg = shift;
     my $r = sub { $f->($first_arg, @_) };
     return @_ ? $r->(@_) : $r;
   };
}
```

Then we call curry() at compile time instead of at run time:

```
BEGIN { *c_imap = curry (\&imap); }
```

Now we can say:

```
*double = c_imap { $_[0] * 2 };
```

and we can still use c_imap() in place of regular imap():

```
$doubles_a = c_imap { $_[0] * 2 } $it_a;
```

PROTOTYPE PROBLEMS

The problem with this technique is that the prototype must be hardwired into curry(), so now it will generate *only* curried functions with the prototype (&;@). This isn't a problem for functions like c_imap() or c_grep(), which would have had that prototype anyway. But that prototype is inappropriate for the curried version of the scale() function from Chapter 6. The uncurried version was:

```
sub scale {
  my ($s, $c) = @_;
  $s->transform(sub { $_[0]*$c });
}
```

curry(\&scale) returns a function that behaves like this:

```
sub {
    my $s = shift;
    my $r = sub { scale($s, @_) };
    return @_ ? $r->(@_) : $r;
}
```

The internals of this function are correct, and it will work just fine, as long as it *doesn't have* a (&;@) prototype. Such a prototype would be inappropriate, since the function is expecting to get one or two scalar arguments. The correct prototype would be ($;$). But if we did:

```
BEGIN { *c_scale = curry(\&scale) }
```

then the resulting c_scale() function wouldn't work, because it would have a (&;@) prototype when we expected to call it as though it had a ($;$) prototype.

We want to call it in one of these two ways:

```
my $double = c_scale(2);
my $doubled_it = c_scale(2, $it);
```

but because c_scale() would have a prototype of (&;@), these both would be syntax errors, yielding:

```
Type of arg 1 to main::c_scale must be block or sub {} (not
constant item)...
```

This isn't a show-stopper. This works:

```
*c_scale = curry(\&scale);
my $double = c_scale(2);
my $doubled_it = c_scale(2, $it);
```

Here the call to c_scale() is compiled, with no prototype, before *c_scale is assigned to; the call to curry() that sets up the bad prototype occurs too late to foul up our attempt to (correctly) call c_scale().

But now we have a somewhat confusing situation. Our curry() function creates curried functions with (&;@) prototypes, and these prototypes may be inappropriate. But the prototypes are inoperative unless curry() is called in a BEGIN block. To add to the confusion, this doesn't work:

```
*c_scale = curry(\&scale);
my $double = eval 'c_scale(2)';
```

because, once again, the call to c_scale() has been compiled after the prototype was set up by curry().

There isn't really any easy way to fix this. The obvious thing to do is to tell curry() what prototype we desire by supplying it with an optional parameter:

```
# Doesn't really work
sub curry {
  my $f = shift;
  my $PROTOTYPE = shift;
  return sub ($PROTOTYPE) {
    my $first_arg = shift;
    my $r = sub { $f->($first_arg, @_) };
    return @_ ? $r->(@_) : $r;
  };
}
```

Unfortunately, this is illegal; ($PROTOTYPE) *does not* indicate that the desired prototype is stored in $PROTOTYPE. Perl 5.8.1 provides a Scalar::Util::set_prototype function to set the prototype of a particular function:

CODE LIBRARY
curry-set_proto

```
# Doesn't work before 5.8.1
use Scalar::Util 'set_prototype';

sub curry {
  my $f = shift;
  my $PROTOTYPE = shift;
  set_prototype(sub {
    my $first_arg = shift;
    my $r = sub { $f->($first_arg, @_) };
    return @_ ? $r->(@_) : $r;
  }, $PROTOTYPE);
}
```

If you don't have 5.8.1 yet, the only way to dynamically specify the prototype of a function is to use string eval:

CODE LIBRARY
curry_eval

```
sub curry {
  my $f = shift;
  my $PROTOTYPE = shift;
  $PROTOTYPE = "($PROTOTYPE)" if defined $PROTOTYPE;
  my $CODE = q{sub PROTOTYPE {
                my $first_arg = shift;
                my $r = sub { $f->($first_arg, @_) };
                return @_ ? $r->((@_) : $r;
              }};
  $CODE =~ s/PROTOTYPE/$PROTOTYPE/;
  eval $CODE;
}
```

7.2.3 More Currying

We can extend the idea of curry() and build a function that generates a generic curried version of another function:

```
sub curry_n {
  my $N = shift;
  my $f = shift;
```

```
  my $c;
  $c = sub {
    if (@_ >= $N) { $f->(@_) }
    else {
      my @a = @_;
      curry_n($N-@a, sub { $f->(@a, @_) });
    }
  };
}
```

curry_n() takes two arguments: a number *N*, and a function *f*, which expects at least *N* arguments. The result is a new function, *c*, which does the same thing *f* does, but which accepts curried arguments. If *c* is called with *N* or more arguments, it just passes them on to *f* and returns the result. If there are fewer than *N* arguments, *c* generates a new function that remembers the arguments that were passed; if this new function is called with the remaining arguments, both old and new arguments are given to *f*. For example:

```
*add = curry_n(2, sub { $_[0] + $_[1] });
```

And now we can call:

```
add(2, 3);      # Returns 5
```

or:

```
*increment = add(1);
increment(8);   # return 9
```

or perhaps more realistically:

```
*csubstr = curry_n(3, sub { defined $_[3] ?
                      substr($_[0], $_[1], $_[2], $_[3]) :
                      substr($_[0], $_[1], $_[2]) });
```

Then we can use any of:

```
$target = "I like pie";
```

 # Just like regular substr

```
$ss = csubstr($target, $start, $length);
csubstr($target, $start, $length, $replacement);
```

```
# Not just like regular substr

# This '$part' function gets two arguments: a start position
# and a length; it returns the appropriate part of $target.

$part = csubstr($target);
my $ss = $part->($start, $length);

# This function gets an argument N and returns that many characters
# from the beginning of $target.

$first_N_chars = csubstr($target, 0);
my $prefix_3 = $first_N_chars->(3);      # "I l"
my $prefix_7 = $first_N_chars->(7);      # "I like "
```

7.2.4 Yet More Currying

Many of the functions we saw earlier in the book would benefit from currying. For example, dir_walk() from Chapter 1:

```
sub dir_walk {
  my ($top, $filefunc, $dirfunc) = @_;
  my $DIR;

  if (-d $top) {
    my $file;
    unless (opendir $DIR, $top) {
      warn "Couldn't open directory $code: $!; skipping.\n";
      return;
    }

    my @results;
    while ($file = readdir $DIR) {
      next if $file eq '.' || $file eq '..';
      push @results, dir_walk("$top/$file", $filefunc, $dirfunc);
    }
    return $dirfunc->($top, @results);
  } else {
    return $filefunc->($top);
  }
}
```

Here we specify a top directory and two callback functions. But the callback functions are constant through any call to dir_walk(), and we might like to specify them in advance, because we might know them well before we know which directories we want to search. The conversion is easy:

CODE LIBRARY
dir-walk-curried

```perl
sub dir_walk {
  unshift @_, undef if @_ < 3;
  my ($top, $filefunc, $dirfunc) = @_;

  my $r;
  $r = sub {
    my $DIR;
    my $top = shift;
    if (-d $top) {
      my $file;
      unless (opendir $DIR, $top) {
        warn "Couldn't open directory $code: $!; skipping.\n";
        return;
      }

      my @results;
      while ($file = readdir $DIR) {
        next if $file eq '.' || $file eq '..';
        push @results, $r->("$top/$file");
      }
      return $dirfunc->($top, @results);
    } else {
      return $filefunc->($top);
    }
  };
  defined($top) ? $r->($top) : $r;
}
```

We can still call dir_walk($top, $filefunc, $dirfunc) and get the same result, or we can omit the $top argument (or pass undef) and get back a specialized file-walking function. As a minor added bonus, the recursive call will be fractionally more efficient because the callback arguments don't need to be explicitly passed.

7.3 reduce() AND combine()

The standard Perl List::Util module provides several commonly requested functions that are not built-in to Perl. These include max() and min() functions, which respectively return the largest and smallest numbers in their argument lists, maxstr() and minstr(), which are the analogous functions for strings; and sum(), which returns the sum of the numbers in a list.

If we write sample code for these five functions, we'll see the similarity immediately:

```
sub max { my $max = shift;
        for (@_) { $max = $_ > $max ? $_ : $max }
        return $max;
    }

sub min { my $min = shift;
        for (@_) { $min = $_ < $min ? $_ : $min }
        return $min;
    }

sub maxstr { my $max = shift;
        for (@_) { $max = $_ gt $max ? $_ : $max }
        return $max;
    }

sub minstr { my $min = shift;
        for (@_) { $min = $_ lt $min ? $_ : $min }
        return $min;
    }

sub sum { my $sum = shift;
        for (@_) { $sum = $sum + $_ }
        return $sum;
    }
```

Generalizing this gives us the reduce() function that is also provided by List::Util:

```
sub reduce { my $code = shift;
        my $val = shift;
        for (@_) { $val = $code->($val, $_) }
        return $val;
    }
```

(List::Util::reduce is actually written in C for speed, but what it does is equivalent to this Perl code.) The idea is that the function will scan the list one element at a time, accumulating a "total" of some sort. We provide a function ($code) that says how to compute the new total, given the old total (first argument) and the current element (second argument). If our goal is just to add up all the list elements, then we compute the total at each stage by adding the previous total to the current element:

```
reduce(sub { $_[0] + $_[1] }, @VALUES) == sum(@VALUES)
```

If our goal is to find the maximum element, then the "total" is actually the maximum so far. Then we compute the total at each stage by taking whichever of the current maximum and the current element is larger:

```
reduce(sub { $_[0] > $_[1] ? $_[0] : $_[1] }, @VALUES) == max(@VALUES)
```

The reduce() function provided by List::Util is easier to call than the preceding one. It places the total-so-far in $a and the current list element into $b before invoking the callback, so that we can write:

```
reduce(sub { $a + $b }, @VALUES)
reduce(sub { $a > $b ? $a : $b }, @VALUES)
```

We saw how to make this change back in Section 4.4, when we arranged to have imap()'s callback invoked with the current iterator value in $_ in addition to $_[0]; this allowed it to have a more map()-like calling syntax. We can arrange reduce() similarly:

```
sub reduce (&@) {
  my $code = shift;
  my $val = shift;
  for (@_) {
    local ($a, $b) = ($val, $_);
    $val = $code->($val, $_)
  }
  return $val;
}
```

Here we're using the global variables $a and $b to pass the total and the current list element. Use of global variables normally causes a compile-time failure under strict 'vars', but there is a special exemption for the variables $a and $b. The exemption is there to allow usages just like this one, and in particular to support the analogous feature of Perl's built-in sort() function. The List::Util version of reduce() already has this feature built in.

If we curry the reduce() function, we can use it to *manufacture* functions like sum() and max():

```
BEGIN {
  *reduce = curry(\&List::Util::reduce);
  *sum = reduce { $a + $b };
  *max = reduce { $a > $b ? $a : $b };
}
```

This version of reduce() isn't quite as general as it could be. All the functions manufactured by reduce() have one thing in common: Given an empty list of arguments, they always return undef. For max() and min() this may be appropriate, but for sum() it's wrong; the sum of an empty list should be taken to be 0. (The sum() function provided by List::Util also has this defect.) This small defect masks a larger one: When the argument list is nonempty, our version of reduce() assumes that the total should be initialized to the first data item. This happens to work for sum() and max(), but it isn't appropriate for all functions. reduce can be made much more general if we drop this assumption. As a trivial example, suppose we want a function to produce the length of a list. This is *almost* what we want:

```
reduce { $a + 1 };
```

But it only produces the correct length when given a list whose first element is 1, since otherwise $val is incorrectly initialized. A more general version of reduce() accepts an explicit parameter to say what value should be returned for an empty list:

```
sub reduce (&$@) {
  my $code = shift;
  my $val = shift;
  for (@_) {
    local ($a, $b) = ($val, $_);
    $val = $code->($val, $_)
  }
  return $val;
}
```

A version with optional currying is:

CODE LIBRARY

reduce

```
sub reduce (&;$@) {
  my $code = shift;
```

```
    my $f = sub {
      my $base_val = shift;
      my $g = sub {
        my $val = $base_val;
        for (@_) {
          local ($a, $b) = ($val, $_);
          $val = $code->($val, $_);
        }
        return $val;
      };
      @_ ? $g->(@_) : $g;
    };
    @_ ? $f->(@_) : $f;
  }
```

The list-length function is now:

```
    *listlength = reduce { $a + 1 } 0;
```

where the 0 here is the correct result for an empty list. Similarly,

```
    *product = reduce { $a * $b } 1;
```

is a function that multiplies all the elements in a list of numbers. We can even use reduce() to compute both at the same time:

```
    *length_and_product = reduce { [$a->[0]+1, $a->[1]*$b] } [0, 1];
```

This makes only one pass over the list to compute both the length and the product. For an empty list, the result is [0, 1], and for a list with one element *x*, the result is [1, x]. List::Util::reduce() can manufacture only functions that return undef for the empty list, and that return the first list element for a single-element list. The length_and_product() function can't be generated by List::Util::reduce() because it doesn't have these properties.

A properly general version of reduce() gets an additional argument that says that the function should return when given an empty list as its argument. In the programming literature, the properly general version of reduce() is more typically called fold():

```
    sub fold {
      my $f = shift;
```

```
          my $fold;
          $fold = sub {
            my $x = shift;
            sub {
              return $x unless @_;
              my $first = shift;
              $fold->($f->($x, $first), @_)
            }
          }
        }
```

Eliminating the recursion yields:

CODE LIBRARY
fold

```
sub fold {
  my $f = shift;
  sub {
    my $x = shift;
    sub {
      my $r = $x;
      while (@_) {
        $r = $f->($r, shift());
      }
      return $r;
    }
  }
}
```

7.3.1 Boolean Operators

In Section 4.3 we saw a system that would search backwards through a log file looking for records that matched a simple query. To extend this into a useful database system, we need to be able to combine simple queries into more complex ones.

Let's suppose that $a and $b are iterators that will produce data items that match queries A and B, respectively. How can we manufacture an iterator that matches the query $A \mid\mid B$?

One way we could do this is to interleave the elements of $a and $b:

CODE LIBRARY
interleave

```
sub interleave {
  my ($a, $b) = @_;
```

```
      return sub {
        my $next = $a->();
        unless (defined $next) {
          $a = $b;
          $next = $a->();
        }
        ($a, $b) = ($b, $a);
        $next;
      }
    }
```

But this has the drawback that if the record sets produced by $a and $b happen to overlap, the interleaved outputs will include some records more than once.

We can do better if we suppose that the records will be produced in some sort of canonical order. This assumption isn't unreasonable. Typically, a database will have a natural order dictated by the physical layout of the information on the disk and will always produce records in this natural order, at least until the data is modified. For example, our program for searching the web log file always produces matching records in the order they appear in the file. Even DBM files, which don't appear to keep records in any particular order, have a natural order; this is the order in which the records will be generated by the each() function.

Supposing that $a and $b will produce records in the same order, we can perform an "or" operation as follows:

CODE LIBRARY
Iterator_Logic.pm

```
package Iterator_Logic;
use base 'Exporter';
@EXPORT = qw(i_or_ i_or i_and_ i_and i_without_ i_without);

sub i_or_ {
  my ($cmp, $a, $b) = @_;
  my ($av, $bv) = ($a->(), $b->());
  return sub {
    if (! defined $av && ! defined $bv) { return }
    elsif (! defined $av) { $rv = $bv; $bv = $b->() }
    elsif (! defined $bv) { $rv = $av; $av = $a->() }
    else {
      my $d = $cmp->($av, $bv);
      if    ($d < 0) { $rv = $av; $av = $a->() }
      elsif ($d > 0) { $rv = $bv; $bv = $b->() }
      else           { $rv = $av; $av = $a->(); $bv = $b->() }
    }
```

```
        return $rv;
      }
    }


  use Curry;
  BEGIN { *i_or = curry(\&i_or_) }
```

i_or_() gets a comparator function, $cmp, which defines the canonical order, and two iterators, $a and $b. It returns a new iterator that returns the next record from either $a or $b in the canonical order. If $a and $b both produce the same record, the duplicate is discarded. It begins by kicking $a and $b to obtain the next record from each. If either is exhausted, it returns the record from the other; if both are exhausted, it returns undef to indicate that there are no more records. $rv holds the record that is to be the return value.

If both input iterators produce records, the new iterator compares the records to see which should come out first. If the comparator returns zero, it means the two records are the same, and only one of them should be emitted. $rv is assigned one of the two records, as appropriate, and then one or both of the iterators is kicked to produce new records for the next call.

The logic is very similar to the merge() function of Section 6.4. In fact, merge() is the stream analog of the "or" operator.

i_or() is a curried version of i_or_(), called like this:

```
  BEGIN { *numeric_or = i_or { $_[0] <=> $_[1] };
          *alphabetic_or = i_or { $_[0] cmp $_[1] };
        }


  $event_times =  numeric_or($access_request_times,
                    numeric_or($report_request_times,
                      $server_start_times));
```

"And" is similar:

```
  sub i_and_ {
    my ($cmp, $a, $b) = @_;
    my ($av, $bv) = ($a->(), $b->());
    return sub {
      my $d;
      until (! defined $av || ! defined $bv ||
             ($d = $cmp->($av, $bv)) == 0) {
        if ($d < 0) { $av = $a->() }
        else        { $bv = $b->() }
      }
```

```
        return unless defined $av && defined $bv;
        my $rv = $av;
        ($av, $bv) = ($a->(), $b->());
        return $rv;
    }
}

BEGIN { *i_and = curry \&i_and_ }
```

7.4 DATABASES

In Section 4.3 we saw the beginnings of a database system that would manufacture an iterator containing the results of a simple query. To open the database we did:

```
        my $dbh = FlatDB->new($datafile);
```

and then to perform a query,

```
        $dbh->query($filename, $value);
```

or:

```
        $dbh->callbackquery(sub { ... });
```

which selects the records for which the subroutine returns true.

Let's extend this system to handle compound queries. Eventually, we'll want the system to support calls like this:

```
        $dbh->select("STATE = 'NY' |
                       OWES > 100 & STATE = 'MA'");
```

This will require parsing of the query string, which we'll see in detail in Chapter 8. In the meantime, we'll build the internals that are required to support such queries.

The internals for simple queries like "STATE = 'NY'" are already done, since that's exactly what the $dbh->query('STATE', 'NY') does. We can assume that other simple queries are covered by similar simple functions, or perhaps by calls to callbackquery(). What we need now are ways to combine simple queries into compound queries.

The i_and() and i_or() functions we saw earlier will do what we want, if we modify them suitably. The main thing we need to arrange is to define a canonical order for records produced by one of the simple query iterators. In particular, we need some way for the i_and() and i_or() operators to recognize that their two argument iterators have generated the same output record.

The natural way to do this is to tag each record with a unique ID number as it comes out of the query. Two different records will have different ID numbers. For flat-file databases, there's a natural record ID number already to hand: the record number of the record in the file. We'll need to adjust the query() function so that the iterators it returns will generate record numbers. When we last saw the query() function, it returned each record as a single string; this is a good opportunity to have it return a more structured piece of data:

CODE LIBRARY
FlatDB_Compose.pm

```perl
package FlatDB_Compose;
use base 'FlatDB';
use base 'Exporter';
@EXPORT_OK = qw(query_or query_and query_not query_without);
use Iterator_Logic;

# usage: $dbh->query(fieldname, value)
# returns all records for which (fieldname) matches (value)
sub query {
  my $self = shift;
  my ($field, $value) = @_;
  my $fieldnum = $self->{FIELDNUM}{uc $field};
  return unless defined $fieldnum;
  my $fh = $self->{FH};
  seek $fh, 0, 0;
  <$fh>;                    # discard header line
  my $position = tell $fh;
  my $recno = 0;

  return sub {
    local $_;
    seek $fh, $position, 0;
    while (<$fh>) {
      chomp;
      $recno++;
      $position = tell $fh;
      my @fields = split $self->{FIELDSEP};
      my $fieldval = $fields[$fieldnum];
      return [$recno, @fields] if $fieldval eq $value;
```

```
      }
    return;
  };
}
```

It might be tempting to try to use Perl's built-in $. variable here instead of having each iterator carry its own synthetic $recno, but that's a bad idea. We took some pains to make sure that a single database filehandle could be shared among more than one query. However, the information for $. is stored inside the filehandle; since we don't want the current record number to be shared among queries, we need to store it in the query object (which is private) rather than in the filehandle (which isn't). An alternative to maintaining a special $recno variable would be to use $position as a record identifier, since it's already lying around, and since it has the necessary properties of being different for different records and of increasing as the query proceeds through the file.

Now we need to manufacture versions of i_and() and i_or() that use the record ID numbers when deciding what to pass along. Because these functions are curried, we don't need to rewrite any code to do this:

```
BEGIN { *query_or  =  i_or(sub { $_[0][0] <=> $_[1][0] });
        *query_and = i_and(sub { $_[0][0] <=> $_[1][0] });
      }
BEGIN { *query_without = i_without(sub { $_[0][0] <=> $_[1][0] }); }
```

The comparator function says that arguments $_[0] and $_[1] will be arrays of record data, and that we should compare the first element of each, which is the record number, to decide which data should come out first and to decide record identity.

Here's a similarly modified version of callbackquery():

```
sub callbackquery {
  my $self = shift;
  my $is_interesting = shift;
  my $fh = $self->{FH};
  seek $fh, 0, SEEK_SET;
  <$fh>;                    # discard header line
  my $position = tell $fh;
  my $recno = 0;

  return sub {
    local $_;
```

```
          seek $fh, $position, SEEK_SET;
          while (<$fh>) {
            $position = tell $fh;
            chomp;
            $recno++;
            my %F;
            my @fieldnames = @{$self->{FIELDS}};
            my @fields = split $self->{FIELDSEP};
            for (0 .. $#fieldnames) {
              $F{$fieldnames[$_]} = $fields[$_];
            }
            return [$recno, @fields] if $is_interesting->(%F);
          }
          return;
        };
    }

    1;
```

In Chapter 8, we'll build a parser that, given this query:

```
    "STATE = 'NY' | OWES > 100 & STATE = 'MA'"
```

makes this call:

```
    query_or($dbh->query('STATE', 'NY'),
             query_and($dbh->callbackquery(sub { $F{OWES} > 100 }),
                       $dbh->query('STATE', 'MA')
                      ))
```

and returns the resulting iterator. In the meantime, we can manufacture the iterator manually.

The one important logical connective that's still missing is "not," which is a little bit peculiar, logically, because its meaning is tied to the original database. If $q is a query for all the people in a database who are male, then query_not($q) should produce all the people from the database who are female. But the query_not function can't do that without visiting the original database to find the female persons. Unlike the outputs of query_and() and query_or(), the output of query_not() is not a selection of the inputs.

One way around this is for each query to capture a reference back to the original database that it's a query on. An alternative is to specify the database explicitly, as $dbh->query_not($q). Then we can implement a more general operator on queries, the so-called *set difference operator*, also known as *without*:

```perl
# $a but not $b
sub i_without_ {
  my ($cmp, $a, $b) = @_;
  my ($av, $bv) = ($a->(), $b->());
  return sub {
    while (defined $av) {
      my $d;
      while (defined $bv && ($d = $cmp->($av, $bv)) > 0) {
        $bv = $b->();
      }
      if ( ! defined $bv || $d < 0 ) {
        my $rv = $av; $av = $a->(); return $rv;
      } else {
        $bv = $b->();
        $av = $a->();
      }
    }
    return;
  }
}

BEGIN {
  *i_without = curry \&i_without_;
  *query_without =
    i_without(sub { my ($a,$b) = @_; $a->[0] <=> $b->[0] });
}

1;
```

If $a and $b are iterators on the same database, query_without($a, $b) is an iterator that produces every record that appears in $a but *not* in $b. This is useful on its own, and it also gives us a base for "not", which becomes something like this:

```perl
sub query_not {
  my $self = shift;
  my $q = shift;
  query_without($self->all, $q);
}
```

$self->all is a database method that performs a trivial query that disgorges all the records in the database. We could implement it specially, or, less efficiently, we could simply use:

```
sub all {
  $_[0]->callbackquery(sub { 1 });
}
1;
```

A possibly amusing note is that once we have query_without(), we no longer need query_and(), since (*a* and *b*) is the same as (*a* without (*a* without *b*)).

7.4.1   Operator Overloading

Perl provides a feature called *operator overloading* that lets us write complicated query expressions more conveniently. Operator overloading allows us to redefine Perl's built-in operator symbols to have whatever meaning we like when they are applied to our objects. Enabling the feature is simple. First we make a small change to methods such as query() so that they return iterators that are blessed into package FlatDB:

```
package FlatDB_Ovl;
BEGIN {
  for my $f (qw(and or without)) {
    *{"query_$f"} = \&{"FlatDB_Compose::query_$f"};
  }
}
use base 'FlatDB_Compose';

sub query {
  $self = shift;
  my $q = $self->SUPER::query(@_);
  bless $q => __PACKAGE__;
}

sub callbackquery {
  $self = shift;
  my $q = $self->SUPER::callbackquery(@_);
  bless $q => __PACKAGE__;
}

1;
```

Then we add:

```
use overload '|'=> \&query_or,
             '&'=> \&query_and,
             '-'=> \&query_without,
             'fallback'=> 1;
```

at the top of `FlatDB.pm`. From then on, any time a `FlatDB` object participates in an | or & operation, the specified function will be invoked instead.

Now, given the following simple queries:

```
my ($ny, $debtor, $ma) =
        ($dbh->query('STATE', 'NY'),
         $dbh->callbackquery(sub { $F{OWES} > 100 }),
         $dbh->query('STATE', 'MA')
        );
```

we'll be able to replace this:

```
my $interesting = query_or($ny, query_and($debtor, $ma))
```

with this:

```
my $interesting = $ny | $debtor & $ma;
```

The operators are still Perl's built-in operators, and so they obey the usual precedence and associativity rules. In particular, & has higher precedence than |.

## CHAPTER 8

PARSING

Parsing is the process of converting an unstructured input, such as a text file, into a data structure. Almost every program that reads input must perform parsing of some type. Long ago when I started writing this book, I was amazed to discover how underappreciated parsing processes are. One editor even worried that parsing might not be a useful application of Perl. But parsing is nearly universal, because almost every program must read an unstructured input, such as a text file, and turn it into a data structure, so that it can do some processing on it.

Programmers have become adept at designing data formats so that parsing is as simple as possible, and they may be unaware that they are doing it. But even Perl's <HANDLE> operator is a rudimentary parser, transforming a character stream into a record stream. For more complicated sorts of inputs, many programmers fall back on a lot of weird hackery. But writing parsers can be straightforward and elegant, even for complex inputs, once you have the right set of tools available.

8.1 LEXERS

Although it isn't absolutely required, parsing is almost always split into two smaller tasks. Consider the process of parsing an English sentence, such as "The bear devoured Joe's tent." Before we can consider the way the words go together, we have to *recognize* the words. At the beginning, all we have is a sequence of characters. We analyze the characters, observing that there are five words, and also a punctuation character, the period. We should probably consider the apostrophe to be part of the word Joe's, although an alternative is to consider Joe's to be a combination of the "words" Joe and 's. We'll probably throw away the whitespace, since that doesn't contribute to the meaning of the sentence except that it allows us to distinguish word boundaries.

A *token* is the smallest part of an input that has a definite meaning. In our English example, the characters devoured have a meaning, but dev and oured don't. devoured is therefore a token; dev and oured aren't. (We could also argue that devoured can be further split, into devour and ed. But there's clearly a limit to how far the meaning can be divided; d and e have no meaning by themselves.)

Computer parsing processes are similar. Given an utterance such as my $terminator = @_ ? shift:$/;, the first thing we usually do is assemble up the unstructured characters of the input into meaningful tokens. Here, the tokens are my, $terminator, =, @_, ?, shift, :, $/, and ;. Alternatively, we could divide some of the tokens a little further; Perl's parser divides $terminator into $ and terminator, and @_ into @ and _, for example. But again, there's a limit to how far we can divide things up without destroying the meaning. When analyzing the meaning of this statement, one simply doesn't consider the meaning of min.

This process of dividing the characters into tokens goes by several names: *tokenization, lexical analysis* or *lexing,* and *scanning.* All these words mean the same thing. The programs that do it are called *tokenizers, lexical analyzers, lexers,* or *scanners.*

One natural way to represent the lexing process is as an iterator of some type. The lexer can generate a sequence of tokens, potentially infinite, to be consumed by some later part of the parsing process.

8.1.1   Emulating the <> Operator

As a very simple example of a lexer, we'll build an iterator that takes a sequence of characters and turns it into a sequence of records. Here's a function that builds iterators that generate sequences of characters:

CODE LIBRARY
Lexer.pm

```
package Lexer;
use base "Exporter";
@EXPORT_OK = qw(make_charstream blocks records tokens iterator_to_stream
                make_lexer allinput);

%EXPORT_TAGS = ('all' => \@EXPORT_OK);

sub make_charstream {
  my $fh = shift;
  return sub { return getc($fh) };
}

# For example:
my $stdin = make_charstream(\*STDIN);
```

If `$chars` is an iterator that generates a sequence of characters, then
`records($chars)` turns it into an iterator that generates a sequence of records:

```
sub records {
  my $chars = shift;
  my $terminator = @_ ? shift : $/;
  my $buffer = "";
  sub {
    my $char;
    while (substr($buffer, -(length $terminator)) ne $terminator
           && defined($char = $chars->())
          ) {
      $buffer .= $char;
    }
    if ($buffer ne "") {
      my $line = $buffer;
      $buffer = "";
      return $line;
    } else {
      return;
    }
  }
}
```

In addition to the character generator, `records()` also gets an optional argument,
a line-terminator string; if not supplied, it defaults to the current value of `$/`,
which is the variable that controls the analogous behavior of the `<...>` operator.
The iterator keeps a buffer with the characters seen so far but not returned, and
appends each new character to the buffer as it appears. When the buffer is seen
to end with the terminator string, it's emptied and the contents are returned to
the caller.

With this formulation, we're in a position to do things that Perl doesn't have
built-in already. For example, people often ask for the ability to set `$/` to a regex
instead of to a plain string. This doesn't work; the "regex" is interpreted as a plain
string anyway. The reason that Perl doesn't have this feature is that it's surprisingly
tricky to implement. It looks easy. For example, we might try implementing it
by changing `records()` as follows:

```
sub records {
  my $chars = shift;
  my $terminator = @_ ? shift : quotemeta($/);
```

```
my $pattern = qr<(?:$terminator)$>;
my $buffer = "";
sub {
  my $char;
  while ($buffer !- /$pattern/
          && defined($char = $chars->())
        ) {
    $buffer .= $char;
  }
  if ($buffer ne "") {
    my $line = $buffer;
    $buffer = "";
    return $line;
  } else {
    return;
  }
}
}
```

If we're expecting inputs with sections that might be terminated either with
"---\n" or with "+++\n", but we don't know which, we can say:

```
my $records = records($chars, qr/-{3}\n|\+3\n/);
```

Inside of records(), the terminator pattern is wrapped up into /(?:-{3}
\n|\+3\n)$/, which looks for the terminator pattern only at the end of the
buffer.

There are two problems with this implementation. One problem is that it's
not very efficient. Reading an input one character at a time into a buffer may be a
good way to perform lexical analysis in C, but in Perl, it's slow. The more serious
problem is that this implementation mishandles a number of regexes that come
up in practice. The simplest example is the regex /\n\n+/, which says that each
record is terminated by one or more following blank lines. Given this input:

    a

    b

(that is, "a\n\n\nb\n") there should be two records: "a\n\n\n" and "b\n". But this
iterator gets a different answer; it produces "a\n\n" and "\nb\n". The problem
here is that the terminator regex could be considered ambiguous. It says that a
record is terminated by two or more newline characters. The iterator has decided

that the first record is terminated by exactly two newline characters, and that the third newline character is part of the *second* record. While this is arguably "correct", it probably isn't what was wanted. The problem occurs because the input is being read character-by-character; when the buffer contains "a\n\n", the terminator pattern succeeds, and the record is split, even though more reading would have generated a longer match.

The same bug causes a more serious problem in a different example. Suppose we're reading an email header and we'd like the iterator to generate logical fields instead of physical lines. Suppose the email header is as follows:

```
Delivered-To: mjd-filter-deliver2@plover.com
Received: from localhost [127.0.0.1] by plover.com
        with SpamAssassin (2.55 1.174.2.19-2003-05-19-exp);
        Mon, 11 Aug 2003 16:22:12 -0400
From: "Doris Bower" <yij447mrx@yahoo.com.hk>
To: webmaster@plover.com
Subject: LoseWeight Now with Pphentermine,Aadipex,Bontriil,PrescribedOnline,shipped
    to Your Door fltynzlfoybv kie
```

There are five fields here; the second one, with the `Received` tag, consists of three physical lines. Lines that begin with whitespace are continuations of the previous line. So if the records we want are email header fields, the terminator pattern is `/\n(?!\s)/`. That is, it's a newline that is not followed by a whitespace.

Note that `/\n[^\s]/` is not correct here, as this says that the following non-whitespace is actually part of the terminator, which it isn't. This would treat the `F` of `From` as the final character of the terminator of the `Received` field; the next field would then begin `rom: "Doris`. In contrast, the assertion `(?!\s)` behaves like part of the preceding `\n` symbol, constraining it to match only certain newline characters instead of all newline characters.

Plugging `/\n(?!\s)/` into `records()` doesn't work, however. The `Received` field is broken into three separate records anyway. What went wrong? Suppose the first `Received` line has been read in completely, including the newline character at the end. The iterator checks to see if the buffer matches `/(?:\n(?!\s))$/` — and it *does* match, because the buffer *does* and with a newline character, and the newline character is *not* followed by whitespace. So the iterator cuts off the line prematurely, without waiting to discover that this wasn't actually an appropriate newline.

We might try to fix this by changing the pattern to `/\n(?=\S)/`, which says that the fields are terminated by newline characters that *are* followed by *non*-whitespace. This does indeed prevent the `Received` field from being split prematurely, because when the first newline comes along, the pattern says that it must be followed by non-whitespace, and it isn't followed by anything. But the pattern also prevents the field from being split in the correct place, and in fact the entire input comes out as one big field. This is because by the time the non-whitespace comes along, the pattern can no longer match at the end of the string, because it requires that the string end with a newline! So we need another approach.

Unfortunately, there doesn't seem to be any good way to solve this problem with the features presently in Perl.

The essential problem is that a pattern match can fail and backtrack for two essentially different reasons. Consider a pattern like /(abcd)+/, and the two target strings "abcde" and "abcda". The regex matches the "abcd" part of both strings, but in different ways. When it matches the string "abcde", it stops at the e because it sees the e and knows the match can't possibly continue. But when it matches the string "abcda" the match stops because the engine runs out of characters after the second "a", and backtracks to the "d".

For most applications, this distinction doesn't matter. But in *this* application, the second situation is quite different, because when the engine runs off the end of the string, we want it to try to read some more data, append it to the end of the target string, and continue. If the engine would tell us whether it reached the end of the string during the matching process, we could write code that would extend the target string and try the match again, but at present that feature is not available, and Perl doesn't give us any good way to distinguish the two situations.

The best we can do at present is to read the entire input into memory at once:

```
sub records {
  my $input = shift;
  my $terminator = @_ ? shift : quotemeta($/);
  my @records;
  my @newrecs = split /($terminator)/, $input;
  while (@newrecs > 2) {
    push @records, shift(@newrecs).shift(@newrecs);
  }
  push @records, @newrecs;
  return sub {
    return shift @records;
  }
}
```

There are a few complications here. We enclose the terminator in parentheses, to prevent split from discarding it. The shift(@newrecs).shift(@newrecs) expression reassembles a record with its terminator. The function does this only when it is sure it has seen the beginning of the *next* record on the input, because it doesn't want to jump the gun and return an incomplete record or a record with an incomplete terminator; hence @newrecs > 2 instead of @newrecs >= 2. When the input is exhausted, the input buffer contains the (possibly incomplete) final record, which is put onto the agenda.

8.1.2 Lexers More Generally

To write a lexer in a language like C, one typically writes a loop that reads the input, one character at a time, and which runs a state machine, returning a complete token to the caller when the state machine definition says to. Alternatively, we could use a program like lex, whose input is a definition of the tokens we want to recognize, and whose output is a state machine program in C.

In Perl, explicit character-by-character analysis of input is slow. But Perl has a special feature whose sole purpose is to analyze a string character-by-character and to run a specified state machine on it; the character loop is done internally in compiled C, so it's fast. This feature is regex matching. To match a string against a regex, Perl examines the string one character at a time and runs a state machine as it goes. The structure of the state machine is determined by the regex.

This suggests that regexes can act like lexers, and in fact Perl's regexes have been extended with a few features put in expressly to make them more effective for lexing.

As an example, let's consider a calculator program. The program will accept an input in the following form:

```
a = 12345679 * 6
b=a*9;  c=0
print b
```

This will perform the indicated computations and print the result, 666666666. The first stage of processing this input is to tokenize it. Tokens are integer numerals; variable names, which have the form /^[a-zA-Z_]\w*$/; parentheses; the operators +, -, *, /, **, and =; and the special directive print. Also, newlines are significant, since they terminate expressions, while other whitespace is unimportant except insofar as it separates tokens that might otherwise be considered a single token. (For example, printb is a variable name, as opposed to print b, which isn't.)

The classic style for Perl lexers looks like this:

```
sub tokens {
  my $target = shift;
```

CODE LIBRARY
tokens-calc

```
    return sub {
      TOKEN: {
        return ['INTEGER', $1]    if $target =~/\G (\d+)        /gcx;
        return ['PRINT']          if $target =~/\G print \b     /gcx;
        return ['IDENTIFIER', $1] if $target =~/\G ([A-Za-z_]\w*) /gcx;
        return ['OPERATOR', $1]   if $target =~/\G (\*\*)        /gcx;
        return ['OPERATOR', $1]   if $target =~/\G ([-+*\/=()])  /gcx;
        return ['TERMINATOR', $1] if $target =~/\G (; \n* | \n+) /gcx;
        redo TOKEN                if $target =~/\G \s+           /gcx;
        return ['UNKNOWN', $1]    if $target =~/\G (.)           /gcx;
        return;
      }
    };
  }
```

There are a few obscure features here. Every Perl scalar may have associated with it a "current matching position," initially the leftmost end of the string. Whenever a scalar is matched against an expression with the /g flag, its current matching position is set to the position at which the regex left off matching. Moreover, if a scalar has a current matching position, then when it's matched against a pattern with /g, the search starts at the current matching position instead of at the leftmost end of the string, effectively ignoring everything to the left of the current matching position.

The current matching position of a scalar can be examined or set with the pos() built-in function. For example:

```
my $target = "123..45.6789...0";
while ($target =~ /(\d+)/g) {
  print "Saw '$1' ending at position ", pos($target), "\n";
}
```

The output is:

```
Saw '123' ending at position 3
Saw '45' ending at position 7
Saw '6789' ending at position 12
Saw '0' ending at position 16
```

In this example, the matching was able to skip past the dots in the string, just as "carrot" =~ /r\w+/ is able to skip past the c and the a. The \G metacharacter anchors each match to occur *only* at the position that the previous match left off;

it's no longer allowed to skip characters at that position. This is what we want for our lexer, because we don't want the lexer to skip forward in the string looking for a numeral when there might be some other token that appears earlier; we want to process the string in strict left-to-right order, skipping nothing.

Our basic strategy is something like this:

```
if ($target =~ /\Gtoken1/g) {
    # do something with token1
} elsif ($target =~ /\Gtoken2/g) {
    # do something with token2
} elsif ...
```

The idea is that we'll search at the current position for something that looks like token1; if we don't find it, we'll look at that position for token2, and so on. Unfortunately, /g has a misfeature that prevents this from working: if the pattern match *fails* in a /g match, the current matching position is destroyed! By the time control reaches the elsif branch, the scalar has forgotten where the search is intended to occur.

We could work around this by using pos to save and restore the current matching position before and after every match, but Perl has another special feature that was introduced just so that we wouldn't have to do that: If the match operator has the /c flag as well as the /g flag, the misfeature is disabled. An unsuccessful match against a /gc pattern leaves the current matching position unchanged, instead of resetting it.

The iterator returned by tokens() uses this strategy. It captures the target string, and then, each time it's called, looks for some sort of token at the current matching position. If it finds one, it returns a value that represents the token; if not, it tries looking for a different kind of token.

The only exceptions to this rule are in the last three lines of the function. If the text at the current position is whitespace (but not newlines, which would have been taken care of by the TERMINATOR line) the function skips the whitespace and tries again. The following line (UNKNOWN) is a catchall for handling unrecognized characters. Alternatively, we might have written the function to throw an exception. Finally, the last line handles the case where the current position is at the very end of the string; as usual, it returns a false value to the caller to indicate that it has no more output.

On our sample input:

```
a = 12345679 * 6
b=a*9; c=0
print b
```

The output is:

```
[IDENTIFIER, "a"]
[OPERATOR, "="]
[INTEGER, "12345679"]
[OPERATOR, "*"]
[INTEGER, "6"]
[TERMINATOR, "\n"]
[IDENTIFIER, "b"]
[OPERATOR, "="]
[IDENTIFIER, "a"]
[OPERATOR, "*"]
[INTEGER, "9"]
[TERMINATOR, ";"]
[IDENTIFIER, "c"]
[OPERATOR, "="]
[INTEGER, "0"]
[TERMINATOR, "\n"]
[PRINT]
[IDENTIFIER, "b"]
[TERMINATOR, "\n"]
```

8.1.3   Chained Lexers

The lexer of the previous section is easy to read and to write, and it's efficient. It has one major drawback, however: the target string must be stored entirely in memory. As we saw, it's quite tricky to use regexes to tokenize an input that hasn't been completely read yet; we might have read some string that ends with print, and tokenized the print as a print operator, only to read another block and discover that it was actually the first five letters of an identifier printmaking. The lexer might similarly misparse ** as * *.

A modified version of the iterator of Section 8.1.1 solves this problem. It gets three arguments. The first is an input iterator, as before. The input iterator will generate strings of input, perhaps a block at a time, or perhaps less or more. The second argument is a label, such as IDENTIFIER or OPERATOR, to include in the output tokens. The third argument is a regex that matches the tokens we want to find. The iterator's output will be a sequence of tokens and strings. When it sees something it recognizes, it converts it into a token, which is a value of the form:

```
[$label, $string]
```

and when it sees something it doesn't recognize, it returns it unchanged, as a plain string. So, for example, the lexer produced by tokens($input, "NUMERAL", qr/\d+/), if given the same preceding sample input, will generate the following items:

```
"a = "
["NUMERAL", 12345679]
" * "
["NUMERAL", 6]
"\nb=a*"
["NUMERAL", 9]
"; c="
["NUMERAL", 0]
"\nprint b\n"
```

Once we have this, what do we do with it? We feed it as input to another lexer iterator, one which passes the NUMERAL tokens through unmodified, but examines the string portions for tokens that match its own regex. If we filter the input with a series of these iterators, we'll get an output stream that will contain the tokens we want, and also some plain strings that represent unrecognized portions of the input.

The code is complicated by the need to hold onto input while looking ahead to make sure that something coming up doesn't change the interpretation of the input we've seen already:

CODE LIBRARY
tokens

```
sub tokens {
  my ($input, $label, $pattern) = @_;
  my @tokens;
  my ($buf, $finished) = ("");
  my $split = sub { split /($pattern)/, $_[0] };
  my $maketoken = sub { [$label, $_[0] ]};
  sub {
    while (@tokens == 0 && ! $finished) {
      my $i = $input->();
      if (ref $i) {              # Input is a token
        my ($sep, $tok) = $split->($buf);
        $tok = $maketoken->($tok) if defined $tok;
        push @tokens, grep $_ ne "", $sep, $tok, $i;
        $buf = "";
      } else {                   # Input is an untokenized string
        $buf .= $i if defined $i; # Append new input to buffer
```

```
                  my @newtoks = $split->($buf);
                  while (@newtoks > 2
                          || @newtoks && ! defined $i) {
                    # Buffer contains complete separator plus complete token
                    # OR we've reached the end of the input
                    push @tokens, shift(@newtoks);
                    push @tokens, $maketoken->(shift @newtoks) if @newtoks;
                  }
                  # Reassemble remaining contents of buffer
                  $buf = join "", @newtoks;
                  $finished = 1 if ! defined $i;
                  @tokens = grep $_ ne "", @tokens;
                }
              }
              return shift(@tokens);
          }
      }
```

The output agenda is @tokens. Tokens are put onto it under three circumstances:

1. When the current input contains so much text that it's clear the function
    has seen an entire token, plus at least one character of what follows it, then
    the token and any preceding non-token text are placed into @tokens. This
    occurs when @newtoks > 2.

2. When the current input is exhausted, a token is extracted from it, if possible,
    and then whatever was found is put into @tokens. This occurs when $i, the
    most recent input, is undefined.

3. When the most recent input is itself a token, passed up from some lower-
    level lexer, we know that the following characters aren't part of *this* token, so
    we can examine the current text in the same way as if it were at the end of
    the input. This occurs when $i the most recent input, is a token; the test is
    if (ref $i).

The input to tokens() is usually another iterator that was built by tokens(). To
get the process started, we could supply an iterator that emits a string containing
the data that is to be tokenized:

```
      sub allinput {
        my $fh = shift;
        my @data;
        { local $/;
```

```
        $data[0] = <$fh>;
    }
    sub { return shift @data }
}
```

We can avoid the need to read the entire input into memory all at once, and use a base iterator that returns one block of data at a time from a filehandle:

```
sub blocks {
    my $fh = shift;
    my $blocksize = shift || 8192;
    sub {
        return unless read $fh, my($block), $blocksize;
        return $block;
    }
}
```

But if we use this, then we must be extremely careful that we don't exercise the problem we saw back in Section 8.1.1, in which a lexer might return a short token when it could have returned a longer one.

We can generalize tokens() a little bit. The code that manufactures the token value, $maketoken, is an anonymous function. We might as well let the user specify the function that performs this task, making it into a callback. Then $label, which isn't used anywhere else, merely becomes a user argument to this callback:

```
sub tokens {
    my ($input, $label, $pattern, $maketoken) = @_;
    $maketoken ||= sub { [ $_[1], $_[0] ] };
    my @tokens;
    my $buf = "";    # set to undef to when input is exhausted
    my $split = sub { split /($pattern)/, $_[0] };
    sub {
        while (@tokens == 0 && defined $buf) {
            my $i = $input->();
            if (ref $i) {
                my ($sep, $tok) = $split->($buf);
                $tok = $maketoken->($tok, $label) if defined $tok;
                push @tokens, grep $_ ne "", $sep, $tok, $i;
                $buf = "";
                last;
```

```
            }

        $buf .= $i if defined $i;
        my @newtoks = $split->($buf);
        while (@newtoks > 2
                || @newtoks && ! defined $i) {
          push @tokens, shift(@newtoks);
          push @tokens, $maketoken->(shift(@newtoks), $label)
                if @newtoks;
        }
        $buf = join "", @newtoks;
        undef $buf if ! defined $i;
        @tokens = grep $_ ne "", @tokens;
      }
    return shift(@tokens);
    }
  }

1;
```

We can call this version of tokens just as before, but now it's more flexible. Formerly, we could have written a whitespace recognizer that generated whitespace tokens:

```
    tokens($input, "WHITESPACE", qr/\s+/)
```

but we would have had to discard these tokens later on, perhaps with igrep, since we weren't really interested in them. With the new formulation, we can write:

```
    tokens($input, "WHITESPACE", qr/\s+/, sub { "" });
```

which represents a whitespace token as an empty string; the empty strings are removed from the output by the iterator itself, so the whitespace just disappears. (If this seems like too much of a trick, it's simple to change the code so that the $maketoken argument is expected to return a *list* of tokens to be inserted into the output, and then have the WHITESPACE maketoken() function return an empty list.)

Similarly, instead of a generic OPERATOR token, it might be convenient to include the operator type and its precedence in the token:

```
    %optype = ('+'  => ['ARITHMETIC', 3],
               '-'  => ['ARITHMETIC', 3],
```

```
            '*'  => ['ARITHMETIC', 4],
            '/'  => ['ARITHMETIC', 4],
            '**' => ['ARITHMETIC', 5],
            'x'  => ['STRING'    , 4],
            '.'  => ['STRING'    , 3],
            ...
          );
      tokens($input, \%optype, qr/\*\*|[-+*\/x.]|.../,
          sub { my $optype = $_[1];
              [ "OPERATOR", @{$optype->{$_[0]}}, $_[0] ]
          });
```

The tokens that come out of this iterator look like ["OPERATOR", "ARITHMETIC", 5, "**"].

   Lexers are easy to write with the chained-lexer technique, but the resulting code is ugly:

```
      my $lexer = tokens(
              tokens(
                tokens(
                  tokens(
                    tokens(
                      tokens($input,
                              'TERMINATOR',
                              qr/;\n*|\n+/,
                            ),
                          'INTEGER',
                          qr/\d+/,
                        ),
                        'PRINT',
                        qr/\bprint\b/,
                      ),
                      'IDENTIFIER',
                      qr|[A-Za-z_]\w*|,
                    ),
                    'OPERATOR',
                    qr#\*\*|[-=+*/()]#,
                  ),
                  'WHITESPACE',
                  qr/\s+/,
                  sub { "" },  # discard
                );
```

But a spoonful of syntactic sugar makes the medicine go down:

```
sub make_lexer {
  my $lexer = shift;
  while (@_) {
    my $args = shift;
    $lexer = tokens($lexer, @$args);
  }
  $lexer;
}
```

Now we can build the lexer with a tidy, tabular piece of code:

```
my $lexer = make_lexer($input,
                    ['TERMINATOR', qr/;\n*|\n+/                    ],
                    ['INTEGER',    qr/\d+/                         ],
                    ['PRINT',      qr/\bprint\b/                   ],
                    ['IDENTIFIER', qr|[A-Za-z_]\w*|                ],
                    ['OPERATOR',   qr#\*\*|[-=+*/()]#              ],
                    ['WHITESPACE', qr/\s+/,         sub { "" } ],
           );
```

Calls to make_lexer() can be chained the same way that calls to tokens() were.

We'll use this lexer later, so let's observe one feature that you might otherwise miss: A semicolon (possibly followed by newlines, but possibly alone) is lexed as a TERMINATOR token, the same as actual newline characters would be.

8.1.4   Peeking

Our lexers need one more feature to be complete. Consider a parser for some kind of expression that has two distinct forms; say a parser for numerals that might look either like "123" or like "-123". These will be tokenized as [INTEGER, "123"] and as [OPERATOR, "-"], [INTEGER, "123"], respectively.

We would like to build the parser to understand both forms, and for reasons of maintenance and modularity we might like to build it from two separate parts, one that handles unsigned integers and one that handles negated integers. A master control will examine the next token in the input. If it's an INTEGER, the master control will invoke the sub-parser for unsigned integers; if it's an OPERATOR the master control will invoke the sub-parser for negated integers. If the next token is anything else, the master parser will signal an error.

The problem is that once the master control has eaten the token at the front of the input stream, the token is gone; the sub-parsers no longer have access to it, and the unsigned integer parser certainly needs it, because the token contains the value of the integer. We could fix this by passing the eaten token to the sub-parsers explicitly. However, this will entail complications in the parsers, which will now have to get their inputs from two separate sources.

A simpler approach is to allow the master parser to put the eaten token back into the input stream, or, alternatively, to allow it to examine the next token in an input *without* removing it from the stream. We'll use the second approach:

```
sub tokens {
  ...
  sub {
    while (@tokens == 0 && ! $finished) {
      ...
    }
    return $_[0] eq 'peek' ? $tokens[0] : shift(@tokens);
  }
}
```

Normally, we invoke a lexer as $lexer->(), which consumes and returns the next token in the input. With this change, we have the option of saying $lexer->('peek'), which returns the next token in the input *without* consuming it; the next call to $lexer->() will return the same token we just peeked at.

An alternative approach is to represent lexers as streams, in the sense of Chapter 6. Turning our generic function-style iterators into lazy streams is easy:

CODE LIBRARY
it2stream.pl

```
use Stream 'node';

sub iterator_to_stream {
  my $it = shift;
  my $v = $it->();
  return unless defined $v;
  node($v, sub { iterator_to_stream($it) });
}

1;
```

If we do this, the "peek" function is just head(), and the "read and discard" function is drop().

8.2   PARSING IN GENERAL

We've finished with lexers, which transform unstructured character sequences into token sequences. Now we'll deal with parsers, which read sequences of tokens and integrate them into complex structures. The result of parsing is the *meaning* of the input, or the *value* of the input. For example, the result of parsing the input 3 + 4 * 5 might be the number 23, which is the meaning or the value of the expression. If the parser is part of a compiler, the value might be a sequence of machine language instructions for calculating $3 + 4 \cdot 5$.

8.2.1 Grammars

The key to parsing is the *grammar*, which describes the structure of a legal input. As a simple example, we'll consider a parser for a very limited set of arithmetic expressions, including only addition, multiplication, and parentheses. Here is the grammar:

```
expression  →  atom '+' expression
expression  →  atom '*' expression
expression  →  '(' expression ')'
expression  →  atom

atom  →  'INT'
atom  →  'VAR'
```

Items in quotes represent literal tokens; items not in quotes represent other parts of the grammar. Both kinds of items are called *symbols*. The first section is the definition of the *expression symbol*. It says that there are four alternative forms for an *expression*. An *expression* might be an atom followed by a + token followed by a complete expression, or it might be an atom followed by a * token followed by a complete expression, or it might be a complete expression enclosed in parentheses, or it might simply be an atom by itself. What's an atom? The second section defines the *atom symbol*: It's either an INT token or a VAR token. The four alternatives in the *expression* definition and the two alternatives in the *atom* definition are sometimes called *clauses* or *productions*. One of the symbols is usually considered more important than the others, and represents the entire structure that we're trying to parse; the other symbols usually represent various sub-structures or special cases. In this case the important symbol is *expression*. This more-important symbol is called the *start symbol*.

The grammar defines all the legal expressions, as follows. Start with the start symbol, *expression*. Apply a production by replacing the symbol on the left side of the production with the symbols on the right; for example, replace *expression* with (*expression*). Repeat until there is nothing left but literal tokens. For example,

```
expression
atom * expression                        # expression clause 2
INT  * expression                        # atom clause 1
INT  * ( expression          ) # expression clause 3
INT  * ( atom + expression   ) # expression clause 1
INT  * ( atom + atom * expression ) # expression clause 2
INT  * ( atom + VAR  * expression ) # atom clause 2
INT  * ( atom + VAR  * atom   ) # expression clause 4
INT  * ( VAR  + VAR  * atom   ) # atom clause 2
INT  * ( VAR  + VAR  * INT    ) # atom clause 1
```

This *derivation* shows that the sequence of tokens INT * (VAR + VAR * INT) is a valid expression. The valid expressions are exactly those for which derivations exist. INT INT INT and INT + + VAR are not valid expressions, according to our grammar, because there are no derivations for them.

Now some jargon: The symbols that appear on the left side of productions, such as *expression* and *atom*, are called *nonterminal symbols* or just *nonterminals*, because a derivation is not complete as long as one of them appears in the result. Conversely, the literal tokens are called *terminal symbols* or just *terminals* because once they appear, they can't be replaced. A sequence of symbols is sometimes called a *sentential form*; if all the symbols are terminals, the sentential form is a *sentence*. So a derivation of a particular sentence consists of a sequence of sentential forms, each of which is obtained from the previous one by the application of one of the productions to one of the nonterminal symbols.

One of the primary jobs of parsing is to determine if a particular sequence of tokens is a sentence according to a given grammar, and, if so, which productions to apply in which order to produce it. In principle, this is simple. The space of all possible sentential forms has a tree structure, and we need only do a tree search on this tree, looking for the sentential form that corresponds to the input tokens. Figure 8.1 shows the top portion of the tree for the *expression* symbol in the example grammar.

The root node is the sentential form that consists only of the start symbol, *expression*. At each node, we obtain the child nodes by replacing the leftmost nonterminal symbol with the right-hand side of one if its productions. When there are no nonterminal symbols, the node is a leaf. A path from the root to

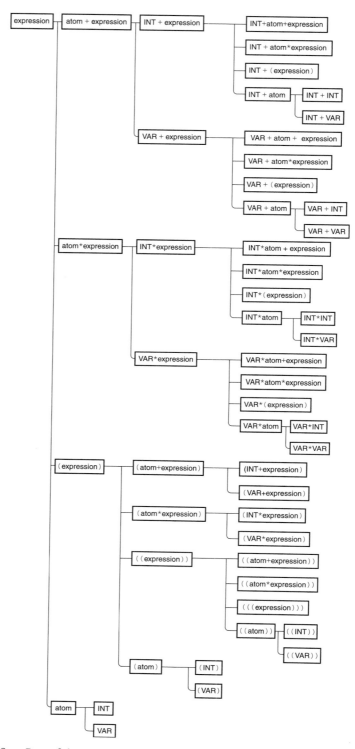

FIGURE 8.1 Part of the search space of all possible expressions.

a particular leaf gives a derivation of the sentence at that leaf. For example, by tracing backwards from the INT+INT leaf to the root, we find a derivation of the sentence INT+INT:

```
expression
atom  '+' expression          # expression clause 1
'INT' '+' expression          # atom clause 1
'INT' '+' atom                # expression clause 4
'INT' '+' 'INT'               # atom clause 1
```

Finding a derivation for a particular sentence, therefore, is equivalent to locating the sentence in the tree, and therefore to a tree search.

Breadth-first search will eventually find the derivation, if it exists, but, as is usual with breadth-first search, consumes a lot of memory, and so isn't used very often. Depth-first search is cheaper, but since the tree is typically infinite, depth-first search can go charging down one of the infinite branches, never to return. To illustrate the potential problem and its solution, here's a particularly simple example grammar:

```
expr → 'A' expr
expr → 'X'
```

An *expr* is either an X token or else an A token followed by a complete *expr*. Expressions (*expr*) in this grammar therefore consist of some number of A's followed by an X. The derivation tree looks like this:

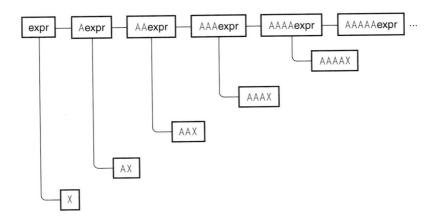

A naive depth-first search will go charging down the topmost branch, looking for a complete sentence, and never find one. It will never investigate any of the other branches. But there's an obvious way to prune the search. Suppose the search is looking for AX. The search first examines the Aexpr node. Each node below this one will begin with A. The target sentence, AX, also begins with A, so the search continues. The next node is AAexpr. Every node below *this* one will begin with AA. The target sentence does not begin with AA, so the search can ignore this entire branch, moving over to the sibling branch, AX. The search then succeeds. The tree is infinite, but the search process can trim out large infinite portions of it.

For an analogous example with a more typical grammar, consider our original grammar example. Suppose the target sentence is simply VAR. The search proceeds down the first branch, *atom+expression*, to the first of its two sub-nodes, which is INT+*expression*. Each node below this one must begin with INT +, and the target sentence does not, so the search can skip all the lower nodes, moving instead to the VAR+*expression* branch. Each node below this one begins with VAR +, and the target sentence does not, so the search again skips all the lower nodes, moving instead to the *atom*expression* branch, which fails similarly. The third branch, (*expression*), fails even more quickly, since the search knows that all the lower nodes on that branch will begin with (, and the target sentence does not. Finally, the search moves to the fourth branch, *atom*, tries the first sub-node, INT, which fails, and then the second sub-node, VAR, which is the sentence that was being sought.

8.2.2 Parsing Grammars

One way to implement a parser is the same way we've done tree search in previous chapters. The search maintains an agenda of sentential forms that need to be investigated. Initially, the agenda contains only the sentential form consisting of just the start symbol. At each stage, the search pops a sentential form off the agenda list. If the sentential form is a sentence, the search succeeds if it is the correct sentence, and continues otherwise. If the sentential form is not a sentence, but begins with some terminal symbols, the search checks to make sure that the target sentence begins with the same terminals. If not, the sentential form is discarded, pruning the search. When there are no sentential forms remaining in the agenda, the search fails.

If the sentential form popped from the agenda is not discarded, the search locates the leftmost nonterminal symbol in the sentential form — let's say the sentential form is VAR + *expression*, so the leftmost nonterminal symbol is *expression*. The search looks up all the productions whose left side is this nonterminal symbol, *expression*. In our example, there are four of these. It adds a new item to the agenda for each one, obtaining the new item by replacing the nonterminal symbol in the left side of the production with the sentential form on the right. In our example, the search adds the four items VAR + *atom* + *expression*, VAR + *atom* * *expression*, VAR + (*expression*), and VAR + *atom* to the agenda. The process then repeats.

Here's sample code, using the make_dfs_search() function of Section 5.3. We will represent a grammar as a hash:

```
expression => [['INT', '+', 'expression'],
               ['INT', '*', 'expression'],
               ['(', 'expression', ')'],
               ['INT'],
              ]
```

Keys are nonterminal symbols; values are arrays of productions. To distinguish a terminal from a nonterminal symbol, we just look it up in the hash:

```
require "make-dfs-search";


sub make_parser_for_grammar {
  my ($start, $grammar, $target) = @_;


  my $is_nonterminal = sub {
    my $symbol = shift;
    exists $grammar->{$symbol};
  };
```

CODE LIBRARY
DFSParser.pm

When the search finds a sentential form, it scans the form to see if it matches the target sentence, stopping at the first nonterminal symbol. If the sentential form is too long or too short, or if one of its leading tokens doesn't match the corresponding token in the target sentence, then the search won't mention it:

```
  my $is_interesting = sub {
    my $sentential_form = shift;
    for my $i (0 .. $#$sentential_form) {
      return 1 if $is_nonterminal->($sentential_form->[$i]);
      return if $i > $#$target;
      return if $sentential_form->[$i] ne $target->[$i];
    }
    return @$sentential_form == @$target ;
  };
```

Given a sentential form, we find the children in the tree by locating the leftmost nonterminal symbol and replacing it with each of its productions from the grammar.

First we locate the leftmost nonterminal symbol:

```
my $children = sub {
  my $sentential_form = shift;
  my $leftmost_nonterminal;
  my @children;

  for my $i (0 .. $#$sentential_form) {
    if ($is_nonterminal->($sentential_form->[$i])) {
      $leftmost_nonterminal = $i;
      last;
```

If the sentential form is too long to match the target, we prune the tree at that point by reporting that it has no children:

```
    } else {
      return if $i > $#$target;
```

Similarly, if the initial tokens of the sentential form don't match the initial tokens of the target sentence, we prune:

```
      return if $target->[$i] ne $sentential_form->[$i];
    }
  }
```

If a node has no nonterminal symbols, it is a leaf and has no children:

```
return unless defined $leftmost_nonterminal; # no nonterminal symbols
```

Having located the leftmost nonterminal symbol, we generate the child nodes by replacing the nonterminal with each of the possible productions for it:

```
  for my $production (@{$grammar->{$sentential_form->[$leftmost_nonterminal]}}) {
    my @child = @$sentential_form;
    splice @child, $leftmost_nonterminal, 1, @$production;
    push @children, \@child;
  }
  @children;
};
```

The parser itself uses make_dfs_search() (See Section 5.3) to do a DFS search of the space of sentential forms. The root node is the sentential form containing only the start symbol:

```
    return sub {
      make_dfs_search([$start], $children, $is_interesting);
    };
  }


  1;
```

To use this, we say something like:

```
  my $parser = make_parser_for_grammar 'expression',
    {
      expression => [['INT', '+', 'expression'],
                     ['INT', '*', 'expression'],
                     ['(', 'expression', ')'],
                     ['INT'],
                    ],

    },
    ['(', 'INT', '*', '(', 'INT', '+', 'INT', ')', ')']
  ;
```

The target sentence here is (INT * (INT + INT)).

```
  my $parses = $parser->();

  while (my $parse = $parses->()) {
    print "@$parse\n";
  }
```

The output is:

```
  expression
  ( expression )
  ( INT * expression )
  ( INT * ( expression ) )
  ( INT * ( INT + expression ) )
  ( INT * ( INT + INT ) )
```

which is indeed a derivation of the target sentence.

If we try parsing a non-sentence, say INT * + INT, we get:

```
expression
INT * expression
```

The target sentence never comes out, because the parser got stuck. It wanted to find a way to make + INT into an expression, but it couldn't.

8.3   RECURSIVE-DESCENT PARSERS

A commonly used technique for parsing by DFS is to move the responsibility for the search back into the Perl function-call mechanism. A parser becomes a function that takes an input stream and examines its front for a certain pattern of tokens and values. If it likes what it sees, it returns two things: the value or meaning it assigns to the tokens, and the unused portion of the input. If the function doesn't like what it sees, it returns false. If a parser represents a compound expression, it may call sub-parsers to help it decide if the input is in the proper form; this is where the DFS arises. Parsers that call each other recursively to parse an input in this way are called *recursive-descent parsers*.

We'll develop a module, Parser.pm, with tools for manufacturing recursive-descent parsers. The module starts off with the usual declarations:

```
package Parser;
use Stream ':all';
use base Exporter;
@EXPORT_OK = qw(parser nothing End_of_Input lookfor
                alternate concatenate star list_of
                operator T
                error action test);
%EXPORT_TAGS = ('all' => \@EXPORT_OK);

sub parser (&);   # Advance declaration - see below
```

8.3.1   Very Simple Parsers

The simplest parser of all consumes no input and always succeeds, yielding the value undef:

```
sub nothing {
  my $input = shift;
```

```
        return (undef, $input);
    }
```

The next simplest just checks for the end of the input:

```
    sub End_of_Input {
      my $input = shift;
      defined($input) ? () : (undef, undef);
    }
```

If the input is undefined (that is, empty), then the function returns success: the value undef, and the remaining unread input, also undef (still empty). Otherwise, the function returns an empty list to indicate failure.

The next-simplest parsers look for single specific tokens. For example, a parser that succeeds if the next token is an INT:

```
    sub INT {
      my $input = shift;
      return unless defined $input;
      my $next = head($input);
      return unless $next->[0] eq 'INT';

      my $token_value = $next->[1];
      return ($token_value, tail($input));
    }
```

If the input is empty, it fails immediately. Otherwise, it examines the token at the head of the input to see if it is an INT token; if not, it fails. But if the next token is an INT token, the function returns the token's numeric value (stored in $token->[1]) and the remaining input. The value returned by this parser is a number, namely the value one would expect the integer token to represent.

Since we'll need many of these token-recognizing functions, we'll build them with a function factory:

```
    sub lookfor {
      my $wanted = shift;
      my $value = shift || sub { $_[0][1] };
      my $u = shift;
      $wanted = [$wanted] unless ref $wanted;
      my $parser = parser {
        my $input = shift;
```

```
      return unless defined $input;
      my $next = head($input);
      for my $i (0 .. $#$wanted) {
        next unless defined $wanted->[$i];
        return unless $wanted->[$i] eq $next->[$i];
      }
      my $wanted_value = $value->($next, $u);
      return ($wanted_value, tail($input));
    };


    return $parser;
  }
```

To generate a function that looks for an [OP +] token, we can call lookfor(['OP', '+']). The generated parser will examine all the elements of $wanted, the argument, and will succeed if all the specified components in $wanted match the actual components of the next input token in $next. To generate the preceding INT function, we could call lookfor(['INT']). lookfor('INT') is a shorthand for lookfor(['INT']).

lookfor() gets an optional second argument, which is a callback function that turns the token into a value, and an optional third argument, which is a user parameter to the callback. The default callback extracts the second element from the token; with the lexers we've been using, this is always the literal text of the token.

The parser() function takes a block of code and builds a parser from it. Right now, it does nothing:

```
    sub parser (&) { $_[0] }
```

Later on, it will have some additional behavior.

8.3.2   Parser Operators

Now that we have some simple parsers, how can we put parsers together? The most obvious thing to do with two parsers is to call them in sequence on the input. Suppose we have the following grammar:

```
    doorbell -> DING DONG
```

We need a parser that looks for DING, and then if it finds DING it looks for DONG, and if it finds DONG, it succeeds. This is called the *concatenation* of the two components.

If we have a parser function that looks for DING and one that looks for DONG, here's
a function to concatenate them into a function that looks for doorbell:

```
sub concatenate {
  my ($p1, $p2) = @_;
  my $parser = parser {
    my $input0 = shift;
    my ($v1, $input1) = $p1->($input0) or return;
    my ($v2, $input2) = $p2->($input1) or return;
    return ([$v1, $v2], $input2);
  }
}
```

The value returned by the concatenation of the two parsers is an array containing
the values returned by the parsers individually. The parser for the doorbell
symbol can be built by saying:

```
$doorbell = concatenate(lookfor('DING'),
                        lookfor('DONG'));
```

If given an input that begins with tokens DING DONG . . . , this parser returns the
value ['DING', 'DONG'] and the remaining tokens.

It's easy to generalize concatenation to more than two parsers:

```
sub concatenate {
  my @p = @_;
  return \&nothing if @p == 0;

  my $parser = parser {
    my $input = shift;
    my $v;
    my @values;
    for (@p) {
      ($v, $input) = $_->($input) or return;
      push @values, $v;
    }
    return (\@values, $input);
  }
}
```

The other important operation on parsers is *alternation*, which looks for an input
in one of several alternative forms. For example, alternate(lookfor('DING'),

lookfor('DONG')) succeeds if the next token in the input is DING *or* DONG and fails otherwise. Here's a two-parser version of alternate():

```
sub alternate {
  my ($p1, $p2) = @_;
  my $parser = parser {
    my $input = shift;
    my ($v, $newinput);
    if (($v, $newinput) = $p1->($input)} { return ($v, $newinput) }
    if (($v, $newinput) = $p2->($input)} { return ($v, $newinput) }
    return;
  };
}
```

The new parser tries running $p1 on the input; if $p1 succeeds, the new parser just returns whatever $p1 returned, effectively behaving like $p1. If $p1 fails, the new parser tries $p2 in the same way, behaving like $p2 instead. If they both fail, then the new parser indicates failure also.

It's even easier to generalize alternate():

```
sub alternate {
  my @p = @_;
  return parser { return () } if @p == 0;
  return $p[0]                if @p == 1;
  my $parser = parser {
    my $input = shift;
    my ($v, $newinput);
    for (@p) {
      if (($v, $newinput) = $_->($input)) {
        return ($v, $newinput);
      }
    }
    return;
  };
}
```

The only fine point here is that if there are no alternatives at all (@p == 0), then alternate() returns a parser that never succeeds (parser { return () }).

8.3.3 Compound Operators

Having written functions to build parsers to handle alternatives and concatenations of other parsers, it's now easy to build more powerful operators for parsers.

For example, we can build an operator that's analogous to the regex * operator. If the parser $P matches a certain kind of input, say DING DONG, then star($P) will be a parser that matches an empty input, DING DONG, DING DONG DING DONG, DING DONG DING DONG DING DONG, and so on. The first cut is:

```
sub star {
  my $p = shift;
  my $p_star;
  $p_star = alternate(concatenate($p, $p_star),
                      \&nothing);
}
```

The idea here is to match an input of the form matched by $p, followed by something else (possibly empty) of the form star($p), or, if we can't find anything acceptable to $p, match nothing.

This function doesn't quite work, because at the time concatenate() is called, its argument $p_star is still undefined. There are several tricks we can use to work around this. The simplest is:

```
sub star {
  my $p = shift;
  my $p_star;
  $p_star = alternate(concatenate($p, parser { $p_star->(@_) }),
                      \&nothing);
}
```

We've replaced $p_star on the right-hand side with a new parser that just calls $p_star on its arguments and returns the result. Behaviorally, the new parser is interchangeable with $p_star itself. But the $p_star on the right isn't evaluated until the new parser is called, by which time $p_star has the right value. This trick goes by the peculiar name of *eta-conversion*.

An alternative formulation would be:

```
sub star {
  my $p = shift;
  my $p_star;
  $p_star = parser { alternate(concatenate($p, $p_star),
                               \&nothing)->(@_) };
}
```

which works for essentially the same reason. But it will be less efficient than the previous version, because it will call `alternate()` and `concatenate()` each time it is called.

Using our parser operators, we can build larger operators whenever it's convenient. A common feature of programming languages is lists of various sorts. For example, Perl has list expressions:

```
@items = ($expression1, $expression2, $expression3);
```

and blocks:

```
$block = sub { $statement1; $statement2; $statement3 };
```

Here's a parser operator for parsing lists of elements separated by some kind of separator sequence:

```
sub list_of {
  my ($element, $separator) = @_;
  $separator = lookfor('COMMA') unless defined $separator;
  return concatenate($element,
                 star($separator, $element));
}


1;
```

Now we can make a parser for lists of expressions:

```
$expression_list = list_of($expression);
```

or for lists of statements:

```
$statement_list = list_of($statement, lookfor('SEMICOLON'));
```

8.4   ARITHMETIC EXPRESSIONS

In Section 8.2, we saw a grammar for a simple subset of arithmetic expressions:

```
expression → atom '+' expression
expression → atom '*' expression
```

```
expression → '(' expression ')'
expression → atom
atom → 'INT'
atom → 'VAR'
```

Let's use an even simpler example, which has only numbers, and no variables:

```
expression → 'INT' '+' expression
expression → 'INT' '*' expression
expression → '(' expression ')'
expression → 'INT'
```

There's also an additional rule that represents an entire input:

```
entire_input → expression 'End_of_Input'
```

We will build a parser for this example, and later add the other required features, like subtraction. Transforming the grammar into a parser is simple. We build one parser function for each nonterminal symbol. We use `alternate()` when a symbol has several alternative definitions, and `concatenate()` when a definition is the concatenation of more than one token or symbol. When the grammar mentions that a symbol might contain a token, we call `lookfor()` to build a parser that looks for that token; when the grammar mentions that a symbol might contain an instance of some other nonterminal symbol, we invoke the parser for that symbol.

To transform the preceding grammar, we first transform the definition of `expression` into a parser for expressions:

```
my $expression;
$expression = alternate(concatenate(lookfor('INT'),
                                    lookfor(['OP', '+']),
                                    $expression),
                        concatenate(lookfor('INT'),
                                    lookfor(['OP', '*']),
                                    $expression),
                        concatenate(lookfor(['OP', '(']),
                                    $expression,
                                    lookfor(['OP', ')'])),
                        lookfor('INT'));
```

Again, this doesn't quite work. We can't use `$expression` in its own definition, because until we've defined it, it's `undef`. The eta-conversion trick works just fine here:

```
use Parser ':all';
use Lexer ':all';

my $expression;
my $Expression = parser { $expression->(@_) };
$expression = alternate(concatenate(lookfor('INT'),
                                    lookfor(['OP', '+']),
                                    $Expression),
                        concatenate(lookfor('INT'),
                                    lookfor(['OP', '*']),
                                    $Expression),
                        concatenate(lookfor(['OP', '(']),
                                    $Expression,
                                    lookfor(['OP', ')'])),
                        lookfor('INT'));
```

Defining a parser for entire_input is simple:

```
my $entire_input = concatenate($Expression, \&End_of_Input);
```

Suppose the input is the string "2 * 3 + (4 * 5)", and we use the lexer of Section 8.1.3:

```
my @input = q[2 * 3 + (4 * 5)];
my $input = sub { return shift @input };

my $lexer = iterator_to_stream(
                make_lexer($input,
                    ['TERMINATOR', qr/;\n*|\n+/               ],
                    ['INT',        qr/\d+/                    ],
                    ['PRINT',      qr/\bprint\b/              ],
                    ['IDENTIFIER', qr|[A-Za-z_]\w*|           ],
                    ['OP',         qr#\*\*|[-=+*/()]#          ],
                    ['WHITESPACE', qr/\s+/, sub { "" }        ],
                )
            );

if (my ($result, $remaining_input) = $entire_input->($lexer)) {
  use Data::Dumper;
```

```
      print Dumper($result), "\n";
    } else {
      warn "Parse error.\n";
    }
```

The parser does succeed, returning the following $result:

```
[
  [
    '2',
    '*',
    [
      '3',
      '+',
      [
        '(',
        [
          '4',
          '*',
          '5'
        ],
        ')'
      ]
    ]
  ],
  undef
]
```

Each of the three-element arrays was returned by concatenate(), which returned an array of the three values that it concatenated. The trailing undef was returned by the End_of_Input() parser and concatenated into the final result by the concatenate() in:

```
    my $entire_input = concatenate($Expression, \&End_of_Input);
```

There are a couple of problems with this result. What we'd most like is to have the parser generate an abstract syntax tree (AST), as in Section 2.2, where each node is labeled with an operator, and has child nodes representing the operands of that operator. We'd like the parser to understand that operators have different precedences — that 2 * 3 + 4 should be parsed the same as (2 * 3) + 4 but differently from 2 * (3 + 4). The parentheses shouldn't appear literally in the output; they should affect only the results of the parse. The value we'd like to get out of the parser for the input "2 * 3 + (4 * 5)" is:

```
[ '+',
  [ '*', 2, 3 ],
  [ '*', 4, 5 ]
]
```

which says that the expression is adding two quantities: the product of 2 and 3, and the product of 4 and 5. Similarly, 2 * 3 + 4 and (2 * 3) + 4 should produce:

```
[ '+', ['*', 2, 3], 4 ]
```

but 2 * (3 + 4) should produce:

```
[ '*', 2, ['+', 3, 4] ]
```

We'll tackle the precedence issue first. There are a few ways to take care of this, but the quickest one is to make a small change to the grammar. We can think of an expression like "2 * 3 + (4 * 5)" as a sum of one or more *terms*, where each term is a product of one or more *factors*. If we rewrite the grammar to express this, the precedence will take care of itself:

```
entire_input → expression 'End_of_Input'

expression → term '+' expression | term

term → factor '*' term | factor

factor → 'INT' | '(' expression ')'
```

The notation:

```
a → b | c
```

is shorthand for the two rules:

```
a → b
a → c
```

so the grammar says that an expression is either a plain term, or a term plus a complete expression. A term is either a plain factor, or a factor times a complete term. Finally, a factor is either an integer token or else a complete expression enclosed in parentheses.

Translating this grammar into code gives us:

```
use Parser ':all';
use Lexer ':all';
my ($expression, $term, $factor);
my $Expression = parser { $expression->(@_) };
my $Term       = parser { $term      ->(@_) };
my $Factor     = parser { $factor    ->(@_) };
$expression = alternate(concatenate($Term,
                                    lookfor(['OP', '+']),
                                    $Expression),
                        $Term);


$term       = alternate(concatenate($Factor,
                                    lookfor(['OP', '*']),
                                    $Term),
                        $Factor);


$factor     = alternate(lookfor('INT'),
                        concatenate(lookfor(['OP', '(']),
                                    $Expression,
                                    lookfor(['OP', ')']))
                        );


$entire_input = concatenate($Expression, \&End_of_Input);
```

The output of the parser on "2 * 3 + (4 * 5)" is now:

```
[
  [
    [
      '2',
      '*',
      '3'
    ],
    '+',
```

```
[
  '(',
  [
    '4',
    '*',
    '5'
  ],
  ')'
]
],
undef
]
```

Not all the problems have been fixed, but the multiplication arguments have been clustered together, as we wanted; 2 is now associated with 3, and 4 with 5. Similarly, "2 * 3 + 4" produces:

```
[
  [
    [
      '2',
      '*',
      '3'
    ],
    '+',
    '4'
  ],
  undef
]
```

with the 2 and 3 correctly grouped; the previous grammar produced this incorrect parse instead:

```
[
  [
    '2',
    '*',
    [
      '3',
      '+',
      '4'
```

```
      ]
    ],
    undef
  ]
```

Now we'll fix the parsers so that they generate proper abstract syntax trees. This isn't hard. All the necessary information is available; we just need to arrange it correctly. In a parser definition like this one:

```
$term      = alternate(concatenate($Factor,
                                    lookfor(['OP', '*']),
                                    $Term),
                       $Factor);
```

the concatenate() operator assembles the values returned by its three arguments in the order they're listed. But for an abstract syntax tree, we want the operator first, not second. Similarly, in:

```
$factor    = alternate(lookfor('INT'),
                       concatenate(lookfor(['OP', '(']),
                                   $Expression,
                                   lookfor(['OP', ')']))
                      );
```

the concatenate() operator assembles all three values, but we're interested only in the middle one, not the parentheses themselves. The value of a factor of the form '(' expression ')' should be the same as the value of the inner expression.

The following function is a little bit like map for parsers generated by concatenate(). It takes a parser and a transformation function, and returns a new parser, which recognizes the same inputs, but whose return value is filtered through the transformation function. It is named T, which is short for "transform":

```
sub T {
  my ($parser, $transform) = @_;
  return parser {
    my $input = shift;
    if (my ($value, $newinput) = $parser->($input)) {
      $value = $transform->(@$value);
      return ($value, $newinput);
```

```
        } else {
          return;
        }
      };
    }
```

For example, to get $factor to throw away the parentheses and return only the inner expression, we replace this:

```
$factor      = alternate(lookfor('INT'),
                     concatenate(lookfor(['OP', '(']),
                                $Expression,
                                lookfor(['OP', ')'])))
                     );
```

with this:

```
$factor      = alternate(lookfor('INT'),
                   T(
                     concatenate(lookfor(['OP', '(']),
                                $Expression,
                                lookfor(['OP', ')'])),
                   sub { $_[1] })
                   );
```

The three values accumulated by concatenate() are passed to the anonymous subroutine, which returns only the second one.

Similarly, to get $term to assemble the operator and operands in that order, we use:

```
$term        = alternate(
                   T(
                     concatenate($Factor,
                                lookfor(['OP', '*']),
                                $Term),
                   sub { [ $_[1], $_[0], $_[2] ]}),
                 $Factor);
```

For the term 3 * 4 the three arguments to the anonymous subroutine will be (3, '*', 4) and the return value will be ['*', 3, 4]. We should make a similar change to the definition of $expression, and we can eliminate the spurious trailing undef by changing `$entire_input` to:

```
my $entire_input = T(concatenate($Expression, \&End_of_Input),
                    sub { $_[0] }
                    );
```

With these changes, the output of the parser, given the input `"2 * 3 + (4 * 5)"`, is perfect:

```
              [
                '+',
                [
                  '*',
                  '2',
                  '3'
                ],
                [
                  '*',
                  '4',
                  '5'
                ]
              ]
```

`"2 * 3 + 4"` and `"(2 * 3) + 4"` both come back as:

```
        [
          '+',
          [
            '*',
            '2',
            '3'
          ],
          '4'
        ]
```

but `"2 * (3 + 4)"`, which is different, comes back as:

```
        [
          '*',
          '2',
          [
            '+',
```

```
        '3',
        '4'
      ]
    ]
```

8.4.1   A Calculator

By adjusting the transformation functions, we can turn our parser into a calculator instead of an abstract-syntax-tree-maker. The value returned by each parser is an abstract syntax tree for some part of the expression. We need to change the parsers to return numeric values instead of AST values. Only two changes are necessary:

```
$expression = alternate(T(concatenate($Term,
                                       lookfor(['OP', '+']),
                                       $Expression),
                          sub { $_[0] + $_[2] }),
                        $Term);
$term       = alternate(T(concatenate($Factor,
                                       lookfor(['OP', '*']),
                                       $Term),
                          sub { $_[0] * $_[2] }),
                        $Factor);
```

The values returned by the parsers are no longer arrays; now they're numbers. When the parser sees an expression like term + expression, instead of building an abstract-syntax-tree node out of the values of the term and the expression, it simply adds the values numerically and returns the sum. Similarly, when computing the value of a term, it just does numeric multiplication on the constituents of the term.

The output for "2 * (3 + 4)" is now just the number 14, and the output for "2 * 3 + 4" and "(2 * 3) + 4" is 10. The parser returns failure when given an input with mismatched or unbalanced parentheses, or any other syntactically incorrect input, such as an input with two consecutive operators or numbers.

8.4.2   Left Recursion

Let's add subtraction and division to the calculator. This requires only small changes to the grammar:

```
entire_input → expression 'End_of_Input'
expression → term '+' expression
```

```
expression → term '-' expression
expression → term
term → factor '*' term
term → factor '/' term
term → factor
factor → 'INT' | '(' expression ')'
```

In the code, the definition of $expression changes from this:

```
$expression = alternate(concatenate($Term,
                                    lookfor(['OP', '+']),
                                    $Expression),
                        $Term);
```

to this:

```
$expression = alternate(concatenate($Term,
                                    lookfor(['OP', '+']),
                                    $Expression),
                        concatenate($Term,
                                    lookfor(['OP', '-']),
                                    $Expression),
                        $Term);
```

and $term changes similarly. We can get the calculator to calculate numeric values by supplying transformation functions like these:

```
$expression = alternate(T(concatenate($Term,
                                      lookfor(['OP', '+']),
                                      $Expression),
                          sub { $_[0] + $_[2] }),
                        T(concatenate($Term,
                                      lookfor(['OP', '-']),
                                      $Expression),
                          sub { $_[0] - $_[2] }),
                        $Term);
```

But now there's a problem: If we ask for the value of "8 - 4", we get the right answer. But if we ask for the value of "8 - 4 - 3", we get 7; the correct answer is 1. What's gone wrong?

If we return to the AST version of the program, we can see the problem. "8 - 4 - 3" is parsed as:

```
[ '-', 8, [ '-', 4, 3 ]]
```

which is the same as the parse of "8 - (4 - 3)". But "8 - 4 - 3" is conventionally understood to mean "(8 - 4) - 3", which parses as:

$$[\ '-', \ [\ '-', \ 8, \ 4], \ 3 \ ]$$

We say that subtraction *associates from left to right* because, in the absence of
parentheses, multiple subtractions are performed from left to right.

   The essential problem is that there are two different ways to understand an
expression like "8 - 4 - 3". We can parse it as an expression ("8 - 4") minus
a term ("3") or as a term ("8") minus an expression ("4 - 3"). The convention
says that it should be the former, but our grammar rule:

$$\text{expression} \rightarrow \text{term '-' expression}$$

says it's the latter. The problem didn't arise for addition; the values of the two
parses were numerically the same because addition is associative, which means
that we get the same answers whether we consider it to associate from left to right
or from right to left.

   It might seem that we could fix this by reversing the order of the expression
and term symbols in the grammar, as follows:

$$\text{expression} \rightarrow \text{expression '+' term}$$
$$\text{expression} \rightarrow \text{expression '-' term}$$
$$\text{expression} \rightarrow \text{term}$$

Then the corresponding parser definition in the code becomes:

```
$expression = alternate(T(concatenate($Expression,
                                       lookfor(['OP', '+']),
                                       $Term),
                          sub { $_[0] + $_[2] }),
                        T(concatenate($Expression,
                                       lookfor(['OP', '-']),
                                       $Term),
                          sub { $_[0] - $_[2] }),
                        $Term);
```

Unfortunately, if we do this, the parser no longer works. The first thing that
the $expression parser does is to look for another expression, so it recurses
forever. Returning to the sentential form trees of Section 8.2.1, we see that this

is because there's a branch that looks like this:

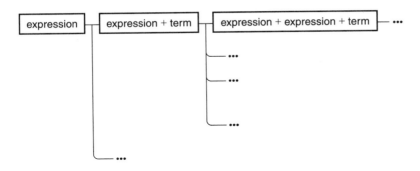

The topmost branch is infinite, so we run the risk that a depth-first search on it will never terminate. We'd been dealing with this risk by pruning the search at each node whose initial terminal symbols failed to match the target sentence. But here, none of the nodes in the topmost branch have any initial terminal symbols, so the pruning doesn't work, and the search *is* infinite.

A grammar rule of the form:

```
symbol → symbol stuff...
```

is called *left-recursive*; recursive-descent parsers hang forever whenever they meet left-recursive grammar rules. In general, left-recursion can be quite complicated; consider:

```
A → B stuff
B → C stuff
C → A stuff
```

Our example is much simpler; the recursion loop involves only one symbol instead of three. Fortunately, there's a technique for eliminating simple loops from a grammar. If we have a set of rules like this:

```
symbol → symbol A | symbol B | X | Y
```

We can transform them into equivalent rules that aren't left-recursive. Let's consider what a *symbol* must begin with. Clearly, it must be an X or a Y. *symbol* might expand to something more complicated that also begins with a *symbol*, but in that case we just have to ask the same question again. So a *symbol* must be an X or a Y followed by a tail of A's and B's. The equivalent grammar is:

```
symbol  →  X symbol_tail  |  Y symbol_tail

symbol_tail  →  A symbol_tail  |  B symbol_tail  |  (nothing)
```

For example, our left-recursive subtraction and addition rule:

```
expression  →  expression '+' term
expression  →  expression '-' term
expression  →  term
```

becomes:

```
expression  →  term expression_tail

expression_tail  →  '+' term expression_tail
expression_tail  →  '-' term expression_tail
expression_tail  →  (nothing)
```

expression_tail here represents the "rest of an expression." A full expression is a single term followed by the rest of an expression; the rest of the expression is either empty, or else a + or - followed by another term followed by the rest of the rest of the expression. If we apply a similar transformation to the *term* rule of the grammar, we get:

```
entire_input  →  expression 'End_of_Input'
expression  →  term expression_tail
expression_tail  →  '+' term expression_tail
expression_tail  →  '-' term expression_tail
expression_tail  →  (nothing)

term  →  factor term_tail
term_tail  →  '*' factor term_tail
term_tail  →  '/' factor term_tail
term_tail  →  (nothing)

factor  →  'INT'
factor  →  '(' expression ')'
```

Now, however, we have another problem. Before, we had rules like:

```
expression → term '+' expression
```

and it was obvious how to compute the value of an expression, given the values of the subterm and the subexpression: Just add them. But what value should we assign to an *expression_tail*? It represents an incomplete expression, such as "+ 3 - 4". When we're parsing an expression like "1 + 3 - 4", the "1" will become the *term* part at the beginning of the *expression* rule, and the "+ 3 - 4" will become the *expression_tail* part at the end of the *expression* rule. The value of the *expression* can't be calculated until we finish parsing the *expression_tail* and assign a value to it, because the value of the *expression_tail* will be passed to the *expression* rule for the computation of *its* value. But the value of an *expression_tail* can't be a number, because it's an incomplete expression; the parser won't know what number it is until it finished parsing the complete expression.

The natural way to represent the result of an incomplete computation such as an *expression_tail* is as a function. An expression tail is like an expression with a blank space at the beginning:

```
_____ + 3 - 4
```

which can be represented as the function:

```
sub { $_[0] + 3 - 4 }
```

When the missing parts of the expression become known, they can be passed as arguments to the function, which will compute the final result. The value of an *expression_tail* will be a function, which, given the missing part of the expression, computes the final result. The action rule for the complete expression will get a *term* value and an *expression_tail* function, and will pass the value to the function to compute the final result.

As an example, let's consider "5 + 7". Let's also disregard multiplication and division for a little while; our grammar will be:

```
expression → term expression_tail
expression_tail → '+' term expression_tail
               | '-' term expression_tail
               | (nothing)
term → 'INT' | '(' expression ')'
```

If "5 + 7" is to be an *expression*, it must be a *term* followed by an *expression_tail*. The *term* is clearly "5", and has a value of 5.

The *expression_tail* matches the first alternative, and is a "+" followed by a *term* followed by another *expression_tail*. The *term* here is clearly "7", and the following expression_tail is empty. The main *expression_tail* represents the partial input "+ 7", and so its value should be a function that adds 7 to its argument: sub { $_[0] + 7 }.

The main *expression* now gets two values, which are 5 and sub { $_[0]+ 7 }. It passes the number to the function; the result is the value of the expression, 12.

To program *expression*, we write:

```
$expression = T(concatenate($Term, $Expression_Tail),
             sub { $_[1]->($_[0]) }
           );
```

It gets the value of the term ($_[0]), which is a number, and the value of the partial expression *expression_tail* ($_[1]), which is a function. It passes the term value to the expression tail function, and returns the result.

The code for *expression_tail* is a little more complicated. Let's consider just the case for the rule:

```
expression_tail → '+' term expression_tail
```

The parser code looks like this:

```
$expression_tail = alternate(T(concatenate(lookfor(['OP', '+']),
                                            $Term,
                                            $Expression_Tail),
                     sub { ... }),
```

Suppose the input has this form:

```
LEFT + term RIGHT
```

Say that $term_value is the number value returned by the $Term parser for the *term* part of the input, and $rest is the function value returned by the $expression_tail parser for the *RIGHT* part of the input. The argument to T() is a function factory that wants to build a new function that represents the + *term RIGHT* part of the input.

The arguments to the function factory are the $term_value and the $RIGHT function (and also the "+" token):

```
sub {
  my ($plus_token, $term_value, $RIGHT) = @_;
```

The job of this function factory is to build another function that given the value of *LEFT*, will return the value of the entire expression. The function we want to build is:

```
        return sub { $RIGHT->($_[0] + $term_value) }
    }
```

The code for the minus rule is almost the same:

```
        T(concatenate(lookfor(['OP', '-']),
                                $Term,
                                $Expression_Tail),
          sub {
            my ($plus_token, $term_value, RIGHT) = @_;
            return sub { $RIGHT->($_[0] - $term_value) }
          }),
```

The code for the "nothing" rule is simple. The "rest" of the expression contains nothing at all. We want a function, which, given the value of the left part of the expression, returns the value of the entire expression. But if the "rest" of the expression is empty, then the value of the left part of the expression *is* the value of the entire expression. So the function we want is just the function that returns its argument unchanged:

```
        T(\&nothing, sub { sub { $_[0] } })
```

The code for the entire expression parser is:

```
    $expression = T(concatenate($Term, $Expression_Tail),
                    sub { $_[1]->($_[0]) }
                   );
    $expression_tail = alternate(T(concatenate(lookfor(['OP', '+']),
                                        $Term,
                                        $Expression_Tail),
                            sub { my ($op, $tv, $rest) = @_;
                                sub { $rest->($_[0] + $tv) }
                            }),
                        T(concatenate(lookfor(['OP', '-']),
                                        $Term,
                                        $Expression_Tail),
                            sub { my ($op, $tv, $rest) = @_;
```

```
                                sub { $rest->($_[0] - $tv) }
                            }),
                    T(\&nothing, sub { sub { $_[0] } })
                );
```

With this structure, the parser works perfectly for all arithmetic expressions. To make it generate ASTs instead of numbers, we use:

```
$expression = T(concatenate($Term, $Expression_Tail),
                   sub { $_[1]->($_[0]) }
               );
$expression_tail = alternate(T(concatenate(lookfor(['OP', '+']),
                                 $Term,
                                 $Expression_Tail),
                     sub { my ($op, $tv, $rest) = @_;
                         sub { [ '+', $tv, $rest->($_[0]) ] }
                     }),
                   T(concatenate(lookfor(['OP', '-']),
                                 $Term,
                                 $Expression_Tail),
                     sub { my ($op, $tv, $rest) = @_;
                         sub { [ '-', $tv, $rest->($_[0]) ] }
                     }),
                   T(\&nothing, sub { sub { $_[0] } })
                );
```

8.4.3   A Variation on `star()`

We can use the `T()` function to improve our definition for `star()`. Formerly, the parser `star(lookfor('INT'))` would have returned a value like [1, [2, [3, [4, undef]]]], because at each stage it's using `concatenate()` to join the values returned by `$p`, its argument, and `$p_star`, the recursive call to itself. We can use `T()` to adjust the value that comes out of `concatenate()` so that the result is [1, 2, 3, 4] instead:

```
sub star {
  my $p = shift;
  my $p_star;
  $p_star = alternate(T(concatenate($p, parser { $p_star->(@_) }),
                      sub { my ($first, $rest) = @_;
```

```
                   defined $rest ? [$first, @$rest] : [$first]
          }),
     \&nothing);
}
```

The function we give to T() is responsible for appending the single value returned by $p to the (possibly empty) list of values returned by $p_star to generate a new list.

Given an input that's unacceptable to $p, star($p) succeeds, consuming none of the tokens, and returns an undefined value, behaving essentially like nothing(). We might prefer for it to return an empty array. In that case, we should use this version:

```
sub null_list {
  my $input = shift;
  return ([], $input);
}

sub star {
  my $p = shift;
  my $p_star;
  $p_star = alternate(T(concatenate($p, parser { $p_star->(@_) }),
                        sub { my ($first, $rest) = @_;
                              [$first, @$rest];
                            }),
                      \&null_list);
}
```

null_list() is like nothing(): It never consumes any input, and it always succeeds. But unlike nothing(), it returns an empty array instead of an undefined value. With this change, we no longer need the special-casery in the transformation function.

Having done this, we can simplify our elimination of left recursion. Instead of converting this:

```
A → A b | c
```

to this:

```
A → c A_tail
A_tail → b A_tail | (nothing)
```

we can convert it to this:

```
A → c star(b)
```

Similarly, this:

```
symbol → symbol A | symbol B
symbol → X | Y
```

becomes this:

```
symbol → (X | Y) star(A | B)
```

With this transformation, our original grammar for expressions:

```
expression → expression '+' term | expression '-' term | term
term → term '*' factor | term '/' factor | factor
factor → 'INT' | '(' expression ')'
```

is transformed to:

```
expression → term star('+' term | '-' term)
term → factor star('*' factor | '/' factor)
factor → 'INT' | '(' expression ')'
```

which is much easier to understand than the version that we saw before, with the artificial *expression_tail* and *term_tail* symbols.

The basic code for the *expression* parser now looks like this:

```
$expression = concatenate($Term,
                          star(alternate(concatenate(lookfor(['OP', '+']),
                                                     $Term),
                                         concatenate(lookfor(['OP', '-']),
                                                     $Term)))));
```

To get this to compute the right values, we'll have the + *term* and - *term* parts return functions that, given the value of the left part of an expression, compute and return the value of the entire expression:

```
concatenate(lookfor(['OP', '+']), $Term)
```

becomes:

```
T(concatenate(lookfor(['OP', '+']), $Term),
   sub { my $term_value = $_[1];
         return sub { $_[0] + $term_value }
      });
```

The code for the - *term* part looks the same, with subtraction substituted for addition.

The parser generated by the star() call will return a list of these addition or subtraction functions. The outermost concatenate() call will produce a parser that expects the value of the leftmost *term* and the list of expression-computing functions returned by the star() parser. If the *expression* is 4+3-5, the arguments to the parser will be the number 4 and the function list (sub { $_[0] + 3 }, sub { $_[0] - 5 }):

```
4                + 3                      - 5


|                 |                        |


4      sub { $_[0] + 3 }      sub { $_[0] - 5 }
```

The outermost parser must compute the complete value of the expression. It does this by passing the leftmost *term* value to the first addition or subtraction function, passing the result to the second addition or subtraction function, and so on, like this:

```
sub { my ($total, $funcs) = @_;
        for my $f (@$funcs) {
          $total = $f->($total);
        }
        $total;
      }
```

The complete parser for expressions is :

```
$expression =
   T(concatenate($Term, star(alternate(T(concatenate(lookfor(['OP', '+']),
                                                      $Term),
                                         sub {
                                           my $term_value = $_[1];
```

```
                                     sub { $_[0] + $term_value };
                                  }),
                        T(concatenate(lookfor(['OP', '-']),
                                        $Term),
                           sub {
                             my $term_value = $_[1];
                             sub { $_[0] - $term_value };
                           }),
                     ))),
      sub { my ($total, $funcs) = @_;
           for my $f (@$funcs) {
             $total = $f->($total);
           }
           $total;
         }
   );
```

The corresponding change to the *term* parser is identical, with multiplication
and division substituted for addition and subtraction.

8.4.4 Generic-Operator Parsers

We've already used this operator parser pattern twice, once in *expression* and once
in *term*. Since operators are common, we might expect to use the same pattern
in the future. We should try to abstract it into a generic function.

In general, we have a grammar where *symbol* can be expanded as *subpart*
OP *subpart* OP ... *subpart*, where OP is left-associative. The parser we just saw
is an example, with *symbol*, *subpart*, and OP being replaced by *expression*, *term*,
and +, respectively. We'll write a function, operator(), which, given a parser
for the subpart, a parser that recognizes the operator, and a callback function
that implements the operator (sub { $_[0] + $_[1] } in the case of addition),
generates a parser for sequences of *subpart* combined with OP. In general we'll
want multiple operators of the same precedence, but to begin with let's assume
there's only one operator at a time. Here's an example of what we want to produce:
the parser for *expression*, with only addition, and not subtraction:

```
$expression =
   T(concatenate($Term, star(T(concatenate(lookfor(['OP', '+']),
                                              $Term),
     sub {
```

```
          my $term_value = $_[1];
          sub { $_[0] + $term_value };
        }),
     )),
          sub { my ($total, $funcs) = @_;
                for my $f (@$funcs) {
                  $total = $f->($total);
                }
                $total;
              }
        );
```

The outline of our operator() function is:

```
sub operator {
  my ($subpart, $op, $opfunc) = @_;
  # Build and return parser like the preceding one
}
```

To construct the operator() function, we start by copying the *expression* parser into the body of sub operator. Then we systematically remove all the *expression*-specific code and replace each removed bit with the corresponding argument:

```
sub operator {
  my ($subpart, $op, $opfunc) = @_;

  # Build and return parser like the earlier one
  T(concatenate($subpart, star(T(concatenate($op,
                                            $subpart),
                        sub {
                          my $subpart_value = $_[1];
                          sub { $opfunc->($_[0], $subpart_value) };
                        }),
                   )),
      sub { my ($total, $funcs) = @_;
            for my $f (@$funcs) {
              $total = $f->($total);
            }
            $total;
          }
    );

}
```

This does work; operator($Term, lookfor(['op', '+']), sub { $_[0] + $_[1] }) does generate a parser for sums of terms. We now need to extend operator() to handle multiple operators of the same precedence. The argument to star() will be an alternation of several sections, rather than a single section. The argument to operator() itself may contain several $opses and $opfuncs. We'll call it like this:

```
operator($Term, [lookfor(['OP', '+']), sub { $_[0] + $_[1] }],
                [lookfor(['OP', '-']), sub { $_[0] - $_[1] }]);

sub operator {
  my ($subpart, @ops) = @_;
  my (@alternatives);
```

First we generate the alternatives that we'll give to star():

```
  for my $operator (@ops) {
    my ($op, $opfunc) = @$operator;
    push @alternatives,
      T(concatenate($op,
                       $subpart),
          sub {
            my $subpart_value = $_[1];
            sub { $opfunc->($_[0], $subpart_value) }
          });
  }
```

Then we build the parser from the alternatives:

```
  my $result =
    T(concatenate($subpart,
                  star(alternate(@alternatives))),
        sub { my ($total, $funcs) = @_;
              for my $f (@$funcs) {
                $total = $f->($total);
              }
              $total;
            });
  }
```

This is a lot of hairy code, but the payoff is excellent. We can stick the hairy operator() function into our parser-generating library and forget about it.

The code to generate the parsers for *term* and *expression* becomes short and transparent:

```
$expression =
  operator($Term,   [lookfor(['OP', '+']), sub { $_[0] + $_[1] }],
                    [lookfor(['OP', '-']), sub { $_[0] - $_[1] }]);

$term =
  operator($Factor, [lookfor(['OP', '*']), sub { $_[0] * $_[1] }],
                    [lookfor(['OP', '/']), sub { $_[0] / $_[1] }]);
```

Now that we have operator(), it's easy to imagine the next step: a parser generator function whose argument is an entire operator precedence table, and that, given a table like this:

```
[
  [['OP', '*'], ['OP', '/']],  # highest precedence
  [['OP', '+'], ['OP', '-']],  # lower precedence
]
```

does the work of the two calls to operator(), or more if we ask it to.

8.4.5   Debugging

Debugging programs containing complex nested functions can be difficult. The Perl interactive debugger isn't very helpful. If $z contains a reference to an anonymous function, the debugger won't give us much useful information about it:

```
    DB<119> x $z
0   CODE(0x849aca0)
      -> &main::__ANON__[arith15.pl:169] in arith15.pl:159-169
```

Just the file and the line numbers in the file. It could easily display the code, but it doesn't; with some extensions it could display the values of the subroutine's lexical variables, but again it doesn't. Internally, the debugger is a tremendous mess, and these improvements probably aren't forthcoming.[1] So we have to fall back on other techniques.

---

[1] Someone looking for a fun project to garner fame and renown in the Perl world would do well to consider replacing the debugger.

The first problem with the debugger's display of anonymous functions is that it's hard to tell them apart. CODE(0x849aca0) doesn't communicate anything intelligible. The easy way to fix this is to have a hash that maps anonymous functions to names or descriptions:

```
$N{$z} = "main parser";
```

Now if we're in the middle of the program and we see a mysterious anonymous function, we can ask for:

```
print $N{$mystery};
```

and get something like:

```
Third alternative of 'expression' symbol
```

A variation on this technique makes the functions into blessed objects with an overloaded stringification operator. The stringification operator simply returns the appropriate element of %N.

Another variation that may not be for everyone, but that I've sometimes used when the functions had little natural significance, is to tie the %N hash and have it *invent* a name when asked for the name of a function that hasn't already had a name assigned:

```
open NAMES, "<", $namefile or die ...;

sub STORE {
  my ($self, $key, $name) = @_;
  $self->{$key} = $name;
}


sub FETCH {
  my ($self, $key) = @_:
  if (exists $self->{$key}) { return $self->{$key} }
  chomp(my $name = <NAMES>);
  $self->{$key} = $name;
  warn "Function had no name; I'll call it '$name'.\n";
  return $name;
}
```

Then you fill up $namefile with twenty or thirty random but evocative nouns, such as:

Máximo Perez
The Train
Luis Melián Lafineur
Olimar
Brimstone
Clubs
The Whale
Gas
The Cauldron
Napoleon
Agustín de Vedia
Nine
The Negro Timoteo
The Flesh Blanket

Even meaningless names can be helpful. They don't tell you what the function does, but they give your memory a peg to hang an association on, and you're likely to recognize a function you've seen before when it comes up again. If you don't like the name that was automatically assigned, you can easily replace it by assigning a different value to %N.

From here it's a small step to having the functions receive their names at their time of manufacture; for example:

```perl
my $CON = 'A';
sub concatenate {
  my $id;
  if (ref $_[0]) { $id = "Unnamed concatenation $CON"; $CON++ }
  else {            $id = shift }

  my @p = @_;
  return \&nothing if @p == 0;
  return $p[0]  if @p == 1;

  my $parser = parser {
    my $input = shift;
    my $v;
    my @values;
    for (@p) {
      ($v, $input) = $_->($input) or return;
```

```
        push @values, $v;
      }
    return values;
  };
  $N{$parser} = $id;
  return $parser;
}
```

Now concatenate() gets an optional initial argument, which is a string that will be used as the name of the parser it generates; for example:

```
$factor       = alternate(lookfor('INT'),
                          T(concatenate("factor : '(' expr ')'",
                                        lookfor(['OP', '(']),
                                        $Expression,
                                        lookfor(['OP', ')']),
                            sub { $_[1] })
                          );
```

We can of course do the same thing to alternate():

```
$factor       = alternate("factor symbol parser",
                          lookfor('INT'),
                          T(concatenate("factor : '(' expr ')'",
                                        lookfor(['OP', '(']),
                                        $Expression,
                                        lookfor(['OP', ')']),
                            sub { $_[1] })
                          );
```

Since $id is a lexical variable, it can be captured and used inside the parser itself:

CODE LIBRARY
Parser::Debug.pm

```
package Parser::Debug;
use base 'Exporter';
use Parser ':all';
@EXPORT_OK = @Parser::EXPORT_OK;
%EXPORT_TAGS = %Parser::EXPORT_TAGS;

my $CON = 'A';
sub concatenate {
  my $id;
```

```
    if (ref $_[0]) { $id = "Unnamed concatenation $CON"; $CON++ }
    else {          $id = shift }

  my @p = @_
  return \&n 11 if @p == 0;
  return $p[ ]  if @p == 1;

  my $parser = parser {
    my $input = shift;
    debug "Looking for $id\n";
    my $v;
    my @values;
    my ($q, $np) = (0, scalar @p);
    for (@p) {
      $q++;
      unless (($v, $input) = $_->($input)) {
        debug "Failed concatenated component    $q/$np\n";
        return;
      }
      debug "Matched concatenated component    $q/$np\n";
      push @values, $v;
    }
    debug "Finished matching $id\n";
    return \@values;
  };
  $N{$parser} = $id;
  return $parser;
}
```

With a suitable definition of debug(), this will generate output like:

```
Looking for factor : '(' expr ')'
Matched concatenated component 1/3
Matched concatenated component 2/3
Matched concatenated component 3/3
Finished matching factor : '(' expr ')'
```

or:

```
Looking for factor : '(' expr ')'
Failed concatenated component 1/3
```

The easiest thing to do in debug() is just to print out the message. But we can do a little better:

```
sub debug ($) {
  return unless $DEBUG || $ENV{DEBUG};
  my $msg = shift;
  my $i = 0;
  $i++ while caller($i);
  $I = "| " x ($i-2);
  print $I, $msg;
}
```

The while caller loop computes the depth to which function calls have been nested. $I is an indentation string that is used to indent the debugging message accordingly. Now the output while parsing an expression like "8 - 3" begins like this:

```
| Looking for Input: expression EOI
| (Next token is INT 8)
| | | | Looking for expression : term star('+'term | '-' term)
| | | | (Next token is INT 8)
| | | | | | | Looking for term: factor star('*'factor | '/' factor)
| | | | | | | (Next token is INT 8)
| | | | | | | | | Looking for factor: INT | '(' expression ')'
| | | | | | | | | (Next token is INT 8)
| | | | | | | | | Trying alternative 1/2
| | | | | | | | | | Looking for token [INT]
| | | | | | | | | | Next token is [INT 8]
| | | | | | | | | | Token matched
| | | | | | | | | | Matched alternative 1/2
| | | | | | | | Matched concatenated component 1/2
...
```

Capturing $id inside the generated parser, as we've done, causes a problem. If we want to change the name of a parser after we've constructed it, we can't, because the name is captured in an inaccessible lexical variable inside the parser. We can change the name in the %N hash, but when the parser prints debug messages, it will still use the old name. One way to fix this is to have the debug messages refer to %N; another way is to provide each parser with a method for changing its name. The %N tactic is easier by far. Using a global variable like this should make you uncomfortable, and when you do it, the first question you should ask is "What if there are several different parsers in one program? Will their overlapping uses of %N collide?" In this case, though, there's no problem. Each anonymous function in the program resides at a different address, which means that the CODE(0x436c1d) strings will all be unique. As long as the parsers don't tamper with hash elements they don't understand, all will be well.

Why would we want to change the name of a parser? We'll see in a minute. Before that, let's note that the names we've been using are formulaic, which means that the next step is to get the parser construction functions to generate the names automatically. We begin by naming the basic parsers:

```
$N{\&End_of_Input} = 'EOI';
$N{\&nothing} = '(nothing)';
$N{$Expression} = 'expression';
$N{$Term} = 'term';
$N{$Factor} = 'factor';
```

Then we fix up concatenate() and alternate() to generate names from the names of their arguments:

```
sub concatenate {
  my @p = @_;
  return \&nothing if @p == 0;
  return $p[0]  if @p == 1;


  my $id = "@N{@p}";

  my $p = parser {
    ...
  };
  $N{$p} = $id;
  return $p;
}

sub alternate {
  my @p = @_;
  return parser { return () } if @p == 0;
  return $p[0]                if @p == 1;
  my $id = join " | ", @N{@p};
```

```
        my $p = parser {
          ...
        };
        $N{$p} = "($id)";
        return $p;
    }
```

Similarly, the description of the parser produced by T() is the same as the description of its argument:

```
    sub T {
      my ($parser, $transform) = @_;
      my $p = parser {
        ...
      };
      $N{$p} = $N{$parser};
      return $p;
    }
```

Now we change lookfor() to name its parsers after the token they're looking for:

```
    sub lookfor {
      my $wanted = shift;
      ...
      $N{$parser} = "[@$wanted]";
      return $parser;
    }
```

Finally, we change star():

```
    sub star {
      my $p = shift;
      my ($p_star, $conc);
      $p_star = alternate(T($conc = concatenate($p, parser { $p_star->(@_) }),
                            sub { my ($first, $rest) = @_;
                                  [$first, @$rest];
                                }),
                          \&null_list);
      $N{$p_star} = "star($N{$p})";
      $N{$conc} = "$N{$p} $N{$p_star}";
      return $p_star;
    }
```

This is why we needed to be able to change the names of parsers. The arguments to concatenate() are the argument $p, whose description, let's say, is P, and the eta-converted version of $p_star, which didn't have a description. The parser that would come out of concatenate() therefore would have a name something like "P ", and the parser that would come out of alternate() would be named something like P | (nothing), neither of which is very helpful. After the parsers are generated, we change the name of the alternation, $p_star itself, to star(P), and the name of the concatenation, temporarily stored in $conc, to P star(P).

The output, including automatically generated names, now looks like this (the input was "8 - 3"):

```
| Looking for expression EOI
| (Next token is INT 8)
| | | | Looking for term star(([OP +] term | [OP -] term))
| | | | (Next token is INT 8)
| | | | | | | | Looking for factor star(([OP *] factor | [OP /] factor))
| | | | | | | | (Next token is INT 8)
| | | | | | | | | Looking for ([INT] | [OP (] expression [OP )])
| | | | | | | | | (Next token is INT 8)
| | | | | | | | | Trying alternative 1/2
| | | | | | | | | | Looking for token [INT]
| | | | | | | | | | Next token is [INT 8]
| | | | | | | | | | Token matched
| | | | | | | | | Matched alternative 1/2
| | | | | | | | Matched concatenated component 1/2
| | | | | | | | Looking for star(([OP *] factor | [OP /] factor))
| | | | | | | | (Next token is OP -)
| | | | | | | | Trying alternative 1/2
```

... looking for multiplicative factors ...

```
| | | | | | | | Failed alternative 1/2
| | | | | | | | Trying alternative 2/2
| | | | | | | | | Looking for nothing
| | | | | | | | | (Next token is OP -)
| | | | | | | | Matched alternative 2/2
| | | | | | | Matched concatenated component 2/2
| | | | | | | Finished matching factor star(([OP *] factor | [OP /] factor))
| | | | Matched concatenated component 1/2
| | | | | Looking for star(([OP +] term | [OP -] term))
| | | | | (Next token is OP -)
| | | | | Trying alternative 1/2
    ...
```

When parsing goes wrong, examination of this debugging output is usually enough to figure out where the problem lies.

8.4.6 The Finished Calculator

Let's finish the calculator now. It starts with the lexer that we saw before:

```
use Parser ':all';
use Lexer ':all';

my $input = allinput(\*STDIN);
my $lexer = iterator_to_stream(
              make_lexer($input,
                  ['TERMINATOR', qr/;\n*|\n+/              ],
                  ['INT',        qr/\d+/                   ],
                  ['PRINT',      qr/\bprint\b/             ],
                  ['IDENTIFIER', qr|[A-Za-z_]\w*|          ],
                  ['OP',         qr#\*\*|[-=+*/()]#         ],
                  ['WHITESPACE', qr/\s+/, sub { "" }       ],
              )
           );
```

The complete grammar for the calculator is:

```
program → star(statement) 'End_of_Input';

statement → 'PRINT' expression 'TERMINATOR'
          | 'IDENTIFIER' '=' expression 'TERMINATOR'

expression → term star('+' term | '-' term)

term → factor star('*' factor | '/' factor)

factor → base ('**' factor | (nothing))

base → 'INT' | 'IDENTIFIER' | '(' expression ')'
```

There are two new grammar rules at the top: *program*, which represents the entire input, and *statement*, which represents a single statement, either a variable assignment or a request to print a result.[2]

---

2   In most modern languages, including Perl and C, statements may have a simpler structure, typically not much different than an expression. For example, in Perl, print $x and $x = $y are both

The grammar for expressions is a little more complicated also. The *factor* symbol no longer represents an atomic expression. Instead, it contains an optional exponentiation operation. Filling the atomic role formerly played by *factor* is a new symbol, *base*, which as before can be a number or a parenthesized expression, and now can also be a variable name.

```
my %VAR;

my ($base, $expression, $factor, $program, $statement, $term);
$Base       = parser { $base->(@_) };
$Expression = parser { $expression->(@_) };
$Factor     = parser { $factor->(@_) };
$Program    = parser { $program->(@_) };
$Statement  = parser { $statement->(@_) };
$Term       = parser { $term->(@_) };

$program = concatenate(star($Statement), \&End_of_Input);

$statement = alternate(T(concatenate(lookfor('PRINT'),
                                     $Expression,
                                     lookfor('TERMINATOR')),
                         sub { print ">> $_[1]\n" }),
                       T(concatenate(lookfor('IDENTIFIER'),
                                     lookfor(['OP', '=']),
                                     $Expression,
                                     lookfor('TERMINATOR')
                                    ),
                         sub { $VAR{$_[0]} = $_[2] }),
                      );
```

When the parser recognizes a complete `print` statement, it prints out the value of the expression. When it recognizes a complete assignment statement, it stores the value of the expression in a hash, %VAR, with the variable's name as a key. (We can prepopulate %VAR with the values of useful constants, such as π.)

The parsers for *expression* and *term* are exactly as before:

```
$expression =
  operator($Term,  [lookfor(['OP', '+']), sub { $_[0] + $_[1] }],
                   [lookfor(['OP', '-']), sub { $_[0] - $_[1] }]);
```

---

expressions, the former returning true or false to indicate success or failure of printing, and the latter returning the value of $y. If we do this, we get the opportunity to do things like $result = print $x and $x = $y = $z, which the calculator won't allow. It would have been both simpler and more useful to write the calculator this way, and I introduced the special *statement* forms solely for variety.

```
$term =
   operator($Factor, [lookfor(['OP', '*']), sub { $_[0] * $_[1] }],
                     [lookfor(['OP', '/']), sub { $_[0] / $_[1] }]);
```

Factors are a little different than in earlier examples, because they may now contain ** operators:

```
$factor = T(concatenate($Base,
                   alternate(T(concatenate(lookfor(['OP', '**']),
                                           $Factor),
                             sub { $_[1] }),
                             T(\&nothing, sub { 1 }))),
            sub { $_[0] ** $_[1] });
```

For an expression like 3 ** 4, we assign a value of 4 to the ** 4 part; the final value computation assigns a value of 81 to the entire 3 ** 4 expression. A missing exponent has a value of 1, so that 3 gets the same value as 3 ** 1. We haven't used operator() here because operator() generates parsers for left-associative operators, and ** is right associative. 2**2**3 means 2**(2**3) = 256, not (2**2)**3 = 64.

```
$base       = alternate(lookfor('INT'),
                        lookfor('IDENTIFIER',
                                sub { $VAR{$_[0][1]} || 0 }),
                        T(concatenate(lookfor(['OP', '(']),
                                      $Expression,
                                      lookfor(['OP', ')'])),
                          sub { $_[1] })
            );
```

The parser for *base* is just like the old parser for *term*, except with an extra clause for handling identifiers. To recover the value of an identifier, we look up the name of the identifier in the %VAR hash. Undefined variables behave like the number 0. Alternatively, we could have the calculator issue a warning message for undefined variables.

The calculator is complete; all we need is to invoke the parser:

```
$program->($lexer);
```

Given the following input:

```
a = 12345679 * 6
b=a*9; c=0
print b
```

it produces the correct output:

```
>> 666666666
```

8.4.7 Error Diagnosis and Recovery

Although the calculator works fine on correct inputs, it fails unpleasantly on erroneous input. If we delete the semicolon from the previous example, yielding:

```
a = 12345679 * 6
b=a*9 c=0
print b
```

then the parser simply fails after the assignment to a, returning an undefined value. No error message is generated.

ERROR-RECOVERY PARSERS

One easy way to put some error handling into the parser is to build a special-purpose sub-parser whose job is to recover from errors. If a statement goes awry, control will pass to the error-recovery parser. The error-recovery parser will try to resynchronize the parser with the input by discarding tokens until it gets to the end of the bad statement, and then restarting the parser from the new position:

```
$statement = alternate(T(concatenate(lookfor('PRINT'),
                                      $Expression,
                                      lookfor('TERMINATOR')),
                          sub { print ">> $_[1]\n" }),
                        T(concatenate(lookfor('IDENTIFIER'),
                                      lookfor(['OP', '=']),
                                      $Expression,
                                      lookfor('TERMINATOR')
                                     ),
                          sub { $VAR{$_[0]} = $_[2] }),
                        error(lookfor('TERMINATOR'), $Statement),
                      );
```

The error() call here generates a new parser, which is a third alternative form for *statement*. If, when trying to parse a statement, the upcoming input fails to

match either of the first two forms, the error-recovery parser returned by error()
will be invoked.

error()'s first argument is another parser whose job is to identify a good place
in the input to restart the parsing process. The error-recovery parser generated by
error() will discard one token at a time until it reaches a point in the input that
is acceptable to error()'s first argument. In this case, a good place to restart is
immediately following a TERMINATOR token, because that is where a new statement
is likely to begin. When the error-recovery parser is ready to continue, it invokes
another parser to continue the job on the remaining input stream; this other
parser is error()'s second argument. In this case, once the error-recovery parser
reaches a newline, it invokes $Statement to start looking for another statement.

The code for error() is fairly straightforward. First we'll see it without
debugging clutter:

```
sub error {
  my ($checker, $continuation) = @_;
  my $p;
  $p = parser {
    my $input = shift;

    while (defined($input)) {
      if (my (undef, $result) = $checker->($input)) {
        $input = $result;
        last;
      } else {
        drop($input);
      }
    }

    return unless defined $input;

    return $continuation->($input);
  };
  $N{$p} = "errhandler($N{$continuation} -> $N{$checker})";
  return $p;
}
```

The essential line is drop($input), which discards a token from the input. This
is done until either the $checker parser (lookfor('TERMINATOR') in the example)
succeeds, or the input is exhausted. Afterward, the error-handler parser continues
by invoking the continuation ($Statement in the example) on the remaining
input.

Here's the version with debugging messages:

```
sub error {
  my ($checker, $continuation) = @_;
  my $p;
  $p = parser {
    my $input = shift;
    debug "Error in $N{$continuation}\n";
    debug "Discarding up to $N{$checker}\n";
    my @discarded;
    while (defined($input)) {
      my $h = head($input);
      if (my (undef, $result) = $checker->($input)) {
        debug "Discarding $N{$checker}\n";
        push @discarded, $N{$checker};
        $input = $result;
        last;
      } else {
        debug "Discarding token [@$h]\n";
        push @discarded, $h->[1];
        drop($input);
      }
    }
    warn "Erroneous input: ignoring '@discarded'\n" if @discarded;
    return unless defined $input;
    debug "Continuing with $N{$continuation} after error recovery\n";
    $continuation->($input);
  };
  $N{$p} = "errhandler($N{$continuation} -> $N{$checker})";
  return $p;
}
```

On our erroneous input, the calculator program performs the assignment to a as instructed on the first line, and then says:

```
Erroneous input: ignoring 'b = a * 9 c = 0
'
>> 0
```

The >> 0 is the result of printing out the value of b in the final line; b was unset and defaulted to 0 because of the syntax error in the previous line.

EXCEPTIONS

Another convenient way to deal with errors is to change the structure of the parsers. Instead of returning undef to indicate a failed parse, they will throw an exception. The exception will include information about what the parser would have accepted and what it saw instead. Error-handler parsers will catch the exceptions, issue error messages, resynchronize, and restart.

First, a brief review of the semantics of exceptions in Perl. Perl's exception-handling mechanism is unfortunately named eval:

```
my $result = eval { ... };
```

Code in the eval is run in exactly the same way as any other code, returning the same result into $result, except that if it throws an exception, the exception will be caught by the eval instead of terminating the program. If the code inside the eval throws an exception, $result becomes undefined.

Exceptions are thrown with the die function. They may be arbitrary data objects. After an exception is caught, the value thrown is placed into the special variable $@.

To rewrite the End_of_Input() parser in this style, we say:

CODE LIBRARY
Parser::Except.pm

```
sub End_of_Input {
  my $input = shift;
  return (undef, undef) unless defined($input);
  die ["End of input", $input];
}
```

If there is no more input, the parser returns a value as before. If there is more input, the parser fails by calling die. The die value includes a string describing what was being sought ("End of Input") and what was found instead ($input).

Here's lookfor():

```
sub lookfor {
  my $wanted = shift;
  my $value = shift || sub { $_[0][1] };
  my $u = shift;
  $wanted = [$wanted] unless ref $wanted;

  my $parser = parser {
    my $input = shift;
    unless (defined $input) {
```

```
      die ['TOKEN', $input, $wanted];
    }

  my $next = head($input);
  for my $i (0 .. $#wanted) {
    next unless defined $wanted->[$i];
    unless ($wanted->[$i] eq $next->[$i]) {
      die ['TOKEN', $input, $wanted];
    }
  }
  my $wanted_value = $value->($next, $u);
  return ($wanted_value, tail($input));
};

  $N{$parser} = "[@$wanted]";
  return $parser;
}
```

If the lookfor()-generated parser sees the token it wants, it returns the same value as the old version. If it sees end-of-input or the wrong token, it throws an exception. As before, the exception value includes a tag indicating what kind of thing was being sought (a TOKEN), and what was found instead ($input). Here it also includes auxiliary information indicating what token was sought.

nothing() requires no changes because it never fails. concatenate() requires no changes, although we have an opportunity to make it simpler. It no longer needs to check to see if its sub-parsers have succeeded and terminate prematurely if one hasn't. It can assume that they all will succeed, because if one doesn't, it will throw an exception that will terminate concatenate() prematurely anyway.

alternate() is the interesting one. When a sub-parser succeeds, it stops and returns the value, as before. When a sub-parser fails, the alternate() parser needs to catch the exception so that it can try the next sub-parser. It installs the exception in an array @failures; if all the sub-parsers fail, @failures will contain the list of reasons why, and alternate() can throw an exception that includes this information:

```
sub alternate {
  my @p = @_;
  return parser { return () } if @p == 0;
  return $p[0]              if @p == 1;

  my $p;
  $p = parser {
```

```
      my $input = shift;
      my ($v, $newinput);
      my @failures;

      for (@p) {
        eval { ($v, $newinput) = $_->($input) };
        if ($@) {
          die unless ref $@;
          push @failures, $@;
        } else {
          return ($v, $newinput);
        }
      }
      die ['ALT', $input, \@failures];
    };
    $N{$p} = "(" . join(" | ", map $N{$_}, @p) . ")";
    return $p;
  }
```

The `die unless ref $@` line is there to propagate any exception that has to do with a programming error, such as division by zero. If we didn't propagate these, then they would get absorbed into the `@failures` array, and might be thrown away.

Finally, we need a function to actually catch exceptions and issue a report. Here's a simple one:

```
sub error {
  my ($try) = @_;
  my $p;
  $p = parser {
    my $input = shift;
    my @result = eval { $try->($input) };
    if ($@) {
      display_failures($@) if ref $@;
      die;
    }
    return @result;
  };
}
```

Its argument $try is a parser; error() returns a new parser that tries $try. If $try succeeds, error() returns its value. If $try fails, error() issues an error report with display_failures() and then calls die to propagate the same exception up to *its* caller.

Here's a rather elaborate implementation of display_failures():

```
sub display_failures {
  my ($fail, $depth) = @_;
  $depth ||= 0;
  my $I = " " x $depth;
  my ($type, $position, $data) = @$fail;
  my $pos_desc = "";

  while (length($pos_desc) < 40) {
    if ($position) {
      my $h = head($position);
      $pos_desc .= "[@$h] ";
    } else {
      $pos_desc .= "End of input ";
      last;
    }
    $position = tail($position);
  }
  chop $pos_desc;
  $pos_desc .= "..." if defined $position;

  if ($type eq 'TOKEN') {
    print $I, "Wanted [@$data] instead of '$pos_desc'\n";
  } elsif ($type eq 'End of input') {
    print $I, "Wanted EOI instead of '$pos_desc'\n";
  } elsif ($type eq 'ALT') {
    print $I, ($depth ? "Or any" : "Any"), " of the following:\n";
    for (@$data) {
      display_failures($_, $depth+1);
    }
  }
}
```

display_failures() is expecting to get at least one argument, which is the exception object, and has the form [$type, $position, $data], where $type is just an identifying string, $position is the position in the input stream at which the error occurred, and the $data is optional and has a form that depends on the $type.

The middle section analyzes the input tokens that appear starting at $position and builds up $pos_desc, a string describing them. The end section examines $type and prints an appropriate message. The case for ALT is the interesting one; in this case $data is an array of all the failure exceptions from the sub-parsers of the alternation. display_failures prints an appropriate header and calls itself recursively to display the sub-failures.

The top-level call of the main parser on the entire input needs to be protected by an eval block, so that the program has a chance to recover from an uncaught exception:

```
my ($val, $rest) = eval { $program->($lexer) };
if ($@) {
  display_failures($@);
}
```

or we could just use:

```
my ($val, $rest) = error($program)->($lexer);
```

Let's consider the example "a = 3; b + 7; c = 5;" and see what comes out:

```
Wanted EOI instead of '[IDENTIFIER b] [OP +] [INT 7] [TERMINATOR ;]...'
```

The parser is reporting that it was unhappy with the "b + 7;" part of the input; it would have preferred to see the input end right after the "a = 3;" part.

We can get better reporting by using the error() function to insert error reporting at appropriate places inside the parser. For example, if we change:

```
$statement = alternate(...);
```

to:

```
$statement = error(alternate(...));
```

then all erroneous statements will be diagnosed. Now the output includes:

```
Any of the following:
  Wanted [PRINT] instead of '[IDENTIFIER b] [OP +] [INT 7] [TERMINATOR ;]...'
  Wanted [OP =] instead of '[OP +] [INT 7] [TERMINATOR ;] [IDENTIFIER c]...'
```

It wanted to see "print" after "a=3;", or else "=" instead of "+" after the "b".

This parser aborts at the first sign of trouble. We could add error recovery to the reporting behavior of `error()` and get the parser to continue and perhaps diagnose more errors.

8.4.8 Big Numbers

As a final improvement, we'll change the calculator to support arbitrarily large numbers. This is trivial; we add:

```
use Math::BigFloat;
```

to the top of the program, and change the part of the parser that assigns a value to an INT token:

```
lookfor('INT')
```

becomes:

```
lookfor('INT', sub { Math::BigFloat->new($_[0][1]) });
```

which passes the token's string representation to `Math::BigFloat`, which constructs a big number object for it. `Math::BigFloat` overloads the normal arithmetic operators to work on arbitrary-precision numbers, so we don't need to change anything else. It would be almost as easy to get the calculator to support complex numbers; we would use `Math::Complex`, and add a line to the lexer to properly interpret constants that matched /\d+i/.

8.5 PARSING REGEXES

As an example that's probably more practical than the calculator, we'll implement a parser for a subset of Perl's regular expressions. In Chapter 6 we saw a program that generated a (possibly infinite) stream of all the strings matched by a certain regex. But it wasn't convenient to use this program. To get a list of the strings matched by /(a|b)*c+/, for example, we had to write the following code:

```
my $z = concat(star(union(literal("a"), literal("b"))),
               plus(literal("c")),
              );
```

What we'd like is to be able to put in a regex in the usual notation and get out the same stream. Our parsing technology will do this. We'll build a parser that can analyze the structure of a regex. As it determines the structure of the regex, it will call the appropriate stream functions to manufacture the stream of matching strings.

First, the lexer. Regexes contain the following operators: + * ? ( ) |. Other than this, they contain atomic expressions, or "atoms," such as w, \r, and \x0d. They also contain other items such as character classes, non-capturing parentheses, lookahead items, and embedded Perl code; we'll ignore these because they're not particularly instructive.

Of these lexical types, the atoms are all syntactically equivalent; any valid regex that contains a w is still valid if the w is replaced by \r or by \x0d. Similarly, the quantifiers +, *, and ? are all syntactically equivalent. This suggests the following lexer:

CODE LIBRARY
regex-parser

```
use Lexer ':all';
use Stream 'node';


my ($regex, $alternative, $atom, $qatoms);


sub regex_to_stream {
  my @input = @_;
  my $input = sub { shift @input };

  my $lexer = iterator_to_stream(
        make_lexer($input,
                 ['PAREN',      qr/[()]/,],
                 ['QUANT',      qr/[*+?]/                      ],
                 ['BAR',        qr/[|]/,                       ],
                 ['ATOM',       qr/\\x[0-9a-fA-F]{0,2} # hex escape
                                 |\\\d+                 # octal escape
                                 |\\.                   # other \
                                 |.                     # other char
                                /x, ],
                  )
          );

  my ($result) = $regex->($lexer);
  return $result;
}
```

Regexes are similar in structure to arithmetic expressions, only with fewer different operators. The lowest-precedence operator is the vertical bar, |. A regex is a series of alternatives separated by vertical bars. Each alternative is a (possibly empty) sequence of (possibly quantified) atoms. For example, in the regex /(a|b)*c+/, there is a single alternative, consisting of two quantified atoms: (a|b)* and c+. The parentheses around a|b group the contents into a single atomic expression. a|b, of course, contains two alternatives, each with one unquantified atom.

The grammar is:

```
regex       → alternative 'BAR' regex  |  alternative
alternative → qatom alternative | (nothing)
qatom       → atom ('QUANT' | (nothing))
atom        → 'ATOM' | '(' regex ')'
```

As before, we define eta-conversions of the parsers so that the parsers can be mututally recursive:

```
use Parser ':all';

my $Regex       = parser { $regex       ->(@_) };
my $Alternative = parser { $alternative->(@_) };
my $Atom        = parser { $atom        ->(@_) };
my $QAtom       = parser { $qatom       ->(@_) };
```

Building the basic parser from the grammar is straightforward:

```
# regex -> alternative 'BAR' regex  |  alternative
$regex = alternate(concatenate($Alternative,
                               lookfor('BAR'),
                               $Regex),
                   $Alternative);
```

This is fine if we want to generate ASTs for regexes. But what we really want is to generate streams of strings. If we assume that the values returned for $Alternative and $Regex are streams, it's easy to generate the result for the entire regex. We use the union() function from Section 6.5.1:

```
use Regex;

# regex -> alternative 'BAR' regex  |  alternative
$regex = alternate(T(concatenate($Alternative,
```

```
                                     lookfor('BAR'),
                                     $Regex),
                          sub { Regex::union($_[0], $_[2])}),
                     $Alternative);
```

If the regex consists of a single alternative, then the list of strings it matches is
the same as the list of strings matched by the single alternative, so nothing extra
needs to be done.

Similarly, the concat() function from Section 6.5.1 takes the streams that
list the strings matched by two regexes and returns the stream of strings that
are matched by the concatenation of two regexes, so it's just what we need to
generate the value of a single alternative:

```
# alternative -> qatom alternative | (nothing)
$alternative = alternate(T(concatenate($QAtom, $Alternative),
                             \&Regex::concat),
                         T(\&nothing, sub { Regex::literal("") }));
```

If the alternative is empty, it matches only the empty string. The call
Regex::literal("") returns a stream that contains the empty string and
nothing else.

```
my %quant;
# qatom -> atom ('QUANT' | (nothing))
$qatom   = T(concatenate($Atom,
                         alternate(lookfor('QUANT'),
                                   \&nothing),
                        ),
             sub { my ($at, $q) = @_;
                   defined $q ? $quant{$q}->($at) : $at });

%quant = ('*' => \&Regex::star,
          '+' => \&Regex::plus,
          '?' => \&Regex::query,
         );
```

For quantified atoms, we get a stream that represents the list of strings matched
by the atom, to which we apply the appropriate quantifier. There might not be
a quantifier, in which case the value of the second element of the concatenation
is undefined, and we return the value of the atom unchanged. Note that %quant
is nothing more than a dispatch table.

We saw `star()` and `plus()` back in Chapter 6, but not `query()`, which is trivial:

```
sub query {
  my $s = shift;
  union(literal(""), $s);
}
```

It matches anything its argument matches, and also the empty string.

```
# atom -> 'ATOM' | '(' regex ')'
$atom = alternate(lookfor("ATOM", sub { Regex::literal($_[0][1]) }),
                  T(concatenate(lookfor(["PAREN", "("]),
                                $Regex,
                                lookfor(["PAREN", ")"]),
                               ),
                    sub { $_[1] }),
                 );
```

Finally, we're down to atoms. If the atom is indeed a single atomic token, then the list of strings contains the value of the token itself; for example, the atomic regex w matches the string `'w'` and nothing else. If the atom is actually a complete regex in parentheses, we call the regex parser recursively and return the value it returns, throwing away the parentheses, just as we did in the arithmetic expression parser.

Calling `Regex::literal()` is a little too simple. When the atom is \x0d, it does *not* match the string `'\x0d'`; it matches the single-character string that contains only a carriage return. We could fix this by passing the token to a string-interpreting function before passing the result to `Regex::literal()`.

Some atoms are more difficult to handle. This parser treats \b, a word-boundary assertion, as an atom. It is atomic, but it certainly doesn't match the string `'\b'`. To handle this properly, we'd have to introduce a new kind of value in our string streams; the new values would denote strings with boundary requirements at the front, the back, or both. When the `concat()` operator tried to put together two strings with boundary requirements at the ends at which they were being joined, it would check the requirements for compatibility. If the requirements were incompatible, `concat()` would skip that pair of strings and move on. The same scheme could handle lookahead and look-behind assertions, although the lexer would have to be extended to understand the notations.

Still, for all its limitations, the string generator performs adequately for a first cut. If we give it the input (a|b)+(c|d*), it cheerfully returns an infinite stream that begins:

a	bbb	abba
b	add	abbb
aa	aac	baaa
ab	abc	baab
ba	bac	baba
bb	bbc	babb
ac	bdd	bbaa
ad	aad	bbab
bc	abd	bbba
bd	bad	bbbb
aaa	bbd	addd
aab	aaaa	aaac
aba	aaab	aabc
abb	aaba	abac
baa	aabb	abbc
bab	abaa	baac
bba	abab	...

8.6   OUTLINES

The regex and calculator examples have many similarities. Here's an example that is quite different. We'll write a program to read in topic outlines and infer a tree structure from the indentation. A typical input looks like this:

```
* Parsing
  * Lexers
    * Emulating the <> operator
    * Lexers more generally
    * Chained Lexers
    * Peeking
  * Parsing in General
    * Grammars
    * Parsing Grammars
  * Recursive-Descent Parsers
    * Very Simple Parsers
    * Parser Operators
    * Compound Operators
```

To keep the problem manageable, we'll make a few simplifying assumptions. Each item occupies exactly one line, and begins with a "bullet" character. The first line is the root of the tree, and will be flush with the left margin; each sub-item will be indented two spaces farther right than its parent.

All the lexers we've seen so far have discarded whitespace. The lexer for this problem mustn't do that because the whitespace is significant. But the input has a very simple lexical structure: each line is an "item," and is separated from the next item by newlines. So the lexer is simply:

CODE LIBRARY
outline-parser

```
use Lexer ':all';
use Stream 'node';

my ($tree, $subtree);
sub outline_to_array {
  my @input = @_;
  my $input = sub { shift @input };

  my $lexer = iterator_to_stream(
        make_lexer($input,
                ['ITEM',         qr/^.*$/m ],
```

```
                                      ['NEWLINE',      qr/\n+/     , sub { "" } ],
                                  )
                              );

                  my ($result) = $tree->($lexer);
                  return $result;
              }
```

The grammar is almost as simple. A tree has a root item, followed by zero or more subtrees. The subtrees must be indented farther to the right than the root item. The grammar will look something like this:

```
        input  →  tree 'End_of_input'
        tree  →  'ITEM' star(subtree)
        subtree  →  tree
```

This isn't exactly right, because it doesn't take into account the indentations. When the parser sees the root item of a new tree, it needs to record that item's indentation; when it tries to parse a subtree, it should succeed if the next item is indented farther right than the previous root, and fail if it isn't. Consider this simple example:

```
        * A
          * B
            * C
          * D
```

Item C here is a sub-item of B, because it's indented farther to the right. At this point, the parser will be looking for sub-items of C. The next item is D. D is not to the right of C, so it is not a sub-item of C. Moreover, it is not to the right of B, so it is not a sub-item of B. But D is to the right of A, so D is a sub-item of A.

The grammar needs to be extended to take the indentations into account:

```
        input  →  tree 'End_of_input'
        tree  →  'ITEM' <<record indentation of root node>> star(subtree)
        subtree  →  <<check indentation of next item>> tree
```

Here, <<record indentation of root node>> is a special version of the null parser. It consumes no input, always succeeds, and returns a meaningless value. But it also examines the item that was just parsed and makes a note of how far it was indented. Similarly, <<check indentation of next item>> also consumes no input and returns a meaningless value. But it also examines the head of the input token stream to make sure that the upcoming item is indented to the right of the current root node. If so, it succeeds, allowing the *subtree* parser to proceed to the real business of parsing the subtree, which it does by calling the *tree* parser recursively. If not, it fails, causing the *subtree* parser to fail also.

Here's the main parser:

```
use Parser ':all';
use Stream 'head';
my $Tree    = parser { $tree->(@_) };
my $Subtree = parser { $subtree->(@_) };


my $LEVEL = 0;
$tree = concatenate(lookfor('ITEM', sub { trim($_[0][1]) }),
                    action(sub { $LEVEL++ }),
                    star($Subtree),
                    action(sub { $LEVEL-- }));

my $BULLET = '[#*ox.+-]\s+';
sub trim {
  my $s = shift;
  $s =~ s/^ *//;
  $s =~ s/^ $BULLET//o;
  return $s;
}
```

The item's string value is passed to trim(), which just trims off the leading whitespace and bullet, if any. The next item in the concatenation is an action() item, which performs the indicated action, incrementing the current indentation level. Then follow zero or more subtrees, and when the parser has finished parsing the subtrees, it invokes another action to put the indentation level back the way it was.

This is action():

```
sub action {
  my $action = shift;
  return parser {
    my $input = shift;
    $action->($input);
    return (undef, $input);
  };
}
```

It takes an action argument and generates a parser that invokes the action, consumes no tokens, and always succeeds.

As it stands, the value returned by *tree* is a list of four items, of which two are the meaningless undefs returned by the action() parsers. As usual, we'll use T() to adjust the return value to the tree structure that we want.

The tree structure we'll construct will be an array. The first element of the array will be the root node, and the other elements will be the subtrees, in order. The tree for this example is ["A", ["B", ["C"]], ["D"]]:

```
    * A
      * B
        * C
      * D
```

The main tree has two subtrees, one rooted at B and one at D. The B subtree has a sub-subtree, with root C.

concatenate() will pass T() four arguments, as noted before; two will be undef. The other two will be $_[0], the string value returned by lookfor(), and $_[2], an array of the subtrees. To assemble these into a tree structure, we just need to make them into a single array:

```
$tree = T(concatenate(lookfor('ITEM', sub { trim($_[0][1]) }),
                      action(sub { $LEVEL++; }),
                      star($Subtree),
                      action(sub { $LEVEL--; })),
          sub { [ $_[0], @{$_[2]} ] });
```

The other half of the parser is easier in some ways, more complicated in others:

```
$subtree = T(concatenate(test(sub {
                              my $input = shift;
                              return unless $input;
                              my $next = head($input);
                              return unless $next->[0] eq 'ITEM';
                              return level_of($next->[1]) >= $LEVEL;
                           }),
                         $Tree,
                        ),
             sub { $_[1] });

sub level_of {
```

```
      my ($space) = $_[0] =~ /^( *)/;
      return length($space)/2;
   }
```

The parser built by test() is like the one built by action(), except that it doesn't always succeed. Instead, it looks at the value returned by the action, and succeeds only if the value is true:

```
   sub test {
     my $action = shift;
     return parser {
       my $input = shift;
       my $result = $action->($input);
       return $result ? (undef, $input) : ();
     };
   }
```

The action here makes sure there is an item coming up, and extracts the text from it. It then uses the level_of() utility function to figure out the nesting depth of the item's text, and returns success if it is far enough to the right, failure if not. If the action succeeds, the *subtree* parser then invokes $Tree to parse the subtree. Note that the item examined by the action is *not* removed from the input stream. If $Tree returns successfully, T() throws away the meaningless value returned by the action, and returns the tree structure from $Tree as the value of the subtree.

This parser is complete. Now we'll make it a little more clever, by having it detect when the entire input is indented (and ignore the uniform indentation if so) and having it handle different amounts of indentation at each level. These two inputs should parse the same:

```
* A                    * A
  * B                      * B
    * C                                  * C
      * D                                  * D
  * E                      * E
    * F                              * F
    * G                              * G
  * H                      * H
    * I                          * I
  * J                      * J
```

Now that indentations vary, the action that records the current indentation level will have to actually examine the current item; simply incrementing a counter is no longer sufficient. We didn't give action() parsers any good way to examine values that have already been parsed, so the easiest way to get what we want is to attach the action to the lookfor('ITEM') parser:

```
my @LEVEL;
$tree = T(concatenate(T(lookfor('ITEM', sub { $_[0] }),
                      sub {
                        my $s = $_[1];
                        push @LEVEL, level_of($s);
                        return trim($s);
                      }),
                    star($Subtree),
                    action(sub { pop @LEVEL })),
          sub { [ $_[0], @{$_[1]} ]},
          );
```

The task of looking up the level of an item and recording it has been delegated to the lookfor('ITEM') parser, since it has easy access to the item's text. We use T() to hang an action on the lookfor() parser. But since T() was designed for use with concatenate(), which returns a list of values, we need to override the normal return value of lookfor() to deliver the entire token instead of just the string data as usual. The string is extracted from the token and assigned to $s, and its level is computed and pushed on a stack. The parser needs to record the levels in a stack because when it finishes parsing the current tree, it will need to recall the level of the parent root. Let's return to the small example:

```
* A
  * B
    * C
  * D
```

While parsing the C tree, the parser will remember that the current root, B, is indented two spaces. When it sees item D, also indented two spaces, it will know that D is not a sub-item of B. This will conclude the parsing of the B subtree, and the action function will pop the stack. The top stack item will then be 0, the indentation of A. Since D is to the right of this, D will be parsed as a subtree of A.

The *subtree* parser is almost identical to the previous version:

```
$subtree = T(concatenate(test(sub {
                                my $input = shift;
                                return unless $input;
```

```
                    my $next = head($input);
                    return unless $next->[0] eq 'ITEM';
                    return level_of($next->[1]) > $LEVEL[-1];
                  }),
                $Tree,),
            sub { $_[1] });
```

The only difference is that the action compares the level of the current item with
the top of the stack rather than with a scalar counter.

level_of() is a little more complicated, because the entire outline might be
indented, and this has to be accounted for:

```
    my $PREFIX;
    sub level_of {
      my $count = 0;
      my $s = shift;
      if (! defined $PREFIX) {
        ($PREFIX) = $s =~ /^(\s*)/;
      }
      $s =~ s/^$PREFIX//o
        or die "Item '$s' wasn't indented the same as the previous items.\n";
      my ($indent) = $s =~ /^(\s*)/;
      my $level = length($indent);
      return $level;
    }
```

$PREFIX is a string of whitespace indicating the indentation of the very first item.
All subsequent indentations are figured relative to this. The $PREFIX is trimmed
off each item before its indentation is figured; if an item doesn't begin with the
same $PREFIX as the others, the parser dies.

Here's the example tree again, and the result of parsing it:

```
    * A                              [ 'A',
        * B                            [ 'B', [ 'C', [ 'D' ] ] ],
              * C                      [ 'E', [ 'F' ], [ 'G' ] ],
               * D                     [ 'H', [ 'I' ] ],
        * E                            [ 'J' ]
             * F                     ]
            * G
        * H
         * I
        * J
```

8.7   DATABASE-QUERY PARSING

In Chapter 4, we saw a simple database system, FlatDB, which supported the combination of simpler queries into more complex ones:

```
query_or($dbh->query('STATE', 'NY'),
         query_and($dbh->callbackquery(sub { $F{OWES} > 100 }),
                   $dbh->query('STATE', 'MA')
                  ))
```

I promised that we would attach this to a parser so that we could simply write something like:

```
complex_query("STATE = 'NY' | OWES > 100 & STATE = 'MA'")
```

and get the same result. The lexer will turn this example into the following tokens:

```
[FIELD, 'STATE']
[OP, '=']
[STRING, 'NY']
[OR]
[FIELD, 'OWES']
[OP, '>']
[NUMBER, 100]
[AND]
[FIELD, 'STATE']
[OP, '=']
[STRING, 'MA']
```

8.7.1 The Lexer

Here's the lexer for our database query language. It has a few novel features:

CODE LIBRARY
dqp.pl

```
use Lexer ':all';

sub lex_input {
```

```
    my @input = @_;
    my $input = sub { shift @input };


    my $lexer = iterator_to_stream(
        make_lexer($input,
            ['STRING', qr/' (?: \\. | [^'] )*  '
                      |" (?: \\. | [^"] )*  " /sx,

                sub { my $s = shift;
                    $s =~  s/.//; $s =~ s/.$//;
                    $s =~  s/\\(.)/$1/g;
                    ['STRING', $s] }            ],

            ['FIELD',  qr/[A-Z]+/                ],
            ['AND',    qr/&/                     ],
            ['OR',     qr/\|/                    ],


            ['OP',     qr/[!<>=]=|[<>=]/,
                sub { $_[0] =~ s/^=$/==/;
                      [ 'OP', $_[0] ] }          ],


            ['LPAREN', qr/[(]/                   ],
            ['RPAREN', qr/[)]/                   ],
            ['NUMBER', qr/\d+ (?:\.\d*)? | \.\d+/x   ],
            ['SPACE',  qr/\s+/, sub { "" }       ],
        )
    );
}
```

Most of this is old hat. The exception is the first rule, which recognizes string constants, which have a fairly complicated lexical structure. First, we'll look at the regex, which is in two parts, one for single-quoted strings and one for double-quoted strings. The two kinds of strings will have identical behavior in this language; we're including them both only to suit the preferences of users for one or the other. The obvious regex to match a single-quoted string is /' .* '/x, but a little thought shows this isn't correct, since it will match 'O'Reilly', which is syntactically incorrect. Really, the characters inside the quotes are forbidden to be quotes themselves, so we want /' [^']* '/x. But now there's no way to write a string that contains a single-quote character, so we introduce backslash escapes. If a backslash appears inside a single-quoted string, the following character is

accepted unconditionally, whether or not it's a quote. The pattern becomes
/'(?: \\. | [^'])* '/sx. (The /s tells the regex engine that it is acceptable
for the . character to match a newline; normally it won't.) The corresponding
pattern for double-quoted strings is similar.

The default method for building a token from a quoted string isn't exactly
what we want, because the input '0\'Reilly' represents the string O'Reilly,
not O\'Reilly. So the STRING rule makes use of a feature we haven't used much
yet, which is the option to specify a token-manufacturing function to replace the
default:

```
sub { my $s = shift;
      $s =~ s/.//; $s =~ s/.$//;
      $s =~ s/\\(.)/$1/g;
      ['STRING', $s] }
```

The token-manufacturing function trims off the leading and trailing quotation
marks, and then expands the backslash escapes. If we wanted to support more
backslash escapes, such as \t for a tab character, this would be the place to do it:

```
sub { my $s = shift;
      $s =~ s/.//; $s =~ s/.$//;
      $s =~ s/\\t/\t/g;
      $s =~ s/\\(.)/$1/g;
      ['STRING', $s] }
```

Note that once a STRING token comes out of the lexer, the parser won't be
able to tell whether it was originally a single-quoted string or a double-quoted
string. Since the two kinds of strings have the same semantics, that's just what
we want; there's no reason for the parser to concern itself with this irrelevant
distinction.

This kind of behavior is typical of lexers. The lexer's job is to convert the
incoming sequence of characters into meaningful tokens, and if two incoming sequences have the same meaning, they should turn into the same tokens.
The Perl lexer does the same thing; by the time the parser gets hold of the
input:

```
$a = "O'Reilly";
```

it can't tell that the input wasn't originally:

```
$a = 'O\'Reilly';
```

instead, or:

```
$a = qq{\x4f\47\x52\x65\151\x6c\x6c\171};
```

for that matter. Similarly, the Perl lexer absorbs the two keywords `for` and `foreach`, which are identical, and grinds both of them down to identical `OPERATOR(FOR)` tokens. By the time the parser gets the input, it doesn't know which one you wrote. We saw another example of this earlier, when the lexer for our calculator treated `/;\n*/` and `/\n+/` as the same kind of token.

The only other lexer rule that's a little different from those we've seen before is `OP`, the rule for matching operators. An operator is one of the following:

```
!= <= >= ==
   <  >  =
```

`==` and `=` are considered the same; we're including both forms as a convenience for the user. The token-manufacturing function transforms `=` to `==`, again eliminating a distinction that is of no concern to the parser.

8.7.2 The Parser

The grammar for the query language is simple, and doesn't contain anything new:

```
complex_query → term star('OR' complex_query)

term → simple_query star('AND' term)

simple_query → 'FIELD' 'OP' 'STRING'
simple_query → 'FIELD' 'OP' 'NUMBER'
simple_query → 'LPAREN' complex_query 'RPAREN'
```

The code for *complex_query* and *term* is completely handled by the `operator()` function we wrote in Section 8.4:

```
use Parser ':all';
use FlatDB_Composable qw(query_or query_and);

my ($cquery, $squery, $term);
my $CQuery = parser { $cquery->(@_) };
my $SQuery = parser { $squery->(@_) };
my $Term = parser { $term->(@_) };
```

```
use FlatDB;

$cquery = operator($Term, [lookfor('OR'), \&query_or]);
$term = operator($SQuery, [lookfor('AND'), \&query_and]);
```

The code for simple_query() is more interesting, because it is the main interface with the flat database library.

Recall that there are three productions for *simple_query*:

```
simple_query  →  'FIELD' 'OP' 'STRING'
simple_query  →  'FIELD' 'OP' 'NUMBER'
simple_query  →  'LPAREN' complex_query 'RPAREN'
```

The third of these is just like several other parsers that we've seen before:

```
# This needs to be up here so that the following $squery
# definition can see $parser_dbh
my $parser_dbh;
sub set_parser_dbh { $parser_dbh = shift }
sub     parser_dbh { $parser_dbh }

$squery = alternate(
            T(concatenate(lookfor('LPAREN'),
                          $CQuery,
                          lookfor('RPAREN'),
                          ),
              sub { $_[1] }),
```

The first two are separate productions because they have different meanings. "STATE = 'NY'" is quite different from "AMOUNT = 0", because the query() method can be used for the first query but not for the second — recall that query() always uses eq to detect matches. Because the FIELD OP NUMBER production must always use callbackquery(), never query(), it's a little simpler and we'll see it first:

```
T(concatenate(lookfor('FIELD'),
              lookfor('OP'),
              lookfor('NUMBER')),
    sub {
      my ($field, $op, $val) = @_;
      my $cmp_code = 'sub { $_[0] OP $_[1] }';
```

```
$cmp_code =~ s/OP/$op/;
my $cmp = eval($cmp_code) or die;
my $cb = sub { my %F = @_;
                    $cmp->($F{$field}, $val)};
$parser_dbh->callbackquery($cb);
}),
```

The callback for the callback query is $cb. $cb sets up a hash %F that maps field names to values, indexes %F to get the value of the appropriate field, and compares the field value with the specified number $val. When $op is ==, the comparison needs to be $F{$field} == $val; when $op is <=, the comparison needs to be $F{$field} <= $val, and so on. There are essentially two ways to do this. One way is to select a function that performs the comparison from a dispatch table:

```
%compare = ('==' => sub { my %F = @_; $F{$field} == $val },
            '<=' => sub { my %F = @_; $F{$field} <= $val },
            '<'  => sub { my %F = @_; $F{$field} <  $val },
            '>=' => sub { my %F = @_; $F{$field} >= $val },
            '>'  => sub { my %F = @_; $F{$field} >  $val },
            '!=' => sub { my %F = @_; $F{$field} != $val },
           );
my $cb = $compare{$op};
```

This technique requires the construction of six anonymous functions, from which we select one to use and discard the other five. The other technique is to generate the desired code by textual substitution at run time; this is what the preceding implementation does. The code for a comparison function is manufactured by replacing OP in sub { $_[0] OP $_[1] } with the actual value of $op, and then using eval to compile the resulting string. $cb then calls the resulting function to actually compare the values. With the eval approach we run the risk of accidentally generating syntactically incorrect code; building Perl code is always fraught with peril because Perl's syntax is so irregular. I chose the eval approach because the peril seemed small in this case, because the code was smaller, and because I didn't like the idea of manufacturing six functions on every call just to throw five of them away.[3]

---

3 One of the technical reviewers ridiculed me extensively for this decision, since the performance difference is negligible. But it wasn't for performance reasons that I disliked the idea of manufacturing six times as many functions as I needed. It was because I'm compulsive.

The $parser_dbh variable in the final line is a bit of a puzzle. callbackquery() is a method, that is called on a database handle object. In order to perform a callbackquery(), the parser needs to know which database to query.

The cleanest way to accomplish this might be to provide each parser with a user-parameter argument, which it would then pass to its sub-parsers. Then we would supply the desired database handle to the top-level parser, and it would percolate down to the T() function in simple_query(), which would use it as the target object of the callbackquery() method. Unfortunately, this would require redesigning all our parser-generation functions to accommodate a new argument format. At present, the argument convention for alternate() and concatenate() is utterly simple and straightforward: You just pass in the parsers you want to alternate or concatenate. If a user-parameter argument were allowed, it would have to be distinguished specially somehow. The alternate() and concatenate() functions wouldn't be able to recognize a user argument just by looking at it, the way they recognized the debugging labels of Section 8.4, because a user argument might have any value at all.

There's an alternative that is preferable in this case. In Chapter 2, we saw how to use user parameters to avoid having to communicate with callbacks via global variables. Now we're going to turn around and use a global variable anyway. But our "global" variable, $parser_dbh, won't be truly global. It will actually be a lexical variable whose scope includes the parser-callback functions. To use the parser, the caller will first set $parser_dbh, then invoke the top-level parser. To avoid requiring that the caller also be in the scope of $parser_dbh, we'll provide a setter function that has access to it:

```
my $parser_dbh;
sub set_parser_dbh { $parser_dbh = shift }
sub     parser_dbh { $parser_dbh }

$squery = alternate(...
            ... $parser_dbh->callbackquery($cb) ...
        );
```

The big drawback of *this* approach is that the parser can't change databases in the middle of a parse without saving $parser_dbh before and restoring it after. For our examples, this isn't important, but it means that we can't easily support queries on more than one database at a time.

With all that out of the way, here's the third production for *simple_query*:

```
T(concatenate(lookfor('FIELD'),
              lookfor('OP'),
```

```
                              lookfor('STRING')),
              sub {
                if ($_[1] eq '==') {
                  $parser_dbh->query($_[0], $_[2]);
                } else {
                  my ($field, $op, $val) = @_;
                  my $cmp_code = 'sub { $_[0] OP $_[1] }';
                  $cmp_code =~ s/OP/$string_version{$op}/;
                  my $cmp = eval($cmp_code) or die;
                  my $cb = sub { my %F = @_;
                                 $cmp->($F{$field}, $val)};
                  $parser_dbh->callbackquery($cb);
                }
              }),
            );
```

There are only two differences between this and the production for numeric comparison. First, there's a special case for when $op is ==. In this case, instead of using the slower and more general callbackquery() to perform the query, we use the simpler and faster query(), which is hardwired to do a string-equality test. Second, in the other cases, when we do use callbackquery(), instead of replacing OP with $op in the comparison function for the callback, we must replace OP with the string version of $op — if $op is <=, the string version is le, and so on. String versions are provided by a simple hash table:

```
my %string_version = ('>'=> 'gt', '>=', => 'ge', '==' => 'eq',
                      '<'=> 'lt', '<=', => 'le', '!=' => 'ne');
```

We need one last function to serve as an entry point from programs that want to use our parser:

```
package FlatDB::Parser;
use base FlatDB_Composable;

sub parse_query {
  my $self = shift;
  my $query = shift;
  my $lexer = main::lex_input($query);
  my $old_parser_dbh = main::parser_dbh();
  main::set_parser_dbh($self);
  my ($result) = $cquery->($lexer);
```

```
        main::set_parser_dbh($old_parser_dbh);
        return $result;
    }
```

Our parser for database queries is now complete.

8.8   BACKTRACKING PARSERS

The parser technique we've seen so far has a serious problem: It doesn't always work. Here's a contrived but very simple example:

```
S -> A B | B c c
A -> a a | a
B -> a b c | a b
```

Now consider the sentence a a b c. *S* will try the first alternative, *A B*. *A* will try its first alternative, a a, which will succeed. Then *B* will try both of its alternatives, each of which will fail, because they begin with a and the remaining input is b c. *B* will report failure, and so *A B* will fail. *S* will then try its second alternative, *B* c c, which will also fail, because the input doesn't end with c c.

But the grammar *does* generate the string a a b c, by the derivation:

```
    S
    A B           # S clause 1
    a B           # A clause 2
    a a b c       # B clause 1
```

Why didn't the parser find the answer? The problem is that after the first alternative for *A* succeeded, the rest of the parse failed. The parser should have tried the second alternative for *A*, since it would have led to success. But that's not how our alternate() function works. Once it commits to an alternative, it's too late for it to come back and try something else. The chosen alternative looked good in the short term. alternate() had no way to find out that its choice turned out bad in the long run, and that the parser called after it failed.

We've seen a number of useful parser examples already, and this problem didn't come up; often it doesn't. But what do we need to do if it does come up?

The alternate() parser can't assume success just because one or another of its alternatives succeeds. It would need to find out if the following parsing succeeded too. If so, then fine; if not, it would need to try another alternative.

8.8.1 Continuations

How can `alternate()` find out if the rest of the parse succeeded? It would need to invoke a parser for the entire rest of the input. We'll pass it one in its argument list.

We'll make each parser responsible for completing the entire parse. Parsers formerly handled a bit of input and then returned. Now they'll get an extra argument, called a *continuation*, for parsing the rest of the input after the bit that they've handled themselves. A parser will look for whatever it normally looks for, and if it is successful, it will invoke the continuation on the rest of the input, returning success if and only if the continuation succeeds.

In the preceding example, *B* is the continuation of *A*. *A* will try the first alternative, a a, which will succeed. *A* will then try its continuation, *B*, on the remaining input, b c; this will fail. So *A* will know that even though a a looked good, it ultimately fails, and is incorrect. *A* will then try the second alternative, a, which will also succeed, so *A* will try the continuation again, this time on the remaining input a b c. *B* will succeed this time, so *A* will report success, having selected the second alternative rather than the first.

With this structure, parsers no longer need to return the unused portion of the input. Instead, they'll pass the unused portion to the continuation. Formerly, parsers got one argument, which was the input stream, and returned two results, which were the calculated value and the remaining input stream. Parsers now get two arguments, which are the input stream and the continuation, and return one result, which is the calculated value.

Here's the rewrite of `alternate()` to handle continuation arguments:

```perl
sub alternate {
  my @p = @_;
  return parser { return () } if @p == 0;
  return $p[0]                if @p == 1;

  my $p;
  $p = parser {
    my ($input, $continuation) = @_;
    for (@p) {
      if (my ($v) = $_->($input, $continuation)) {
        return $v;
      }
    }
    return;  # Failure
  };
  $N{$p} = "(" . join(" | ", map $N{$_}, @p) . ")";
  return $p;
}
```

$p tries the alternatives (the elements of @p) in order. When one leads to a complete successful parse, the resulting value is returned. If an alternative fails, $p tries the next alternative.

Note that $p doesn't have to invoke the continuation itself. It just passes the continuation to the chosen alternative; the chosen alternative will take care of invoking the continuation if it succeeds.

Who actually invokes the continuation? Parsers generated by lookfor() invoke the continuation:

```perl
sub lookfor {
  my $wanted = shift;
  my $value = shift || sub { $_[0] };
  my $u = shift;
  $wanted = [$wanted] unless ref $wanted;
  my $parser = parser {
    my ($input, $continuation) = @_;
    return unless defined $input;

    my $next = head($input);
    for my $i (0 .. $#$wanted) {
      next unless defined $wanted->[$i];
      return unless $wanted->[$i] eq $next->[$i];
    }
    my $wanted_value = $value->($next, $u);

    # Try continuation
    if (my ($v) = $continuation->(tail($input))) {
      return $wanted_value;
    } else {
      return;
    }
  };

  $N{$parser} = "[@$wanted]";
  return $parser;
}
```

The process of checking the next token to see if it's what was expected is exactly the same, and, as before, if this fails, then the parser fails and returns false. But if it succeeds, the lookfor() parser doesn't immediately return success. Instead, it invokes the continuation to try to parse the rest of the input. It returns success only if the continuation succeeds as well.

The null parser is still simple. It does nothing, passing the buck to the continuation. If the continuation succeeds, nothing() is happy; if not, nothing() reports the failure to its caller:

```
sub nothing {
    my ($input, $continuation) = @_;
    return $continuation->($input);
}
```

CODE LIBRARY
nothing-continuation

The End_of_Input() parser doesn't change at all. It doesn't even get a continuation, because there's nothing left to do after End_of_Input() is finished. It just checks to make sure that the input is exhausted, succeeding if it is.

concatenate() is a little trickier. Suppose we have:

```
S -> Z blah de blah
Z -> A B
```

Here Z is the concatenation of A and B; the continuation of Z is a parser for blah de blah. What does Z do?

Clearly, the first thing it needs to do is to invoke the parser for A. But what is the continuation for A? It's B, followed by blah de blah. So the continuation for A is a parser that invokes B with blah de blah as *its* continuation. The code may make this clearer:

```
sub concatenate2 {
  my ($A, $B) = @_;
  my $p;
  $p = parser {
    my ($input, $continuation) = @_;
    my ($aval, $bval);
    my $BC = parser {
      my ($newinput) = @_;
      return unless ($bval) = $B->($newinput, $continuation);
    };
    $N{$BC} = "$N{$B} $N{$continuation}";
    if (($aval) = $A->($input, $BC)) {
      return ([$aval, $bval]);
    } else {
      return;
```

CODE LIBRARY
concatenate2-cont

```
          }
        };
        $N{$p} = "$N{$A} $N{$B}";
        return $p;
      }
```

The parser for *A B* gets a continuation, which is a parser for blah de blah. It builds a new parser, $BC, which invokes *B*, telling *B* that it is followed by blah de blah. It then invokes *A*, giving it the continuation $BC. If both *A* and *B* succeed, it packages the two values into an array and returns the array.

This concatenates only two parsers. To concatenate more than two, we call concatenate2() repeatedly:

```
sub concatenate {
    my (@p) = @_;
    return \&nothing if @p == 0;
    my $p0 = shift @p;

    return concatenate2($p0, concatenate(@p));
}
```

T() doesn't change significantly. The parser it builds expects a continuation argument, which it passes along:

```
sub T {
    my ($parser, $transform) = @_;
    my $p = sub {
        my ($input, $continuation) = @_;
        if (my $v = $parser->($input, $continuation)) {
            $v = $transform->(@$v);
            return $v;
        } else {
            return;
        }
    };
    $N{$p} = $N{$parser};
    return $p;
}
```

There's one final detail: Where does the first continuation come from? This is almost the simplest part of the whole operation. Say the top-level symbol is *S*.

Like all parsers, the parser S expects two arguments: the upcoming input, and the continuation parser. The upcoming input, of course, is the entire input. The continuation of S is simply the End_of_Input() parser.

With these changes, the parser from the beginning of the section succeeds:

```
...
$S = alternate(concatenate($A, $B),
               concatenate($B, lookfor('c'), lookfor('c')));

my $results = $S->($input, \&End_of_Input);
```

$results is assigned a value representing the correct parse, $S \rightarrow A\ B \rightarrow a\ B \rightarrow$ a a b c.

8.8.2 Parse Streams

We introduced continuations to solve the problems caused by alternate(), not really knowing whether an alternative has succeeded until the following parsers reached the end of the input. Another way to solve the problem is to change the parsers so that instead of returning a single result from the first parse they find, they return *all* the results from *all* possible parses. Since this would be a big waste of time in the event that the caller cared about only the first parse, we would want to do it in a lazy fashion, returning a stream of possible parses.

This solves the problem too, because in this model, alternate() returns a stream that is the lazy merge of the streams returned by its arguments; if any of these streams is empty, it is ignored. concatenate() is responsible for combining two streams of parses into a stream of concatenations; if either input is empty, so is the output. If the first argument to alternate() succeeds but some later-concatenated part of the parsing process fails, that later part will return an empty stream, the concatenation with the successful alternative will be empty, and alternate() will effectively skip that alternative.

Before we see the changes to the parser constructors themselves, here are some utility functions we'll need. single() manufactures a stream of length 1, with specified head and empty tail:

```
sub single {
  my $v = shift;
  node($v, undef);
}
```

We saw union() before; it gets a list of streams, and produces a single stream formed by appending the arguments end-to-end. sunion() is similar, except that its argument is a stream of streams rather than a list of streams:

```
sub sunion {
  my ($s) = @_;
  my $cur_stream;
  while ($s && ! $cur_stream) {
    $cur_stream = head($s);
    $s = tail ($s);
  }
  return undef unless $cur_stream;

  return node(head($cur_stream),
            promise { sunion(node(tail($cur_stream), $s)) }
            );
}
```

Note that this is unsuitable if parsers might produce an infinite stream of possible parses; if so, we'd need to use a different version of sunion() that mingled the argument streams instead of appending them end-to-end.

lookfor() is the same as before, except that it returns an empty stream on failure and a singleton stream on success:

```
sub lookfor {
  ...
  my $parser = parser {
    ...
    for my $i (0 .. $#$wanted) {
      next unless defined $wanted->[$i];
      unless ($wanted->[$i] eq $next->[$i]) {
        return undef;
      }
    }
    my $wanted_value = $value->($next, $u);
    return single([$wanted_value, tail($input)]);
  };

  $N{$parser} = "[@$wanted]";
  return $parser;
}
```

Similarly, `End_of_input()` and `nothing()` return singleton streams when they succeed:

```
sub End_of_Input {
  my $input = shift;
  defined($input) ? () : single(["EOI", undef]);
}

sub nothing {
  my $input = shift;
  return single([undef, $input]);
}
```

`alternate()` becomes much simpler; it's merely a call to `union()` to join together the streams returned by its argument parsers:

```
sub alternate {
  my @p = @_;
  return parser { return undef } if @p == 0;
  return $p[0]                   if @p == 1;

  my $p;
  $p = parser {
    my $input = shift;
    union(map $_->($input), @p);
  };
  $N{$p} = "(" . join(" | ", map $N{$_}, @p) . ")";
  return $p;
}
```

`concatenate()`, however, is trickier. To concatenate parsers S and T, we must first call S on the main input, returning a stream of [$svalue, $input1] pairs. We then call T on each of the $input1 values, producing a stream of [$tvalue, $input2] pairs. The parser produced by `concatenate()` then produces a stream of [[$svalue, $tvalue], $input2] pairs for each $tvalue and its corresponding $svalue:

```
sub concatenate2 {
  my ($S, $T) = @_;
  my $p;
```

```
$p = parser {
  my $input = shift;
  my $sparses = $S->($input);
  sunion(transform {
    my ($sv, $input1) = @{$_[0]};
    my $tparses = $T->($input1);
    transform {
      my ($tv, $input2) = @{$_[0]};
      [[$sv, $tv], $input2];
    } $tparses;
  } $sparses);
};
$N{$p} = "@N{$S, $T}";
return $p;
}
```

This concatenates only two parsers; to concatenate more than two, we repeat the process as necessary:

```
sub concatenate {
  my @p = @_;
  return \&null if @p == 0;
  my $p = shift @p;
  return $p      if @p == 0;

  my $result = concatenate2($p, concatenate(@p));
  $N{$result} = "@N{$p, @p}";
  return $result;
}
```

Finally, T needs to be changed to apply its transformation function to each of the values returned by its argument parser:

```
sub T {
  my ($parser, $transform) = @_;
  my $p = parser {
    my $input = shift;
    transform {
      my ($v, $input1) = @{$_[0]};
      [$transform->($v), $input1];
```

```
    } $parser->($input);
  };
  $N{$p} = $N{$parser};
  return $p;
}
```

8.9   OVERLOADING

The recursive-descent parsing system works well, and it's easy to compose small parsers into bigger ones and to capture common patterns in larger parser-generating functions, such as operator() of Section 8.4.4. But the notation looks awful. We can clean this up a little bit by using Perl's operator-overloading feature, introduced in Chapter 7.

The most frequently-used parser operators have been concatenate(), alternate(), and T(). We'll overload three operators to invoke these functions, so that what we once wrote as:

```
$factor      = alternate(lookfor('INT'),
                     T(
                       concatenate(lookfor(['OP', '(']),
                                 $Expression,
                                 lookfor(['OP', ')'])),
                      sub { $_[1] })
                    );
```

will become:

```
$factor = lookfor('INT')
        | lookfor(['OP', '(']) - $Expression - lookfor(['OP', ')'])
              >> sub { $_[1] }
        ;
```

which looks almost exactly like the grammar rules it represents. The - is used for concatenation, the | is of course used for alternation, and the >> replaces T(), because it visually suggests that the value from the parser on the left is being passed into the function on the right. The precedences of these three operators just happen to have the order we need: - has higher precedence than both | and >>, so a | b - c >> d means a | ((b - c) >> d), which is almost always what we want.

The remaining syntactic clutter is mostly the calls to lookfor(). If we want to trim this as well, it's easy: just give lookfor() a shorter name:[4]

```
sub _ { @_ = [@_]; goto &lookfor }

$factor = _("INT")
        | _('OP', '(') - $Expression - _('OP', ')')
                >> sub { $_[1] }
        ;
```

To pull this off, we must engage the Perl overloading features by turning parsers into objects blessed into a class that defines the operators. We'll change the formerly trivial parser() function to do that:

```
package Parser;

sub parser (&) { bless $_[0] => __PACKAGE__ }
```

We have the Parser class overload the relevant operators:

```
use overload '-'  => \&concatenate2,
             '|'  => \&alternate2,
             '>>' => \&T,
             '""' => \&overload::StrVal,
             ;
```

I've used concatenate2() and alternate2() here just in case I someday want to have a place to hang some extra semantics on the overloaded operators. In the meantime, these binary functions just call their more general counterparts:

```
sub concatenate2 {
  my ($A, $B) = @_;
  concatenate($A, $B);
}

sub alternate2 {
  my ($A, $B) = @_;
  alternate($A, $B);
}
```

---

4 It would be nice to get rid of the parentheses as well, but we can't, because _ $x - $y means _($x - $y), rather than _($x) - $y as we'd like.

The function associated with the "" (*stringification*) pseudo-operator is invoked by Perl when a `Parser` object needs to be converted to a string. This occurs in debugging messages and also whenever we use a parser as a key to the debugging names in the `%N` hash. The function `\&overload::StrVal` restores the default behavior of converting the `Parser` objects to strings of the form `Parser=CODE(0x83bb36c)`. An alternative would be to associate the stringification operator with a function that looks up the parser's name in the `%N` hash:

```
use overload '""'=> \&parser_name;

sub parser_name {
   my $parser = shift;
   my $key = overload::StrVal($parser);
   exists($N{$key}) ? $N{$key} : $key;
}
```

If we did this, we would never need to refer explicitly to `%N` in debugging messages; just printing out a parser as if it were a string would print the name assigned to it from the `%N` hash.

There are a few technical problems associated with the change. The assignment:

```
$parser = $A - $B - $C
```

is not exactly equivalent to:

```
$parser = concatenate($A, $B, $C) ;
```

but rather to:

```
$parser = concatenate(concatenate($A, $B), $C) ;
```

If the values returned by `$A`, `$B`, and `$C` are a, b, and c, the first parser would have returned `[a, b, c]`, but the overloaded version will return `[[a, b], c]`. It might seem that we could fix this by having `concatenate()` flatten its first argument. But a little thought shows that this won't work, because `$A - $B` would try to flatten a, which would be an error. And `concatenate()` can't have a policy of flattening its first argument whenever the first argument is an array reference, because `$A` might actually return a legitimate array reference value.

Probably the best way to handle this is to leave `concatenate()` mostly alone and let it return values like `[[[a, b], c], d]`. Almost all compound values returned by concatenate() are passed through T() anyway, so we'll let T() take care of undoing the nesting of the values. But we need some way to signal to T() the difference between a value returned by $A - $B - $C, where [[a, b], c] needs to be flattened to [a, b, c], and the same value returned by $A - $C, where $A happened to return an array reference [a, b], which doesn't need to be flattened. A solution is to tag the pairs returned by concatenate so that T() can recognize them. Instead of:

```
for (@p) {
  ($v, $input) = $_->($input);
  push @values, $v;
}
return (\@values, $input);
```

we have:

```
for (@p) {
  ($v, $input) = $_->($input);
  push @values, $v;
}
return (bless(\@values => 'Pair'), $input);
```

We must also add code to T() to recognize and flatten lists of these special Pair objects:

```
my ($value, $newinput) = $parser->($input);
# Flatten nested lists returned by concatenate()
my @values;
while (ref($value) eq 'Pair') {
  unshift @values, $value->[1];
  $value = $value->[0];
}
unshift @values, $value;
$value = $transform->(@values);
return ($value, $newinput);
```

Only a few other changes need to be made. Expressions like:

```
T(\&nothing, sub { 1 })
```

don't translate as they should. The corresponding expression,

```
\&nothing >> sub { 1 }
```

doesn't work, because \&nothing is not an overloaded Parser object. (It hasn't been blessed.) The solution is simple; instead of using \&nothing directly, provide a blessed version:

```
bless($nothing = \&nothing, "Parser");
$N{$nothing} = "(nothing)";
```

and then use $nothing instead of \&nothing:

```
$nothing >> sub { 1 }
```

With the new syntax, the parser for the final calculator example of Section 8.4.6 becomes:

```
$program = star($Statement) - $Parser::End_of_Input;


$statement = _("PRINT") - $Expression - _("TERMINATOR")
                >> sub { print ">> $_[1]\n" }
          | _("IDENTIFIER") - _('OP', '=')
                          - $Expression - _("TERMINATOR")
             >> sub { $VAR{$_[0]} = $_[2] };



$expression = $Term - star(_('OP', '+') - $Term
                          >> sub { my $term = $_[1];
                                   sub { $_[0] + $term } }

                      |
                      _('OP', '-') - $Term
                          >> sub { my $term = $_[1];
                                   sub { $_[0] - $term } }

                     )
    >> sub { my ($first, $rest) = @_;
             for my $f (@$rest) {
                $first = $f->($first);
             }

             $first;
           };


$term = $Factor - star(_('OP', '*') - $Factor
```

```
                                              >> sub { my $factor = $_[1];
                                                       sub { $_[0] * $factor } }
                                    |
                                  _('OP', '/') - $Factor
                                          >> sub { my $factor = $_[1];
                                                   sub { $_[0] / $factor } }
                              )
                >> sub { my ($first, $rest) = @_;
                         for my $f (@$rest) {
                           $first = $f->($first);
                         }
                         $first;
                       };


      $factor = $Base - (
                          _('OP', '**') - $Factor >> sub { $_[1] }
                          |
                          $Parser::null >> sub { 1 }
                        )
          >> sub { $_[0] ** $_[1] };
      $base = _("INT")
            | lookfor('IDENTIFIER', sub { $VAR{$_[0][1]} })
            | _('OP', '(') - $Expression - _('OP', ')')
                    >> sub { $_[1] }
          ;
```

The overloaded version is substantially less bulky and much easier to read.

DECLARATIVE
PROGRAMMING

Beginning programmers often wish for a way to simply tell the computer what they want, and have the computer figure out how to do it. Declarative programming is an attempt to do that. The idea is that the programmer will put in the specifications for the value to be computed, and the computer will use the appropriate algorithm.

Nobody knows how to do this in general, and it may turn out to be impossible. But there are some interesting results we can get in specific problem domains. Regular expressions are a highly successful example of declarative programming. You write a pattern that represents the form of the text you are looking for, and then sit back and let the regex engine figure out the best way of locating the matching text.

Searching in general lends itself to declarative methods: the programmer specifies what they are searching for, and then lets a generic heuristic searching algorithm look for it. Database query languages are highly visible examples of this; consider SQL, or the query language of Chapter 8. The programming language Prolog is an extension of this idea to allow general computations.

We've seen searching in some detail already, so in this chapter we'll look at some other techniques and applications of declarative programming.

9.1   CONSTRAINT SYSTEMS

Suppose you wrote a program to translate Fahrenheit temperatures into Celsius:

```
sub f2c {
  my $f = shift;
  return ($f - 32) * 5/9;
}
```

Now you'd like to have a program to perform the opposite conversion, from Celsius to Fahrenheit. Although this calculation is in some sense the same, you'd have to write completely new code, from scratch:

```
sub c2f {
  my $c = shift;
  return 9/5 * $c + 32;
}
```

The idea of constraint systems is to permit the computer to be able to run this sort of calculation in either direction.

9.2   LOCAL PROPAGATION NETWORKS

One approach that seems promising is to distribute the logic for the calculation among several objects in a *constraint network* as shown in Figure 9.1.

There is a node in the network for each constant, variable, and operator. Lines between the nodes communicate numeric values between nodes, and they are called *wires*. A node can set the value on one of its wires; this sends a notification to the node at the other end of the wire that the value has changed. Because values are propagated only from nodes to their adjacent wires to the nodes attached at the other end of the wire, the network is called a *local propagation network*.

A constant node has one incident wire, and when the network is started up, the constant node immediately tries to set its wire to the appropriate constant

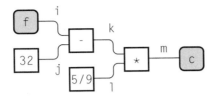

FIGURE 9.1 A constraint network for turning Fahrenheit temperatures to Celsius and back.

value. In the network shown in Figure 9.1, wire j initially has the value 32, and wire l initially has the value 5/9.

The nodes marked with variable names, c and f in this example, are input-output nodes. Initially, they do nothing, but the user of the program has the option to tell them to set their incident wires to certain values; that is how the user sends input into the network. If an input-output node notices that its incident wire has changed value, it announces that fact to the user; that's how output is emitted from the network.

We'll use the network of Figure 9.1 to calculate the Celsius equivalent for 212 Fahrenheit. We start by informing the f node that we want f to have the value 212. The f node obliges by setting the value of wire i to 212.

The change on wire i wakes up the attached - node, which notices that both of its input wires now have values: Wire i has the value 212 and wire j has the value 32. The - node performs subtraction; it subtracts 32 from 212 and sets its output wire k to the difference, 180.

The change on wire k wakes up the attached * node, which notices that both of *its* input wires now have values: Wire k has the value 180 and wire l has the value 5/9. The * node performs multiplication; it multiplies 180 by 5/9 and sets its output wire m to the product, 100.

The change on wire m wakes up the attached input-output node c, which notices that its input wire now has the value 100. It announces this fact to the user, saying something like:

    c = 100

which is in fact the Celsius equivalent of 212 Fahrenheit.

What makes this interesting is that the components are so simple and so easily reversible. There's nothing about this process that requires that the calculation proceed from left to right. Let's suppose that instead of calculating the Celsius equivalent of 212 Fahrenheit, we wanted the Fahrenheit equivalent of 37 Celsius. We begin by informing the c input-output node that we want the

value of *c* to be 37. The c node will set wire *m* to value 37. This will wake up the
* node, which will notice that two of its three incoming wires have values: *l* has
value 5/9 and *m* has value 37. It will then conclude that wire *k* must have the
value 37/(5/9) = 66.6, and set wire *k* accordingly.

The change in the value of wire *k* will wake up the attached - node, which
will notice that the subtrahend *j* is 32 and the difference *k* is 66.6, and conclude
that the minuend, *i*, must have the value 98.6. It will then set *i* to 98.6. This
will wake up the attached f node, which will announce something like:

```
f = 98.6
```

which is indeed the Fahrenheit equivalent of 37 Celsius.

It's no trouble to attach more input-output nodes to the network to have it
calculate several things at once. For example, we might extend the network as
shown in Figure 9.2.

Now setting c to 37 causes values to propagate in two directions. The 37 will
propagate left along wire *m* as before, eventually causing node f to announce the
value 98.6. But wire *m* now has three ends, and the 37 will also propagate right-
ward, causing the - node to set wire *p* to 310.15, which is the value announced
by the k node. The output looks something like:

```
f = 98.6
k = 310.15
```

which are the Fahrenheit and kelvin equivalents of 37 Celsius. Alternatively,
we could have set node k to 0, which would have resulted in wire *m* being set
to −273.15. Node c would announce that fact, and the * node would also

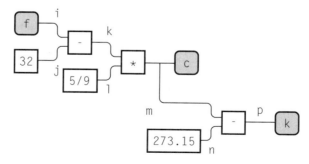

FIGURE 9.2   A constraint network for interconverting Fahrenheit, Celsius, and
absolute temperatures.

take note; eventually wire i would be set to -459.67, and the output from the entire network would be:

```
c = -273.15
f = -459.67
```

which are the Celsius and Fahrenheit temperatures of absolute zero.

9.2.1   Implementing a Local Propagation Network

Clearly we will have two kinds of objects: wires and nodes. Wires store values. When a wire's value is set by a node, the wire remembers the value and also which node was responsible for setting it. This is so that the node can change or retract the value later. If the wire didn't remember the original source of its information, it wouldn't be able to distinguish the situation where the source changed its mind from the situation in which it was being given conflicting information. We'd like it to diagnose the latter but not the former:

```
package Wire;

my $N = 0;
sub new {
  my ($class, $name) = @_;
  $name ||= "wire" . ++$N;
  bless { N => $name, S => undef, V => undef, A => [] } => $class;
}
```

The $name here is used for debugging purposes; we can supply a name to the constructor, or else the constructor will auto-generate one. V will be the stored value, initially undefined. S will be the identity of the node that supplied the stored value ("settor"), also initially undefined. A is a list of attached nodes. When the wire's value changes, it will notify the attached nodes.

It's common to need to manufacture several wires at once, so here's a utility function that does that:

```
sub make {
  my $class = shift;
  my $N = shift;
  my @wires;
```

```
        push @wires, $class->new while $N--;
        @wires;
    }
```

`Wire->make(5)` returns a list of five new wires.

The principal `Wire` method is set, which assigns a value to a wire:

```
sub set {
    my ($self, $settor, $value) = @_;
    if (! $self->has_settor || $self->settor_is($settor)) {
        $self->{V} = $value;
        $self->{S} = $settor;
        $self->notify_all_but($settor, $value);
    } elsif ($self->has_settor) {
        unless ($value == $self->value) {
            my $v = $self->value;
            my $N = $self->name;
            warn "Wire $N inconsistent value ($value != $v)\n";
        }
    }
}
```

The normal case is if the wire had no value before (`! $self->has_settor`) or if the old settor is changing the value, in which case the wire remembers the new value and the settor, and then calls `notify_all_but()` to notify the other attached nodes that the value has changed.

The other case of interest occurs when some other node, not the original settor, tries to notify the wire of a new value. In this case, if the old and new values are the same, all is well, and nothing need be done. But if the values differ, the wire should issue a diagnostic message. This might occur, for example, if we set the Fahrenheit input of a network to 212, and then tried to set the Celsius input to something other than 100.

The `notify_all_but()` function takes care of notifying the attached nodes of a change in value:

```
sub notify_all_but {
    my ($self, $exception, $value) = @_;
    for my $node ($self->attachments) {
        next if $node == $exception;
        $node->notify;
    }
}
```

When a wire is set to a certain value, it notifies all its attached nodes of the change *except* the one that set the value in the first place; this avoids infinite loops.

The accessors for attachments are trivial:

```
sub attach {
  my ($self, @nodes) = @_;
  push @{$self->{A}}, @nodes;
}


sub attachments { @{$_[0]->{A}} }
```

The other `Wire` accessor methods are similarly trivial:

```
sub name {
  $_[0]{N} || "$_[0]";
}


sub settor { $_[0]{S} }
sub has_settor { defined $_[0]{S} }
sub settor_is { $_[0]{S} == $_[1] }
```

The only unusual method here is `settor_is()`. `$wire->settor_is($node)` asks if the wire's settor is `$node`, and returns true if so. Note that objects can be compared for identity with the `==` operator; this actually compares the underlying machine addresses at which the objects are stored.

The opposite of `set()` is `revoke()`, which allows the settor node to revoke a previously set value:

```
sub revoke {
  my ($self, $revoker) = @_;
  return unless $self->has_value;
  return unless $self->settor_is($revoker);
  undef $self->{V};
  $self->notify_all_but($revoker, undef);
  undef $self->{S};
}


1;
```

As far as the attached nodes are concerned, a revocation of a value is the same as setting the value to `undef`.

The final methods in the Wire class are the ones that query a wire for its current value. The code is short, but a little tricky. They're *almost* straightforward accessors, simply returning the value of $self->{V} or its definedness:

```
sub value { my ($self, $querent) = @_;
            return if $self->settor_is($querent);
            $self->{V};
        }
sub has_value { my ($self, $querent) = @_;
            return if $self->settor_is($querent);
            defined $_[0]{V};
          }
```

The exception is if the wire's settor is asking about the value. In this case, the wire returns undef, indicating that it doesn't know. This is necessary to support revocation of values. To see the reason for this, consider an adder node with addend wires *A* and *B*, and sum wire *C*. Suppose *A* and *B* have been set to 1 and 2 by some other components; the adder node itself then sets the sum *C* to 3. Now suppose the value of *B* is revoked. The adder node receives a notification and inspects the values of the wires. If not for the special case in value(), it would learn that *A* had value 1 and *C* had value 3, and conclude that *B* must have value 2, a conclusion that is no longer warranted. To avoid this, wire *C* will report a value of 3 to any *other* node that asks, but if the adder itself asks, the wire will say undef, meaning "If you're not sure what my value is supposed to be, then I'm not sure either."

We'll use an abstract class to represent nodes. We could subclass this to make the various node types, but since most of the node behavior is the same in all node types, we won't bother; the variable part of the behavior can be specified by supplying an anonymous function that will be stored in the node object.

Here's the generic constructor:

CODE LIBRARY
Node.pm

```
package Node;
my %NAMES;
sub new {
  my ($class, $base_name, $behavior, $wiring) = @_;
  my $self = {N => $base_name . ++$NAMES{$base_name},
              B => $behavior,
              W => $wiring,
             };
  for my $wire (values %$wiring) {
    $wire->attach($self);
  }
```

```
    bless $self => $class;
  }
```

The constructor's first argument is a node type name, such as adder, which is used to construct a name for debugging. The important arguments are the other two. $behavior is a function that is invoked when one of the attached wires changes values; it is the responsibility of $behavior to calculate new values and to propagate them through the network. $wiring is a hash whose values are the wires themselves; each wire is associated with a name, through which $behavior will access it.

The primary method is notify(). When a node is notified that a wire has changed, it builds a hash of its current wire values, and passes the hash to its behavior function:

```
sub notify {
  my $self = shift;
  my %vals;
  while (my ($name, $wire) = each %{$self->{W}}) {
    $vals{$name} = $wire->value($self);
  }
  $self->{B}->($self, %vals);
}
```

The rest of the Node methods are simple utilities, intended to be used by the behavior function:

```
sub name {
  my $self = shift;
  $self->{N} || "$self";
}
```

wire() takes a name and returns the associated wire object:

```
sub wire { $_[0]{W}{$_[1]} }

sub set_wire {
  my ($self, $wire_name, $value) = @_;
  my $wire = $self->wire($wire_name);
  $wire->set($self, $value);
}

sub revoke_wire {
  my ($self, $wire_name) = @_;
```

```
        my $wire = $self->wire($wire_name);
        $wire->revoke($self);
    }
```

We're finally at the meat of the program; we're ready to see the components themselves. Here's the behavior function for an adder:

```
{
  my $adder = sub {
    my ($self, %v) = @_;
    if (defined $v{A1} && defined $v{A2}) {
      $self->set_wire('S', $v{A1} + $v{A2});
    } else {
      $self->revoke_wire('S');
    }
    if (defined $v{A1} && defined $v{S}) {
      $self->set_wire('A2', $v{S} - $v{A1});
    } else {
      $self->revoke_wire('A2');
    }
    if (defined $v{A2} && defined $v{S}) {
      $self->set_wire('A1', $v{S} - $v{A2});
    } else {
      $self->revoke_wire('A1');
    }
  };

# continues...
```

An adder has three wires: two addends, named A1 and A2, and a sum, named S. When it receives a notification, it checks to see if A1 and A2 both have values; if so, it sets S to be the sum. If not, it revokes any value that it might have given to S; note that if S has no value, or if some other component was responsible for setting S, the revocation is harmless, because of the way we defined the Wire::revoke() method. There are two analogous blocks of code for inferring the two addends from the sum.

The function to build an adder node gets three wires as arguments and invokes Node::new() to build a node with those three wires and the adder behavior function:

```
# continued...

sub new_adder {
  my ($a1, $a2, $s) = @_;
```

```
Node->new('adder',
          $adder,
          { A1 => $a1, A2 => $a2, S => $s });
  }
}
```

The behavior function for a multiplier node is a little more complicated. Not only does it need to infer a product from the two factors, and vice versa, but when a factor is 0, it can infer the product even without the other factor:

```
{
  my $multiplier = sub {
    my ($self, %v) = @_;
    if (defined $v{F1} && defined $v{F2}) {
      $self->set_wire('P', $v{F1} * $v{F2});
    } elsif (defined $v{F1} && $v{F1} == 0) {
      $self->set_wire('P', 0);
    } elsif (defined $v{F2} && $v{F2} == 0) {
      $self->set_wire('P', 0);
    } else {
      $self->revoke_wire('P');
    }

# continues...
```

The price of this free inference, however, is that the wires can be in an inconsistent state, which corresponds to a division by zero. If one factor is zero while the product is nonzero, the node won't be able to reason backwards, and will become upset:

```
# continued...

    if (defined $v{F1} && defined $v{P}) {
      if ($v{F1} != 0) {
        $self->set_wire('F2', $v{P} / $v{F1});
      } elsif ($v{P} != 0) {
        warn "Division by zero\n";
      }
    } else {
      $self->revoke_wire('F2');
    }
```

```
         if (defined $v{F2} && defined $v{P}) {
           if ($v{F2} != 0) {
             $self->set_wire('F1', $v{P} / $v{F2});
           } elsif ($v{P} != 0) {
             warn "Division by zero\n";
           }
         } else {
           $self->revoke_wire('F1');
         }

     };

     # continues...
```

The function for building a multiplier node, `new_multiplier()`, is similar to `new_adder()`:

```
     # continued...

     sub new_multiplier {
       my ($f1, $f2, $p) = @_;
       Node->new('multiplier', $multiplier,
               { F1 => $f1, F2 => $f2, P => $p });
     }
   }
```

We could go on and build a subtraction node, but there's no need.

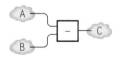

This network fragment expresses the constraint $A - B = C$. But that's the same as $C + B = A$, so the network shown below expresses the same thing.

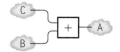

With the transformation shown above, our Fahrenheit-to-Celsius network becomes the network shown here.

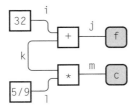

But for convenience, we could define:

```
# S - M = D
sub new_subtractor {
  my ($s, $m, $d) = @_;
  new_adder($d, $m, $s);
}


# V / S = Q
sub new_divider {
  my ($v, $s, $q) = @_;
  new_multiplier($q, $s, $v);
}
```

if we wanted.

Now all we need are constant nodes and input-output (IO) nodes. Constants, as you would expect, are very simple:

```
sub new_constant {
  my ($val, $w) = @_;
  my $node = Node->new('constant',
                       sub {},
                       {'W' => $w},
                      );
  $w->set($node, $val);
  $node;
}
```

The two arguments here are $val, the constant value, and $w, the outgoing wire. The behavior function is trivial and does nothing. The only fine point is that the constructor needs to notify the attached wire of the outgoing constant value immediately after constructing the node, before anything else happens in the network.

Most of the code for IO nodes is for announcing changes in values on the one attached wire. $announce is a curried function. Its argument is the name of the IO node, and it returns a behavior function for that node:

```
{
  my $announce = sub {
    my $name = shift;
    sub {
      my ($self, %val) = @_;
      my $v = $val{W};
      if (defined $v) {
        print "$name : $v\n";
      } else {
        print "$name : no longer defined\n";
      }
    };
  };

  # continues...
```

The IO node itself is an ordinary node with this announcing behavior:

```
  # continued...

  sub new_io {
    my ($name, $w) = @_;
    Node->new('io',
                $announce->($name),
                { W => $w });
  }
}
```

There are two utility functions exposed to the main program for setting and revoking the values of IO nodes:

```
sub input {
  my ($self, $value) = @_;
  $self->wire('W')->set($self, $value);
}
```

```
sub revoke {
  my $self = shift;
  $self->wire('W')->revoke($self);
}
```

We can now build local propagation networks:

```
my ($F, $C);
{ my ($i, $j, $k, $1, $m) = Wire->make(5);
  $F = new_io('Fahrenheit', $i);
  $C = new_io('Celsius', $m);
  new_constant(32, $j);
  new_constant(5/9, $1);
  new_adder($i,$k,$j);
  new_multiplier($k,$1,$m);
}
```

And now we can use the network to calculate values:

```
input($F, 212);
        Celsius : 100
input($F, 32);
        Celsius : 0
revoke($F);
        Celsius : no longer defined
input($C, 37);
        Fahrenheit : 98.6
input($F, 100);
        Wire wire3 inconsistent value (100 != 98.6)
revoke($C);
        Fahrenheit : no longer defined
input($F, 100);
        Celsius : 37.7777777777778
```

We can extend the network to handle kelvins by adding:

```
my ($F, $C);
my $K;
{ my ($i, $j, $k, $1, $m) = Wire->make(5);
  $F = new_io('Fahrenheit', $i);
  $C = new_io('Celsius', $m]);
```

```
    new_constant(32, $j);
    new_constant(5/9, $l);
    new_adder($i,$k,$j);
    new_multiplier($k,$l,$m);
    my ($n, $p) = Wire->make(2);
    $K = new_io('kelvin', $n);
    new_constant(273.15, $p);
    new_adder($m, $p, $n);
}
```

The final adder node expresses the constraint that $C + 273.15 = K$. Note that the wire $m has been attached to three nodes, as shown here.

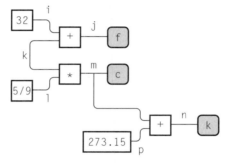

These definitions of local propagation networks are quite verbose, but it's easy to imagine attaching a front-end that would allow the programmer to enter the desired constraints in ordinary algebraic notation:

```
C = (F+32)*5/9 ;
K = C + 273.15 ;
```

The front-end would have a parser for expressions like the ones we've already seen. The output from the parser would be a constraint network corresponding to the input expressions. Central to the parser would be productions like these, that would build up the appropriate constraint network as the input expression was analyzed:

```
$expression = operator($Term,
                       [lookfor(['OP', '+']),
```

```
sub { my $sum = Wire->new;
      new_adder($_[0], $_[1], $sum);
      return $sum;
    }
[lookfor(['OP', '-']),
  sub { my $difference = Wire->new;
        new_adder($difference, $_[1], $_[0]);
        return $difference;
      }
);
```

9.2.2 Problems with Local Propagation

If you've ever seen a discussion of local propagation networks before, you've probably seen the Fahrenheit-Celsius converter example. There's a good reason for this: It's one of the few examples for which local propagation actually works.

Let's consider a different problem, almost as simple. Suppose we're building a drawing system. A horizontal line has two endpoints at (x_1, y) and (x_2, y). Its center point is at (c, y), and its length is l. y is independent of the other parameters, but any two of x_1, x_2, c, and l determine the other two. We might reason that the center point is the one that is the same distance from each endpoint, and define the center point with the equation:

$$c - x_1 = x_2 - c$$

The length, of course, is the distance between the endpoints:

$$x_2 - x_1 = l$$

These two constraints yield the network shown here.

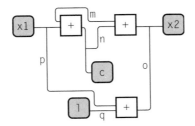

If we set x_1 to 3 and c to 5, everything works out. The 5 is propagated along wire n to the leftmost + node, which sets wire m to 2. This value, plus the 5 reaching the upper-right + node along wire n, causes wire o to be set to 7, which is reported as the value of x_2. Wire o, carrying 7, and wire p, carrying x_1's value of 3, arrive at the lower + node, allowing the network to deduce that the value of l is 4.

But suppose instead we set x_1 to 3 and x_2 to 7. The two values arrive at the lower + node, allowing the calculation of l as before. But there's a problem in the upper part of the diagram. Each of the two upper + nodes has only one defined input. Neither m nor n is defined, and each is needed for the deduction of the other one. Since wire n defines the value of c, the network has failed. Similarly, although the network above can compute x_2 from x_1 and l, it fails to compute c.

This kind of problem often arises when local constraint networks contain loops. In general, we can't avoid constraints that result in loops, so we need another technique.

One technique that's commonly used in such cases is called *relaxation*. We tell the network to *guess* a value for c, and to compute the consequences of the guess. In general, this will result in an inconsistent network. In the preceding example, we might guess that c is 0. This means that n is 0, and then the two upper addition nodes can compute values for wire m. The leftmost one computes that m is -3, and the rightmost one that m is -7. These are inconsistent, so the network averages them, getting -4, and tries that out as a value for m. If m is -4, then the two addition nodes want to set wire n to -1 and to 11, respectively. So the network once again tries the average, 5, for n. This time, the two addition nodes agree that m should be 2 — so the relaxation is complete, and has solved the constraint equations.

As with nearly all numerical techniques, relaxation is fraught with peril. Sometimes the relaxation process will diverge: Instead of reaching the correct value, the successive steps produce more and more grossly incorrect values. Sometimes the relaxation process converges slowly to the correct values, getting closer and closer but never quite making it.

Getting local propagation networks to work well is an active research area. I introduced the technique because it's an interesting exercise and a good introduction to the idea of constraint systems. But for the rest of the chapter, we're going to go a different way.

9.3 LINEAR EQUATIONS

As a large example, we'll develop a system, called `linogram`, for drawing diagrams.

Diagrams are usually drawn with a WYSIWYG structured drawing system. The big drawback of this kind of system is that if you want to change the diagram globally, you essentially have to start over. For example, suppose you were drawing a family tree, and you decided to represent each person with a rectangle 0.75 inches wide by 0.5 inches tall. You get the diagram done, but then you learn that the diagram will need to be printed in landscape mode, rather than portrait mode. You want to make the boxes shorter, to fit on the shorter page, but wider, to fit the text in — say 1 inch wide and only 0.4 inches tall. Also, you want to see how the diagram looks if the corners of the boxes are rounded off.

In the typical structured drawing system, you'd have to manually adjust each box and the text inside it. In a declarative drawing system, however, this kind of change is easy. A diagram is like a program, and there is a definition in the program that describes the kind of box you want to use for a person. By changing the definition, you change every box of that type in the entire diagram.

In the declarative drawing system, you can tell the computer to calculate the positions and sizes of drawing elements based on the positions and sizes of other elements. So, for example, you can easily tell the system that you want all the squares to be made into rectangles, or all the straight arrows made into curved arrows, or all the parts of the diagram that represent widgets to be drawn with three round knobs instead of two square knobs, just by changing a small part of the description of the diagram.

Since the input to the declarative system is a plain text file, it's also easy to get another program to generate diagrams as output.

If we're going to describe objects by giving constraints, we need some way of solving the constraints to figure out where the objects actually are. As we saw, local propagation won't do it. In general, the problem is very difficult, because constraints are equations, so solving constraints means solving equations. If solving equations were easy, we wouldn't have to suffer through four years of high school algebra learning how to do it, and we wouldn't need mathematicians to figure it out.

For general geometric problems, we have to solve general sorts of equations; these may involve higher algebra, or even trigonometry. There is one kind of equation, however, that's easy to solve. Linear equations are easy. The solution of:

$$ax + b = c$$

is:

$$x = \frac{c - b}{a}$$

Because diagrams usually involve many straight lines, linear equations usually do most of what we want. The kind of curves that appear in diagrams are unusually simple and highly constrained. It may require advanced mathematics to find the intersection of a lemniscate and a cardioid, but how often do you draw a diagram with a lemniscate and a cardioid? Diagrams do involve circles (which potentially opens up a can of trigonometric worms), but typically the circle is used as just another kind of box. If we allow drawing elements to be attached to circles only at the "corners" (the northmost, northwestmost, etc. points) then the circle is essentially an octagon as far as the equations are concerned; then once we figure out where the corners are located, we can join them with curves instead of straight sides.

9.4   linogram: A DRAWING SYSTEM

The entities with which our program deals are called *features*. A feature represents something like a box or a line. It might contain sub-features; for example, a box feature contains four sub-features that represent its four sides. A feature also contains a list of constraint equations that define the relationships between its sub-features; for example, in a box feature, the top and left sides are constrained to start at the same point.

The input to the drawing system will be a specification for a large compound feature, called the *root feature*, which represents the entire drawing. Here's an example specification for a root feature:

```
box F, plus, con32, times, C, con59;
line i, j, k, l, m;
number hspc, vspc, boxht, boxwd;

constraints {
  boxht = 1; boxwd = 1;
  hspc = 1 + boxwd; vspc = 1 + boxht;

  F.ht = boxht; F.wd = boxwd;

  plus = F + (hspc, 0);
  con32 = plus + (hspc, 0);
  times = plus + (0, vspc);
  C = times + (hspc, 0);

  con59 + (hspc, 0) = times;
```

```
    i.start = F.e;       i.end = plus.nw;
    j.start = plus.e;   j.end = con32.w;
    k.start = plus.sw; k.end = times.nw;
    l.start = con59.e; l.end = times.sw;
    m.start = times.e; m.end = C.w;

    F.nw = (0,0);
}
```

The first three lines declare the sub-features of the root feature; it contains six boxes, five lines, and four numbers. Numbers are primitive, and don't contain sub-features. The numbers hspc and vspc will be used to determine the amount of space between the boxes. If we want to move all the boxes closer together in the horizontal direction, we will need only to change the definition of hspc to a smaller value. Similarly, boxht and boxwd will be the height and width of each of the six boxes.

The constraints section is the really interesting part. It's a list of linear equations that specify the sizes and relative locations of the boxes and lines. The first four equations define the four numeric parameters boxht, boxwd, hspc, and vspc. hspc represents the minimum center-to-center horizontal separation of two nearby boxes, so it's defined in terms of boxwd: The distance between the two centers is the width of one box, plus one unit of space.

The next two equations define the height and the width of the F box by establishing constraints on its subfeatures F.ht and F.wd. The definition of the box type (which we'll see later) contains a declaration like:

```
    number ht, wd;
```

to say that every box has these two properties, and other declarations that relate these numbers to the positions of the four sides.

The next equation,

```
    plus = F + (hspc, 0);
```

constrains the size, shape, and position of the plus box. The (hspc, 0) is called a *tuple expression* and represents a displacement. The constraint says that the box plus is exactly like F, only displaced eastward by hspc units and southward by 0 units. Internally, this will translate into a series of constraints that force each of plus's four corners and four sides to be hspc units east and 0 units south of the corresponding corners and sides of F.

Although this equation looks like an assignment, it isn't; it's a declaration. If linogram knows about F, it can deduce the corresponding information about plus — or vice versa. It can also deduce complete information about both from partial information. For example, if only the left side of F and the top side of plus are known, then the other sides of the two boxes can all be deduced: The left side of plus is like the left side of F, and the top side of F is like the top side of plus.

We could also have written this equation in any of these mathematically equivalent forms:

```
F + (hspc, 0) = plus;
plus + (-hspc, 0) = F;
plus - F = (-hspc, 0);
plus - (hspc, 0) - F = 0;
```

Sometimes it's convenient to write equations like this. For example, suppose we have four features, A, B, C, and D. We're not sure where A, B, and C are, but we know that we want D's position relative to C to be the same as B's position relative to A — if B is one furlong due north of A, we want D one furlong due north of C, or whatever. It's quite straightforward and intuitive to express it like this:

```
D - C = B - A;
```

Or suppose we wanted point Z to be one-third of the way from X to Y along the straight line between them:

```
Z - X = 1/3 * (Y - X);
```

In addition to a height and a width, every box has thirteen more subfeatures: four lines and nine points. The lines represent the four sides, and are named top, bottom, left, and right. The points aren't strictly necessary, but they're convenient. They are the four corner points, called nw, ne, sw, and se, the midpoints of the four sides, called n, s, e, and w, and the center point, called c.

Similarly, a line contains two sub-features, called start and end, that denote its two endpoints.

The next few declarations in our specification define the endpoints of the five lines i through m.

The declarations:

```
i.start = F.e;      i.end = plus.nw;
```

constrain line i to start at the midpoint of F's east side, and to end at the northwest corner of box plus.

Finally, we have to tell the program the absolute location of at least one of the features, or it won't be able to figure out where anything is located. We force the issue by attaching the northwest corner of box F arbitrarily to (0,0), although it doesn't really matter; we could as easily have attached any other point of any of the boxes.

In addition to these manifest constraints, there are a large number of hidden constraints that we don't see, inherent in the definitions of the box and line types. For example, the definition of box has, among others,

```
top.start = left.start;
nw = top.start;
top.start + wd = top.end;
n = top.center;
...
```

and the definition of line has:

```
center = (start + end)/2;
```

Again, although this looks like an assignment, it isn't; it's symmetric. If the start and end points of the line are known, the center will be calculated from them; if the start and center are known instead, the position of the end point will be calculated instead. Any two of the points imply the third.

The program's strategy for drawing a diagram is as follows. First it will read in the definition of the root feature, including the implied definitions of common sub-features such as box. It will accumulate a large set of linear constraint equations. These will include the explicit constraints, as well as many automatically generated implicit constraints. If the root feature contains a box named F, then it will also include F's constraints implicitly, in the form of equations like these:

```
F.top.start = F.left.start;
F.nw = F.top.start;
F.top.start + F.wd = F.top.end;
F.n = F.top.center;
...
```

In fact, since F itself contains several sub-features, it will inherit constraints from these. F's top side is a line, so F will inherit the constraint:

```
top.center = (top.start + top.end)/2;
```

from the definition of line; this will in turn be inherited by the root feature as:

```
F.top.center = (F.top.start + F.top.end)/2;
```

After accumulating all the constraint equations, the program will solve the equations. The result will be a complete description of where every part of each feature is located.

Associated with each feature will be one or more drawing functions. The program will invoke the drawing functions for each feature, passing them a hash containing the relevant variables. It's up to the drawing functions to generate the appropriate output. The output might be instructions in PostScript to be sent to a printer, or perhaps a "canvas" object containing a bitmap of the finished diagram.

Before we go any further with the main program, let's look at the definitions of the simpler sub-features such as boxes, which will be instructive. The simplest features that the program deals with are numbers, which are atomic. These are the only features whose definitions are built into the program. All other features are defined by a library file that specifies the feature's sub-features, constraints, and drawing methods.

After a number, the simplest feature is a point, which has x and y coordinates, but no constraints on them:

```
define point {
  number x, y;
}
```

When linogram wants to draw a feature, its default behavior is to recursively draw all the feature's sub-features. Thus it draws a point by trying to "draw" the two numbers x and y. Numbers are considered to be invisible, so the aggregate behavior for drawing a point is also to do nothing. The simplest visible feature is a line, which has start and end points:

```
define line {
  point start, end, center;
  constraints { center = (start + end)/2; }
  draw { &draw_line; }
}
```

As mentioned before, a line also has a center point, for convenience; it's constrained to be halfway between the start and end points (see Figure 9.3).

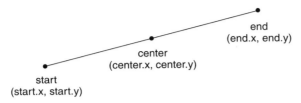

FIGURE 9.3 A line and its subfeatures.

The draw section is new. The declaration shown here is the name of a Perl subroutine responsible for drawing the feature. The & is a lexical marker that indicates that this is the name of a subroutine. When invoked, the subroutine will be passed a hash that indicates the positions of the sub-features of the line:

```
("start.x" => 5, "start.y" => 3,
 "end.x" => 3, "end.y" => 7,
 "center.x" => 4, "center.y" => 5,
)
```

If any of the sub-features are unknown, they'll be omitted from the hash; in that case, the function should complain. Since this chapter is about declarative programming, and not about graphics, we'll weasel out of doing any actual drawing, and use the following drawing function, which claims to draw lines even though it doesn't really draw anything. It does, however, give us a clear description of the line it *would have* drawn, which is enough to see whether the program is doing what it should be doing:

```perl
sub draw_line {
  my $env = shift;
  my $GOOD = 1;
  for my $k (qw(start.x start.y end.x end.y)) {
    unless (defined $env->{$k}) {
      warn "Can't draw line because '$k' is missing\n";
      $GOOD = 0;
    }
  }
  if ($GOOD) {
    print "Drawing line from ($env->{'start.x'}, $env->{'start.y'})
           to ($env->{'end.x'}, $env->{'end.y'})\n";
  }
}
```

Given the preceding hash, this will produce the output:

```
Drawing line from (5, 3) to (3, 7)
```

Even though we weaseled out of the drawing, creating a diagram in PostScript is barely more difficult. We would need to generate output something like this:

```
50 30 moveto 30 70 lineto stroke
```

This is almost the same, but there are a (very) few additional complications that I didn't want to have to consider, so we'll stick with the weasel drawing technique.

The other possible inhabitants of a draw section are the names of some of the sub-features that make up the feature. Only these sub-features will be drawn. If there is no draw section at all, the default is to draw all the sub-features.

We have enough machinery now to define boxes directly, but linogram's standard library goes through a set of intermediate definitions first. The top and bottom sides of a box are constrained to be horizontal, and it's convenient to define a new feature type to represent a horizontal line:

```
define hline extends line {
    number y, length;
    constraints {
        start.y = end.y;
        start.y = y;
        start.x + length = end.x;
    }
}
```

This defines a new type, called hline, which has all of the sub-features and constraints that an ordinary line has, and some additional ones. The start and end points must have the same y-coordinate, and an hline also has an additional sub-feature, called y, which is defined to be equal to this y-coordinate. If we were trying to specify the location of a box F, this would allow us to abbreviate F.top.start.y as simply F.top.y, which is more natural. An hline also has a length, which is the distance between the endpoints. In general, the length of a line is not a linear function of the positions of the endpoints (because $length = \mathrm{sqrt}((end.x - start.x)^2 + (end.y - start.y)^2)$) and computing one point given the length and the other endpoint requires trigonometry, which linogram won't do. But for horizontal lines, the calculation is trivial.

The constraints in this definition are adjoined to those inherited from line, which imply the position of the center point of an hline, even though we never

mentioned it explicitly. The draw section is also inherited from line, so that the
Perl draw_line function will be used for hline as well.

Vertical lines are almost exactly the same:

```
define vline  extends line {
  number x, height;
  constraints {
    start.x = end.x;
    start.x = x;
    start.y + height = end.y;
  }
}
```

Now we're ready to define box. It has a lot of machinery, but none of it is new:

```
define box {
  vline left, right;
  hline top, bottom;
  point nw, n, ne, e, se, s, sw, w, c;
  number ht, wd;

  constraints {
    left.start  = top.start;
    right.start = top.end;
    left.end    = bottom.start;
    right.end   = bottom.end;

    nw = left.start;
    ne = right.start;
    sw = left.end;
    se = right.end;
    n = top.center;
    s = bottom.center;
    w = left.center;
    e = right.center;

    c = (n + s)/2;

    ht = left.height;
    wd = top.length;
  }
}
```

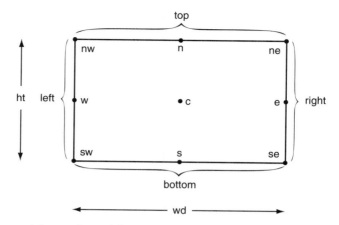

FIGURE 9.4   A box and its subfeatures.

A box has a left and a right side, which are vlines, and a top and a bottom side, which are hlines. It has nine named points, which are identical to various parts of the four sides, except for c, the center, which is halfway between the north and south points. It also has a height and a width, which are the same as the lengths of the left and top sides, respectively (see Figure 9.4). We didn't need to require that ht = right.height; this is already implicit in the other equations, although it wouldn't have hurt to put it in.

The box definition doesn't contain a draw section. The default behavior is for linogram to draw a box by drawing each of its fifteen sub-features. For the nine points and the two numbers, this does nothing at all; the other four sub-features are the four sides, which linogram draws by calling draw_line. Each box will therefore result in four calls to draw_line, which is just what we want.

To define a square, we need only write:

```
define square extends box {
  constraints { ht = wd; }
}
```

which defines a square to be the same as a box but with the height and width constrained to be equal. Another common constituent of diagrams is an arrow. From linogram's point of view, this is nothing more than an oddly-drawn line:

```
define arrow extends line {
  draw { &draw_arrow; }
}
```

An arrow has a start and end point, just like a line; these are the start and end points of the arrow's shaft. The draw_arrow function is responsible for drawing the shaft (which it can do by calling draw_line) and then filling in the two whiskers at the endpoint.

If we're feeling creative, we might go on:

```
define golden_rectangle extends box {
  constraints { ht * 1.618 = wd; }
}

define circle {
  number r, d;
  point c, nw, n, ne, e, se, s, sw, w;
  constraints {
    d = 2*r;

    n = c - (0, r);
    s = c + (0, r);
    e = c + (r, 0);
    w = c - (r, 0);

    se = c + ( r, r)/1.4142;
    sw = c + (-r, r)/1.4142;
    ne = c + ( r,-r)/1.4142;
    nw = c + (-r,-r)/1.4142;
  }
  draw { &draw_circle; }
}

define diamond extends box {
  line nw_side(start=n, end=w),
       sw_side(start=s, end=w),
       ne_side(start=n, end=e),
       se_side(start=s, end=e);
  draw { nw_side;
         sw_side;
         ne_side;
         se_side;
  }
}
```

The `nw_side(start=n, end=w)` declaration in the last definition is a short-hand for:

```
line nw_side;
constraints { nw_side.start = n;
              nw_side.end = w;
            }
```

linogram has a few other features, but we'll see them in the course of seeing the program code. The program code comprises three major classes and several less-important classes. The three major classes are `Constraint`, which represents constraints; `Type`, which represents feature types such as box and line; and `Value`, which represents the value of an expression as it is being converted to a set of constraints. We'll see constraints and equations first.

9.4.1   Equations

The heart of linogram will be the module that solves systems of linear equations. The usual way to do this is to represent the system as a matrix, and then perform sequences of matrix transformations on it until the matrix is in a canonical form; this is called *Gaussian elimination*. Methods for doing this are well studied, and also available on CPAN. But for various reasons, the CPAN modules I found for solving linear equations didn't seem to be what I wanted, so I'll develop one here.

An `Equation` object is a hash. The equation:

$$14x + 9y - 3.5z = 28$$

is represented by the hash:

```
{ "x" => 14,
  "y" => 9,
  "z" => -3.5,
  ""  => -28,
}
```

The values 14, 9, and -3.5, are called the *coefficients* of x, y, and z, respectively. The -28 is the *constant part*. It's negative because the equation is actually:

$$14x + 9y - 3.5z - 28 = 0$$

The "" key in the hash is mandatory because every linear equation has a constant part, even if the constant part is 0. The equation:

$$x = 0$$

corresponds to the hash:

```
{ "x" => 1,
  "" => 0,
}
```

and the trivial equation $0 = 0$ is represented by the hash { "" => 0 }.

Manipulating equations through these hashes is straightforward and easy to debug, although slow. If speed is an issue, the Equation module of the program should be replaced with one that uses a more abbreviated representation of equations, perhaps one implemented in C.

The constructor function takes an argument hash and puts it into a canonical form:

CODE LIBRARY
Equation.pm

```
sub new {
  my ($base, %self) = @_;
  $class = ref($base) || $base;
  $self{""} = 0 unless exists $self{""};
  for my $k (keys %self) {
    if ($self{$k} == 0 && $k ne "") { delete $self{$k} }
  }
  bless \%self => $class;
}
```

If the constant part is missing, the constructor sets it to 0; if the coefficients of any of the variables are 0, they are deleted. For example, ->new("x" => 0, "y" => 1), which represents $0x + 1y = 0$, is turned into { "y" => 1, "" => 0 }.

ref($base) || $base

One idiom used here and elsewhere that you may not have seen is the ref($base) || $base trick. The goal is to write a function that can be called as either an object or a class method, either as:

```
Equation->new(...)
```

or as;

```
$some_equation->new(...)
```

In the former case, $base is the string Equation, and ref $base is false, since $base is a string rather than a reference. $class is therefore set equal to $base. In the latter case, $base is the object $some_equation, and ref($base) is the class into which $some_equation was blessed. $class is therefore set equal to $some_equation's class. This is convenient when we'll be writing several other constructor methods that might get an Equation object as an argument and will want to create another object similar to it. For example, here's a method that makes a copy of an Equation object:

```
sub duplicate {
  my $self = shift;
  $self->new(%$self);
}
```

Note that:

```
# WRONG!
sub duplicate {
  my $self = shift;
  Equation->new(%$self);
}
```

doesn't work properly if its argument is an object of a class derived from Equation. The correct code creates a new object from the same derived subclass; the incorrect code creates a new Equation object regardless.

SOLVING EQUATIONS

For convenience, we set up a constant for the important trivial equation $0 = 0$:

```
BEGIN { $Zero = Equation->new() }
```

Equations have three important accessors. One retrieves the coefficient of a given variable:

```
sub coefficient {
  my ($self, $name) = @_;
```

```
    $self->{$name} || 0;
  }
```

The second recovers the constant part:

```
# Constant part of an equation
sub constant {
    $_[0]->coefficient("");
}
```

The other returns the names of all the variables that the equation mentions:

```
sub varlist {
    my $self = shift;
    grep $_ ne "", keys %$self;
}
```

All equations can be scaled and added. If an equation is known to be true, you can multiply its constant and its coefficients by any number n, and the resulting equation is also true. For example, if:

$$14x + 9y - 3.5z = 28$$

then we can scale all the numbers by 2 and get:

$$28x + 18y - 7z = 56$$

which is equivalent.

If we have two equations that are true, we can add them together and get another true equation. For example, suppose we have:

$$x = 13$$
$$2y = 7$$

we can add these, getting:

$$x + 2y = 20$$

These two operations are fundamental to all methods of solving linear equations. For example, suppose we have:

$$x + y = 12$$
$$x - y = 2$$

If we add these two equations together, the $+y$ in the first and the $-y$ in the second cancel, yielding:

$$2x = 14$$

which we can then scale (by 1/2) to yield:

$$x = 7$$

We can then scale this by -1, yielding:

$$-x = -7$$

When we add this last equation to the very first equation, the x's cancel, and we're left with:

$$y = 5$$

And in fact $x = 7$, $y = 5$ is the solution of the equations.

The most important function in the `Equation` module is `arithmetic()`, which scales and adds equations:

```
sub arithmetic {
  my ($a, $ac, $b, $bc) = @_;
  my %new;
  for my $k (keys(%$a), keys %$b) {
    my ($av) = $a->coefficient($k);
    my ($bv) = $b->coefficient($k);
    $new{$k} = $ac * $av + $bc * $bv;
  }
  $a->new(%new);
}
```

Given two equations, $a and $b, and two numbers, $ac and $bc, `arithmetic()` scales $a by $ac, scales $b by $bc, and adds the two scaled equations together. Built atop this base are several simpler utility functions. For example, to add two equations together, we use `arithmetic()`, with both scale factors set to 1:

```
sub add_equations {
  my ($a, $b) = @_;

  arithmetic($a, 1, $b, 1);
}
```

Similarly, to subtract one equation from another is the same as adding them, but with the second one negated:

```
sub subtract_equations {
  my ($a, $b) = @_;

  arithmetic($a, 1, $b, -1);
}
```

Scaling a single equation is yet another special case, where the second equation is zero:

```
sub scale_equation {
  my ($a, $c) = @_;
  arithmetic($a, $c, $Zero, 0);
}
```

Now suppose we have two equations:

$$ax + \text{some other stuff} = c$$
$$bx + \text{more stuff} = d$$

Here we can eliminate x from the first equation by scaling the second by $-a/b$ and adding the result to the first equation. The function `substitute_for()` is for eliminating a variable from an equation. The call:

```
$first->substitute_for("x", $second);
```

eliminates variable "x" from equation `$first` in this way, by combining it with an appropriately scaled version of `$second`:

```
# Destructive
sub substitute_for {
```

```
    my ($self, $var, $value) = @_;
    my $a = $self->coefficient($var);
    return if $a == 0;
    my $b = $value->coefficient($var);
    die "Oh NO" if $b == 0;   # Should never happen

    my $result = arithmetic($self, 1, $value, -$a/$b);
    %$self = %$result;
  }
```

If $a is zero, then the first equation didn't contain the variable we were trying to eliminate, so nothing needs to be done. The "Oh NO" case occurs when the second equation doesn't contain the variable we're trying to eliminate; in this case there's no way to use it to eliminate the variable from the first equation. Note that the function is destructive: It modifies $self in place.

The cost of eliminating a variable like x is that the resulting equation might be more complicated than what we started with, depending on what else is in the equation we're using to reduce it. If we're not careful, we might even get stuck in an infinite loop. Suppose we had:

$$x + y = 3$$
$$y + z = 5$$

and we scale the second equation by -1 and add it to the first, to eliminate y:

$$x - z = -2$$

If we then add *this* equation to the second one to eliminate z, we're back where we started.

We'll adopt a simple strategy that prevents infinite loops. We'll take the first equation and use it to completely eliminate one of its variables from all the other equations. The variable will be present in that first equation only, so as long as we don't use the first equation again, we can't possibly reintroduce that variable. We'll then move to the second equation and use *it* to eliminate one of *its* variables from all the other equations. We'll repeat this for each equation.

To that end, here's a method that returns an arbitrarily chosen variable from an equation:

```
sub a_var {
  my $self = shift;
```

```
    my ($var) = $self->varlist;
    $var;
}
```

Let's see a small example of how this works. Consider the equations:

$$A: \quad x + 2y = 8$$
$$B: \quad 2y + z = 10$$
$$C: \quad x + y + 2z = 13$$

First we use A to eliminate x from the other two equations. For equation B there is nothing to do; eliminating x from C leaves:

$$A: \quad x + 2y = 8$$
$$B: \quad 2y + z = 10$$
$$C: \quad -y + 2z = 5$$

Now we use B to eliminate y from the other two equations. Eliminating y from A leaves:

$$A: \quad x - z = -2$$
$$B: \quad 2y + z = 10$$
$$C: \quad -y + 2z = 5$$

Eliminating y from C leaves:

$$A: \quad x - z = -2$$
$$B: \quad 2y + z = 10$$
$$C: \quad 2.5z = 10$$

Finally, we use C to eliminate z from the other two equations:

$$A: \quad x = 2$$
$$B: \quad 2y = 6$$
$$C: \quad 2.5z = 10$$

At this point we have finished one complete pass through all the equations, so we are done. There's a final step that needs to be done to put the equations in standard form: We must adjust the coefficients to 1:

$$A: \quad x = 2$$
$$B: \quad y = 3$$
$$C: \quad z = 4$$

but this is a simple scaling operation.

Solving entire systems of equations is the job of the `Equation::System` module, whose objects represent whole systems of equations:

```
package Equation::System;

sub new {
  my ($base, @eqns) = @_;
  my $class = ref $base || $base;
  bless \@eqns => $class;
}
```

In the course of solving a system of equations, we often find that some of them are redundant. The way this appears in the mathematics is that we reduce an equation and find that we have nothing left. (That is, nothing but $0 = 0$, which adds no useful information.) We can detect such a ghostly equation with `Equation::is_tautology`:

```
package Equation;

sub is_tautology {
  my $self = shift;
  return $self->constant == 0 && $self->varlist == 0;
}
```

In such a case, we'll replace the ghostly equation with `undef`.

The important accessor for an `Equation::System` recovers the current list of equations, ignoring the ones we have nulled out:

```
package Equation::System;

sub equations {
  my $self = shift;
  grep defined, @$self;
}
```

A typical operation on a system of equations will be to transform each equation in some way:

```
sub apply {
  my ($self, $func) = @_;
  for my $eq ($self->equations) {
    $func->($eq);
  }
}
```

Now we're ready to see Equation::System::solve, the end product of all this machinery.

```
sub solve {
  my $self = shift;
  my $N = my @E = $self->equations;
  for my $i (0 .. $N-1) {
    next unless defined $E[$i];
    my $var = $E[$i]->a_var;
    for my $j (0 .. $N-1) {
      next if $i == $j;
      next unless defined $E[$j];
      next unless $E[$j]->coefficient($var);
      $E[$j]->substitute_for($var, $E[$i]);
      if ($E[$j]->is_tautology) {
        undef $E[$j];
      } elsif ($E[$j]->is_inconsistent) {
        return ;
      }
    }
  }
  $self->normalize;
  return 1;
}
```

The main loop selects an equation number i, selects one if its variables, $var, and then scans over all the other equations j reducing each one to remove $var. If the result is the trivial equation $0 = 0$, equation j is nulled out.

After each reduction, we test the resulting equation to make sure it makes sense. If we get an equation like $1 = 0$, we know something has gone wrong.

This will occur if the original equations were inconsistent. For example:

$$start.y = 1;$$
$$y = 2;$$
$$start.y - y = 0;$$

Eliminating *start.y* from the others yields:

$$start.y = 1;$$
$$y = 2;$$
$$-y = -1;$$

Then using the second equation to eliminate *y* from the others yields:

$$start.y = 1;$$
$$y = 2;$$
$$0 = 1;$$

which is no good, because it says that $0 = 1$. The Equation::is_inconsistent method detects bad equations like $0 = 1$ that have no variables, but whose constant part is nonzero:

```
package Equation;

sub is_inconsistent {
  my $self = shift;
  return $self->constant != 0 && $self->varlist == 0;
}
```

When the main loop is finished, we hope that the equations in the system have been reduced to the point where they contain only one variable each. As we saw, the equations might need one final adjustment. An equation like this:

$$2y = 6$$

should be adjusted to this:

$$y = 3$$

The `Equation::System::normalize` method adjusts the equations in this way:

```
package Equation::System;

sub normalize {
  my $self = shift;
  $self->apply(sub { $_[0]->normalize });
}
```

To normalize a single equation, we scale it appropriately:

```
package Equation;

sub normalize {
  my $self = shift;
  my $var = $self->a_var;
  return unless defined $var;
  %$self = %{$self->scale_equation(1/$self->coefficient($var))};
}
```

An equation like $y = 3$ is so simple that even the computer understands what it means. We say that this equation *defines* the variable y. The `defines_var()` method reports on whether an equation defines a variable:

```
sub defines_var {
  my $self = shift;
  my @keys = keys %$self;
  return unless @keys == 2;
  my $var = $keys[0] || $keys[1];
  return $self->{$var} == 1 ? $var : () ;
}
```

To define a variable, an equation must have the form *var = val*, and so must contain exactly two keys. One is the name of the variable; the other is the empty string. Moreover, the coefficient of the one variable must be 1. If all this is true, `defines_var()` returns the name of the variable so defined. The value of the variable can be recovered with - `$equation->constant`. (The minus sign is because $y = 7$ is represented as $y - 7 = 0$, which is { y => 1, "" => -7 }.)

The main entry to the equation-solving subsystem for outside functions is the `values()` method. This takes a system of equations, solves the equations, and returns a hash that maps the names of known variables to their values:

```
package Equation::System;

sub values {
  my $self = shift;
  my %values;
  $self->solve;
  for my $eqn ($self->equations) {
    if (my $name = $eqn->defines_var) {
      $values{$name} = -$eqn->constant;
    }
  }
  %values;
}


1;
```

CONSTRAINTS

linogram will have another class, called Constraint, which represents constraints. Since constraints are essentially equations, Constraint will be a derived class of Equation:

CODE LIBRARY
Constraint.pm

```
package Constraint;
use Equation;
@Constraint::ISA = 'Equation';
```

Constraint adds a few utility methods to Equation that make more sense in the context of linogram than in the general context of equation solving. The most important is qualify(). A type like hline contains the constraint $start.y - y = 0$. But when considered as part of a box, the hline has a name like top or bottom, and the constraint, when translated into the context of the box, turns into $top.start.y - top.y = 0$. qualify() takes a constraint and a name prefix and produces a new, transformed constraint:

```
sub qualify {
  my ($self, $prefix) = @_;
  my %result = ("" => $self->constant);
```

```
      for my $var ($self->varlist) {
        $result{"$prefix.$var"} = $self->coefficient($var);
      }
      $self->new(%result);
    }
```

Constraint's other methods are simple things. In some places inside linogram,
constraints are used as if they were expressions; when there is an expression with
an addition in the drawing specification, we have to add together constraints.
We'll see this in more detail later; in the meantime, new_constant() manufactures
a constraint like $0 = 0$ or $0 = 1$ that plays the role of a constant expression:

```
    sub new_constant {
      my ($base, $val) = @_;
      my $class = ref $base || $base;
      $class->new("" => $val);
    }
```

add_constant() adds a constant to a constraint, transforming something like
$x = 0$ to something like $x = 3$, and mul_constant() multiplies a constraint
by a constant, transforming something like $x = 3$ to something like $4x = 12$:

```
    sub add_constant {
      my ($self, $v) = @_;
      $self->add_equations($self->new_constant($v));
    }
```

```
    sub mul_constant {
      my ($self, $v) = @_;
      $self->scale_equation($v);
    }
```

All the other methods of Constraint are inherited from Equation.
   Analogous to Constraint, there is a Constraint_Set class that is derived
from Equation::System. It's even simpler than Constraint. It has only one extra
method:

```
    package Constraint_Set;
    @Constraint_Set::ISA = 'Equation::System';

    sub constraints {
```

```
        my $self = shift;
        $self->equations;
    }


    1;
```

9.4.2 Values

In the course of reading and parsing the specification, we'll need to deal with expressions. We saw the parsing end of this in detail in Chapter 8. The question that arises is what the values of the expressions will be; the answer turns out to be quite interesting. Values are not always numbers. For example, consider:

```
point P, Q;
P + (2, 3) = Q;
```

Here we have an expression P + (2, 3). The value of this expression isn't a simple number. It implies parts of two constraints, involving $P.x$ and $P.y$. Later on, these partial constraints must be combined with Q to yield the complete constraints, which are $P.x + 2 = Q.x$ and $P.y + 3 = Q.y$.

One of linogram's main classes is Value, which represents the value of an expression. Value is where the most interesting arithmetic takes place inside of linogram. Values come in three kinds. Value::Constant represents a scalar constant value such as 3. Value::Tuple represents a lone tuple, such as (2, 3), or a sum of tuples. And Value::Feature represents a feature type, even a scalar feature type, such as P or Q or P + (2, 3). Value itself is an abstract base class, and doesn't represent anything; it's there only to provide methods that are inherited by the other classes, primarily for doing arithmetic.

Value objects have one generic accessor, called kindof(), which returns CONSTANT, TUPLE, or FEATURE, depending on what kind of object it is called on. The other methods are arithmetic. The entry to these from the parser is via a quartet of operation methods called add(), sub(), mul(), and div(), which are just thin wrappers around the real workhorse, op():

```
sub add { $_[0]->op("add", $_[1]) }
sub sub { $_[0]->op("add", $_[1]->negate) }
sub mul { $_[0]->op("mul", $_[1]) }
sub div { $_[0]->op("mul", $_[1]->reciprocal) }
```

Note that subtraction and division are defined in terms of addition and multiplication, which cuts down on the amount of work we need to do for op().

op() itself is driven by a dispatch table because otherwise it would be quite complicated. The dispatch table is indexed by the operation name (either add or mul) and by the kinds of the two operands. It looks like this:

```perl
package Value;

my %op = ("add" =>
            {
             "FEATURE,FEATURE"     => 'add_features',
             "FEATURE,CONSTANT"    => 'add_feature_con',
             "FEATURE,TUPLE"       => 'add_feature_tuple',
             "TUPLE,TUPLE"         => 'add_tuples',
             "TUPLE,CONSTANT"      => undef,
             "CONSTANT,CONSTANT"   => 'add_constants',
             NAME => "Addition",
            },
          "mul" =>
            {
             "FEATURE,CONSTANT"    => 'mul_feature_con',
             "TUPLE,CONSTANT"      => 'mul_tuple_con',
             "CONSTANT,CONSTANT"   => 'mul_constants',
             NAME => "Multiplication",
            },
          );
```

Addition, surprisingly, turns out to be more complicated than multiplication. This is because we've restricted our system to linear operations, which means that multiplication is forbidden, except to multiply by constant values. Given two Value objects and an operation tag, op() consults the dispatch table, dispatches the appropriate arithmetic function, and returns the result:

```perl
sub op {
  my ($self, $op, $operand) = @_;
  my ($k1, $k2) = ($self->kindof, $operand->kindof);
  my $method;
  if ($method = $op{$op}{"$k1,$k2"}) {
    $self->$method($operand);
  } elsif ($method = $op{$op}{"$k2,$k1"}) {
```

```
            $operand->$method($self);
        } else {
        my $name = $op{$op}{NAME} || "'$op'";
        die "$name of '$k1' and '$k2' not defined";
        }
    }
}
```

The two operands are $self and $operand. op() starts by finding out what sorts of values these are, using kindof, which returns CONSTANT for Value::Constant objects, TUPLE for Value::Tuple objects, and so forth. It then looks in the dispatch table under the operator name ("add" or "mul") and the value kinds. If it doesn't find anything, it tries the operands in the opposite order, since a function for adding a tuple to a feature is the same as one for adding a feature to a tuple; this cuts down on the number of functions we have to write. If neither operand order works, then the op function fails with a message like "Addition of 'CONSTANT' and 'TUPLE' not defined".

The only other generic methods in Value are for negate(), which is required for subtraction, and reciprocal(), which is required for division. negate() passes the buck to a general scaling method, which will be defined differently in each of the various subclasses:

```
sub negate { $_[0]->scale(-1) }
```

reciprocal() is even simpler, because in general it's illegal. You're not allowed to divide by a tuple (what would it mean?) or by a feature (since this would mean that the equations were nonlinear; consider $x = 1/y$) so the default reciprocal() method dies:

```
sub reciprocal { die "Nonlinear division" }
```

You *are* allowed to divide by a constant, so Value::Constant::reciprocal() will override this definition.

CONSTANT VALUES

Of the three kinds of Value, we'll look at Value::Constant first, because it's by far the simplest. Value::Constant objects are essentially numbers. The object is a hash with two members. One is the kind, which is CONSTANT; the other is the numeric value. The constructor accepts a number and generates a Value::Constant value with the number inside it:

```
package Value::Constant;
@Value::Constant::ISA = 'Value';

sub new {
  my ($base, $con) = @_;
  my $class = ref $base || $base;
  bless { WHAT => $base->kindof,
          VALUE => $con,
        } => $class;
}

sub kindof { "CONSTANT" }

sub value { $_[0]{VALUE} }
```

To perform the scale() operation, we multiply the constant by the argument:

```
sub scale {
  my ($self, $coeff) = @_;
  $self->new($coeff * $self->value);
}
```

Division is defined for constants, so we must override the fatal reciprocal() method with one that actually performs division. The reciprocal of a constant is a new constant with the reciprocal value:

```
sub reciprocal {
  my ($self, $coeff) = @_;
  my $v = $self->value;
  if ($v == 0) {
    die "Division by zero";
  }
  $self->new(1/$v);
}
```

Finally, the dispatch table contains two methods for operating on constants. One adds two constants, and the other multiplies them:

```
sub add_constants {
  my ($c1, $c2) = @_;
```

```
      $c1->new($c1->value + $c2->value);
    }


    sub mul_constants {
      my ($c1, $c2) = @_;
      $c1->new($c1->value * $c2->value);
    }
```

TUPLE VALUES

Tuples represent displacements. A tuple like (2, 3) represents a displacement of 2 units in the x direction (east) and 3 units in the y direction (south). As we'll see, linogram isn't restricted to two-dimensional drawings, so (2, 3, 4) could also be a legal displacement. Although it's unlikely that any four-dimensional beings will be using linogram, there's no harm in making it as general as possible, so internally, a tuple is a hash. The keys are component names (x, y, and so forth) and the values are the components. The tuple (2, 3) is represented by the hash { x => 2, y => 3 }. (2, 3, 4) is represented by the hash { x => 2, y => 3, z => 4 }. The tuple class itself doesn't care what the component names are, although this version of linogram will refuse to generate tuples with any components other than x, y, and possibly z.

One possibly fine point is that tuple components need not be numbers; they might be arbitrary Values. A tuple like (3, hspc) will have a y component that is a Value::Feature. It's even conceivable that we could have a tuple whose components are other tuples. We'll take some pains to forbid this last possibility, since it doesn't seem to have any meaning in the context of drawings.

Here is the constructor, which gets a component hash and returns a tuple value object:

```
    package Value::Tuple;
    @Value::Tuple::ISA = 'Value';

    sub kindof { "TUPLE" }

    sub new {
      my ($base, %tuple) = @_;
      my $class = ref $base || $base;
      bless { WHAT => $base->kindof,
              TUPLE => \%tuple,
            } => $class;
    }
```

It has a few straightforward accessors:

```
sub components { keys %{$_[0]{TUPLE}} }
sub has_component { exists $_[0]{TUPLE}{$_[1]} }
sub component { $_[0]{TUPLE}{$_[1]} }
sub to_hash { $_[0]{TUPLE} }
```

To perform subtraction on tuples, we will need a scale() operation that multiplies a tuple by a number. This is done componentwise; 2 * (2, 3) is (4, 6):

```
sub scale {
    my ($self, $coeff) = @_;
    my %new_tuple;
    for my $k ($self->components) {
      $new_tuple{$k} = $self->component($k)->scale($coeff);
    }
    $self->new(%new_tuple);
}
```

Note that we must use $self->component($k)->scale($coeff) rather than $self->component($k) * $coeff, because the component value might not be a number.

Adding tuples will also be done componentwise. We want to make sure that the user doesn't try to add tuples with different components. It's not clear what (2, 3) + (2, 3, 4) would mean, for example. This function takes two tuples and returns true if their component lists are identical:

```
sub has_same_components_as {
  my ($t1, $t2) = @_;
  my %t1c;
  for my $c ($t1->components) {
    return unless $t2->has_component($c);
    $t1c{$c} = 1;
  }
  for my $c ($t2->components) {
    return unless $t1c{$c};
  }
  return 1;
}
```

Adding two tuples is one of the functions from the dispatch table:

```
sub add_tuples {
  my ($t1, $t2) = @_;
  croak("Nonconformable tuples") unless $t1->has_same_components_as($t2);

  my %result ;
  for my $c ($t1->components) {
    $result{$c} = $t1->component($c) + $t2->component($c);
  }
  $t1->new(%result);
}
```

The other dispatch table function that can return a tuple involves multiplying a tuple by a constant. This is a simple application of `scale()`:

```
sub mul_tuple_con {
  my ($t, $c) = @_;

  $t->scale($c->value);
}
```

FEATURE VALUES

The code for handling feature values isn't much longer than the code for handling tuples or constants, but it's more complex, because arithmetic of features is more complex. This is partly because it's not really clear what it should mean to add two boxes together.

What *does* it mean to add two boxes together? Suppose that A and B are hlines, and that we have the constraint $A = B$, or, equivalently, $A - B = 0$, which involves a subtraction of two hline features. What does this mean?

A contains several intrinsic constraints, including A.start.x + A.length = A.end.x, and B similarly contains B.start.x + B.length = B.end.x. The end value of $A - B$ must contain both of these constraints. The subtraction won't affect them at all. We will need to carry along all the intrinsic constraints from both input features into the result, but these intrinsic constraints don't otherwise participate in the arithmetic.

But the end value also must include some constraints that relate the two inputs, such as A.end.y - B.end.y = 0, A.end.x - B.end.x = 0, and so on. We'll call these *synthetic constraints*, because they must be synthesized out of information that we find in the input values.

A feature value has two parts, the *intrinsic constraints* and the *synthetic constraints*. Each is a set of constraints. The intrinsic constraints are those contributed by the definitions of the features themselves, and are internal to particular features. The synthetic constraints are those derived from the structure of the expression and the interactions between the features in the expression. The intrinsic constraints don't participate in arithmetic, while the synthetic constraints do participate in arithmetic.

When we want to add (or subtract) two boxes, we unite their two intrinsic constraint sets into a single set, which becomes the intrinsic constraint set of the result. But to combine the two synthetic constraint sets, we perform arithmetic on *corresponding* synthetic constraints. To keep track of which synthetic constraints correspond, each one is labeled with a string. A synthetic constraint that involves the start.x components of two hlines will be labeled with the string start.x and will be combined with the start.x components of any other lines involved in the expression. Synthetic constraint sets will therefore be hashes.

INTRINSIC CONSTRAINTS

Intrinsic constraint sets are represented by the class Intrinsic_Constraint_Set. An intrinsic constraint set is a simple container class that holds a list of Constraint objects:

```
package Intrinsic_Constraint_Set;

sub new {
  my ($base, @constraints) = @_;
  my $class = ref $base || $base;
  bless \@constraints => $class;
}

sub constraints { @{$_[0]} }
```

It has only a few methods. One is a map-like function for invoking a callback on each constraint in the set, and returning the set of the results:

```
sub apply {
  my ($self, $func) = @_;
  my @c = map $func->($_), $self->constraints;
  $self->new(@c);
}
```

This is used by qualify(), which qualifies all the constraints in the set:

```
sub qualify {
  my ($self, $prefix) = @_;
  $self->apply(sub { $_[0]->qualify($prefix) });
}
```

Last is union(), which takes one or more intrinsic constraint sets and generates a new set that contains all the constraints in the input sets:

```
sub union {
  my ($self, @more) = @_;
  $self->new($self->constraints, map {$_->constraints} @more);
}
```

SYNTHETIC CONSTRAINTS

Synthetic_Constraint_Set is more interesting, because it supports arithmetic rather than mere aggregation. As mentioned earlier, a synthetic constraint set is represented by a hash, because each constraint in the set has a label that is used to determine which constraints in other sets it will fraternize with. For convenience, the constructor accepts either a regular hash or a reference to a hash:

```
package Synthetic_Constraint_Set;

sub new {
  my $base = shift;
  my $class = ref $base || $base;
  my $constraints;
  if (@_ == 1) {
    $constraints = shift;
  } elsif (@_ % 2 == 0) {
    my %constraints = @_;
    $constraints = \%constraints;
  } else {
    my $n = @_;
    require Carp;
    Carp::croak("$n arguments to Synthetic_Constraint_Set::new");
  }

  bless $constraints => $class;
}
```

It has the usual accessors:

```
sub constraints { values %{$_[0]} }
sub constraint { $_[0]->{$_[1]} }
sub labels { keys %{$_[0]} }
sub has_label { exists $_[0]->{$_[1]} }
```

Also a method for appending another constraint to the set:

```
sub add_labeled_constraint {
  my ($self, $label, $constraint) = @_;
  $self->{$label} = $constraint;
}
```

It has another map-like function that applies a callback to each constraint and returns a new set with the results. This method leaves the labels unchanged:

```
sub apply {
  my ($self, $func) = @_;
  my %result;
  for my $k ($self->labels) {
    $result{$k} = $func->($self->constraint($k));
  }
  $self->new(\%result);
}
```

This function seems to be a good target for currying, but I decided to postpone that change.

Like `Intrinsic_Constraint_Set`, `Synthetic_Constraint_Set` also has a method for qualifying all of its constraints:

```
sub qualify {
  my ($self, $prefix) = @_;
  $self->apply(sub { $_[0]->qualify($prefix) });
}
```

Unlike `Intrinsic_Constraint_Set`, whose constraints are not involved in arithmetic, `Synthetic_Constraint_Set` has a method for scaling all of its constraints:

```
sub scale {
  my ($self, $coeff) = @_;
```

```
        $self->apply(sub { $_[0]->scale_equation($coeff) });
}
```

Yet another map-like function takes *two* synthetic constraint sets and applies the callback function to pairs of corresponding constraints, building a new set of the results:

```
sub apply2 {
  my ($self, $arg, $func) = @_;
  my %result;
  for my $k ($self->labels) {
    next unless $arg->has_label($k);
    $result{$k} = $func->($self->constraint($k),
                          $arg->constraint($k));
  }
  $self->new(\%result);
}
```

This function will be used for addition of features. apply2() will be called to add the matching constraints from the sets of its two operands.

This brings up a fine point: What if the labels in the two sets don't match? For example, what if we have:

```
line L;
hline H;
L + H = ... ;
```

Here H will have synthetic constraints:

$$\text{center.x} \Rightarrow \text{H.center.x} = 0$$

$$\text{center.y} \Rightarrow \text{H.center.y} = 0$$

$$\text{end.x} \quad \Rightarrow \text{H.end.x} = 0$$

$$\text{end.y} \quad \Rightarrow \text{H.end.y} = 0$$

$$\text{length} \Rightarrow \text{H.length} = 0$$

$$\text{start.x} \Rightarrow \text{H.start.x} = 0$$

$$\text{start.y} \Rightarrow \text{H.start.y} = 0$$

$$\text{y} \quad\quad \Rightarrow \text{H.y} = 0$$

but L will be missing a few of these, and will have only:

$$center.x \Rightarrow L.center.x = 0$$

$$center.y \Rightarrow L.center.y = 0$$

$$end.x \quad \Rightarrow L.end.x = 0$$

$$end.y \quad \Rightarrow L.end.y = 0$$

$$start.x \quad \Rightarrow L.start.x = 0$$

$$start.y \quad \Rightarrow L.start.y = 0$$

What happens to H's *length* and *y* constraints? The right thing to do here is to discard them. The result set is:

$$center.x \Rightarrow L.center.x + H.center.x = 0$$

$$center.y \Rightarrow L.center.y + H.center.y = 0$$

$$end.x \quad \Rightarrow L.end.x + H.end.x = 0$$

$$end.y \quad \Rightarrow L.end.y + H.end.y = 0$$

$$start.x \quad \Rightarrow L.start.x + H.start.x = 0$$

$$start.y \quad \Rightarrow L.start.y + H.start.y = 0$$

Thus, the result of adding an hline and a line is just a line. Similarly if we try to equate an hline and a vline, the resulting expression contains synthetic constraints only for the parts they have in common. The horizontalness and verticalosity are handled by the intrinsic constraint sets instead. There should probably be a check to make sure that the two operands in an addition are of compatible types, but that's something for the next version. In the meantime, the code in apply2() silently discards constraints with labels present in one but not both argument sets.

The final method in Synthetic_Constraint_Set is a special one for handling arithmetic involving features and tuples. Adding a feature to a tuple is interesting. The trick here is that the tuple's *x* component must be added to all the synthetic constraints that represent *x* coordinates, and similarly for the *y* component. (And similarly also the *z* component in a three-dimensional drawing.) Suppose we had:

```
hline H;
H + (3, 4) = ...
```

The synthetic constraint set for H is:

$$center.x \Rightarrow H.center.x = 0$$
$$center.y \Rightarrow H.center.y = 0$$
$$end.x \quad \Rightarrow H.end.x = 0$$
$$end.y \quad \Rightarrow H.end.y = 0$$
$$length \quad \Rightarrow H.length = 0$$
$$start.x \quad \Rightarrow H.start.x = 0$$
$$start.y \quad \Rightarrow H.start.y = 0$$
$$y \qquad \Rightarrow H.y = 0$$

The synthetic constraint set of the sum is:

$$center.x \Rightarrow H.center.x + 3 = 0$$
$$center.y \Rightarrow H.center.y + 4 = 0$$
$$end.x \quad \Rightarrow H.end.x + 3 = 0$$
$$end.y \quad \Rightarrow H.end.y + 4 = 0$$
$$length \quad \Rightarrow H.length = 0$$
$$start.x \quad \Rightarrow H.start.x + 3 = 0$$
$$start.y \quad \Rightarrow H.start.y + 4 = 0$$
$$y \qquad \Rightarrow H.y + 4 = 0$$

How do we decide whether a synthetic constraint represents an x or a y coordinate? linogram assumes that any feature named x is an x coordinate, and that any feature named y is a y coordinate. The tuple's x component should be combined with any synthetic constraint whose label ends in .x or is plain x. This selective combination is handled by yet another map-like function, apply_hash():

```
sub apply_hash {
  my ($self, $hash, $func) = @_;
  my %result;
  for my $c (keys %$hash) {
    my $dotc = ".$c";
```

```
    for my $k ($self->labels) {
      next unless $k eq $c || substr($k, -length($dotc)) eq $dotc;
      $result{$k} = $func->($self->constraint($k), $hash->{$c});
    }
  }
  $self->new(\%result);
}
```

Each component of the argument hash has a label, $c. The function scans the labels of the constraints in the set, which are indexed by $k. If the constraint label matches the tuple component label, the callback is invoked and its return value is added to the result set. The labels match if they are equal (as with x and x) or if the constraint label ends with a dot followed by the tuple label (as with start.x and x.) The dot is important, because we don't want a label like max or box to match x.

FEATURE-VALUE METHODS

Now we can see the methods for operating on feature-value objects. The objects themselves contain nothing more than an intrinsic and a synthetic constraint set:

```
package Value::Feature;
@Value::Feature::ISA = 'Value';

sub kindof { "FEATURE" }

sub new {
    my ($base, $intrinsic, $synthetic) = @_;
    my $class = ref $base || $base;
    my $self = {WHAT => $base->kindof,
                SYNTHETIC => $synthetic,
                INTRINSIC => $intrinsic,
               };
    bless $self => $class;
}
```

There's another very important constructor in the Value::Feature class. Instead of building a value from given sets of constraints, it takes a Type object, which represents a type such as box or line, figures out what its constraint sets should be, and builds a new value with those constraint sets:

```
sub new_from_var {
  my ($base, $name, $type) = @_;
  my $class = ref $base || $base;
  $base->new($type->qualified_intrinsic_constraints($name),
             $type->qualified_synthetic_constraints($name),
          );
}
```

Value::Feature naturally has two accessors, one for the intrinsic and one for the synthetic constraint sets:

```
sub intrinsic { $_[0]->{INTRINSIC} }
sub synthetic { $_[0]->{SYNTHETIC} }
```

For its scaling operation, it passes the buck to the synthetic constraint set. The intrinsic constraints don't participate in arithmetic, so they remain the same:

```
sub scale {
  my ($self, $coeff) = @_;
  return
    $self->new($self->intrinsic,
               $self->synthetic->scale($coeff),
              );
}
```

The four other methods are the ones from the dispatch table. To add two features, we unite their intrinsic constraint sets, and add corresponding constraints from their synthetic constraint sets:

```
sub add_features {
  my ($o1, $o2) = @_;
  my $intrinsic = $o1->intrinsic->union($o2->intrinsic);
  my $synthetic = $o1->synthetic->apply2($o2->synthetic,
                                         sub { $_[0]->add_equations($_[1]) },
                                        );
  $o1->new($intrinsic, $synthetic);
}
```

Adding constraints is performed by add_equations(), which is inherited from Equation.

As with tuples, multiplying a feature by a constant is trivial, since it's the same as scale():

```
sub mul_feature_con {
    my ($o, $c) = @_;
    $o->scale($c->value);
}
```

Adding a feature to a constant isn't hard, once we decide what it should mean. The current version of linogram adds the constant to each synthetic constraint. This happens to be correct for features that represent numbers, since, as we'll see, they have a single synthetic constraint with label "". But it doesn't make much sense for most other features. Probably this function should contain a type check to make sure that its feature argument represents a scalar, but that isn't present in this version:

```
sub add_feature_con {
    my ($o, $c) = @_;
    my $v = $c->value;
    my $synthetic = $o->synthetic->apply(sub { $_[0]->add_constant($v) });
    $o->new($o->intrinsic, $synthetic);
}
```

Once again, the intrinsic constraints don't participate in arithmetic, so they're unchanged.

The final method is for adding a feature to a tuple. We use the apply_hash() function that was specifically intended for adding features to tuples. Its callback argument is complicated by the fact that tuple components might not be simple numbers. If the component *is* a simple number (a Value::Constant object), then we use the add_constant() method as in the previous function:

```
sub add_feature_tuple {
    my ($o, $t) = @_;
    my $synthetic =
        $o->synthetic->apply_hash($t->to_hash,
                              sub {
                                  my ($constr, $comp) = @_;
                                  my $kind = $comp->kindof;
                                  if ($kind eq "CONSTANT") {
                                      $constr->add_constant($comp->value);
```

If the tuple component is a feature, we assume that it's a scalar, which has only a single constraint, with label "":

```
      } elsif ($kind eq "FEATURE") {
        $constr->add_equations($comp->synthetic->constraint(""));
```

If the tuple component is another tuple, we croak, because that's not allowed. This freak tuple should have been forbidden earlier, but there's little harm in adding more than one check for the same thing:

```
      } elsif ($kind eq "TUPLE") {
        die "Tuple with subtuple component";
      } else {
        die "Unknown tuple component type '$kind'
      }
    },
  );
  $o->new($o->intrinsic, $synthetic);
}


1;
```

Once again, the intrinsic constraints are unchanged because they don't participate in arithmetic.

9.4.3 Feature Types

Where do the constraints come from? If the equation solver is the heart of linogram, then its liver is the parser, which parses the input specification, including the constraint equations. The result of parsing is a hierarchy of feature types such as box and line. These are Perl objects from the class Type. Each type of feature is represented by a Type object, which records the sub-features, the constraints, and the other properties of that kind of feature object.

   To construct a new type, we call Type::new:

```
package Type;

sub new {
  my ($old, $name, $parent) = @_;
  my $class = ref $old || $old;
```

```
    my $self = {N => $name, P => $parent, C => [],
                O => {}, D => [],
               };
    bless $self => $class;
  }
```

$name is the name of the new type. $parent is optional, and, if present, is a Type object representing the type from which the new type is extended. For example, the parent of vline is line; the parent of line is undefined. The parent type is stored under member P for "parent"; the name is stored under N.

The other members of the Type object are:

- **C**: The constraints defined for the object.

- **O**: The sub-features of the type. This is a hash. The keys are the names of the sub-features, and the values are the Type objects representing the types of the sub-features.

- **D**: A list of "drawables," either Perl code references or sub-feature names.

SCALAR TYPES

Type has a subclass, Type::Scalar, which represents trivial types, such as number, that have no constraints and no sub-features. linogram has no scalar types other than number, but a future version might introduce some.

Sometimes these types behave a little differently from compound types such as points and boxes, so it's convenient to put their methods into a separate class. One principal difference is the trivial is_scalar method, which returns true for a scalar type object and false for a nonscalar object. Type::Scalar also overrides the methods that are used to install constraints and sub-features into type objects:

```
        package Type::Scalar;
        @Type::Scalar::ISA = 'Type';
        sub is_scalar { 1 }

        sub add_constraint {
          die "Added constraint to scalar type";
        }

        sub add_subfeature {
          die "Added subfeature to scalar type";
        }
```

We should never be extending scalar types like number with sub-features or constraints, so overriding these methods provides us with early warning if something is going terribly wrong.

Type METHODS

The simplest Type method says that types are not scalars, except when the method is overridden by the Type::Scalar version of the method:

```
package Type;

sub is_scalar { 0 }
```

Many of the accessor methods on Type objects are straightforward; for example:

```
sub parent { $_[0]{P} }
```

But in some cases, an accessor needs to be referred up the derivation chain to the parent type. For example, a vline has a sub-feature named start, but it's not stored in the type object for vline; it's inherited from line. So if we want find out about the type of the start sub-feature of vline, we must search in line. Moreover, a vline has a sub-feature named start.x, which is the x sub-feature of the start sub-feature. The subfeature method handles all of these situations:

```
sub subfeature {
  my ($self, $name, $nocroak) = @_;
  return $self unless defined $name;
  my ($basename, $suffix) = split /\./, $name, 2;
  if (exists $_[0]{O}{$basename}) {
    return $_[0]{O}{$basename}->subfeature($suffix);
  } elsif (my $parent = $self->parent) {
    $parent->subfeature($name);
  } elsif ($nocroak) {
    return;
  } else {
    Carp::croak("Asked for nonexistent subfeature '$name' of type '$self->{N}'");
  }
}
```

`$type->subfeature($name)` returns the type of the sub-feature of `$type` with name `$name`. If `$name` is a compound name, which contains a dot, it is split into a `$basename` (the component before the first dot) and a `$suffix` (everything after the first dot); the `$basename` is looked up directly, and the `$suffix` is referred to a recursive call to `subfeature`. If the specified type does not contain a sub-feature with the appropriate basename, then its parent object is consulted instead. If there is no parent type, then the requested sub-feature doesn't exist, and the function croaks. This is because the error is most likely to be caused by an incorrect specification in the drawing, asking for a nonexistent sub-feature. To disable the croaking behavior, the user of the function can pass the optional third parameter, which makes the function return false instead. An example of this is the simple `has_subfeature` method, which returns true if the target has a sub-feature of the specified name, and false if not:

```
sub has_subfeature
  {
    my ($self, $name) = @_;
    defined($self->subfeature($name, "don't croak"));
  }
```

The recursion in `subfeature()` is in two different directions. Sometimes we recurse from a feature to one of its sub-features, and sometimes we recurse up the type inheritance tree to the parent type. Suppose `$box`, `$hline`, `$line`, `$point`, and `$number` are the Type objects that represent the indicated types. Let's see how the call `$box->subfeature("top.start.x")` is resolved:

```
$box->subfeature("top.start.x")
```

`$box` has a sub-feature called `"top"`, which is an `hline`, so the call is referred to the sub-feature type:

```
$hline->subfeature("start.x");
```

`$hline` has no sub-feature called `"start"`, so the call is referred to the parent type:

```
$line->subfeature("start.x");
```

`$line` does have a sub-feature called `"start"`, which is a `point`, so the call is referred to the sub-feature type:

```
$point->subfeature("x");
```

$point does have a sub-feature called "x", which is a number, so the call is referred to the sub-feature type:

```
$number->subfeature(undef);
```

The call reaches the base case and returns $number, which is indeed the type of the top.start.x feature of box.

A similar process occurs in the Type::constraints method, which delivers an array of all the constraints of a type, including those implied by the sub-features and the parent type:

```
sub constraints {
  my $self = shift;
```

First the function obtains the constraints inherent in the type itself:

```
my @constraints = @{$self->{C}};
```

Then it obtains the constraints that are inherited from the parent type, and, via recursion, from all the ancestor types:

```
my $p = $self->parent;
if (defined $p) { push @constraints, @{$p->constraints} }
```

Then it obtains the constraints that it gets from its sub-features, including any constraints that *they* inherit from their ancestor types:

```
while (my ($name, $type) = each %{$self->{O}}) {
  my @subconstraints = @{$type->constraints};
  push @constraints, map $_->qualify($name), @subconstraints;
}
\@constraints;
}
```

constraint_set() is the same, except that it returns a Constraint_Set object instead of a raw array reference:

```
sub constraint_set {
  my $self = shift;
  Constraint_Set->new(@{$self->constraints});
}
```

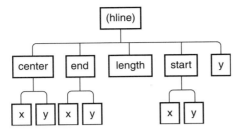

FIGURE 9.5   The subfeatures of a feature form a tree structure.

These constraints are precisely the intrinsic constraints that are used by
Value::Feature objects, so we have:

```
sub intrinsic_constraints {
  my $constraints = $_[0]->constraints;
  Intrinsic_Constraint_Set->new(@$constraints);
}
```

The new_from_type method of Value::Feature actually wants the *qualified*
intrinsic constraints:

```
sub qualified_intrinsic_constraints {
  $_[0]->intrinsic_constraints->qualify($_[1]);
}
```

As usual, the synthetic constraints for a type are rather more interesting. In
the absence of any other information, an expression like P is interpreted as the
constraint $P = 0$. Later, the $P = 0$ might be combined with a $Q = 0$ to
produce $P + Q = 0$ or $P - Q = 0$, and we'll see that we can treat $P = Q$ as
if it were $P - Q = 0$. So figuring out the synthetic constraints for a type like
point involves locating all the scalar type subfeatures of point, and then setting
each one to 0.

The recursive auxiliary method all_leaf_subfeatures() recovers the
names of all the scalar sub-features of the given type (see Figure 9.5). Its name
refers to the fact that the sub-feature relation makes each type into a tree. The
scalar sub-features are the leaves of the tree.

```
sub all_leaf_subfeatures {
  my $self = shift;
  my @all;
  my %base = $self->subfeatures;
  while (my ($name, $type) = each %base) {
```

```
        push @all, map {$_ eq "" ? $name : "$name.$_"}
            $type->all_leaf_subfeatures;
      }
      @all;
    }
```

The function starts by getting all the direct sub-features. These include those defined directly by the target type and also those defined by its ancestor types. Some of these sub-features might be compound features and have sub-features of their own, and some might be leaves. The function loops over them to do the recursion on each one. It qualifies the names appropriately and adds the information to the result array. The special case in the map is to avoid extra periods from appearing at the end of the key names in some cases.

To build the synthetic constraint set for a particular type, we locate all the scalar sub-features and make a constraint for each one. If *name* is the name of a scalar subfeature, we introduce the synthetic constraint that has *name* = 0 with label *name*:

```
    sub synthetic_constraints {
      my @subfeatures = $_[0]->all_leaf_subfeatures;
      Synthetic_Constraint_Set->new(map {$_ => Constraint->new($_ => 1)}
                                        @subfeatures
                                      );
    }

    sub qualified_synthetic_constraints {
      $_[0]->synthetic_constraints->qualify($_[1]);
    }
```

All but one of the remaining Type methods are accessors, most of them fairly simple:

```
    sub add_drawable {
      my ($self, $drawable) = @_;
      push @{$self->{D}}, $drawable;
    }
```

subfeatures() returns all the direct sub-features of a type, but not the sub-sub-features. For box, it will return top and nw, but not top.center or nw.y:

```
    sub subfeatures {
      my $self = shift;
```

```
  my %all;
  while ($self) {
    %all = (%{$self->{O}}, %all);
    $self = $self->parent;
  }
  %all;
}
```

The function that retrieves the list of drawable sub-features and drawing functions for a type recurses up the type inheritance tree using subfeatures(). It doesn't need to recurse into the sub-features, because the drawing method will do that itself. We'll see the drawing method later; here's the drawables() method, which returns a list of the drawables:

```
sub drawables {
  my ($self) = @_;
  return @{$self->{D}} if $self->{D} && @{$self->{D}};
  if (my $p = $self->parent) {
    my @drawables = $p->drawables;
    return @drawables if @drawables;
  }

  my %subfeature = $self->subfeatures;
  my @drawables = grep ! $subfeature{$_}->is_scalar, keys %subfeature;
  @drawables;
}
```

If the type definition contains an explicit drawable list, the method returns it. If not, it uses the drawable list of its parent object, if it has one. If the type has no parent type, the method generates and returns the default, which is a list of all the sub-features that aren't scalars. There's no point returning scalars, since they're not drawable, so they're filtered out.

New sub-features are installed into a type with add_subfeature(). Its arguments are a name and a sub-feature type:

```
sub add_subfeature {
  my ($self, $name, $type) = @_;
  $self->{O}{$name} = $type;
}
```

Similarly, new constraints are installed into a type with add_constraints(). Its arguments are Value::Feature objects. The method extracts the constraints from the values and inserts them into the `Type` object:

```
sub add_constraints {
  my ($self, @values) = @_;
  for my $value (@values) {
    next unless $value->kindof eq 'FEATURE';
    push @{$self->{C}},
      $value->intrinsic->constraints,
      $value->synthetic->constraints;
  }
}
```

I've left the most important `Type` method for the end. It's the most important method in the entire program, because it's the method that actually draws the picture. Its primary argument is a `Type` object. When invoked for the root type, it draws the entire picture. It's a little longer than the other methods, so we'll see it a bit at a time:

```
sub draw {
  my ($self, $env) = @_;
```

The primary argument, `$self`, is the type to draw. The other argument is an *environment*, which belongs to an `Environment` class we didn't see. The environment is nothing more than a hash with the names and values of the solutions of the constraints.[1] The initial call to draw(), which draws the root feature, omits the environment, because the equations haven't been solved yet; the missing `$env` parameter triggers draw() to solve the equations:

```
unless ($env) {
  my $equations = $self->constraint_set;
  my %solutions = $equations->values;
  $env = Environment->new(%solutions);
}
```

The rest of the function does the actual drawing. It scans the list of drawables for the feature being drawn. If the drawable is a reference to an actual drawing

---

[1] In an earlier version of this program, the environment parameter was more interesting. Features could contain local variables that didn't participate in the constraint solving (and which therefore didn't have to be linear) and parameters passed in from the containing feature. In the interests of clear exposition, I trimmed these features out.

function, the function is invoked, and is passed the environment:

```
for my $name ($self->drawables) {
  if (ref $name) {              # actually a coderef, not a name
    $name->($env);
```

Otherwise, the drawable is the name of a sub-feature on which the draw() method is recursively called. The function recovers the type of the sub-feature. It also uses the Environment::subset() method to construct a new environment that contains only the variables relevant to that sub-feature:

```
  } else {
    my $type = $self->subfeature($name);
    my $subenv = $env->subset($name);
    $type->draw($subenv);
  }
}
}

1;
```

For completeness, here is Environment::subset():

CODE LIBRARY
Environment.pm

```
package Environment;
sub subset {
  my ($self, $name) = @_;
  my %result;
  for my $k (keys %$self) {
    my $kk = $k;
    if ($kk =~ s/^\Q$name.//) {
      $result{$kk} = $self->{$k};
    }
  }
  $self->new(%result);
}
```

9.4.4 The Parser

We're now ready to see the core of linogram, which is the parser that parses drawing specifications. First, the lexer, which is straightforward:

CODE LIBRARY
linogram.pl

```
use Parser ':all';
use Lexer ':all';
```

```
    my $input = sub { read INPUT, my($buf), 8192 or return; $buf };

    my @keywords = map [uc($_), qr/\b$_\b/],
      qw(constraints define extends draw);

    my $tokens = iterator_to_stream(
      make_lexer($input,
                 @keywords,
                 ['ENDMARKER',  qr/__END__.*/s,
                  sub {
                    my $s = shift;
                    $s =~ s/^__END__\s*//;
                    ['ENDMARKER', $s]
                  } ],
                 ['IDENTIFIER', qr/[a-zA-Z_]\w*/],
                 ['NUMBER', qr/(?: \d+ (?: \.\d*)?
                                 | \.\d+)
                                (?: [eE]  \d+)? /x ],
                 ['FUNCTION',   qr/&/],
                 ['DOT',        qr/\./],
                 ['COMMA',      qr/,/],
                 ['OP',         qr|[-+*/]|],
                 ['EQUALS',     qr/=/],
                 ['LPAREN',     qr/[(]/],
                 ['RPAREN',     qr/[)]/],
                 ['LBRACE',     qr/[{]/],
                 ['RBRACE',     qr/[}]\n*/],
                 ['TERMINATOR', qr/;\n*/],
                 ['WHITESPACE', qr/\s+/, sub { "" }],
      ));
```

Only a few of these need comment. IDENTIFIER is a simple variable name, such as box or start. Compound names like start.x will be assembled later, by the parser.

ENDMARKER consists of the sequence __END__ and *all* the following text up to the end of the file. The lexer preprocesses this to delete the __END__ itself, leaving only the following text.

Several similar definitions for the CONSTRAINTS, DEFINE, EXTENDS, and DRAW tokens are generated programmatically, and are inserted at the beginning of the lexer definition via the @keywords array.

Whitespace, as in earlier parsers, is discarded.

PARSER EXTENSIONS

The parser module used in `linogram` is based on our functional parser library of Chapter 8, with some additions. Suppose that `$A` and `$B` are parsers. Recall the following features supplied by the parser of Chapter 8:

- `empty()` is a parser that consumes no tokens and always succeeds.

- `$A - $B` ("*A*, then *B*") is a parser that matches whatever `$A` matches, consuming the appropriate tokens, and then applies `$B` to the remaining input, possibly consuming more tokens. It succeeds only if both `$A` and `$B` succeed in sequence.

- `$A | $B` ("*A* or *B*") is a parser that tries to apply `$A` to its input, and, if that doesn't work, tries `$B` instead. It succeeds if either of `$A` or `$B` succeeds.

- `star($A)` matches zero or more occurrences of whatever `$A` matches; it is equivalent to `empty() | $A - star($A)`.

- `_(...)` is a synonym for `lookfor([...])`, which builds a parser that looks for a single token of the indicated kind. If the next token is of the correct kind, it is consumed and the parser succeeds; otherwise the parser fails.

- `$A >> $coderef` is a synonym for `T($A, $coderef)`, a parser that applies `$A` to its input stream, and then uses `$coderef` to transform the result returned by `$A` into a different form. It assumes that `$A` is a concatenation of other parsers.

To these operations, we'll add a few extras:

- `option($item)` indicates that the syntax matched by the `$item` parser is optional. It builds a parser equivalent to:

    ```
    $item | empty()
    ```

- `labeledblock($label, $contents)` is for matching labeled blocks like:

    ```
    draw {
      ...
    }
    ```

    and:

    ```
    define line {
      ...
    }
    ```

It's equivalent to:

```
$label - _('LBRACE') - star($contents) -_('RBRACE')
    >> sub { [ $_[0], @{$_[2]} ] }
```

- `commalist($item, $separator)` is for matching comma-separated lists of items. The `$separator` defaults to `_('COMMA')`. It is otherwise equivalent to:

```
$item - star($separator - $item >> sub { $_[1] })
        - option($separator)
    >> sub { [ $_[0], @{$_[1]} ] }
```

The first `sub` throws away the values associated with the separators, leaving only the values of the items. The second `sub` accumulates all the item values into a single array, which is the value returned by the `commalist` parser.

- `$parser > $coderef` is like `$parser >> $coderef`, except that it doesn't assume that `$parser` is a concatenation. Instead of assuming that the value returned by `$parser` is an array reference, and passing the elements of the array to the coderef, it passes the value returned by `$parser` directly to `$coderef` as a single argument.

- `$parser / $condition` is like `$parser`, with a side condition on the result. It runs `$parser` as usual, and then passes the resulting value to the coderef in `$condition`. If the condition returns true, the parser succeeds, and the final result is the same value originally returned by `$parser`. If the coderef returns false, the parser fails.

%TYPES

The main data structure in `linogram` is `%TYPES`, which is a hash that maps known type names to the `Type` objects that represent them. When the program starts, `%TYPES` is initialized with two predefined types:

```
my $ROOT_TYPE = Type->new('ROOT');
my %TYPES = ('number' => Type::Scalar->new('number'),
             'ROOT'   => $ROOT_TYPE,
            );
```

Initially, `linogram` knows about the type `number`, which is a trivial type with no sub-features and no constraints, and the type `ROOT`, which represents the entire diagram.

PROGRAMS

A program in linogram is a series of subtype definitions and feature and constraint declarations which together define the root type. As subtype definitions are encountered, the corresponding Type objects are manufactured and installed in %TYPES. As feature and constraint declarations are encountered, they are installed into the root type object.

The top-level parser looks like this:

```
$program = star($Definition
              | $Declaration
                > sub { add_declarations($ROOT_TYPE, $_[0]) }
              )
            - option($Perl_code) - $End_of_Input
        >> sub {
          $ROOT_TYPE->draw();
        };
```

The $definition parser will take care of manufacturing new type objects and installing them into %TYPES. When a declaration is parsed, add_declarations() will install it into the root type object $ROOT_TYPE. The program may be followed with an optional section of plain Perl code, which is a convenient place to stick auxiliary functions like draw_line. When the parser finishes parsing the entire specification, it invokes the draw method on the root type object, drawing the entire diagram.

$perl_code is an optional section at the end of the drawing specification. It's an arbitrary segment of Perl code, separated from the rest of the specification with the endmarker __END__:

```
$perl_code = _("ENDMARKER") > sub { eval $_[0];
                                    die if $@;
                                  };
```

The lexer has already trimmed off the endmarker itself. The Perl code is then passed to eval, which compiles the Perl code and installs it into the program.

DEFINITIONS

$definition is a parser for a block of the form:

```
define point { ... }
```

or:

```
define hline extends line { ... }
```

We use the `labeledblock` function to construct this parser:

```
$definition = labeledblock($Defheader, $Declaration)
  >> sub { ... } ;
```

`$declaration` is the parser for a declaration, which will see shortly. `$defheader` is the part of the definition block before the curly braces:

```
$defheader = _("DEFINE") - _("IDENTIFIER") - $Extends
  >> sub { ["DEFINITION", @_[1,2] ]};

$extends = option(_("EXTENDS") - _("IDENTIFIER") >> sub { $_[1] }) ;
```

The value from the `$definition` parser is passed to a postprocessing function that is responsible for constructing a new `Type` object and installing it into %TYPES; the code is all straightforward. For a definition that begins `define hline extends line`, `$name` is `hline` and `$extends` is `$line`:

```
$definition = labeledblock($defheader, $Declaration)
  >> sub {
    my ($defheader, @declarations) = @_;
    my ($name, $extends) = @$defheader[1,2];
    my $parent_type = (defined $extends) ? $TYPES{$extends} : undef;
    my $new_type;

    if (exists $TYPES{$name}) {
      lino_error("Type '$name' redefined");
    }
    if (defined $extends && ! defined $parent_type) {
      lino_error("Type '$name' extended from unknown type '$extends'");
    }

    $new_type = Type->new($name, $parent_type);

    add_declarations($new_type, @declarations);

    $TYPES{$name} = $new_type;
  };
```

DECLARATIONS

A declaration takes one of three forms. One is the declaration of one or more sub-features:

```
hline top, bottom;
```

Two others are constraints and draw sections:

```
constraints { ... }
draw { ... }
```

Here's the declaration parser:

```
$declaration = $Type - commalist($Declarator) - _("TERMINATOR")
                  >> sub { ... }
             | $Constraint_section
             | $Draw_section
             ;
```

A $type is the same as an identifier, with the side condition that it must be mentioned in the %TYPES hash:

```
$type = lookfor("IDENTIFIER",
            sub {
            exists($TYPES{$_[0][1]}) || lino_error("Unrecognized type '$_[0][1]'");
            $_[0][1];
            }
          );
```

A declaration might declare more than one variable, as with:

```
hline top, bottom;
```

Each of the sub-parts of the declaration is called a *declarator*; the preceding declaration has two declarators. In its simplest form, a declarator is nothing more than a variable name:

```
$declarator = _("IDENTIFIER")
               - option(_("LPAREN")  - commalist($Param_Spec) - _("RPAREN")
                     >> sub { $_[1] }
                 )
```

```
>> sub {
   { WHAT => 'DECLARATOR',
     NAME => $_[0],
     PARAM_SPECS => $_[1],
   };
};
```

The optional section in the middle is for a parenthesis-delimited list of "parameter specifications." A declarator might look like this:

```
... F(ht=3, wd=boxwid), ...
```

which is equivalent to:

```
... F, ...
F.ht = 3;
F.wd = boxwid;
```

The sub { $_[1] } discards the parentheses; the parameter specifications are packaged into the resulting value under the key PARAM_SPECS. The format of a parameter specification is simple:

```
$param_spec = _("IDENTIFIER") - _("EQUALS") - $Expression
  >> sub {
    { WHAT => "PARAM_SPEC",
      NAME => $_[0],
      VALUE => $_[2],
    }
  }
  ;
```

Thus the value manufactured for the declarator F(ht=3, wd=boxwid) looks like this:

```
{ WHAT => 'DECLARATOR',
  NAME => 'F',
  PARAM_SPECS =>
    [ { WHAT => 'PARAM_SPEC',
        NAME => 'ht',
        VALUE => (expression representing constant 3),
      },
```

```
        { WHAT => 'PARAM_SPEC',
          NAME => 'wd',
          VALUE => (expression representing variable 'boxwid'),
        },
      ]
}
```

We haven't yet seen the representation for expressions.

The `$declaration` parser gets a type name and a list of declarators and manufactures a declaration value; later on, the add_declarations() function will install this declaration into the appropriate Type object. The declaration value is manufactured as follows:

```
$declaration = $Type - commalist($Declarator) - _("TERMINATOR")
            >> sub { my ($type, $decl_list) = @_;
                    unless (exists $TYPES{$type}) {
                        lino_error("Unknown type name '$type' in declaration '@_'\n");
                    }
                    for (@$decl_list) {
                      $_->{TYPE} = $type;
                      check_declarator($TYPES{$type}, $_);
                    }
                    {WHAT => 'DECLARATION',
                     DECLARATORS => $decl_list };
                  }

          ....

      | $Constraint_section
      | $Draw_section
      ;
```

The construction function checks to make sure the type used in the declaration actually exists. It then installs the type into each declarator value, transforming:

```
{ WHAT => 'DECLARATOR',
  NAME => 'F',
  PARAM_SPECS => [ ... ],
}
```

into:

```
{ WHAT => 'DECLARATOR',
  NAME => 'F',
  PARAM_SPECS => [ ... ],
  TYPE => $type,
}
```

Each declarator is also checked to make sure the names in its parameter specifications are actually the names of sub-features of its type. box F(ht=3) passes the check, but box F(age=34) fails, because boxes don't have ages. This check is performed by check_declarator():

```
sub check_declarator {
  my ($type, $declarator) = @_;
  for my $pspec (@{$declarator->{PARAM_SPECS}}) {
    my $name = $pspec->{NAME};
    unless ($type->has_subfeature($name)) {
      lino_error("Declaration of '$declarator->{NAME}' "
                . "specifies unknown subfeature '$name' "
                . "for type '$type->{N}'\n");
    }
  }
}
```

Declarator values are combined into declaration values; a typical declaration value, for the declaration box C, F(ht=3, wd=boxwid);, looks like this:

```
{ WHAT => 'DECLARATION',
  DECLARATORS =>
    [ { WHAT => 'DECLARATOR',
        NAME => 'C',
        PARAM_SPECS => [],
        TYPE => 'box',
      },
      { WHAT => 'DECLARATOR',
        NAME => 'F',
        PARAM_SPECS =>
          [ { WHAT => 'PARAM_SPEC',
              NAME => 'ht',
```

```
                VALUE => (expression representing constant 3),
            },
            { WHAT => 'PARAM_SPEC',
              NAME => 'wd',
              VALUE => (expression representing variable 'boxwid')
            },
        ]
      TYPE => 'box',
    },
  ]
}
```

The other two kinds of declarations we've seen before have been constraint and draw sections, which have their own productions in the grammar:

```
$declaration = ...
              | $Constraint_section
              | $Draw_section
              ;
```

The overall structure of a constraint section is a block, labeled with the word constraints:

```
$constraint_section = labeledblock(_("CONSTRAINTS"), $Constraint)
  >> sub { shift;
            { WHAT => 'CONSTRAINTS', CONSTRAINTS => [@_] }
        };
```

A constraint is simply an equation, which is a pair of expressions with an equal sign between them:

```
$constraint = $Expression - _("EQUALS") - $Expression - _("TERMINATOR")
  >> sub { Expression->new('-', $_[0], $_[2]) } ;
```

The value of the constraint is not actually a Constraint object, but rather an Expression object. Since the constraint $A = B$ is semantically equivalent to $A - B = 0$, we compile it into an expression that represents A - B and leave it at that. The finished value for a constraint section, say for:

```
constraints { start.x = end.x;
              start.x = x;
              start.y + height = end.y;
}
```

is the hash:

```
{ WHAT => 'CONSTRAINTS',
  CONSTRAINTS =>
    [ (expression representing start.x - end.x),
      (expression representing start.x - x),
      (expression representing start.y + height - end.y),
    ]
}
```

The third sort of declaration is a draw section, which might look like this:

```
draw { &draw_line; }
```

or like this:

```
draw { top; bottom; left; right; }
```

Once again, it is a labeled block, very similar to the definition of the constraint section:

```
$draw_section = labeledblock(_("DRAW"), $Drawable)
  >> sub { shift; { WHAT => 'DRAWABLES', DRAWABLES => [@_] } };
```

Since there are two possible formats for a drawable, however, the definition of $drawable is a little more complicated than the definition of $constraint:

```
$drawable = $Name - _("TERMINATOR")
              >> sub { { WHAT => 'NAMED_DRAWABLE',
                         NAME => $_[1],
                       }
                     }
          | _("FUNCTION") - _("IDENTIFIER") - _("TERMINATOR")
              >> sub { my $ref = \&{$_[1]};
                       { WHAT => 'FUNCTIONAL_DRAWABLE',
                         REF => $ref,
                         NAME => $_[1],
                       };
                     };
```

The first clause handles the case where the drawable is the name of a sub-feature of the feature being defined, say top;. In this case we construct the value:

```
{ WHAT => 'NAMED_DRAWABLE',
  NAME => 'top',
}
```

The other clause handles the case where the drawable is the name of a Perl function, say &draw_line;. In this case we construct the value:

```
{ WHAT => 'FUNCTIONAL_DRAWABLE',
  NAME => 'draw_line',
  REF => \&draw_line,
}
```

The NAME member here is just for debugging purposes; only the reference is actually used. Drawables of both types may be mixed in the same draw section. A draw section like draw { top; &draw_line; } turns into the value:

```
{ WHAT => 'DRAWABLES',
  DRAWABLES => [ { WHAT => 'NAMED_DRAWABLE',
                   NAME => 'TOP',
                 },
                 { WHAT => 'FUNCTIONAL_DRAWABLE',
                   NAME => 'draw_line',
                   REF => \&draw_line,
                 },
               ]
}
```

When a complete type definition has been parsed, several values will be available: the type name; the name of the parent type, if there is one; and the list of declarations. The parser function manufactures a new type object from class Type, and calls add_declarations() to install the declarations into the new object.

add_declarations() is rather complicated, because it has many different branches to handle the different kinds of declarations. Each branch individually is simple, which argues for a dispatch table structure:

```
my %add_decl = ('DECLARATION' => \&add_subfeature_declaration,
                'CONSTRAINTS' => \&add_constraint_declaration,
                'DRAWABLES' => \&add_draw_declaration,
```

```
                          'DEFAULT' =>  sub {
                             lino_error("Unknown declaration kind '$[1]{WHAT}'");
                          },
                        );

    sub add_declarations {
      my ($type, @declarations) = @_;

      for my $declaration (@declarations) {
        my $decl_kind = $declaration->{WHAT};
        my $func = $add_decl{$decl_kind} || $add_decl{DEFAULT};
        $func->($type, $declaration);
      }
    }
```

Sub-feature declarations to `Type` objects are added by this function, which loops over the declarators, adding them one at a time:

```
    sub add_subobj_declaration {
      my ($type, $declaration) = @_;
      my $declarators = $declaration->{DECLARATORS};
      for my $decl (@$declarators) {
        my $name = $decl->{NAME};
        my $decl_type = $decl->{TYPE};
        my $decl_type_obj = $TYPES{$decl_type};
```

`$decl_type` is the name of the type of the sub-feature being declared; `$decl_type_obj` is the `Type` object that represents that type. The first thing the function does is record the name and the type of the new sub-feature:

```
        $type->add_subfeature($name, $decl_type_obj);
```

Unless the declarator came with parameter specifications, the function is done. If there were parameter specifications, the function turns them into constraints and adds them to the type's list of constraints:

```
        for my $pspec (@{$decl->{PARAM_SPECS}}) {
          my $pspec_name = $pspec->{NAME};
          my $constraints = convert_param_specs($type, $name, $pspec);
          $type->add_constraints($constraints);
        }
      }
    }
```

convert_param_specs() turns the parameter specifications into constraints. We'll see this function later, after we've discussed the way in which expressions are turned into constraints.

```
sub add_constraint_declaration {
  my ($type, $declaration) = @_;
  my $constraint_expressions = $declaration->{CONSTRAINTS};
  my @constraints
    = map expression_to_constraints($type, $_),
        @$constraint_expressions;
  $type->add_constraints(@constraints);
}
```

This function is invoked to install a constraints block into a type object. The contents of the constraints block have been turned into Expression objects, but these objects are still essentially abstract syntax trees, and haven't yet been turned into constraints. The function expression_to_constraints() performs that conversion. add_constraints() then inserts the new constraints into the type object's constraint list. We'll see expression_to_constraints() later, along with the other functions that deal with expressions.

The third sort of declaration is a draw section, whose contents are drawables. These are installed into a type object by add_draw_declaration():

```
sub add_draw_declaration {
  my ($type, $declaration) = @_;
  my $drawables = $declaration->{DRAWABLES};

  for my $d (@$drawables) {
    my $drawable_type = $d->{WHAT};
    if ($drawable_type eq "NAMED_DRAWABLE") {
      unless ($type->has_subfeature($d->{NAME})) {
        lino_error("Unknown drawable feature '$d->{NAME}'
      }
      $type->add_drawable($d->{NAME});
    } elsif ($drawable_type eq "FUNCTIONAL_DRAWABLE") {
      $type->add_drawable($d->{REF});
    } else {
      lino_error("Unknown drawable type '$type'");
    }
  }
}
```

There are two branches here, for the two kinds of drawables. One is a functional drawable, typified by &draw_line; here we insert a reference to the Perl draw_line function into the drawables list. The other kind of drawable is a named drawable, which is the name of a sub-feature; here we insert the name into the drawables list. The only real difference in handling is that we make sure that the name of a named drawable is already known.

EXPRESSIONS

The expression parser is similar to the ones we saw in Chapter 8. Its output is essentially an abstract syntax tree, blessed into the Expression class. Expressions appear in constraints and on the right-hand sides of parameter specifications. The grammar is:

```
$expression = operator($Term,
                       [_('OP', '+'), sub { Expression->new('+', @_) } ],
                       [_('OP', '-'), sub { Expression->new('-', @_) } ],
                      );


$term = operator($Atom,
                 [_('OP', '*'), sub { Expression->new('*', @_) } ],
                 [_('OP', '/'), sub { Expression->new('/', @_) } ],
                );
```

which is nothing new. Expressions, as mentioned before, are nothing more than abstract syntax trees. Expression::new() is trivial:

```
package Expression;

sub new {
  my ($base, $op, @args) = @_;
  my $class = ref $base || $base;
  unless (exists $eval_op{$op}) {
    die "Unknown operator '$op' in expression '$op @args'\n";
  }
  bless [ $op, @args ] => $class;
}
```

The $atom parser accepts the usual numbers and parenthesized compound expressions. But there are a few additional atoms of interest:

```
package main;

$atom = $Name
      | $Tuple
      | lookfor("NUMBER", sub { Expression->new('CON', $_[0][1]) })
      | _('OP', '-') - $Expression
          >> sub { Expression->new('-', Expression->new('CON', 0), $_[1]) }
      | _("LPAREN") - $Expression - _("RPAREN") >> sub {$_[1]};
```

The _('OP', '-') production handles unary minus expressions such as -A; this is compiled as if it had been written 0-A.

$name is a variable name, possibly a compound variable name containing dots; it is turned into an expression object containing ['VAR', $varname]:

```
$name = $Base_name
      - star(_("DOT") - _("IDENTIFIER") >> sub { $_[1] })
      > sub { Expression->new('VAR', join(".", $_[0], @{$_[1]})) }
      ;

$base_name = _"IDENTIFIER";
```

Similarly, a number is turned into an expression object containing ['CON', $number]. (CON is an abbreviation for "constant.")

$tuple is a tuple expression, which we saw before in connection with the constraint:

```
plus = F + (hspc, 0);
```

The (hspc, 0) is a tuple expression. Syntactically, a tuple is a parenthesized, comma-separated list of expressions. But its parser has some interesting features:

```
$tuple = _("LPAREN")
       - commalist($Expression) / sub { @{$_[0]} > 1 }
       - _("RPAREN")
```

The side condition sub { @{$_[0]} > 1 } requires that the comma-separated list have more than one value in it. This prevents something like (3) from ever being parsed as a 1-tuple.

The value of the tuple expression is generated as follows:

```
>> sub {
  my ($explist) = $_[1];
  my $N = @$explist;
  my @axis = qw(x y z);
  if ($N == 2 || $N == 3) {
    return [ 'TUPLE',
              { map { $axis[$_] => $explist->[$_] } (0 .. $N-1) }
           ];
  } else {
    lino_error("$N-tuples are not supported \n");
  }
} ;
```

This does two things. First, it checks to make sure that the tuple has exactly two or three elements. For two-dimensional diagrams, only 2-tuples make sense.

3-tuples are supported because linogram might as easily be used for three-dimensional diagrams. One would have to write another standard library, including definitions like:

```
define point { number x, y, z; }
```

and with replacement drawing functions that understood about perspective. But once this was done, linogram would handle three-dimensional diagrams as well as it handles two-dimensional ones. Many of the standard library definitions would remain exactly the same. For example, the definition of line would not need to change; a line is determined by its two endpoints, regardless of whether those endpoints are considered to be points in two or three dimensions. n-tuples for n larger than three are forbidden until someone thinks of a use for them.

The value returned from the tuple parser for a tuple such as (5, 12) is:

```
[ 'TUPLE',
  { x => 5,
    y => 12,
  }
]
```

For 3-tuples, there is an additional z member of the hash. The special treatment of the names x, y, and z comes ultimately from here.

The result of parsing an expression, as mentioned before, is an abstract syntax tree. For the expression x + 2 * y, the tree is:

```
[ '+', ['VAR', 'x'],
       ['*', ['CON', 2],
             ['VAR', 'y'],
       ],
]
```

which should be familiar.

When constraint and parameter declarations are processed, they contain these raw Expression objects. Later, expressions need to be converted to constraints. This is probably the most complicated part of the program. The process of conversion is essentially evaluation, except that instead of producing a number result, the result is an object from class Value. This evaluation is performed by the function expression_to_constraints():

```
sub expression_to_constraints {
    my ($context, $expr) = @_;
```

Variables in an expression have associated types, and to map from a variable's name to its type we need a context. To see why, consider the following example:

```
define type_A {
   number age;
   age = 4;
}

define type_B {
   box age;
   age = 4;
}
```

The constraint age = 4 in the first definition makes sense, but the same constraint in the second definition does not make sense because 4 is not a box. More generally, the meaning of a constraint might depend in a complex way on the types of the variables it contains. So expression_to_constraints requires a context that maps variable names to their types. This is nothing more than a Type object; the mapping is performed by Type::subfeature().

Continuing with the evaluation function:

```
unless (defined $expr) {
  Carp::croak("Missing expression in 'expression_to_constraints'");
}
my ($op, @s) = @$expr;
```

Here we break up the top-level expression into an operator $op and zero or more subexpressions, @s. We then switch on the operator type. It might be a variable, a constant, a tuple, or some binary operator such as + or *:

```
if ($op eq 'VAR') {
  my $name = $s[0];
  return Value::Feature->new_from_var($name, $context->subfeature($name));
```

If it's a variable, we build a new Value::Feature object of the indicated name and type. new_from_var(), which we saw earlier, is responsible for manufacturing the appropriate set of constraints.

```
} elsif ($op eq 'CON') {
  return Value::Constant->new($s[0]);
```

If the expression is a constant, the code is simple; we build a Value::Constant object.

Tuples are where things start to get interesting. As we saw earlier, tuples are *not* required to be constants; (hspc + 3, 2 * top.start.y) is a perfectly legitimate tuple. Since the components of a tuple may be arbitrary expressions, we call expression_to_constraints() recursively:

```
} elsif ($op eq 'TUPLE') {
  my %components;
  for my $k (keys %{$s[0]}) {
    $components{$k} = expression_to_constraints($context, $s[0]{$k});
  }
  return Value::Tuple->new(%components);
}
```

There should probably be a check here to make sure that the resulting component values are not themselves tuples. At present, ((1, 2), (3, 4)), which is illegal, is not diagnosed until later, when the malformed tuple participates in an arithmetic operation.

If the argument expression was neither a tuple, a variable, nor a constant, then it's a compound expression. We start by evaluating the two operands:

```
my $e1 = expression_to_constraints($context, $s[0]);
my $e2 = expression_to_constraints($context, $s[1]);
```

We then dispatch an appropriate method to combine the two operands into a single expression. When the operator is +, we use the add method, and so on:

```
my %opmeth = ('+' => 'add',
              '-' => 'sub',
              '*' => 'mul',
              '/' => 'div',
             );

my $meth = $opmeth{$op};
if (defined $meth) {
  return $e1->$meth($e2);
} else {
  lino_error("Unknown operator '$op' in AST");
}
}
```

This is what connects the parser with the arithmetic functions from class Value.

The one important function we haven't seen is convert_param_specs(), which takes the parameter specifications in a declaration like hline L(end=Q+R) and converts them to constraints. The arguments are a context, the sub-feature type (hline in the example), and a parameter specification value, something like:

```
{ WHAT => 'PARAM_SPEC',
  NAME => 'end',
  VALUE => [ '+', ['VAR', 'Q'],
                  ['VAR', 'R'],
           ],
}
```

The only fine point here is that parameter specifications are asymmetric. The name end on the left side is interpreted as a sub-feature of L, but the named Q and R on the right side are interpreted as sub-features of the outer context in which L is being defined. convert_param_specs() builds a new Value::Feature object for the left side by making two calls to subfeature(), one to find

the type of the feature that's being defined, L in the example, and then one
more to find the type of the parameter name, end in the example. It uses the
expression_to_constraints() function to convert the right-hand side, and then
subtracts right from left to produce the final constraint:

```
sub convert_param_specs {
  my ($context, $subobj, $pspec) = @_;
  my @constraints;
  my $left = Value::Feature->new_from_var("$subobj." . $pspec->{NAME},
                                 $context->subfeature($subobj)
                                 ->subfeature($pspec->{NAME})
                                );
  my $right = expression_to_constraints($context, $pspec->{VALUE});
  return $left->sub($right);
}
```

Our walk through the code is now complete.

9.4.5   Missing Features

linogram is missing a few valuable features. Some are easier to fix than others.
It doesn't support varying thickness lines, colored lines, or filled boxes. These
are easy to add, and in fact an earlier version of linogram supports them; I took
the feature out for pedagogical reasons. The technical support for the feature was
to allow "parameter" declarations, like this:

```
define line {
  point x, y;
  param number thickness = 1;
  param string color = "black";
  draw { &draw_line; }
}
```

A parameter is just another sub-feature, except that it doesn't participate in
the system of linear equations. Like any other sub-feature, it may be constrained
by the root feature or some other feature that includes it. The following root
feature definition draws a vertical black line crossed by a horizontal red line:

```
vline v;
hline h(color="red");
constraints { v.center = h.center; }
```

The color="red" parameter specification overrides the default of "black". The parameter values are then included in the environment hash that is passed to the drawing functions. When draw_line sees that the color is specified as "red" it is responsible for drawing a red line instead of a black one.

With the parameter feature, we can support the placement of objects that contain text:

```
define text extends box {
  param string text = "";
  param number font_size = 9;
  param string font = "courier";
  draw { &draw_text }
}
```

and now we have something that has a top, bottom, left, northwest corner, and so forth, like a box, but whose four sides are invisible. Instead, the draw_text function is responsible for placing the text appropriately, or for issuing an error message if it doesn't fit.

The value of a parameter must be completely determined before the constraint system is solved, either by a declaration like hline h(color="red"), or by a specified default. If neither is present, it is a fatal error.

Parameters can be used for other applications:

```
define marked_line extends vline {
  hline mark;
  param number markpos = 50;
  constraints {
    mark.length = 0.02;
    mark.center = (center.x, start.y + markpos/100 * height);
  }
}
```

This defines a feature that is a vertical line with a horizontal tick mark across it. By default, the tick mark is halfway up the line, but this depends on the value of *markpos*, which can be between 0 and 100 to indicate a percentage of the way to the end of the vline. If *markpos* is 100, the tick mark is at the end of the vline; if *markpos* is 75, the tick mark is one-quarter of the way from the end.

If *markpos* were not a param, the definition would be illegal, because the expression markpos/100 * height is nonlinear. But parameters do not participate in linear-equation solving. The rules for parameters say that *markpos* must be specified somewhere before the equation solving begins. Suppose it has been specified to be 75. Then the constraint is effectively:

```
mark.center = (center.x, start.y + 75/100 * height);
```

which *is* linear. This feature lends a great deal of flexibility to the system.

One major feature that is missing is splines. A spline is a curved line whose path is determined by one or more control points. The spline wiggles along, starting at its first control point and heading towards the second, then veering off toward the third, and so on, until it ends at the last control point. The main impediment here is that unlike the other features we've seen, the number of control points of a spline isn't known in advance. We could conceivably get around this by defining a series of spline types:

```
define spline2 {
  point p1, p2;
  draw { &draw_spline; }
}

define spline3 extends spline2 {
  point p3;
}

define spline4 extends spline3 {
  point p4;
}


  . . .
```

but this is awfully clumsy. What linogram really needs to support features like splines and polygons is a way to specify a parametrizable array of features and their associated constraints, perhaps something like this:

```
define polygon(N) {
  point v[N];
  line s[N];
  constraints {
    when j is 1 .. N   { s[j].start = v[j]; }
    when j is 1 .. N-1 { s[j].end   = v[j+1]; }
    s[N].end = v[1];
  }
}
```

There are a few missing syntactic features. A declaration like:

```
number hsize = 12;
```

would be convenient, as would equations with multiple equals signs:

```
A.sw = B.n = C.s;
```

9.5   CONCLUSION

linogram is a substantial application, one that might even be useful. I have been using the venerable pic system, developed at Bell Labs, for years, and it convinced me that defining diagrams by writing a text file of constraints is a good general strategy. But I've never been entirely happy with pic, and I wanted to see what else I could come up with.

I also wanted to finish the book with a serious example that would demonstrate how the techniques we've studied could be integrated into real Perl programs. linogram totals about 1,300 lines of code, counting the parsing system we developed in Chapter 8, but not counting comments, whitespace, curly braces, and the like. It would have been very difficult to build without the techniques of earlier chapters. The parsing system itself was essential; the clean design of the parsing system depends heavily on the earlier work on lazy streams and iterators. We used recursion and dispatch tables throughout to reduce and reorganize the code. Although the program doesn't use any explicit currying or memoization, there are several places where the code would probably be improved by its introduction — the functions based on apply(), and the subfeature() function spring to mind.

INDEX

Special Characters

A

B

FUNCTION INDEX

A NOTE ABOUT
THE COVER

The pictures on the cover are significant for two reasons.

Around 1994 I started dating a woman who was a quilter. Quilting is a traditional American craft in which the quilter takes small scraps of fabric and sews them together into *patches*, then sews the patches into *blocks*. Eventually the blocks are assembled into a quilt top, which is sandwiched with some stuffing to make the complete quilt. The layers of the sandwich are sewn together, with the stitching forming patterns; this stitching is the actual *quilting*.

Quilts are like programs in some ways. They are built up from smaller bits that work together. The programs in this book are even more like quilts, because this book is about building programs from small prefabricated standard parts and by plugging variations into stock patterns.

There are many traditional designs for quilt blocks, with colorful names like Flying Geese, Corn and Beans, Broken Dishes, Log Cabin, Courthouse Steps, Underground Railroad, Bear Claw, and so on. But after seeing a lot of quilts and pictures of quilts, it occurred to me that there might be a lot of block designs that nobody used, and that perhaps had never been seen.

I was curious about this, and I also wanted to impress my new girlfriend, so I wrote a suite of Perl programs to generate all the quilt blocks of a certain type: sixteen "half-square-triangle" patches arranged into a square with 90-degree rotational symmetry. Then I printed out the result:

http://perl.plover.com/hop/quilt/composites/bindexs.jpg

(I made a mistake in my output; one block appears twice. Can you find the duplicate?)

I was delighted, because the results confirmed my suspicions: there *are* a lot of excellent but rarely-seen quilt blocks.

The cover of the book shows the development of one of these blocks, starting from the half-square triangle patch, then four such patches joined together, then a complete block with 90-degree rotational symmetry, and then a larger piece formed by joining four blocks together. This reminds me of the way the functions in this book take functions as inputs and use them as components in larger and more complicated assemblages.

I was even more delighted when the quilter and I got married. She made the program output into a real quilt and gave it to me as a wedding present. There are pictures here:

```
http://perl.plover.com/hop/quilt/
```

The other reason that the cover pictures are significant is that since my original goal in writing the programs was to impress my girlfriend, the cover pictures are therefore part of the output of the most successful Perl programs I've ever written. I wish all my programs achieved their design goals so spectacularly.